THE TRUE CRIME BOOKS COLLECTION

60 DISTURBING TRUE CRIME STORIES ABOUT MURDER AND MAYHEM (5-IN-1 BOOK)

BY

JACK ROSEWOOD

ISBN: 978-1-64845-136-2

CONTENTS

DISCLAIMER i

PREFACE..1

TRUE CRIME STORIES – BOOK 1...**3**

Introduction..5

Chapter 1:   The Wrongful Murder Conviction of Gary Gauger............................6

Chapter 2:   The Case of the Youthful Murderers, Cindy Collier and Shirley Wolf... 13

Chapter 3:   The Execution of Troy Davis 20

Chapter 4:   Daphne Abdela, the "Baby-Faced Killer" 25

Chapter 5:   The Murder of Helle Crafts 32

Chapter 6:   The Murder of Virgil Lamar Ware 40

Chapter 7:   Wanda Holloway, the Killer Cheerleader Mom 44

Chapter 8:   The Murder of Scott Amedure 53

Chapter 9:   Katherine Knight, the Cannibal Queen 61

Chapter 10:   The Strange Life of the Lobster Boy, Grady Stiles Junior 71

Chapter 11:   The Murder of Marlene Warren 76

Chapter 12:   The Phoenix Canal Murders.. 80

Conclusion 84

TRUE CRIME STORIES – BOOK 2... **85**

Introduction.. 87

Chapter 1:   The Cold Murder Case of Nova Welsh 89

Chapter 2:   Michael MacGregor and Tanya Bogdanovich, the Canadian "Thrill Kill" Couple 96

Chapter 3:   The Murder of Timothy Wiltsey 105

Chapter 4:   The Jeffrey Franklin Murder Spree 114

Chapter 5:   The Anthony Barbaro School Shooting 120

Chapter 6:   The Murder of Harold Sasko 127

Chapter 7:   The Murder of the Doss Family 134

Chapter 8:   The Teen Hatchet Killers, Antonio Barbeau and Nathan Paape. 139

Chapter 9:   Cody Alan Legebokoff, the Canadian Country Boy Killer........... 146

Chapter 10:   The Murder of Robbie Middleton 154

Chapter 11:   The Portland Machete Murder 161

Chapter 12:   The Murder of Cassie Jo Stoddart 165

Conclusion 169

TRUE CRIME STORIES – BOOK 3 ....**171**

Introduction 173

Chapter 1:   The Abduction and Murder of Samantha Knight 175

Chapter 2:   The Murder of Zoe Hastings 184

Chapter 3:   Mayhem on the Camino de Santiago 189

Chapter 4:   The Unicorn Killer 195

Chapter 5:   The Lyle and Marie McCann Murder Case 205

Chapter 6:   Mesac Damas, the Voodoo Family Annihilator 213

Chapter 7:   The Disappearance of Ben Smart and Olivia Hope 220

Chapter 8:   The Murder of Susan Morris 226

Chapter 9:   Cheyenne Rose Antoine, the Social Media Murderess 233

Chapter 10:   Bevan Spencer von Einem and "The Family" Murders 240

Chapter 11:   The Covina Massacre 249

Chapter 12:   The Murder of Kristy Manzanares 253

Conclusion 256

TRUE CRIME STORIES – BOOK 4 ....**257**

Introduction 259

Chapter 1:   The Murder of Shanda Sharer 261

Chapter 2:   The Mysterious Murder Case of Roland T. Owen 273

Chapter 3:   The Wolf Family Murders 281

Chapter 4:   The Granny Murders 288

Chapter 5:   The Monster of Walmart, Donald Smith 299

Chapter 6:   The Aussie Femme Fatales, Jemma Lilley and Trudi Lenon 303

Chapter 7:   The Thomas J. Grasso Murder Case 307

Chapter 8:   The Murder of Kiaya Campbell 314

Chapter 9:   The Soham Murders 318

Chapter 10:   The Kapil Dogra Rape Case 328

Chapter 11:   The Murder of Shayla O'Brien/Elsie Scully-Hicks 332

Chapter 12:   The Murder of Ame Lynn Deal 336

Conclusion 341

TRUE CRIME STORIES – BOOK 5 343

Introduction 345

Chapter 1:   The Hi-Fi Murders 347

Chapter 2:   The Elizabeth Haysom Murder Case 357

Chapter 3:   The Murders of Debbie Ackerman and Marian Johnson 366

Chapter 4:   India's Crime of the Century—The Murders of Aarushi Talwar
               and Hemraj Banjade 373

Chapter 5:   Krystal Bell and the Texas Killing Fields 383

Chapter 6:   The Emmett Till Murder Case 387

Chapter 7:   The Bizarre Case of Orion Krause 397

Chapter 8:   The Disappearance of Susan Powell 401

Chapter 9:   The Mysterious Death of Rebecca Zahau 409

Chapter 10:   The Marco Flores Murder Case 414

Chapter 11:   The Execution of Joe Arridy 418

Chapter 12:   The Wannabe Serial Killer, William Inmon 424

Conclusion 427

EPILOGUE 428

FREE BONUS BOOKS

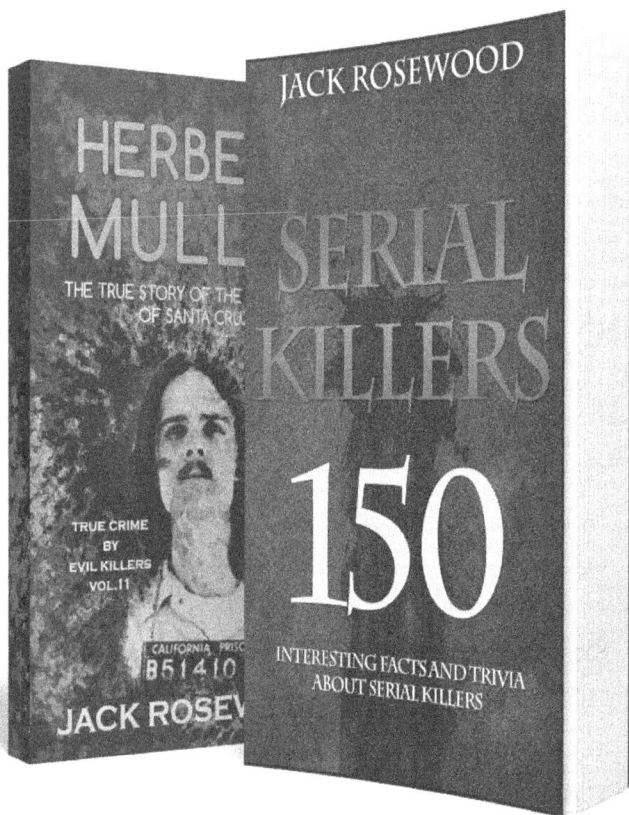

DISCLAIMER

This crime anthology biography includes quotes from those closely involved in the twelve cases examined, and it is not the author's intention to defame or intentionally harm anyone involved. The interpretation of events leading up to these crimes is the author's, based on research into the true crime murders. Any comments made about the psychopathic or sociopathic behavior of criminals involved in any of these cases are the sole opinion and responsibility of the person quoted.

PREFACE

True crime is more than a genre—it's a window into the darkest corners of the human experience. Within *The True Crime Books Collection: Sixty Disturbing True Stories About Murder And Mayhem (Five-in-One Book)*, you'll find stories that defy explanation, challenge assumptions, and force you to confront uncomfortable truths. The cases we explore in these volumes are not merely headlines or courtroom transcripts. They are reminders of what happens when ordinary lives collide with extraordinary horror.

The stories included in this collection are drawn from my previously released books—*True Crime Stories Volumes Nine, Ten, Eleven,* and *Twelve*—along with an all-new, never-before-published title, *Volume Thirteen*.

The crimes detailed here are shocking in their brutality and many remain unresolved or riddled with contradictions. They gripped the public imagination, sometimes decades after the fact. They sparked national debates, influenced legal history, and revealed the chilling unpredictability of human behavior.

Each volume in this anthology includes twelve stories. Every story aims to present the facts as they are known, while respecting the complexities of the individuals involved.

Some, like the case of Gary Gauger, illustrate the terrifying fallibility of the justice system. Wrongfully convicted of killing his parents, Gauger's story reminds us that not all who wear the title "criminal" are guilty.

Others, like Katherine Knight, uncover a level of savagery that defies comprehension—a woman who butchered her partner and attempted to serve him as a meal. Stories like that of Daphne Abdela, dubbed "The Baby-Faced Killer," offer a glimpse into juvenile crime and its moral gray zones.

Other cases stretch across decades and continents, such as the Camino de Santiago disappearance, or "The Unicorn Killer," Ira Einhorn, who eluded justice for years after murdering his girlfriend. Some, like the case of the Covina Massacre, show the strange contradiction of festive moments turned deadly.

Others still remain etched in memory due to the cultural reverberations they caused, like the tragic story of Emmett Till, a fourteen-year-old whose murder helped ignite the Civil Rights Movement.

The anthology also confronts rare cases where mental illness, abuse, and neglect form part of the puzzle—stories like Joe Arridy, a man with the mental capacity of a child, wrongfully executed for a crime he likely did not commit. Or Ame Lynn Deal, a little girl whose suffering went unnoticed, her death exposing systemic failures in child protection.

There are no happy endings in true crime. But there are lessons—many of them painful, some deeply instructive. We ask difficult questions in these pages. How could this have happened? Who failed to act? Why was justice delayed, denied, or distorted? And perhaps most haunting: could this happen again?

Even if you're a true crime fan, many of these stories won't be easy to read. Yet they invite reflection, demand accountability, and, in some small way, offer remembrance for those who can no longer speak for themselves.

As you turn the pages of these volumes, remember: each case once lived on front pages and in breaking news alerts. But beyond the headlines were real people, real consequences, and real communities changed forever. We owe it to them to look closely, question deeply, and never forget.

TRUE CRIME STORIES

BOOK 1

INTRODUCTION

In the following book, you will read about twelve crime cases that caused media sensations when they took place and still garner attention due to their strange and sometimes bizarre circumstances.

You will read about two men who went through the American legal system—Gary Gauger and Troy Davis—and were convicted of murder and sentenced to death. Both men had plenty of supporters who believed they were innocent, but in the end, only one was proven innocent while the other died on death row.

The problem of youth crime is also profiled in this volume. You will read about the brutal and senseless murder that two California girls committed in 1983 just for "fun." Similar to that case is that of a privileged New York girl who had it all but decided to throw it all away for some street cred and to see what it was like to kill someone.

You will also read about several truly bizarre crimes that shocked people around the world when they happened. The Australian female cannibal Katherine Knight is profiled, along with the strange and tragic story of the carnival sideshow "freak" known as the "Lobster Boy." You will also learn about a conservative "cheerleader mom" who was so determined to see her daughter succeed that she was willing to murder to ensure it.

All of these cases are captivating and disturbing at the same time. They demonstrate that humans can be extremely creative and destructive at the same time. Many of the criminals profiled in this book truly thought of new ways to bring misery to others, while some stayed with tried and true methods.

CHAPTER 1:

THE WRONGFUL MURDER CONVICTION OF GARY GAUGER

The famed English jurist Sir William Blackstone wrote in 1765 that, "It is better that ten guilty persons escape than that one innocent suffer." Those words have been used and sometimes abused in the centuries since by criminal defense lawyers and prison reform advocates who have argued that too many innocent people linger in prisons.

In the United States, the above quote has been used quite frequently, and as much as many Americans like to believe that theirs is the best legal system, and it may in fact be, the reality is that—unfortunately—innocent people are sent to prison even in the United States.

It is hard to say for sure what the actual percentage is of innocent persons convicted of crimes in the United States, but relevant evidence in the form of exonerations shows that it is a persistent, if not major, problem. A look at some of the more notable wrongful convictions in the United States demonstrates that both men and women are subject to errors in the criminal justice system.

Many of the women who have been found to be wrongfully convicted of murder were sent to prison for killing their children. Sabrina Butler was convicted in 1980 for killing her son and sent to Mississippi's death row. After years of appeals, Butler was finally fully exonerated in 1995.

Like Butler, Patricia Stallings was convicted of killing her son in 1990 and sentenced to life in prison, but she was later exonerated.

Notable men to be wrongfully convicted of murder in the United States include Adrian Thomas, who was convicted of murdering his son in 2008. Thomas' conviction was largely based on a confession he made that was later considered coerced. The son was eventually determined to have died from sepsis, which led to Thomas' complete exoneration.

Finally, one of the more high-profile murder conviction exonerations in recent years was that of Wisconsinite Steven Avery, who is the subject of the Netflix documentary *Making a Murderer*. Avery was convicted of a rape and murder that took place in 1985, but he was fully exonerated when the true perpetrator was found. Avery was later convicted of another murder in 2007, though, and now sits in a Wisconsin prison with a life sentence.

Less than three hours away from Avery's home, another wrongful murder conviction case took place in northern Illinois in the mid-1990s, and that's the one we're going to explore here.

On April 8, 1993, seventy-four-year-old Morris Gauger and his seventy-year-old wife Ruth were found murdered by their forty-one-year-old son, Gary, on their rural McHenry County, Illinois, property.

Gary first found his father lying on the ground.

"I thought he'd had a stroke or heart attack, fallen down and hit his head," Gary later recalled, but when he noticed a substantial amount of blood on his father's body, he realized the situation was grave and called 911 for an ambulance.

Gary searched his parents' home for his mother but could not find her, so he checked the trailer on the property that Ruth used for selling Indian rugs. To Gary's horror, he found his mother sprawled on the floor of the trailer, bloodied and dead.

When the McHenry County Sheriff's Department showed up at the Gauger farm, they immediately went to work assessing the situation. Both Morris and Ruth showed signs of being badly beaten, and it appeared that they both had their throats slit.

The coroner's report would later confirm that both Morris and Ruth died from having their throats slit.

Once the initial shock of what they saw had worn off a bit, the McHenry County deputies focused on the only person alive at the scene—Gary Gauger.

The sheriff's deputies put Gary into the back of a squad car and began their long, intense interrogation.

Gary Gauger was the only suspect they needed.

The Confession

To the average person who has never been through the American criminal justice system, an accused's confession to a crime is perhaps the best piece of evidence and indicator of that person's guilt. After all, why would an innocent person confess to a crime they didn't commit, right?

The truth is that things are much different in the real world. Detectives beating the accused during interrogations that continue until a confession is made is mostly a thing of the past, but in place of those methods, investigators have grown more intelligent in their craft.

Most major police departments in the United States require their officers to have college degrees, and even many of the smaller departments expect the same background from prospective employees, especially if they hope to make detective.

Today's American police officers are neither dumb nor uneducated.

Most detectives are well-versed in the law and know where the "line" is and how to skirt it without breaking any laws.

In addition to their formal education, seasoned veteran police officers develop keen abilities to manipulate and trick suspects of crimes.

For an average person with no criminal background, such as Gary Gauger, a police interrogation can be a very intimidating and traumatic experience, even if that person is totally innocent.

When the McHenry County deputies placed Gary into the back of one of their squad cars, they believed they had the Gaugers' killer. Statistically speaking, they were right to believe so because most violent crimes are perpetrated by someone who knows the victim. To the McHenry County detectives, it looked like a sure case of domestic violence. They reasoned that Gary had little going on in his life and that killing his parents would be a sure way for him to move forward financially.

After sitting in the back of the squad car for a few hours, Gary was then brought to the sheriff's department for a more in-depth interrogation.

"I told the police everything I know," Gary recalled. "They showed up between 11 and noon. I sat in the squad car until 4 [p.m.], They took me to the police station in Woodstock, the county seat. And I was questioned from 4 o'clock until 10 o'clock the next morning."

Gary's interrogation at the police station lasted for at least eighteen hours. During that interrogation, the detectives used all of the psychological weapons in their arsenal.

The overarching tactic was the classic "good cop, bad cop" routine, where one detective basically does a lot of yelling and calling the accused a piece of dirt. The "good cop" then usually steps in and appeals to the conscience of the accused, hoping to elicit a confession in the process.

The bad cop in this case told Gary that if he didn't confess, a jury would find him guilty and surely send him to death row, instilling fear in the suspect.

The good cop intervened and told Gary that he knew it was all some type of big mistake and that if he confessed then everyone could move on with their lives.

The process cycled through several times before Gary finally broke down and confessed.

"They were basically trying to convince me that I killed my parents and, for a while, through lack of sleep, incessant interrogation, not being really able to think on my own for 10 seconds at a time, they had me believing that I must have had a blackout and that I killed my parents," said Gary.

As soon as he confessed, Gary knew he'd made a big mistake. Unfortunately for him, it was a mistake that he could not take back and one that almost ended his life.

The Trial

As Gary Gauger languished in the McHenry County Jail for nearly a year, he was confronted with the reality that he might never see the outside world again. The prosecutor was pushing for the death penalty, and although Illinois is considered to be a liberal state politically speaking, McHenry County is fairly conservative, so the death sentence was a possibility.

The only evidence that the prosecution had was Gary's confession: they had no physical evidence tying him to the murders, and there were no witnesses to the crimes.

It turned out that Gary's confession would be enough.

Gary Gauger was convicted of his parents' murders and sentenced to death on January 11, 1994.

Gary was immediately transferred to the Illinois Department of Corrections to meet his fate in the death chamber at the Menard Correctional Center in Chester, Illinois. But just when it looked like it would be the end of the road for Gauger, he received a couple of reprieves.

The first good news that Gary received was that his death sentence was reduced to life in prison by the appellate courts. By the mid-1990s, Illinois was moving closer to abolishing the death penalty, which ultimately helped Gauger. The next major news that Gary received was that the Illinois Court of Appeals deemed his confession to the police inadmissible in March 1996.

The appellate court's decision to deem his confession inadmissible essentially stripped the prosecution of its sole solid piece of evidence. Although McHenry County officials desired a retrial, they recognized that without a confession, they possessed insufficient evidence, compelling them to dismiss the charges against Gary.

Gary Gauger was released from prison in October 1996.

Gauger's release was only the end of one chapter in this story that has many unexpected twists and turns. The McHenry County prosecutors still believed that Gary had murdered his parents, and some in the community agreed with that sentiment.

Just when it seemed as though the true killers of the Gaugers would never be caught, a federal investigation of organized crime gangs in northern Illinois uncovered the murderers.

The Outlaws Motorcycle Club

Throughout the 1990s, the otherwise bucolic peace of northern Illinois was routinely interrupted by violence between warring organized crime factions. In this case, the factions were not mafia-related or cartels from south of the border, but homegrown crime gangs on Harley Davidson motorcycles.

Northern Illinois became the scene of a turf war between the "one percenter" motorcycle "clubs" the Hells Angels and Outlaws.

In the world of motorcycle enthusiasts, the term "one percenter" is used to refer to the one percent of all bikers who make their own rules and are therefore "outlaws." Since just before World War II, outlaw bikers have formed "clubs" that evolved in the following decades to become highly organized crime organizations with international reach. The biggest and most well-known of all biker gangs is the Hells Angels, which formed in 1948 in California. After their formation, the Hells Angels opened chapters across the United States and are now on nearly every continent.

Even older than the Hells Angels, and almost as big, is the Outlaws, who formed in 1935 in a suburb of Chicago, Illinois.

Both gangs are known for their violence and criminal activity, and they share a deep hatred for each other. One of the patches worn on the vests of many Outlaws members is the letters ADIOS, which is said to stand for "Angels Die in Outlaw States."

Needless to say, biker gangs are very territorial.

Traditionally, the Outlaws have claimed states in the Midwest and Southeast, while the Hells Angels have claimed the West and upper Midwest. Essentially, the Mississippi River was the dividing line between their territories, but by the late 1970s, the Hells Angels began slowly to expand into Outlaw states.

The result was numerous acts of extreme violence.

There was a shootout at the annual Sturgis biker rally one year between the two gangs, and an especially gruesome case where members of the Outlaws were suspected of murdering and beheading a Hells Angel in North Carolina.

Still, despite the immense hostility between the two gangs, the Outlaws never set foot in California, and the Hells Angels never entered Illinois—until the 1990s.

The Hells Angels wanted a piece of the lucrative gun and drug trade in Chicago, so they "patched over" a "support" club in the Windy City. A support club is basically a puppet club that the main gang controls while hoping to steer clear of any criminal activity. A "patch over" is when the gang decides to make the support club fully "patched" members of their gang.

When the Outlaws learned that the Hells Angels patched over another club in their backyard, they were not pleased, to say the least. The Outlaws responded by bombing the Hells Angels' Chicago clubhouse in 1994 and then shot to death the president of the chapter. The Outlaws then followed up their violence in Chicago by murdering the president of a Hells Angels support club in Rockford, Illinois.

It turns out that the Gaugers were some of the first victims and essentially collateral damage in the war between the Outlaws and Hells Angels in the 1990s.

Morris Gauger was a skilled mechanic who often worked on motorcycles in his spare time for some extra cash. Over the years, he got to know a number of Outlaws members, who gladly paid for his services. The gang members never gave the Gaugers any problems, but in April 1993, two low-ranking members thought they could score big.

Randall Miller and James Schneider wanted to impress more influential members of the organization. The two men also had expensive crystal meth habits and overheard other Outlaws members who claimed that the Gaugers kept a lot of cash at their residence—thirty thousand dollars, to be exact.

Except there was nowhere near that kind of money at the Gauger farm.

After Miller and Schneider arrived at the Gauger farm, they separated the couple and began beating them to find out where the cash was. When the Gaugers failed to cooperate, the bikers cut their throats.

They netted an entire fifteen dollars from the double murder.

When the violence escalated between the Hells Angels and Outlaws in Illinois, the FBI and the ATF conducted a far-ranging investigation of both clubs. However, since the Outlaws were the main gang in the region, and most of the violence was perpetrated by them, the investigation focused on their chapters in northern Illinois and Wisconsin.

In the late 1990s, the United States Attorney's office handed down indictments of seventeen high-ranking Outlaws members in Illinois and Wisconsin. The members were charged with a plethora of federal crimes relating to several offenses, which included armed robbery, drug trafficking, arson, bombings, and six murders.

Morris and Ruth Gauger were included in the Outlaws' body count.

The brotherhood and criminal code often claimed by Outlaws bikers quickly went out the window when Schneider learned that he was looking at spending the rest of his life in prison or possibly the death penalty. His attorneys made a deal with the federal prosecutors whereby he would relate the full details of the Gaugers' murders and then agree to testify against Outlaws members in other cases for a reduced sentence.

Gary Gauger could finally see the light at the end of the tunnel.

A Full Pardon

After Gary was released from prison in 1996, he found himself in a virtual legal limbo. The McHenry County prosecutors believed he was still guilty and planned to re-charge him if they could find any new evidence.

Many of the Gaugers' neighbors also doubted Gary's innocence.

After the Outlaws' trials, though, most people began to realize that Gary Gauger was the victim of the most unfortunate of circumstances.

The Illinois Appellate Court reversed Gauger's conviction and ordered a new trial in March 1996, ruling that the statements made during his interrogation were inadmissible because they were the "fruit of an unlawful arrest," lacking probable cause. All charges against Gauger were dismissed by the State's Attorney and he was released in October 1996. Gary Gauger was finally given a full pardon in 2002 after the Outlaws were sent to prison.

In the years since Gary has been out of prison, he has maintained a low profile. He became an organic farmer in rural McHenry County, where he still lives today.

CHAPTER 2:

THE CASE OF THE YOUTHFUL MURDERERS, CINDY COLLIER AND SHIRLEY WOLF

Youth violence is a phenomenon that, for the most part, is unique to the modern world. Although young people have engaged in crime throughout history, their crimes have become increasingly brazen, violent, and devoid of remorse in recent decades. During tougher times in history, young people often stole food or money to help make ends meet, but the juvenile offenders of today often kill for no other reason than the thrill of the kill.

Youth gangs have become a major issue in many countries during the last forty years, which has left authorities scratching their heads over how to deal with the growing problem. Experts have tried to isolate the reasons that lead to youth violence, but it seems there are too many.

Some youths commit violent acts due to peer pressure and/or in order to join a gang or other group that serves as a surrogate family.

Other kids have been known to lash out in revenge against bullies or other people who they believe have wronged them in some way.

Still, there are cases where juveniles have committed horrendous acts of violence for no apparent reason other than pure sadism. These are the most difficult to understand and also probably the most difficult to predict. There have been a number of these types of cases that have made headlines around the world.

In 1993 in the United Kingdom, two ten-year-old boys, Robert Thompson and James Venables, abducted and brutally murdered three-year-old James Bulger. The world was shocked when the mug shots of Bulger's killers showed not two creepy-looking hardened criminals but two baby-faced boys.

The trial of Venables and Thompson revealed both boys to be sociopaths who had no remorse for their terrible crime. The trial never uncovered a motive for the murder.

Also in 1993, in upstate New York, thirteen-year-old Eric Smith murdered four-year-old Derrick Robie in an equally brutal and perplexing crime. Smith was convicted and sent to prison for the murder, but he never gave a reason for his heinous act.

About ten years before Eric Smith, Robert Thompson, and James Venables entered the annals of crime history, two girls in California committed an equally disturbing murder.

On the evening of June 14, 1983, fifteen-year-old Cindy Lee Collier and her new best friend, fourteen-year-old Shirley Catherine Wolf, set out to murder someone, anyone, just for "fun." Unlike the other child killers mentioned above, Collier and Wolf had no problem telling the authorities why they committed the murder, which made the case even more disturbing.

Two Troubled Lives

You've probably heard of the "nature versus nurture" debate at some point during your life. The two arguments are that a person's life is largely the result of either their upbringing or genes. Essentially, the nurture argument is one that posits the environment is the biggest determining factor in a person's life, while the nature argument gives more credence to hereditary factors.

The debate will probably never be settled, and most people today believe that life is so complicated that both certainly affect a person's destiny. With that said, those born into desperate situations are starting with one strike against them.

Cindy Collier and Shirley Wolf were definitely the victims of bad environments.

Cindy Collier was born into a home with little supervision or direction. Although her parents were married when she was born, they divorced when she was one, and her father left the area. Cindy never knew her father and never had a strong male figure in her life.

Although Cindy claims she was raped on more than one occasion as a child, there is little evidence to suggest she was abused by family members.

But sometimes neglect can be just as bad as physical or sexual abuse.

With no adult supervision, Cindy did whatever she wanted and ran wild on the streets of Sacramento, California. As a child, Cindy racked up arrests for burglary, assault, theft, and drugs. Eventually, she earned her first stretch in the juvenile hall at the age of twelve and was in some type of state institution for most of the time thereafter.

When she wasn't in a juvenile hall or halfway house, Cindy was a terror in the public school system. When she was in the ninth grade, Cindy was already 5'9 and weighed 140 pounds, which she used to intimidate other kids, both girls and boys.

"Cindy was one of those girls that nobody would mess with," said former classmate David Silva. "If she didn't like somebody, she'd yell at them and push them around."

As bad as Cindy Collier's early years were, Shirley Wolf's were significantly worse.

Wolf was born and spent her first few years in the Queens borough of New York, New York. She lived in a high-crime neighborhood and was surrounded by chaos, both in her home and on the streets. Shirley ran away for the first time at just six years old but returned within a few hours.

In 1976, Shirley's father moved the family to the Sacramento, California area, but the change did little to help the young girl's situation.

Sexual abuse was a regular part of life in the Wolf household, as Shirley was abused by both her father and grandfather. Shirley was raped daily by her dad, and when she reached puberty, her dad bought her birth control pills so that he could keep up the unnatural acts with no repercussions.

"I was really scared," Shirley later said. "I was really frightened to lose my virginity, plus my honor and my pride. That's something I don't forgive my dad for."

Shirley eventually summoned the courage to go to the police about the sexual abuse, which led to a full investigation and her dad's arrest.

But the criminal justice system was very different in 1970s America. The "get tough on crime" philosophy had not yet entered the mainstream, and there was little consideration for victims' rights.

Shirley's dad was only given a 100-day sentence in the county jail, but worst of all, the court ruled that Shirley should be taken from the family. The confused kid became a ward of the state and was shuffled around various foster and group homes in the Sacramento area.

The system clearly failed Shirley Wolf.

The Two Meet

In the early summer of 1983, Cindy Collier was out of the system and living with her mother in suburban Sacramento. For Cindy, the summer was a time when she had even more time on her hands, which meant that there were plenty of ways for her to get into trouble. When most kids her age were playing a summer sport, at camp, vacationing with their parents, or working part-time jobs such as mowing lawns and babysitting, Cindy spent her days drinking alcohol, smoking pot, and getting into trouble.

She had few "normal" friends from school, but she also knew just about every local kid who was in a group home—except Shirley Wolf.

On the morning of June 14, 1983, Cindy woke up and left her mom's house to find something to do. After checking out some local spots popular with juvenile delinquents but finding no one around, Cindy made her way to a local halfway house to meet with some friends. When she got to the halfway house, she talked with those friends and then met Shirley Wolf.

The two girls were immediately drawn to each other.

Cindy later articulated their connection when she told the police, "Shirley's exactly like me. She has the same childhood."

After spending a couple of hours at the halfway house talking, Shirley signed out for the day, and the two girls went walking around Sacramento looking for something to do. Almost immediately, their plans turned to murder.

The pair decided that they would steal a car, kill the owner, and run away and live happily ever after. It was clearly a plan full of more holes than a net, but to two disturbed and mentally scarred teenage girls, it seemed like a good idea.

Perhaps the most remarkable part is that they put the plan into action less than eight hours after they met.

The Murder of Anna Brackett

As the two girls spent the day together, they added more details to the plan. If the plan had not ended in the death of an innocent person, it would have been laughable. They decided that it was important to mask their identities, so they came up with the brilliant idea of dyeing their hair as "disguises." Actually, the idea of dyeing their hair as part of their disguises was not so flawed in itself, but they didn't take the next logical step of committing the crime in a location where they were not well known.

Instead, the pair went to the Auburn Green subdivision where Collier lived with her mother and was known around the neighborhood.

A simple dye job would've done little to mask her identity.

The girls seemed to have had no real plan other than to somehow gain access to a home and then kill the occupant. To do this, the rough-looking and not-so-neatly dressed duo went house to house, either asking to use the phone or requesting a drink of water.

A seventy-year-old retiree named Joe Becker allowed them into his home to use his phone and to drink some water. The girls didn't attack Becker, probably because he was still a relatively healthy male who could defend himself, but they left an enduring impression on him and his wife.

"But after they left, my wife felt so contaminated by them that she immediately washed the glass and scrubbed the phone with alcohol—before we knew anything about the murder," recalled Becker.

As Collier and Wolf continued on their diabolical journey in the neighborhood, eighty-five-year-old Anna Brackett was waiting patiently for a call from her son.

Anna Brackett was a retired seamstress and great-grandmother who grew up in a very different America than Collier and Wolf. Brackett lived through both world wars and the Great Depression, so turmoil and loss were nothing foreign to her. With that said, Anna was very trusting and a generally good-natured woman.

If there was anyone Collier and Wolf could take advantage of, it would be Anna Brackett.

On the night in question, Anna was waiting to receive a call from her fifty-two-year-old son Carl, telling her that he was on his way there to bring her to her weekly bingo game. When she heard the knock at the door, she probably thought it was Carl who had just decided to drive there without calling.

Anna let Collier and Wolf into her home to use the phone, but as soon as they had feigned making a phone call, they attacked the elderly woman like she was a prey animal on the African savannah. According to the confession of the duo, Collier threw Anna to the ground, and then Wolf began stabbing her repeatedly until she died.

The two juvenile murderers then left Anna in a pool of blood in the kitchen and began searching for the keys to a 1970 Dodge they saw parked in the driveway. They looked for several minutes but were unable to find the keys, so they ran out the back door with some loose change, covered in blood.

They then walked the short distance to Collier's home.

The duo didn't get their getaway car, but possibly there would be another day.

The Arrests and Trials

As Collier and Wolf were making their escape, Carl Brackett saw the motley duo walking down the road. He thought they looked a little out of place considering their age and the time of day, but he quickly put it out of his mind and continued to his mother's home.

He was horrified by what he found there.

When the Placer County Sheriff's Department arrived at Anna's home, they quickly determined that Carl was not a suspect. When Carl told the investigators about the two strange teenage girls walking through the neighborhood, they at first thought that there was no connection.

Then the sheriff's department received eleven calls about the girls. Some of the callers were familiar with Cindy Collier, so the detectives decided to follow up on the lead by paying a visit to her home. They didn't think there was anything to the sightings, instead believing that it was probably just a coincidence, since there was no way two teenage girls would commit an act of cold-blooded murder.

When the detectives arrived at the Collier home, they found the girls in the basement having a slumber party as though nothing had happened. Still not believing there was any connection, the detectives nonchalantly asked Wolf if she had anything to do with Anna Brackett's murder, to which she calmly answered, "Yes."

The detectives were floored by the revelation, but their disbelief at the situation only increased when they brought both girls into the police station.

Although not forthcoming at her home, Collier opened up once she was at the police station, and what she said was truly disturbing.

"To honestly tell you the truth, we didn't feel any badness," said Collier. "Then after we did it, we wanted to do another one. We just wanted to kill someone. Just for fun."

Wolf added, "We both felt excited. I had done something I had never done before."

As the detectives continued the disturbing interviews of the two junior psychopaths, Wolf's diary was uncovered, which illuminated the unsettling mindset of the girls even more.

"Today, Cindy and I ran away and killed an old lady. It was lots of fun."

"Killing for fun" is a phrase one would expect an adult male serial killer to use, not two teenage girls. But it was painfully clear to the police, the courts, the media, and the public that these were not two ordinary girls.

Justice for the duo moved swiftly. Their trials took place about a month after they were arrested, with quite foreseeable outcomes. Both were found guilty of first-degree murder as juveniles and sentenced to the California Youth Authority with indeterminate sentences.

In 1983, the "get tough on crime" attitude was beginning to sweep through the United States, but at that point, juveniles were rarely tried as adults, no matter how heinous their crimes.

After the Murder

Although Cindy Collier and Shirley Wolf developed an immediate and deep bond, they were separated after their arrests and never saw each other again.

Collier did nine years and was released in 1992. She later married, had four children, and now lives a quiet life in northern California.

Things did not work out so well for Shirley Wolf, though.

Wolf tried to escape from custody numerous times and, as a result, was given more time. She did twelve years altogether, the last couple in an adult prison. She was released in 1995 and has had numerous legal and drug problems since. She reportedly tried to contact her father, who molested her repeatedly as a child, but was rebuffed.

Shirley Wolf's whereabouts are currently unknown.

Collier's and Wolf's crime and their lives were so disturbing that their case was the subject of numerous magazine articles and true crime investigation television shows throughout the 1980s. Joan Merriam wrote the definitive book of the case titled *Little Girl Lost: A True Story of Shattered Innocence and Murder,* and in 1993, a fictionalized version of the case was made into a film titled *Fun* starring Alicia Witt.

CHAPTER 3:

THE EXECUTION
OF TROY DAVIS

Capital punishment has always been a polarizing issue. Ancient Greek and Roman philosophers discussed the efficacy, or lack thereof, of killing convicted criminals, and in modern times, the debates have only become more intense. The consequence is that the United States is the only Western nation-state that still executes some of its criminals, but even in the U.S., the death penalty is a much-nuanced issue.

Since the United States is a federal republic that gives a large amount of power to its individual states, the use of the death penalty is not uniform across the country. In the modern era, states in the upper Midwest and New England have, for the most part, prohibited the death penalty, while states in the South and West have traditionally had death penalty statutes.

Generally speaking, the more politically liberal states, such as New York and Massachusetts, have not had the death penalty. However, there are exceptions to this, as California has had the death penalty for all of the modern era.

In total, the death penalty is used in thirty-one of the fifty states as well as by the federal government.

When it comes to the death penalty debate, the opposition is usually the most vocal.

One of the most notable arguments death penalty opponents make is that it is a violation of the Eighth Amendment to the United States Constitution, which prohibits the use of "cruel and unusual punishment" by the courts. Those who use this argument have pointed to several "botched" executions as examples.

Still, states that are ardent in their use of the death penalty simply change methods to counter this argument.

Perhaps the best argument that death penalty opponents make is that innocent people are executed. This argument is difficult to prove since no one executed in the modern era has yet been definitively proven innocent posthumously. With that said, it is still a reasonable argument to assume at least one innocent person has been executed in recent years.

The potential execution of an innocent person is the background for the next case. The person on death row was a troubled young man named Troy Davis, and although there was little doubt that he lived a rough life and associated with a bad crowd, there were doubts about his guilt right up until the time when he was ultimately executed.

An Aimless Guy

Davis grew up in the working class, in the predominantly Black neighborhood of Cloverdale in Savannah, Georgia. Like many of his friends, Davis did not know his father very well, although his mother did what she could to instill positive values in her son.

As a young child, Davis seemed to be headed in the right direction because he never got into trouble and was generally respectful of his elders around the neighborhood.

But as Davis entered his teen years, things began to change.

Troy began running with a tough crowd in the Cloverdale neighborhood and showed little interest in school. Although he was an athletic and well-developed teen, Davis did not play sports and performed very poorly in his classes. His mother pleaded with him to shape up, and though he respected her immensely, she was often gone working long hours. Eventually, Troy dropped out of high school in the eleventh grade, but he continued his education on the streets of Savannah.

Davis quickly gained respect with his peers in Cloverdale by using his athletic build to intimidate and assault those who got out of line with him. His violence earned him the nickname "RAH," which stood for "rugged as hell."

In 1988, Troy Davis was clearly headed down a dark path.

Davis' criminal behavior led to his arrest in 1988 for carrying a concealed gun that had a filed-off serial number. The offense landed Davis in the county jail, charged with a felony. He was looking at potentially serving a couple of years in either a state or federal prison for the charge. Lucky for Davis, he had a good lawyer who was able to successfully argue that the court should be lenient on his client due to his age and the fact that he had no criminal record.

The prosecutor agreed and allowed Troy to plead guilty to a misdemeanor, which meant that he avoided prison time.

For many people, the situation would have been a wake-up call to clean up one's life and get new friends, but Davis instead immersed himself deeper in the criminal underbelly of Savannah's Cloverdale neighborhood.

It would be a choice that Davis would soon come to regret.

Death at Burger King

On the evening of August 18, 1989, Troy Davis and some of his friends were drinking heavily. They began drinking in the afternoon and then took their binge to a house party in the Cloverdale neighborhood. After consuming even more alcohol at the party, Davis and a friend left, which is when the first confrontation of the night took place.

Some of the eyewitness reports of the chain of events that led to the murder of twenty-seven-year-old off-duty policeman Mark MacPhail Senior are sketchy, and others are conflicting, but a reasonable account of what happened can be gleaned from the reports.

When Davis and his friend Daryl Collins left the party in Cloverdale in Collins' car, they met another car on the street. According to the witnesses at the scene, either Davis or Collins fired a gun into the other car after a verbal altercation. Sixteen-year-old Michael Cooper was shot in the confrontation.

Fortunately, Cooper sustained only minor injuries in the attack.

At this point, the combination of alcohol, peer pressure, adrenaline, and a lack of intelligence took control of Davis' and Collins' thinking processes. Most people would call it a night after shooting into a car and go home and lie low.

Most people wouldn't have shot into a car.

Instead, Davis and Collins decided to go to the nearest Burger King for some burgers before they went home.

This is where the narrative of events gets fuzzy.

What is known is that MacPhail, who was moonlighting as a security guard at the Burger King, stopped a homeless man from being pistol-whipped by another man in the parking lot of the restaurant at about 1 a.m. on August 19. As MacPhail struggled with the assailant, he was shot in the heart and face and died at the scene.

MacPhail left behind a wife and two children.

Since MacPhail was a police officer, the Savannah Police Department, the Chatham County Sheriff's Department, and the Georgia State Police quickly mobilized to catch the fallen officer's killer.

Eyewitnesses to the crime described seeing a young Black man wearing a white T-shirt first assaulting the homeless man and then shooting MacPhail. A further inquiry led investigators to Sylvester "Redd" Coles, who was a local small-time criminal with a penchant for violence.

Coles was acquainted with Davis and Collins as they were all from the same neighborhood, but they were not known to be friends. In fact, some said they were rivals. When the investigators tracked down Coles later in the day on August 19, he told them that Troy Davis was MacPhail's killer. Later, both Davis and Collins would claim that Coles was the killer.

The Capture and Trial

Despite Coles´ questionable background, the investigators believed his story, so they focused all of their energy on Troy Davis. First, they went to Davis' mother's house and conducted a search without a warrant that was later unsuccessfully challenged in court. They retrieved a pair of bloody shorts that didn't play much of a role in Davis' trial but did serve to get an arrest warrant.

While the police were searching Davis' mother's home, Davis was hiding out in Atlanta.

The investigators didn't know exactly where Troy Davis was, but they had a feeling his family knew, and they also believed he was probably somewhere in the Cloverdale neighborhood. The local law enforcement decided to put the heat on every drug dealer, sex worker, pimp, fence, and gang banger in Cloverdale to capture Davis. Since Davis was in Atlanta, law enforcement's efforts did not directly lead to Davis' arrest, but the heat put on the local criminal underworld was quite intense.

The local criminals began threatening Davis' family.

Finally, after negotiating with the police, Troy Davis returned to Savannah and turned himself in on August 23. Davis was promptly charged with capital murder—he would face the death penalty if convicted.

After nearly two years of pre-trial motions and hearings, Troy Davis' capital murder trial finally got underway. For the most part, the prosecution had a circumstantial case against him, but it was a strong circumstantial case nonetheless. The prosecutors called thirty-four witnesses, several of whom testified to having seen Davis either assault the homeless man or kill MacPhail.

In terms of forensic evidence, the murder weapon was never recovered, but prosecution experts testified that the bullets that killed MacPhail may have come from the same gun that wounded Cooper earlier in the evening.

Davis did not have the money for a lawyer, so he was given a court-appointed attorney, which is usually not a good situation in most courtrooms in the United States. With that said, Davis' defense team put up a spirited defense and questioned how eyewitnesses could definitively identify their client from across a parking lot at 1 a.m. They also pointed out that the other potential suspect, Sylvester Coles, bore a resemblance to Troy Davis.

The defense called six witnesses to testify, which included Davis' mother, who stated that she was with her son most of the night until he left for Atlanta. Davis also took the stand in his own defense and was adamant that the killer was Sylvester Coles.

The jury didn't believe Troy Davis' mama. On August 30, 1991, he was convicted of MacPhail's murder and sentenced to death.

After Troy Davis was sent to Georgia's death row, his case went into an automatic appeal process, which is where it began to gather attention. Eventually, calls for clemency and/or a new trial became frequent. Davis' supporters argued that a man should not be executed with so little physical evidence pointing toward his guilt. Most of Davis' supporters were from the left wing of the political spectrum and included anti-death penalty activists, but former Georgia Republican United States Congressman Bob Barr also stated publicly that he believed Davis should be given a new trial.

The merits of the case were argued in numerous appeals and resulted in three stays of execution, including a final denial of clemency by the Georgia Board of Pardons and Paroles, and on the day of the execution, a rejection by the United States Supreme Court. However, unlike the Gary Gauger case profiled in this book, there was no "smoking gun" that proved another person was MacPhail's killer. This profound difference in outcomes—exoneration versus execution—reveals a chilling juxtaposition and serves to highlight an unsettling truth about the death penalty: once a sentence is carried out, it is final, even if doubt persists.

On September 21, 2011, Troy Davis was executed by lethal injection.

CHAPTER 4:

DAPHNE ABDELA,
THE "BABY-FACED KILLER"

The epidemic of senseless youth violence has already been profiled in this book with the case of Cindy Collier and Shirley Wolf. As shown in that case, the life course of the two teenage girls almost seemed inevitable. They both came from extremely difficult familial situations in which abuse was common and where they received no proper moral foundation or direction.

The majority of youth criminals come from similar situations. Youth criminals are often frustrated with life and strike out indiscriminately against anyone who happens to be in their vicinity. The origins of their rage can often be traced to abuse, neglect, and poverty.

But that is not always the case.

Sometimes, the suburbs and wealthy urban neighborhoods produce children who are every bit as violent as those from low-income neighborhoods. Notable privileged youth criminals include the so-called "Billionaire Boys Club" that operated in southern California during the 1980s, and Erik and Lyle Menendez, who gunned down their parents in 1989.

Although the crimes of the Billionaire Boys Club and the Menendez brothers were extremely brutal and difficult for the average person to fathom, they did have motives—greed.

The next case concerns a child of privilege who didn't kill for greed as the Menendez brothers did, but just for the "fun" of it, more like Cindy Collier and Shirley Wolf. On the night of May 22, 1997, a fifteen-year-old child of wealth named Daphne Abdela spiced up her seemingly boring life when she and her boyfriend killed a man just for the thrill.

The Daphne Abdela murder case shocked people around the world. They wondered how a girl so young, who "had it all," could be so cold and brutal.

The reasons why Abdela committed the brutal murder will probably never be known, but the details of her life and the crime that made her infamous are part of the public record.

A Spoiled Brat

In many ways, the first few months of Daphne Abdela's life were a story of contrasts and extremes. Little is known about her biological parents, but it is believed they died in an accident. It is thought that the infant orphan had no extended family who could care for her, so she was made a ward of the state and placed for adoption.

The difficulties that Daphne faced in her first few months of life quickly dissipated, though, when she was adopted by a wealthy, worldly family.

Daphne's adopted father was Angelo Abdela, who was a wealthy Israeli corporate executive. Abdela made millions in lucrative investments in the Middle East, Europe, and North America, which allowed him to buy properties in many different countries and to move to the United States.

Abdela's money also allowed him to move in crowds with the "beautiful people."

Through his connections, Angelo met and married a French model named Catherine, and the two decided to live in the exclusive New York City neighborhood of Central Park West. The couple had everything most people would want: money, a nice home, and influential and interesting friends.

But one thing was missing—children.

The couple decided to adopt a child in the early 1980s, and through their connections, were able to adopt a toddler girl they named Daphne.

Besides the nice home in Central Park West, the Abdelas spoiled Daphne with things of which most kids could only dream. She was sent to the best and most expensive schools in New York City, and between school years and during Christmas breaks, the Abdelas brought Daphne on expensive trips to Europe, Asia, and the Middle East.

Daphne's former model mother made sure that her daughter was always wearing the trendiest and most expensive clothes, and her father usually bought her whatever she wanted.

Things went well in the Abdela house until Daphne hit puberty in the mid-1990s. At that point, Daphne began rebelling by talking back to her parents and breaking their rules. The Abdelas were not worried very much at first, as they believed that their daughter was just going through a normal teenage rebellious phase. They figured that if they gave her enough space, it would come to an end.

But things got exponentially worse when Daphne turned fifteen.

The depth of Daphne's troubles will probably never be known, but the rebellious attitude she exhibited starting at the age of thirteen was amplified when she began experimenting with drugs and alcohol around the same time. Although she was sent to the finest schools in New York City, there was no shortage of drugs or alcohol in any of the schools Daphne attended. If anything, the affluent children she was around had money to buy strong strains of marijuana and to purchase expensive drugs such as cocaine.

And most rich people have a well-stocked bar in their homes.

By the age of fifteen, Daphne was a full-blown alcoholic. She rarely went to school, and even her normally permissive parents knew something had to be done, so they took her out of school and enrolled her in an outpatient treatment center.

Daphne was not pleased with the situation.

Christopher Vasquez

Before Daphne was placed in full-time treatment by her parents, she met a kid her own age at the prestigious Beekman School named Christopher Vasquez. Although he also attended the pricey private school, Vasquez came from the east side of Manhattan and was there on a scholarship. Normally, his family would not have been able to pay for the tuition, but his grades, combined with the fact that he fit into several categories the Beekman administrators were looking for to diversify their student population, meant that he could attend alongside the children of some of New York City's elite.

The fact that Vasquez was Hispanic and from a poor neighborhood attracted Daphne to him. Friends said that Daphne was always looking to build some sort of "street cred," and that she felt Vasquez would help her attain it.

The reality was that Chris Vasquez was anything but a thug or a tough guy.

Before becoming involved with Daphne, Vasquez was described by most who knew him as a bespectacled, nerdy kid who was polite and friendly but socially awkward. According to his family members, Chris lacked confidence and was diagnosed with an anxiety disorder.

When Vasquez transferred to the Beekman School, he was a fish out of water, and his anxiety issues only seemed to get worse—until he met Daphne Abdela.

Vasquez was glad to make a new friend in the unfamiliar environment, and Abdela believed that her new friend from the wrong side of the tracks would give her instant street cred.

"She always tried acting like she was from a bad neighborhood," a friend of the pair later said.

The friendship between Vasquez and Abdela soon became a romance. The pair spent their days skipping class, rollerblading, and drinking booze in Central Park. It became clear, though, to those who knew the pair, that Abdela was the one in charge. She manipulated Vasquez to get what she wanted, but for Vasquez, the situation was not so bad: he finally had a girlfriend who presumably showed a genuine interest in him. But Abdela wanted more.

She wanted to be a murderer.

Strawberry Fields Forever

May 22, 1997, began like most other days for Daphne Abdela. After having breakfast, she grabbed her roller blades and walked the short distance from her apartment to Central Park to meet Vasquez. When Vasquez first saw Abdela that day, he thought they would spend the day rollerblading and drinking.

But Abdela had other ideas.

Shortly after the two met up, Abdela reached into her pocket and pulled out a switchblade knife.

"I'm gonna slice someone," Abdela nonchalantly told her boyfriend.

Vasquez later claimed he thought little of the knife or Abdela's statement. She was always trying to act tough, so her actions on that day were nothing out of the ordinary. After showing Vasquez the knife, Abdela then suggested that they walk over to a section of the park known as "Strawberry Fields," which was named for murdered musician John Lennon, who lived across the street at the time of his death.

Abdela knew that there was usually a crowd in Strawberry Fields passing various types of alcohol around in a circle and that there was never any age requirement. When the pair came upon a drinking circle, Abdela immediately noticed forty-four-year-old Michael McMorrow.

In 1997, Michael McMorrow was a bit of a troubled and confused man. He was a somewhat successful real estate agent in New York City who made decent money, but most other aspects of his life were a mess. He had never married nor had children, and at the time was living at his mother's house nearby. McMorrow's big problem was booze. Like most people consumed with the ravages of alcoholism, McMorrow lost relationships and money to the addiction, and on the day in question, it ultimately cost him his life.

As the bottle of booze made its way around the circle, Abdela squeezed her way in next to McMorrow. Despite the vast age difference, the two were fairly well-acquainted, as they had shared beer and liquor on numerous occasions in the park. The two were even friendly enough that Abdela referred to McMorrow affectionately as "Irish."

But as the bottle made its way around the circle, Abdela didn't look at McMorrow with affection. She eyed him the way a predator views its quarry—with a cold, calculating indifference, knowing that, in a short while, he would be dead.

When the alcohol began to take effect, Abdela asked McMorrow if he would like to join her and Vasquez for a more intimate drinking session near the pond. McMorrow agreed, and within minutes the three were passing a bottle around near the pond, with Abdela flirting with the middle-aged man by rubbing on him and kissing his cheeks.

At this point, Vasquez became enraged by what he saw, which was apparently Abdela's plan, and he attacked the older man with a knife and several punches to the head and body. As soon as the attack began, Abdela helped by kicking McMorrow's legs out from underneath him, rendering him defenseless against Vasquez's battering.

The forensic evidence shows that the blitzkrieg-style attack happened so fast that McMorrow was unable to defend himself. Neither Abdela nor Vasquez suffered any wounds from the assault. The two teenagers pummeled the older alcoholic relentlessly until he quit moving.

Then Abdela ordered Vasquez to disembowel their victim so they could sink his corpse in the pond.

The Capture and Trial

After Vasquez waded a few feet into the pond and sank McMorrow's body, he and Abdela walked the short distance back to her apartment, soaking wet and covered in blood.

Unknown to Abdela, her father had called the police when she failed to come home at her 10 p.m. curfew. Daphne had missed plenty of curfews before this day, but Angelo was tired of his daughter's behavior, and it was well past midnight. He reasoned that if his out-of-control daughter wouldn't listen to him, then maybe she would listen to the police.

Little did Angelo Abdela know what his little girl was up to that night.

As the police were searching the area for Daphne, and her parents were up waiting, worried and wondering, the murderous duo made their way back to the apartment building around 1 a.m. Abdela and Vasquez then went to the back of the building on the ground floor, where there was a community washroom. There, they proceeded to strip naked and wash the blood off each other. As they were cleaning up, the police showed up, tipped off by the doorman who thought the sight of two bloody and wet teenagers was odd.

When questioned about what they were doing, Abdela calmly told the police that they were cleaning up after a rollerblading accident. With that explanation, the police left, and Vasquez went home.

What happened next in this already troubling and bizarre case makes the entire situation even more difficult to comprehend.

After Daphne went back to her apartment, she argued with her dad for a while before he went to bed. Daphne then called 911 and told the operator that there was a body in the pond in Central Park.

The call was traced back to the Abdela home, which led both uniformed police officers and plainclothes detectives to visit the Abdelas.

Angelo knew that this time his daughter was in serious trouble. He exhorted Daphne to say nothing until he got her a lawyer, but the young murderer would have none of it.

She wanted to talk.

As she calmly sat eating a bowl of macaroni and cheese in her family's living room, Daphne Abdela confessed to everything. To verify her story, the police brought her to Central Park, where they dragged McMorrow's body from the pond.

The average New York City police officer, both uniformed and detective, sees a lot of violent crime throughout their career, but those on hand when McMorrow's corpse was pulled from the pond were astonished and perplexed by the entire situation.

They were even more astounded when Abdela went into a bizarre display of histrionics.

"I tried to help you! I tried to give you CPR!" she yelled at the corpse.

Abdela was quickly brought to a juvenile detention facility, and Vasquez was picked up a short time later.

Like the Collier and Wolf case, the murder of Michael McMorrow quickly became a media sensation. The perpetrator's ages combined with Daphne's "baby face" contributed to making this one of the more followed crime cases of the late 1990s. An added element to this case, which was missing in Collier and Wolf's case, was the privileged background of Abdela.

Daphne Abdela's background led many to speculate that she would be able to buy her way out of any significant punishment and that the less fortunate Vasquez would probably shoulder most of the legal blame. As the two defendants' cases worked their way through the courts over the period of about a year and a half, both were certified as adults.

Daphne Abdela and Chris Vasquez were looking at doing significant prison time, possibly the rest of their lives, in tough New York state prisons.

Vasquez was the first of the pair to go to trial. His defense was essential to point the finger at Abdela. His lawyers argued that the wealthier and more sophisticated girl held a Svengali-like influence over their client, who was out of his league at the Beekman School and suffered from mental health issues. They admitted that Vasquez was there when McMorrow was murdered, but that he played a diminished role and that he never knew what Abdela had planned.

The jury partially agreed with Vasquez's defense.

In December 1998, the jury acquitted Vasquez of the most serious charge, second-degree murder, but found him guilty of first-degree manslaughter. Chris Vasquez was sentenced a month later to up to ten years in prison.

As soon as Vasquez was convicted of manslaughter, Daphne Abdela's expensive team of lawyers set about to get their client the best possible plea bargain. After some haggling with the prosecutors, Abdela agreed to plead guilty to first-degree manslaughter and was sentenced to up to ten years in state prison.

Some people, namely Michael McMorrow's family, believed that the teen killers got off easy, but most in New York City were willing to turn the page. Although the murder was senseless and extremely brutal, Abdela and Vasquez were quite young and should get another chance, most argued. Besides, they were both going to tough state prisons and would have felony convictions on their records for the rest of their lives, so neither killer got off scot-free.

Both Abdela and Vasquez were denied parole twice, but the pair were eventually paroled in 2004. In the years since, Vasquez has maintained a low profile, but Abdela's name has been in the news on more than one occasion.

Abdela was charged with terroristic threats in 2004 and was involved in a lawsuit over a 2009 car accident.

The case of Daphne Abdela appears to show that, no matter how many advantages some people are given, they will find a way to throw it all away.

CHAPTER 5:

THE MURDER OF
HELLE CRAFTS

There is a common notion when it comes to murder that, if there is no body, then there can be no conviction. In the past, this was largely true throughout most of the United States; in fact, many states had statutes that specifically stated that a person could not be charged with first-degree murder without the corpse of the victim.

The reason for this can be traced back to early American history, and actually back to Great Britain, where plenty of safeguards were written into laws to protect innocent people from falling victim to zealous prosecutors. The reasoning was that if a person simply decided to leave town without telling anyone, a prosecutor with an axe to grind could simply charge someone with the missing person's murder, even if it was not known that a murder had taken place.

For most of American history, the citizens were fine with such laws. Cases where a murder potentially happened but no corpse could be found were extremely rare, and in the few cases where the evidence seemed to overwhelmingly point toward murder, the prosecutor could usually charge the person with a lesser murder or manslaughter statute.

But things began to change in the late 1960s.

As the United States' crime rate dramatically rose from the late 1960s until the early 1980s, people began demanding harsher sentences for criminals. On the other hand, criminals became more sophisticated, and organized crime became more prevalent.

Americans were inundated with grisly news stories of bodies being chopped up, dumped at sea, and burned so that the perpetrators could avoid first-degree murder charges. Soon, the disgust and fear that these stories generated in Americans was replaced with anger that these criminals seemed to be giving a metaphorical middle finger to the American justice system and, in essence, the American people.

Something had to change.

Actually, a couple of major things took place that led to many states revising their first-degree murder statutes regarding the presence of the victim's body. First, the "get tough on crime" attitude took hold of the United States during the 1980s. The states and the federal government enacted new laws and statutes that made it easier for criminal defendants to be prosecuted for first-degree murder, even when the victim's body was not available. Second, advances in forensic science made the first point moot at times. By the 1980s, crime scene investigators had mastered the use of the chemical luminol to identify washed-away blood evidence at crime scenes. The uncovering of a large amount of blood could definitively determine that there was no way a person could survive the loss, which many courts began to consider as a reasonable substitute when no body was present.

Still, there was no way of knowing whose blood it was.

That changed in the late 1980s when DNA profiling was first used in a criminal case in the United Kingdom. By the early 1990s, DNA profiling gave investigators the ability to identify the source of blood and other biological evidence, which meant that murder cases could be built against defendants without a body.

A murder that took place on November 19, 1986, in Connecticut eventually made legal history as the first first-degree murder case to be successfully prosecuted in that state without a body.

Besides the precedent-setting investigation, prosecution, and verdict, the case was made for the tabloids of the era. The defendant was a handsome airline pilot who was accused of murdering his beautiful wife and disposing of her body in a wood chipper.

The details proved to be a partial inspiration for the 1996 film *Fargo* and helped bring the now-famed forensic investigator Henry Lee to prominence through his work on the case.

Helle Nielsen and Richard Crafts

Helle Nielsen was born in a small town in northern Denmark in 1947. Although Denmark escaped most of the ravages of World War II, things were still tough for most Danes in the first few years after the war, so the Nielsens often had to save money by avoiding luxury items and travel.

For young Helle, though, the lack of money or the ability to travel was never a major concern because she was enthralled in a world of books. Unlike many other kids, Helle actually enjoyed attending school, which is where she developed interests in history and languages. She showed an especially high aptitude for foreign languages.

By the time she graduated from the Danish equivalent of high school, Helle had mastered French, English, and German in addition to her native Danish and the other Scandinavian languages of Norwegian and Swedish.

Helle then moved to England to study at a university where she blossomed into a sophisticated, cultured, and very attractive young woman. She had no difficulty meeting men of a similar quality, but still in her twenties, Helle wanted to travel and see some more of the world, so she took a position as a nanny in France. Although she liked her job, Helle wanted to see more of the world, so after a friend mentioned that she might consider working as an airline attendant, she applied for and was hired by an airline in Europe in the late 1960s.

The slim, trim, sophisticated blonde found airline work to her liking, and after working in Europe for a couple of years, she applied to what was at the time one of the biggest airlines in the world—Pan American World Airways.

Richard Crafts was born ten years before Helle, and almost from the start, it looked like he would do great things in his life. Richard was never a physically imposing individual—as an adult, he only stood five feet, eight inches—and he was usually not the best looking guy in the room, especially around his fellow pilots, but there is no doubt that he possessed a considerable amount of charisma. Other men respected Richard's opinions and ideas, and he never had problems meeting women.

But unlike Helle Nielsen, Richard Crafts never liked school very much.

Crafts was pushed into attending college after he graduated high school, but he was quickly bored with the curriculum and dropped out.

Lucky for Richard, he grew up in an era in the United States when a person didn't need to go to college to get a good job. There were several options available to young people who wanted to enter the workforce immediately after high school, the military being one of the most popular.

Richard joined the United States Marine Corps in 1956 and received extensive training as a pilot. It was in the Marines where Richard learned how to fly a variety of different aircraft, and it was also where he worked in covert operations for the CIA. During Crafts' time with the Marines in the 1960s, he flew several missions over Southeast Asia for the infamous Air America airlines. Crafts' time with Air America gave him his first sense of real danger, and some close to him would later say that it instilled a sense of paranoia in him that played a role in Helle's murder.

After Crafts was honorably discharged from the Marines, he returned to the United States, where he worked for some smaller airlines before landing a job with Eastern Airlines.

By the early 1970s, Richard Crafts was well on his way to having a successful career and life. Then he met Helle Nielsen.

The Marriage

When Richard returned stateside, he picked up where he left off regarding women. Crafts found it easy to attract women earlier in his life, but once he became a commercial airline pilot, things got even easier. After dating several women, he became engaged to an attractive young flight attendant.

The flight attendant was not Helle Nielsen.

Although Crafts was engaged, his eyes continued to wander until he eventually began cheating on his fiancée. One of the women he was seeing behind his fiancée's back was a young Danish flight attendant. Richard was immediately captivated by Helle's natural beauty and sophistication, while Helle was equally attracted to Craft's charisma and confidence. Crafts was honest with Nielsen about his engagement: he told her that he had no plans to end it.

Helle and Richard fought over the situation while continuing to see other people. Then Helle learned that she was pregnant.

Needless to say, Richard was not happy.

Despite their obvious issues and the fact that their relationship had begun under a cloud of deception, Richard agreed to marry Helle. Around the time Helle gave birth to their first child, Andrew, in 1975, Richard and Helle married. The couple was more than financially stable and able to afford a nice home in the exclusive New York City suburb of Newtown, Connecticut.

The change in the couple's marital status, though, did little to alleviate their difficulties. Due to the nature of their work, both were gone from home a lot, and Richard soon returned to his womanizing ways.

There were also rumors that Helle had more than one tryst with other men.

Still, the couple managed to stay together, and Helle even gave birth to another son, Thomas, in 1979, and a daughter, Kristina, in 1980.

When Helle wasn't working, she dedicated much of her time to her children, driving them to activities and helping them with their homework. Friends of the

Crafts said that Helle was an excellent mother and truly enjoyed raising her kids. Richard, on the other hand, was for the most part aloof toward the family.

When Richard wasn't working or chasing after his next sexual conquest, he spent most of his free time developing an extensive gun collection. Collecting guns is a fairly common pastime in the United States, but for Richard Crafts, it seemed to coincide with a carefully crafted persona he had tried to build over the years. He often told anyone who would listen about his covert operations with Air America during the Vietnam War and often implied that he was still working with one or more intelligence agencies.

Crafts was also a part-time police officer in the area.

The position he took was in a small town with little crime. The department didn't even have enough money to give Crafts his own car, so he went out and bought one with his own money.

Helle was not happy with the purchase.

In fact, by the mid-1980s, Helle was not happy with much of what her husband did. Friends of the couple said they argued constantly, and some claimed to have seen Helle with bruises and black eyes on more than one occasion.

The marriage was clearly dysfunctional, and Richard obviously had many inner demons to deal with, so many of Helle's friends were not surprised when they learned she had disappeared off the face of the earth on the evening of November 19, 1986.

The Disappearance

On the evening of November 19, Helle Crafts flew into John F. Kennedy International Airport in New York City after working flights in Europe. There was a snowstorm brewing that had the potential to turn into an early winter blizzard, so Helle quickly rendezvoused with the other flight attendants in her carpool to beat the weather.

According to her co-workers, Helle said little on the nearly two-hour drive to Newtown. When they arrived at the house, they all noticed the lights were on, and Helle said, "Oh, Richard's home," before saying goodbye and walking into the house.

Helle's friends never saw her again.

It will probably never be known for sure what happened next, unless Richard gives a full confession before he dies, but a chronology of the events was created by the prosecutors based on the circumstantial and forensic evidence available.

Because Richard bought several items that were instrumental in his concealment of the crime, it is believed that the murder was premeditated. He sent all three of their children to friends' homes for the night so that when Helle returned, he could kill her, move the body, and clean up the scene without anyone knowing.

After she entered the house, Helle went straight to the couple's bedroom, presumably to sleep after the long flight from Europe. Instead, she was met by Richard, who beat her to death with a blunt object. Richard then put her body in a freezer in the house and went out and ran some errands that were related to concealing the crime.

First, he bought some cleaning supplies.

Most importantly, he picked up a wood chipper he had reserved days earlier in a neighboring town.

As Crafts was running his errands, he was glad to see that it was still snowing. He believed that the snow would help conceal his crime, or at least slow the investigation once the authorities began looking for Helle. Crafts was under no illusions when it came to what he had done; he knew that there would be an extensive search for his wife, and he would no doubt be the prime suspect in her disappearance.

But Crafts believed that if there was no body, there was no way he could be convicted.

Richard went back to his home and retrieved his wife's corpse from the freezer before any of his children returned. He then drove a few miles to what he believed was an isolated location on the shore of Lake Zoar.

It is not known if Crafts dismembered Helle at their home or at Lake Zoar, but experts later testified that he would've needed to dismember the body to get it all into the wood chipper. No doubt he knew that freezing the body would leave less of a mess in terms of blood, but once he put her body parts in the chipper, it would leave a pile of flesh and bones.

Richard hoped that the fresh snowfall would conceal his heinous act.

As Crafts was placing his wife's body parts in the wood chipper, a pickup truck drove slowly by. Crafts did not let the driver worry him, though, as he quickly completed his nefarious task and made it home in time to meet his children.

In the days after Helle's disappearance, her friends began to grow suspicious when she didn't return any of their calls and failed to report to work without notifying anyone of an intended absence. It just did not fit the usually punctual and thoughtful Nordic's character. Before too long, Helle's friends' suspicions were amplified when they asked Richard where their friend was.

Richard told some of Helle's friends that she had moved back to Denmark, while to others he said she was in the Canary Islands, and to some he exclaimed that he had no idea where she was.

None of it made sense to her friends, especially when they contacted the Nielsen family in Denmark and learned that they had not heard from Helle in some time.

The Investigation and Arrest

In the days after Helle's disappearance, after Richard had related multiple stories about his wife's whereabouts, Helle's friends began contacting the local police department. The Newtown Police Department was initially indifferent to Helle's friends' pleas as they countered that the attractive woman probably met another man in some exotic location and would eventually return once she'd had her fun. The police also knew Richard Crafts from his part-time work with police departments in the area, which led them to think that he was not capable of murder.

Believing that there was much more to the case, Helle's friends next went to her divorce lawyer for answers.

They were surprised to learn that the Crafts had more than the average marriage problems. Yes, there were infidelities and possible physical abuse, but Helle's lawyer also contended that she was genuinely in fear for her life.

Helle's lawyer was particularly disturbed by one conversation he'd had with her when she told him, "If something happens to me, please don't assume it was an accident."

At this point, few familiar with the Crafts believed her disappearance was an accident.

After meeting with Helle's lawyer, a private investigator named Keith Mayo came forward with even more evidence. Mayo had been working with Helle's divorce lawyer to compile evidence against Richard, whom he had caught cheating with another woman. But Mayo's investigation revealed far more than infidelity on Richard's part. Mayo learned that the Crafts' nanny noticed a dark red spot on the carpet in the couple's bedroom, which Richard had replaced as soon as she mentioned it.

Mayo also learned about some questionable purchases Crafts had made in neighboring towns in the days before Helle's disappearance.

Instead of bringing the evidence to the local police, who were indifferent to the case, Mayo brought his findings to the Connecticut State Police, who arrested Richard Crafts for murder in January 1987.

Resolution

In the United States, a defendant in a criminal trial has a right to a "speedy trial" according to the Sixth Amendment of the United States Constitution. What exactly constitutes a speedy trial has been challenged in numerous cases that have gone all the way to the Supreme Court, but the definition remains a bit ambiguous.

And defendants are not always helped by a speedy trial.

The longer a case takes, the more witnesses' memories erode, and still others may change their stories altogether. For Richard Crafts, a speedy trial would've actually served him best since he was held without bail, and advances in forensic science were being made that ultimately ensured that he would be convicted of his wife's murder.

Crafts' defense was that he simply did not kill his wife and, in fact, there was little to no evidence that she was dead. His lawyers called few witnesses and instead focused their energies on taking apart the prosecution's case.

The prosecution's case was predominantly circumstantial, but there were plenty of circumstances that pointed toward Richard's guilt. A number of witnesses were called who testified that Richard was both abusive towards Helle and a serial philanderer, which established a motive for murder. Next, the prosecutors showed that Crafts rented a freezer and a wood chipper just days before his wife disappeared. The man who saw Crafts using the chipper at the lake then positively identified him in court. Although less than an ounce of human remains was recovered from the pile at the lake, a document with Helle's name was found among the remains.

A chainsaw with blood and human remains was also found near the lake.

As Richard Crafts sat in the county jail waiting for his trial, advances in DNA profiling allowed investigators to positively identify the blood on the chainsaw as belonging to Helle Crafts.

Despite the plethora of circumstantial evidence stacked against him, Crafts' first trial ended in a hung jury in the summer of 1988.

A new trial was ordered in which the prosecutors were able to use their DNA evidence against Crafts. The result was that Richard Crafts was found guilty of first-degree murder in November 1989. Crafts was the first person in Connecticut history to be convicted of first-degree murder without the victim's body. He was sentenced to fifty years in prison but was paroled in 2020 due to "statutory good time."

CHAPTER 6:

THE MURDER OF
VIRGIL LAMAR WARE

The 1960s were a turbulent time in the United States. People were fiercely divided over cultural issues, racial tensions were high, and violence from both the far left and right wings of the political spectrum was commonplace. The era of civility that characterized 1950s America was long gone, and in its place was a cultural change that most people didn't understand or want.

Of course, some locations in the country were more adversely affected than others.

The major cities were often the locations of political violence, and California became ground zero for the "Counter-Culture Revolution," while the many battles in the Civil Rights Movement, both legal and illegal, played out in the Deep South.

On September 15, 1963, Birmingham, Alabama, became the site of extreme violence in America's growing cultural war.

After the Supreme Court's ruling in the case *Brown v. Board of Education* made segregation illegal, the states that practiced segregation in their schools and other public spaces were ordered to dismantle the system. Some of the border states, such as West Virginia, quickly complied, but states in the Deep South militantly opposed any changes. The federal government used force to integrate some schools, most notably in 1954 at Little Rock Central High School, but the process to integrate all public spaces in the South proved to be arduous and at times violent.

Many people in the North and on the left wing of the political spectrum believed that they needed to speed the process up, so thousands of volunteers descended on the Deep South to protest and to help Black people register to vote.

Mississippi was the primary target of many of these activists, but Alabama was a close second.

Alabamans are traditionally very conservative people, and although most were not happy to see segregation end, they were willing to follow the law and accept the Supreme Court's judgment.

A minority of White Alabamans decided to turn to violence.

Membership in the Ku Klux Klan in Alabama exploded after *Brown v. Board of Education* became the law of the land, and by 1963, it had thousands of members statewide, divided into scores of secret cells. Klansmen promoted their ideas through violence by committing numerous acts of arson, assault, and even murder throughout the 1960s.

The most publicized act of Klan violence in Alabama during the period was when the 16th Street Baptist church in Birmingham was bombed, which left four young Black girls dead.

The Klan bombing of the church led to an intense FBI investigation of the Klan, which resulted in several arrests and convictions. But unknown to most, on that same day, another Black youth named Virgil Lamar Ware also lost his life due to the political and racial violence that had engulfed the state of Alabama.

Three Young Lives

Although some of the factors that led to Virgil Ware's murder were similar to the bombing of the 16th Street Baptist church, there were several notable differences. In the church bombing, the perpetrators were well-seasoned veterans of Alabama's race war who had long histories of violence, whereas Virgil's killers were teenagers not unlike him. The church bombing was also a well-planned attack meant to intimidate those who believed in desegregation, while Virgil's killing was not a premeditated murder.

With that said, Virgil lost his life on that day because he ended up in the wrong place at the wrong time.

At the time of his murder, Virgil Ware was much like most thirteen-year-old boys in the United States. He liked to play sports and was not a fan of school, although his attendance was good, and he was not a problem for his teachers. Like nearly every kid in Alabama at the time, he attended a segregated school in Birmingham, which was said to be the most segregated city in the United States. Despite the political and racial turmoil that was happening all around him, Virgil avoided conflict in the volatile city. Like most people of both races, Virgil Ware just wanted to live his life.

Living his life included doing odd jobs around the neighborhood for cash, which eventually landed him a paper route, but there was one issue—he needed a bike for a paper route.

On the morning of September 15, Virgil's brother suggested that they go to another neighborhood where they could buy a used bike for Virgil at a reasonable cost. Not sensing what was taking place around them, the two boys headed out on their mission.

In many ways, sixteen-year-olds Michael Lee Farley and Larry Joe Sims were not very different from Virgil Ware. Like Ware, Farley and Sims were reasonably ambitious for their age and did various odd jobs to earn spending money. Farley and Sims were also good students and were Boy Scouts who had attained the prestigious rank of Eagle Scout.

Farley was the leader of the pair, and neither one was known to harbor much animosity toward Black people. Sims' father was a manager at an area Sears store who, although not a liberal in the modern sense, was clearly not a militant segregationist.

The pair also lived not far from Ware.

But it may as well have been a world away in 1963 Birmingham, because Farley and Sims were White.

On the morning in question, Farley and Sims had attended a pro-segregation rally in Birmingham where fiery speeches were given by local leaders of the Ku Klux Klan and the White Citizens' Council.

After listening to the speeches, Farley and Sims were fired up and ready for action.

A Deadly Chance Encounter

When the pro-segregation rally concluded, Farley started up his motorcycle, and Sims got on the back. The pair were planning on going straight home, but they decided to stop at a store. There, they heard about the church bombing and retaliatory rock-throwing attacks by groups of Black youths. Even more fired up now, the pair rode around their neighborhood for a while until they noticed something out of place—two Black boys riding a bicycle.

The two Black boys were Virgil Ware and his brother James. Virgil was riding on the handlebars of the bike with James pedaling, unaware that they were about to be attacked.

Farley spotted the Ware brothers and alerted Sims to the outsiders. They later told the court that they believed the Ware brothers were in their neighborhood either to start fights with White kids or to steal. Like most young men in the American South, both Farley and Sims were well-acquainted with firearms, and on that day, Farley pulled out a new .22 caliber handgun he'd bought. After admiring the gun for a few minutes, he handed it to Sims and told him that he would drive up close to the two Black kids, and then he should fire a couple of shots from his gun to scare them.

The right-handed Sims fired from his left hand, with disastrous consequences.

"I thought I was shooting at the ground," Sims recalled. "I remember pop-pop, and then thinking, oh, no, I might have hit [Virgil] in the leg."

In fact, he shot Virgil twice, once in the head and once in the chest, leaving him dead at the scene.

After the shooting, Farley and Sims fled to their homes.

The Aftermath

Farley and Sims were quickly tracked to their parents' homes and charged with first-degree murder. It was big news that they were being charged at all for killing a Black person, but the most severe charge of first-degree murder caused commotion throughout the state of Alabama. Black and White people in favor of integration saw the charges as progress, while segregationists believed that the Jefferson County officials were offering Sims and Farley up as sacrifices to placate the mob.

Sims went to trial first in front of an all-White jury. The jury acquitted Sims of the most serious charges but convicted him of second-degree manslaughter. Farley then pleaded guilty to second-degree manslaughter. The youths were sentenced to seven months in jail, but the sentence was suspended, and they were placed on two years' probation instead.

The lenient verdict hurt the impoverished Ware family, who initially had no money to buy a headstone for Virgil. He eventually got one in 2004.

Farley and Sims moved on with their lives. Farley has lived in the area for most of his life and has become a recluse due to publicity from the case. Sims went on to college at Auburn University, and instead of continuing on to graduate school to avoid the draft for the Vietnam War, he volunteered.

"I was aware that it was people from poorer families, like [Virgil's], that were being sent to fight the war. I needed to see the war from the grunts-eye view," said Sims about his decision to volunteer.

Today, Birmingham is a much different place, but memories and ghosts of the turbulent 1960s persist.

CHAPTER 7:

WANDA HOLLOWAY, THE KILLER CHEERLEADER MOM

In the 1999 dark comedy film *Drop Dead Gorgeous*, Kirstie Alley plays a mom obsessed with her beauty pageant daughter's success. Throughout the film, she sabotages her daughter's rivals to the point of committing murder, which ultimately backfires, resulting in her daughter's death and her own prison time. Most who watch the film enjoy the dark humor, as it pokes fun at Middle Americans' tendency sometimes to go to extreme lengths for their children.

Of course, in the real world, most parents know where to draw the line when it comes to their children. Some will affix a "proud parent of a (enter school here) honor student" to the bumper of their car, and most are willing to spend generous amounts of money and time on their children's success.

There are cases where angry parents have gotten into shouting matches with referees and/or coaches at high school sporting events, and in some rare cases, those confrontations have even ended in assaults.

But murder to benefit a kid's social status—that only happens in movies, right?

Think again.

It just so happens that *Drop Dead Gorgeous* had a kernel of reality to it and was at least partially inspired by a real-life plot by an ambitious cheerleader mom who wanted to kill her daughter's primary rival.

During the Christmas holiday season of 1990, prim and proper Texas housewife Wanda Holloway hired a hitman to kill her thirteen-year-old daughter's primary rival on her school's cheerleading squad. The bizarre case shook the foundation of a quiet, conservative Houston suburb and revealed the extremes that some in Middle America would go to for their children's success. If human lives weren't in jeopardy, it would have been an entirely laughable affair, but Wanda Holloway was deadly serious when she embarked on her diabolical plot.

The Holloways

In 1990, Wanda Holloway was an attractive thirty-seven-year-old mother of two. She grew up in the working-class, conservative Houston suburb of Channelview, Texas, which is known more for its views of oil refineries belching smoke than of any waterway. As a child, Wanda's father did a good job providing for her and her siblings, but her family lived an austere life devoid of most luxuries many other kids her age enjoyed.

Wanda was brought up in a strict Christian evangelical household where many of the children's school activities were curtailed if they were viewed as a negative influence.

Cheerleading was one of those negative influences.

Despite Wanda's pleas, her parents never let her become a cheerleader. They reasoned that it was not very ladylike to jump around and wear the uniforms that cheerleaders did, even in the 1960s. Wanda was truly disappointed that her parents forbade her from joining the cheerleading squad, but she kept her resentments to herself.

Instead, she let the resentments fester for decades.

Although Wanda was forbidden from being a cheerleader, her parents allowed and encouraged her to partake in other activities. Wanda read biblical scripture and sang in her church's choir. She displayed a natural aptitude for the piano, which she carried with her well into adulthood.

Wanda also learned how to present herself in an effective way at an early age.

Wanda benefited from natural good looks, and she magnified her attractiveness by always being well-dressed and well-spoken. Wanda's fashion sense was stylish yet conservative, and she spoke perfect English, albeit with an East Texas accent.

According to one of her daughter's junior high school teachers, Wanda was "very refined, spoke good English, and was beautifully attired."

When Wanda graduated from high school, she did what many young women did in her situation at the time and looked for a husband. Wanda was certainly intelligent enough to study at most universities, but her ultimate goal was to have a Rockwellesque family.

And Wanda was not willing to settle for just any guy.

Her good looks, neat appearance, and sophisticated personality attracted many suitors, some of whom were fairly wealthy. By 1990, Wanda was on her third husband and had established a fair amount of personal wealth from her second and third husbands. She also gave birth to a son, Shane, and a daughter, Shanna. Interestingly, Wanda never had to leave Channelview to build her dream life, although by 1990, she lived in the city's priciest subdivision. It was located just a few short blocks from her childhood home.

Ultimately, Wanda was driven by a desire to "show up" Channelview. She wanted to show the people of her hometown how a girl from a humble background could become one of the wealthiest and most influential women in the city.

Wanda wanted respect and was willing to do whatever it took to get it.

When Wanda gave birth to Shanna in 1977, she saw it as another opportunity to prove her worth to the people of Channelview. From the time Shanna was born, Wanda groomed her to be the cheerleader that she could never be. Essentially, Wanda lived vicariously through her daughter.

Wanda bought Shanna her first cheerleader kit at the age of five and began paying for expensive gymnastics lessons. Wanda drove Shanna to all of her cheerleading and gymnastics practices and usually stayed for the duration of the practice so she could critique her daughter when they got home. After they got home, Wanda would force Shanna to practice some more. For Shanna, cheerleading became the entirety of her life. She was allowed little time to just "hang out" with other kids her own age; everything revolved around her being the top cheerleader in Channelview.

For the most part, Shanna was cooperative with her mother and usually never showed any displeasure about the long hours of practicing or her lack of social life. Still, a parent can only push a kid so far before something happens. Eventually, the excessive practice began to take its toll physically on Shanna as she began to rack up numerous injuries.

But Wanda Holloway was not going to let some injuries get in the way of her dreams.

Wanda continued to push Shanna to the point where she made her practice and compete even when she was injured. But instead of making Shanna the best cheerleader in Channelview, Wanda's daughter began to tire of cheerleading.

"At some point, it clicked; this isn't fun," said Shanna in an interview with *People* magazine. "But I was so close to my mom. She was my world, and I wanted to please her."

There was no discussion in the Holloway home: Shanna would be a cheerleader whether she liked it or not.

But sometimes things don't go as planned, even when one seemingly plans for everything. After all her efforts, Wanda was sure that Shanna would make her junior high cheerleading squad. Wanda had watched the junior high squad practice, and she was also familiar with the other seventh-grade girls Shanna would compete against for a spot on the squad.

She knew that Shanna was virtually assured a spot. Before Shanna even tried out for the junior high squad, Wanda was already planning her daughter's next move to the high school squad and beyond.

But Shanna had to try out for the team first.

Wanda dutifully brought Shanna to the tryouts and followed that up by schmoozing with the judges to ensure that her daughter would make the team.

Within a few days, however, Wanda got the earth-shattering news that Shanna did not make the team. The news depressed Wanda, who set about to rectify the snub by making Shanna practice even more intensely. Shanna, on the other hand, was less worried about the situation. Her interest in cheerleading had long since evaporated, and she was more interested in other things, such as music, boys, and shopping at the local mall.

But Wanda would not accept defeat.

As she trained her reluctant daughter for the next tryout in a year, Wanda Holloway learned that a girl who lived a few houses away named Amber Heath had made the team. Wanda was incensed that her beautiful, athletic daughter had been passed over in favor of Amber, who she believed was much less attractive and far less capable.

So, Wanda increased Shanna's training regimen for another year until the tryouts began once more for the junior high cheerleading squad. But Shanna didn't make the cut in eighth grade, either, although Amber Heath did.

At this point, Wanda Holloway decided to take matters into her own hands.

A Bizarre Plot

Wanda's disappointment simmered, then turned to raw hatred when Shanna was kept off the cheerleading squad for a second straight year. For whatever reason, Wanda's wrath was directed at Amber Heath and her mother, Verna. It's not like there weren't other girls chosen ahead of Shanna, and the coaches had never given Wanda the impression that Amber was the last girl picked and Shanna was the first one out.

But in Wanda Holloway's mind, she knew the score.

To Wanda, Verna Heath was at the head of a conspiracy to deprive Shanna of her rightful spot on the squad. Really, though, this was all about Wanda and how she was living vicariously through her daughter. Wanda's dreams of seeing her daughter lead cheers in high school and then possibly college seemed to be coming to an end unless she did something drastic.

"I could see my mom was agitated. She felt Verna was trying to get in the way of my becoming a cheerleader," Shanna later recalled.

As the months went by, things only seemed to get worse.

Since the Heaths lived just a few doors down from the Holloways, Wanda saw quite a bit of Verna and Amber, and so was repeatedly reminded of her own failures. Wanda Holloway would not stand for this level of disrespect—she was a woman of action who was going to do something about it.

By late 1990, Wanda Holloway was fully committed to taking care of her daughter's—and therefore her—rivals. To this day, it is not clear what exactly Wanda hoped to get out of the bizarre plot that followed. She was never clear during her sentencing on why she intended to kill Verna and Amber Heath, but it seems as though she believed initially that doing so would get Shanna on the cheerleading squad. After the plot developed, though, it appears that revenge and hate were the primary motives.

Wanda knew that she could never kill the Heaths herself. She was just too prim and proper to perform such a dirty act, so she had to find a hired gun. Since Wanda had never been involved in any illegal activity, she had no underworld contacts and didn't know how to approach someone with such a proposition.

Then she remembered Terry Harper.

Terry Harper was a former brother-in-law of Wanda's. She'd had limited contact with him in the years leading up to Christmas 1990, but from what Wanda remembered of him, she thought he could help her with her problem.

Harper was no master criminal or a member of any organized crime group, but he was known around Channelview as a bit of a tough guy and a thug. Over the years, Harper had accumulated a criminal record, but it was far from the type of resume a hit man would normally have: misdemeanor assaults and disorderly conducts were it. Terry had never done any time in a state or federal prison and didn't live his life as a criminal.

But Terry Harper was known to have financial difficulties.

A string of failed marriages had left Harper in financial ruin and earned him the enmity of most of his children. Although Terry may not have been a professional criminal, he was prone to violence and was probably desperate for money, Wanda reasoned.

In the days before Christmas, Wanda called Terry to talk about old times, and after discussing their families for a few minutes, she asked to meet him about a possible business venture. Since Harper had problems finding regular work in the area, he gladly agreed to meet Wanda. He was, however, a bit confused when they met because she insisted they talk in her car.

Wanda wasted no time letting Terry know about her bizarre murder plot and the role that she had envisioned for him in it. Harper was taken aback when Wanda coldly and with a straight face told him how she wanted both Amber and Verna Heath dead. As Terry protested the whole affair, Wanda appealed to Terry's love for his niece.

After all, Wanda reasoned, it was all about Shanna.

But Terry Harper knew that, in reality, it was all about Wanda.

In Wanda's tunnel-vision quest to eliminate her and her daughter's rivals, she miscalculated how ordinary people would react to such a diabolical plot. She just assumed that she could appeal to Terry Harper's greed, and if that didn't work, then she could tug at his heartstrings.

She clearly miscalculated Terry Harper.

If she had taken the time to talk to her former brother-in-law in the years before the murder plot, then she would have known that he had left his wild ways long behind him and was now a practicing Christian.

Before leaving Wanda's car, Harper told her, "I don't do anything like that, and I don't know anyone who would do a thirteen-year-old child."

Instead of taking a step back and realizing the situation she was creating was not a good idea, or at least recognizing that Terry Harper was not on board with the plot, in the typical fashion of a person truly lacking in self-awareness, Wanda Holloway continued.

Wanda told Terry she would get back to him real soon. "I thought, fine," Terry recalled. "I just wanted to get out of the car."

To say that Terry Harper was disturbed by his conversation with Wanda Holloway would be an understatement. He wanted nothing to do with a murder plot, and he was angry and upset that his former sister-in-law would consider him for such a devious mission. After going home and thinking about the situation for some time, Terry decided to tell his brother Tony, Wanda's ex-husband.

Tony realized that although he was no longer married to Wanda, she was still the mother of his daughter, and that going to the authorities would subject her and her family to public shame—and she may possibly end up in jail. He asked Terry if she was serious and questioned if maybe Wanda was just venting and letting off some steam.

Terry was adamant that she was *dead* serious.

Tony told his brother that there was no other choice. If she decided to go through with the plot without him, then Terry would be at least partially responsible for any deaths. Tony also told Terry that he would be looking at prison time if the authorities learned that he knew of the plot but said or did nothing.

On Christmas Eve 1990, Terry Harper learned that Wanda was not joking or venting about murdering Verna Heath. She asked Terry again if he would help her eliminate the issue living a few doors down, and surprisingly, he agreed.

What Wanda didn't know was that, after the first time she'd solicited Terry to murder the Heaths, he'd told his brother and then gone to the Harris County Sheriff's Department.

The sheriff's department told Terry to go along with the plot and that they would give him a "wire" to wear and record all their conversations.

Once Terry agreed to be Wanda's hitman, their phone conversations shifted to specifics concerning how the deed would be done and payment. Wanda agreed to pay Terry $2,500 for the murder of Verna Heath, but most of the money would be paid after it was done. She agreed to give Terry a down payment of jewelry in the meantime.

On January 14, 1991, Terry went to the Holloway home to discuss the final details of the hit with Wanda and to receive his down payment of jewelry. After discussing the hit for a few minutes, Terry offered his former sister-in-law a final chance to extricate herself from the situation by asking her if she still wanted to go through with it.

She answered with an emphatic, "Yes."

The Harris County Sheriff's Department arrived at the Holloway home the next day and arrested Wanda for solicitation of first-degree murder.

A Media Sensation

As soon as the local Houston media outlets began reporting the details of the bizarre "cheerleader mom murder plot," the story was picked up throughout the United States. Reporters thronged to Channelview to understand how a conservative, middle-class mother could be driven to create such a diabolical plot. Though people searched in Wanda's past for answers, few came.

Since no one was physically hurt in the murder plot, and Wanda was considered a pillar of the community and not a flight risk, she was given bail and allowed to return home. Needless to say, things were pretty tense around Channelview. The Holloways lost their membership at a local country club, and in an era long before Facebook, they were "unfriended" by most people they knew, usually through silence.

But Wanda had more important things to think about than the local social scene. She was looking at spending a good portion of her life in prison if convicted.

The pre-trial hearings dragged on for several months until the trial finally began.

The only defense that Wanda's lawyers put up was that she was set up by Tony and Terry Harper. They argued that Tony was a bitter ex and that he wanted nothing more than to see Wanda in prison.

The jury didn't buy it and found Wanda Holloway guilty of solicitation of first-degree murder. She was sentenced to fifteen years in the Texas Department of Corrections.

As Wanda was about to be whisked away to prison, fate stepped in to help the defeated cheerleader's mom. It was revealed that one of the jurors should have been ruled ineligible under Texas law because he was on probation. Wanda was once more released on bail, but the Harris County prosecutors were determined to try the case again.

The pre-trial hearings for the second trial went on for years instead of months. The drawn-out nature of the second trial proved to be beneficial for Wanda, though, as many in the community began to tire of the endless media presence in their once-quiet town. The outcry to throw the book at Wanda had dissipated, and the prosecution was willing to make a deal with the cheerleader mom.

At the urging of her lawyers, Wanda agreed to plead guilty in September 1996 to solicitation to commit murder and received a ten-year prison sentence.

But fate stepped in once more.

In March 1997, the judge allowed Wanda to be released from prison after serving six months. She was placed on probation for ten years and ordered to pay a $10,000 fine. She later also settled with the Heath family for $150,000 as part of a civil lawsuit.

Some believe that Wanda Holloway got away with near murder, but she did spend some time behind bars, was bankrupted as a consequence of the case, and most importantly, she had her beloved reputation forever tarnished.

Wanda Holloway would never again be Channelview's favorite daughter.

The Aftermath

Wanda Holloway's murder plot deeply affected the lives of several people and left an enduring mark on America's pop culture landscape.

Although Wanda claimed to have committed her crime on behalf of her daughter, it was Shanna who suffered the most as a result. Shanna was ostracized at school and around Channelview because of her mom's actions. She spent the remainder of her teen years withdrawn and depressed, and for a long time would not forgive her mother. In her adulthood, Shanna blossomed into a beautiful young woman, graduated from college, and now works as a teacher. She also married and started her own family.

Today, Shanna has repaired her relationship with Wanda, but the two never talk about the murder plot. Shanna's children all know their grandmother, but they have yet to learn about Granny's lurid past.

Perhaps they will learn about it from Hollywood?

Besides being partially the inspiration for *Drop Dead Gorgeous*, Wanda's murder plot has been featured in numerous true crime television shows. The case was also depicted in a 1992 made-for-television film on the ABC network titled *Willing to Kill: The Texas Cheerleader Story*. The success of that movie led executives at the premium cable television network HBO to produce their own fictionalized version of the story, *The Positively True Adventures of the Alleged Texas Cheerleader-Murdering Mom*, starring Holly Hunter as Wanda Holloway.

More than likely, the incredibly scandalous nature of this case will lead to more movies, films, and books, so stay tuned.

CHAPTER 8:

THE MURDER OF
SCOTT AMEDURE

Every decade in recent American history can be characterized by distinct cultural traits and fads. For instance, the 1970s era is remembered for the "golden age of sitcoms," disco, and clothing styles that have thankfully not yet made a comeback, while the 1980s were typified by the "new wave" music style and hairstyles that could only be done with a lot of hairspray and/or gel. For those of us who remember the 1990s, whether we would like to or not, it is impossible to forget the grunge music, angst, and, of course, the talk shows.

If you were to spend a day at home watching television during the 1990s, talk shows were about all you could find. Talk shows were on standard television stations and cable, and ran from early in the morning until late in the evening. By the middle of the decade, talk shows had largely replaced game shows as the number two most popular types of daytime television programs after soap operas.

Television talk shows began long before bands like Nirvana and Pearl Jam were household names, though.

Phil Donahue is largely credited with starting the talk show phenomenon in the late 1970s, and then Geraldo Rivera followed up on Donahue's style with more controversial topics. However, it was Morton Downey Junior who gave birth to the style of talk shows that were so prevalent in the 1990s and led to the term "trash TV."

On Downey's show, titled the *Morton Downey Junior Show*, he routinely found not just the most controversial subjects and people to put on display, but also the most reprehensible. The result was usually designed chaos where Downey and the audience shouted insults at the guests, who often did the same, and sometimes were willing to use violence.

Although Downey's show was canceled in 1989, former Cincinnati mayor Jerry Springer decided to try his hand at the format with *The Jerry Springer Show*.

53

Springer's show, which began in 1991 and is still on today, established the tempo for the rest of the talk show craze of the 1990s and effectively set the bar at a very low level.

Springer cornered the market as the trashiest of all talk shows, but there were scores of others who were willing to use some of his tactics for ratings.

One of the less trashy talk shows of the 1990s that was still willing to use some of Downey Junior's and Springer's tactics was *The Jenny Jones Show*, hosted by Jenny Jones. Instead of focusing on bizarre topics, people, and situations, Jones' show usually featured people going through relationship problems, although controversial topics that were in the news were also covered.

With that said, Jenny Jones was not above "trashing it up" from time to time.

The subject of the March 6, 1995, taping of *The Jenny Jones Show* was "secret crushes." The producers of the show thought it would be a ratings hit to ambush some of their guests with the realization that their secret crush was of the same sex. One of the guests on that taping, Jonathan Schmitz, was told that a friend of his had a deep crush on him and that he would be given an all-expenses-paid trip to Chicago to appear on the show and learn the identity of his secret crush. When he got to the show, he learned the person was a male friend named Scott Amedure.

Three days after the taping, Schmitz killed Amedure.

Amedure and Schmitz

Both Amedure and Schmitz grew up in metropolitan Detroit and were living near each other in the suburb of Lake Orion, Michigan, in the mid-1990s. Although their social circles overlapped to a certain degree, the two men lived very different lives.

Scott Amedure lived openly as a gay man and by all accounts relished the nightlife. When Amedure was not at work, he could often be found in a Detroit-area gay club, drinking and mixing it up with other men. Amedure was in good shape and was fairly good-looking, so he could easily find dates in the local gay community. Still, his eyes sometimes wandered to men who were not known to be gay.

Jonathan Schmitz was a straight man who often came off to many as possibly being gay. Although in good shape, Schmitz was a bit short and small-framed and sometimes displayed "feminine" mannerisms, which led many to think he was a homosexual or bisexual. Despite what many thought, Schmitz was never known to have had any sexual encounters with men, and when he first met Amedure in late 1994, he was still reeling from being dumped by his female fiancée.

Besides being unlucky in love, Jonathan Schmitz had some other very apparent troubles.

Schmitz had a history of bipolar disorder and was known to binge drink and smoke a lot of marijuana. Friends and family believed that Schmitz was trying to self-medicate to deal with some of his darker mental issues. Despite his issues, Schmitz was known to be a helpful, solid friend who could be counted on in a pinch.

It was in one of those situations where Amedure and Schmitz first met.

Donna Riley was a mutual friend of Amedure's and Schmitz's, and one day, when she was having trouble with her car, she called reliable Jonathan Schmitz to take a look at it. While Schmitz was there, Scott Amedure showed up for an unannounced visit and met Schmitz in the process. Schmitz thought Amedure was a nice guy, but Amedure developed an immediate crush on Schmitz.

The crush would prove to be fatal.

The Taping

Amedure became enamored with Schmitz and began constantly talking about him around their mutual friend, Riley. For her part, Riley did nothing to discourage Amedure's crush by telling him that Schmitz was straight; in fact, she gave him hope by questioning Schmitz's sexuality and telling Amedure that things could change. To make matters worse, Riley began contacting the plethora of talk shows around at the time with the story of her gay friend's unrequited love in the hopes that they would get on television.

Donna Riley was clearly a drama queen.

Finally, after pitching Amedure's quandary to every talk show host from Rikki Lake to Sally Jesse Raphael, producers from *The Jenny Jones Show* contacted her and said that they would be interested in flying her, Amedure, and Schmitz to Chicago to be on an episode about "same-sex crushes." Riley was thrilled with the news, but she knew that there was little chance that Schmitz would cooperate if he knew that Amedure was the one who wanted him.

At this point, there is disagreement over what happened next.

Schmitz claimed that when the producers of the show contacted him, they implied that the crush was a female, but the producers later said in court that they told him it could be a "man or woman."

According to Schmitz's family and friends, after speaking with the producers of *The Jenny Jones Show*, he was convinced that the crush was either his ex-fiancé or a woman he had recently met at work. Jonathan was looking forward to the trip to Chicago and bought new clothes for the show.

Jonathan Schmitz was ready to meet his secret crush.

The trio was put on separate flights and housed in different hotel rooms the night before the taping so that Jonathan wouldn't notice what was happening and potentially back out of the show. Although the episode was never aired, thanks to the wonders of modern technology, it is now available on a number of different internet sites.

It was clearly a very awkward segment.

The segment began with Riley and Amedure seated, explaining the situation to an overwhelmingly female audience. Riley and Amedure related to Jones the situation in which the latter met Schmitz. The first few minutes of the segment were relatively tame until Jones started pressing Amedure about what he found physically attractive in Schmitz. Amedure responded that he liked how Schmitz was fit and in shape, but apparently that was not enough because Jones kept at him to relate more sordid details about any fantasies he had.

Apparently, Amedure had spilled his guts to the producers beforehand, who in turn gave Jones all the spicy details.

"I thought about tying him up to my hammock," Amedure finally responded.

Amedure's response got a round of laughs and applause from the audience.

Just when it looked as though Jones couldn't get anything more out of the segment, she invited out Schmitz, who had been seated backstage in a soundproof room.

When Schmitz came out to meet Amedure, his eyes immediately went to Riley. It was clear that his initial thought was that Riley was his secret admirer, although he didn't look very pleased at that prospect. As the moment clearly became awkward, that feeling intensified when Amedure stepped forward and embraced Schmitz in a very uneasy hug.

"Did you think Donna had the crush on you?" Jones asked Schmitz.

Before Schmitz could answer, Jones continued, "Well, guess what? It's Scott that has the crush."

"You lied to me," responded Schmitz with an awkward smile.

The noticeably confused Schmitz then became even more visibly upset when Jones revealed all the lurid details of Amedure's sexual fantasy. Jones then asked Schmitz if he would like to reciprocate the feelings.

"I'm definitely heterosexual," replied Schmitz.

Back in Michigan

In the days following the taping, Schmitz's anger over the ambush interview began to simmer. According to his friends and family, he was angry that Riley and Amedure had put him out there like that, and that when the show aired, he would be a laughingstock at work and around town.

Still, by most accounts, Schmitz was willing to forget about the whole situation.

Then, on March 9, Schmitz found a particularly lurid note tacked to the door of his apartment.

"If you really want to get it off, I'm the only one with the right tool," it said, and it was signed by Scott Amedure.

Schmitz found the note after he returned home from a night of heavy drinking. The booze combined with his already-simmering rage drove the young man into the world of homicidal fantasies. He had twice now been made a fool of by Amedure.

Jonathan Schmitz was set on getting revenge.

When Schmitz woke up on the morning of March 10, he immediately set about to put his murderous plan into action. First, he went to his bank and withdrew several hundred dollars, and then went to a gun store and bought a shotgun. Next, he had a few drinks to steel his nerves. Once he felt ready to proceed, Schmitz then drove over to Amedure's house to confront him about the note.

Schmitz left his gun in the car and walked up to the door and talked to Amedure for a few minutes. According to Schmitz, Amedure thought the entire situation was humorous and actually tried to seduce him one last time.

That was more than Schmitz could handle.

Schmitz went back and sat in his car for several minutes before getting his gun and returning to the house to shoot Amedure twice in the chest, killing him. The killer then drove to another location where he called 911 and admitted to the murder.

The Trials

Almost immediately, due to a combination of the lurid details surrounding the case and the fact that talk show television was involved, it became a media sensation. Some in the gay community believed that Amedure was the victim of homophobia or possibly even a hate crime, while many across the country began thinking that it was time to clamp down on "trash TV."

For his part, Jonathan Schmitz was looking at doing some serious time behind bars. He was immediately charged with first-degree murder, and although the state of Michigan does not have the death penalty, if convicted, he was looking at spending the rest of his life behind bars. And on the merits of the case, there would seem to be little defense that Schmitz could muster.

But this was the 1990s.

Schmitz had two things going for him in 1996 when he finally went on trial. First, the gay political lobby was not as powerful then as it is today. Although some in the gay community looked at this case as an issue to rally behind, there was never a coherent message put forth. Schmitz was not an avowed "homophobe," and it did not appear that he killed Amedure because he was gay but rather because he hit on a man who was not. Also, Americans were much less sympathetic to gay rights causes at that time, and many men and potential jurors may have been somewhat sympathetic to Schmitz's reaction to Amedure's sexual advances to a certain degree.

But more importantly, Americans were growing tired of talk shows by the mid-1990s.

Yes, the shows were extremely popular, but they were popular in the same way that people gooseneck when they drive by an accident scene—it is just so bad that you have to look at it for yourself to see if it is real. By the time Schmitz killed Amedure, talk show hosts were viewed in a similar light as lawyers and mafia goons.

Schmitz's lawyers were good enough to recognize these cultural currents, and so the defense they devised was two-tiered: it would comprise a modified "gay panic defense" and put *The Jenny Jones Show* on trial.

The first part of Schmitz's defense was a modified "gay panic defense," which has been attempted many times in American courtrooms, usually unsuccessfully. Essentially, the gay panic defense holds that a person cannot be held legally sane due to unwanted sexual advances by a person of the same sex. It held that the advances bring out a homosexual panic in the defendant, who is temporarily unable to tell right from wrong.

The defense has been tried very few times in American history, with the best outcomes for the defendants coming in a couple of cases where the charges of first-degree murder were dropped to manslaughter. In most of those cases, there were also other factors that were considered.

Since Schmitz's lawyers knew that defense alone would not win their client's freedom, they combined the gay panic defense with a "diminished capacity" defense. Schmitz's attorneys argued that their client's well-known battles with bipolar disorder and chemical addiction, combined with a homosexual panic, led to the events on March 10, 1995. Jonathan Schmitz was clearly in a fragile mental state when the situation began to unravel, which Amedure exploited, but even more to blame than the victim was *The Jenny Jones Show*.

Although Schmitz's fragile mental state was the underlying factor in Scott Amedure's murder, Schmitz's lawyers argued, the catalyst was the ambush segment on *The Jenny Jones Show*. The producers of the show and even Jenny Jones were called to testify as witnesses for the defense.

"I hope this changes the talk shows, they're absolutely rotten," said Jonathan Schmitz's father, Allyn Schmitz, in an interview during his son's trial. "Had [Jenny Jones] not done this, this would never have happened."

Although one can never really know if the murder was the direct result of the show, many in the public agreed with Allyn Schmitz's sentiments.

That was what the defense was betting on.

The defense strategy was partially successful. When the verdict was announced on November 13, 1996, it was clearly mixed. Schmitz was found not guilty of first-degree murder but guilty of the slightly lesser charge of second-degree murder. In later interviews with jury members, it was revealed that ten of the twelve jurors believed Schmitz was guilty of first-degree murder, but two of the jurors remained unconvinced that the act was truly premeditated. They argued that since Schmitz did not immediately kill Amedure when he first went to his house on the day of the murder, then he truly did not plan to kill him that day.

Although the victory was a victory of sorts for Schmitz and his legal team, the reality was that Jonathan was now a convicted murderer who would have to spend a large part of his adult life behind bars.

The judge handed Schmitz a twenty-five to fifty-year prison sentence.

Like most people who are convicted of felonies in the United States, Schmitz appealed his conviction and sentence and was given a new trial in 1999, but that trial ended with the same verdict and sentence as the first.

Most people believed that the resolution of the case was fair, but many still held "trash TV" partially responsible and thought that *The Jenny Jones Show* should be held more accountable.

Scott Amedure's family was willing to do their part to achieve that. In 1999, Amedure's family sued *The Jenny Jones Show*, Telepictures, which produced the show, and Warner Bros. for the wrongful death of Scott Amedure. The family was initially awarded $25 million, but that was later overturned on appeal.

Schmitz quietly did his time in some of Michigan's toughest prisons. He avoided troubles with other inmates and staff and was awarded parole after serving nearly twenty years behind bars. Schmitz was paroled from the prison in Jackson, Michigan, in August 2017, and he continues to keep a low profile.

For Jenny Jones, Amedure's murder proved to be a double-edged sword. The controversy and media attention following the murder proved to be a ratings boom for the show, but the criminal and civil trials brought those ratings back down to reality. The show limped along until it was canceled in 2003.

But the talk show format was dead long before 2003, and many experts point to the murder of Scott Amedure as the beginning of the end.

CHAPTER 9:

KATHERINE KNIGHT, THE CANNIBAL QUEEN

In modern, industrialized societies, extreme acts of violence involving cannibalism and necrophilia are extremely rare in peacetime. Sure, there have been cases where people such as Jeffrey Dahmer and Ted Bundy engaged in those activities, but they are outliers, which is partly the reason why they are so well-known today.

It would seem that the Dahmers and Bundys of the world are aberrations in history—not just in the modern world, but throughout all periods of "civilization."

That assumption is false.

There are numerous instances of individuals partaking in cannibalism and other violent activities that run counter to modern norms, but during their time were accepted and even sanctioned by important people.

In fifteenth-century central Mexico, the Aztecs were given a princess from the city-state of Culhuacan to cement an alliance between the two peoples. The king of Culhuacan believed that he was giving his daughter to marry one of the Aztec princes, so he was horrified when he learned that instead they killed her, flayed the skin from her body, and wore it in a ceremony.

During the period of the Dark Ages in Western Europe (the sixth through the ninth centuries CE), violence was a way of life, and warlords would often behead opposing warlords and craft their skulls into ornate drinking vessels. In the Germanic legendary cycle known as the *Nibelungenlied*, which originated during the Dark Ages, the heroine Kreimhild murdered the villainous Attila's children and then dismembered their bodies and put their flesh in his food.

One can find many more stories like these throughout history, and as the story of Kreimheld shows, women are just as capable of committing such atrocious acts.

The normally laid-back nation of Australia was shocked when it learned that one of its female citizens committed a series of acts on February 29, 2000, that would have made the Aztecs proud. On that day, forty-five-year-old Katherine Mary Knight committed a murder, despoiled the corpse, and then tried to eat it.

A Life of Violence and Shame

Katherine Knight was born on October 24, 1955, in the small town of Aberdeen in New South Wales, Australia. Aberdeen is located about 150 miles north of Australia's largest city, Sydney, but it may as well be a world away. The small town is what many would call "provincial" due to its rural, working-class nature. Aberdeen is also very conservative politically and socially speaking, and has been traditionally resistant to change.

Despite living in a socially conservative area of Australia, Katherine's parents did not practice traditional "family values." Both of Katherine's parents were guilty of numerous infidelities and, as a result, they eventually had to move from the conservative small town.

The man who was married to Katherine's mother when she was born was not her biological father. Katherine's family moved around quite a bit, as her stepfather was never able to hold down a good job. The stress of low-paying jobs took a toll on the family, which eventually led to Katherine and her siblings being sent to live with different family members.

Katherine eventually went to live with her biological father, Ken Knight, who taught her very little other than how to use violence as a tool to get what you want. Ken drank heavily and physically and sexually abused Katherine's mother, although Katherine claimed he never abused her.

Katherine has claimed that several other members of her extended family sexually abused her until the age of eleven. When Katherine wasn't being abused by her family members, she was largely ignored. Her parents never spent time with her, helping her with her schoolwork or doing other normal things that parents do with their children. Katherine's tough childhood helped create an angry, rebellious teen that few wanted to be around.

At school, Katherine was known as a violent bully who would attack other students, both girls and boys, over the slightest of perceived insults. Katherine was also known to assault teachers if they got involved. By the age of fifteen, Katherine was spending more time in the principal's office or suspended than she did in class, and when she was in class, she never paid attention—or possibly, she had a learning disability that was never diagnosed. Barely able to read and knowing that college was a pipe dream, Katherine decided to drop out of school at the age of fifteen. Needless to say, her parents were rather ambivalent toward her decision, other than to tell her that if she wasn't in school, then she needed to find work if she wanted to keep living in their house.

Katherine immediately found work at a place that seemingly defined her life and contributed to the crime that shocked a nation.

She found work at a slaughterhouse.

The Many Loves of Katherine Knight

As an adult, Katherine Knight can best be described as an average-looking woman. She was also never known to have a stellar personality, and she was not very sophisticated, cultured, or worldly, but she was always in a relationship with a man.

There were a couple of reasons why, despite her average looks and not very impressive personality, Katherine always had a significant other. The fact that she always worked in abattoirs certainly played in her favor, since it is traditionally a male-dominated profession. Sure, women work in slaughterhouses around the world, but most who do are in the office—Katherine worked on the kill floor with men all day long.

Katherine's past and personality also had a lot to do with her ability to wrangle men. She learned at an early age that people are little more than commodities to be used and then traded in when necessary. Katherine had also picked up different types of manipulation skills, which she then modified in adulthood to locate and seduce men.

And Katherine didn't land just any men.

Most of the men Katherine was involved with were similar to her in many ways: at best average looks, little education, and not much in terms of prospects. Katherine was smart enough to know what type of men she could land, so she didn't waste time with "high market value" men.

She also never received a good template of what a healthy relationship looked like.

Katherine spent her entire childhood either watching or being subjected to various forms of abuse. It was normal for the adults around her, even the ones who professed to love each other, to denigrate, debase, and abuse one another.

In the mind of Katherine Knight, no one was ever going to abuse her again, and if need be, she would, in fact, become the predator.

Knight's first serious relationship in adulthood came not long after she turned eighteen. She met a local twenty-two-year-old man named David Kellet, whom she believed would provide her with a good, stable life. Kellet was an over-the-road truck driver who made pretty good money, so Katherine's choice seemed to be a good one.

But Katherine could not control her anger.

To outsiders, the couple looked normal, but beyond the façade, a storm was brewing. Katherine's violent attitude manifested itself gradually, with verbal fights evolving into threats, but just before the couple married, things began to get much worse.

The couple liked to drink at local bars, and Katherine, in particular, was known to be a heavy drinker. Needless to say, Katherine and David were not hanging out at upscale bars but at working-class establishments where fistfights were quite common. Although David Kellet was not known for being a brawler, his mouth got him into some problems in the bars around Aberdeen.

Nearly every time David was about to get into a physical confrontation, Katherine would intervene by throwing punches at David's adversaries. Because of this, Katherine developed somewhat of a fearsome reputation around town.

"You better watch this one, or she'll fucking kill you," Katherine's mother told David on their wedding day in 1974.

Kellet should have heeded his mother-in-law's warning.

The two began their booze-laden marriage with Katherine threatening David's life on their wedding night due to not enough sex. From there, the marriage quickly took a downward trajectory. Katherine routinely beat David with her fists, frying pans, and whatever improvised weapon she could find around the house. The police were called on at least one occasion, but in the era before domestic violence was an issue—and since Katherine was a woman—no charges were ever filed.

Despite all of this, the couple welcomed a daughter to their family in 1976, but the abuse persisted. Finally, Kellet had had enough, so he left Katherine and their daughter, Melissa Ann, and moved to another state.

When Kellet left, it temporarily sent Katherine over the edge.

Not long after Kellet left her, Katherine took their baby in a stroller around town, violently shaking it as she walked. Concerned citizens eventually called the police, and Katherine was brought to a mental hospital, where she spent several weeks before being allowed to leave on her own recognizance. Not long after she was released, Katherine left her baby on a train track and then threatened several people nearby with an axe. Melissa Ann was saved by a local transient, and Katherine was returned to the mental hospital once more, only to sign herself out again the next day.

After her second stint in the mental hospital, Katherine was determined to find the perceived source of all her problems—David Kellet. To carry out her plan, Katherine slashed a woman's face with one of her slaughterhouse knives and then made her drive to Kellet's home. Along the way, they had to stop for gas, which allowed the woman to escape. But Katherine then took a teenage worker hostage. The police were able to negotiate a relatively peaceful end to the situation, but not before Katherine admitted to a plan to kill Kellet and his mother.

For whatever reason, the police never charged Knight with any crimes related to the violent incident. Even stranger, Kellet left his girlfriend and moved back in with Katherine. The couple moved to suburban Brisbane, Queensland, and even had another daughter.

Then, for reasons still unknown, Katherine left Kellet one day in 1984.

Next on Katherine Knight's list of lovers was a thirty-eight-year-old miner named David Saunders.

After leaving Kellet, Katherine moved back to Aberdeen with her two daughters to be close to her dysfunctional family and to go back to the original abattoir where her glorious career began. Not long after returning to work, Katherine was injured on the job, which eventually led to her receiving disability. To most people, being on disability is a bad thing, but to Katherine Knight, the situation allowed her to pursue her other primary interests in life—drinking, men, and violence.

While drinking in the local bars in 1986, Katherine met Saunders. She was immediately attracted to the strapping miner who seemed to exude every bit of the testosterone-laden persona that she so desired. The relationship was contentious for the first year, but far from the ultra-violence that Katherine wielded against Kellet.

But Katherine was just getting warmed up.

About a year into their relationship, the couple was having a heated argument when Katherine did something so horrible that many would find it unforgivable. It was also something that could land one in prison today in many jurisdictions. While they were arguing, Katherine reached down and grabbed David's pet dingo puppy and threatened to cut its throat. Perhaps David was unaware of what his girlfriend was capable of and didn't think she would do anything, but he was wrong.

Katherine cut the innocent animal's throat as if it were a pig in the slaughterhouse.

The sadistic act caused David to temporarily break things off with Katherine, but he kept taking her back, and she got more violent every time. Similar to the

65

situation with Kellet, Katherine beat Saunders with her fists, frying pans, and whatever else was available.

Ever a glutton for punishment and possibly a true masochist, Saunders kept taking Katherine back, and in 1988, even had a daughter with her. Believing that he should do the "right thing," Saunders bought a small house in the area for the growing family, and like a good partner, he let the woman do the decorating.

Katherine's taste in home décor reflected her violent personality—one could only describe her attempt at interior design as "early medieval." Animal skins, traps, and various weapons adorned the walls of Saunders' small house, which made it look more like a museum or a teenage boy's fantasy than a quiet family home.

At this point, weapons began playing an ever-increasing role in Katherine's life. Besides the various knives, daggers, and swords she had strewn about the house, she always slept with at least a few knives close to her bed. She and David lived in a very low-crime area of Australia, but Katherine insisted that she needed the weapons for her protection.

David began growing more fearful for his life and decided to leave his family to go into hiding in 1989. Katherine searched for her missing paramour for several months but was unable to find him. As a parting shot, Katherine contacted the local police and told them that David had threatened her life.

The police responded by putting a restraining order on David Saunders.

Katherine wasted little time finding a new beau and, within months of being dumped by Saunders, she was already deeply involved with forty-three-year-old John Chillingworth. Knight met Chillingworth on the job at a slaughterhouse, so the two seemingly had something important in common. The couple welcomed a baby boy, whom they named Eric, into their family—Katherine's fourth child and first boy.

Ever the jealous woman, Katherine Knight turned violent on her lovers when she even remotely suspected that one might be cheating on her. Most of her former lovers claim that the accusations were baseless, but also pointed out that the same rules never applied to her. In her relationship with Chillingworth in particular, Knight was said to have spent more time with other men.

Spending time with other men is how Katherine Knight met her final and most tragic lover in a long list.

John Price was a local miner who was the same age as Katherine when they began their affair in 1991. Price was well aware of Knight's well-earned bad reputation, but either due to desperation or the fact that he thought she had changed, he decided to let her move into his home in the town of Scone in 1995. Like with her other relationships, this one began benign enough, but as it progressed, it became more violent.

Once again, Knight unleashed a torrent of violence and abuse on her partner. With Price, though, Knight added a new wrinkle to her devious acts in 1998. After what seemed like just another shouting match, Katherine retreated to the bedroom. Price was surprised that Knight seemed to give up so easily, but he did not push the situation and left her alone.

Then, days later, John learned why Katherine ended their argument so abruptly.

It turns out that she was on the phone with John's boss, informing him that John had stolen some expired medicine from the job site.

John was immediately terminated from his well-paying job, which put him in a difficult situation. Once he learned how his boss found out, he took the bold step of kicking Katherine out of his home. At that point, John should have left well enough alone and never talked to Katherine again—they had no children together, and the house was in his name. But John Price was a lonely man, and he had a difficult time meeting women, so he agreed to start seeing Katherine again.

It was a decision that cost him his life and nearly the lives of his children.

Just Like the Aztecs

The on-again, off-again relationship between Katherine Knight and John Price continued into the new millennium. Following her typical relationship pattern, Katherine's verbal assaults evolved into outright violence. Despite the verbal and physical abuse, John kept taking Katherine back.

In early February 2000, John allowed Katherine back into his life once more, but was stabbed in the chest by Katherine for all his troubles.

Still, he kept seeing her.

Finally, on February 29, everything came to a head. Perhaps John knew that Katherine had something particularly sinister planned for him, or maybe he was finally tired of her abuse. Whatever the reason, he went to the local police station that morning to get a restraining order on Katherine. Since Katherine's reputation preceded her in the area, the police were well aware of her potential for violence. They agreed with Price that a restraining order would be a good idea, but added that he should leave the house immediately to avoid more confrontations. Price agreed that leaving would probably be a good idea, but he couldn't since his children lived at the house.

Meanwhile, while Price was planning his exit from the contentious relationship, Katherine was planning some things of her own.

All evidence indicates that Katherine clearly planned her partner's murder. She sent John's children to stay at a neighbor's, and what took place after was far from spontaneous or done in the heat of passion.

After going to the police station and running some other errands around town, John came home in the evening, watched some television, and then turned in for bed around eleven because he had to get up for work early the next day. Not long after John went to bed, Katherine arrived at the house, and it was as if the two had never had any problems. They talked for a few minutes and then had sex. After their tryst, John fell asleep while Katherine took a shower. She then watched some television before putting her appalling plan into action.

In the early morning hours of March 1, Katherine mercilessly stabbed John with a butcher knife while he slept. Although at a clear disadvantage, the athletic Price was able to wake up and fight his attacker off to a certain extent. Forensic evidence shows that after John fended off the initial attack, he tried to make his way out of the house, presumably to get help. He made it just outside the front door, but he collapsed there from the loss of blood. Katherine then dragged John back inside and finished him off with a few more stabs.

Then Katherine summoned her inner Aztec.

Knight next put her slaughterhouse skills to good use by flaying the skin off of John's body and hanging it over a doorway in the house.

A fifteenth-century Aztec couldn't have done better.

She then butchered his remains and cooked some of his internal organs. The evidence shows that Knight attempted to eat some of John's body parts, but even more disturbing is the fact that she apparently meant to "share" John with others. She set three places at the dinner table. The authorities believe one was meant for her, and the other two were for John's children.

She apparently planned to feed John to his children.

Price lived in a neighborhood where the houses and yards are small and where sound travels well. It was also a small town where everyone knew each other, so when the deadly assault began in the middle of the night, its noise was heard by several neighbors. Most in the neighborhood were well aware of Katherine Knight's violent reputation, so many went back to sleep, but one neighbor called the police in the morning when he noticed John's truck still in the driveway.

When the police received the call about a possible disturbance at John Price's home, they were reminded of Price's visit to them on the previous day.

They immediately knew something bad had happened.

They first found Katherine passed out on a couch, the result of taking several sleeping pills, but when they looked around more, they were horrified to find John's skin hanging from a doorway. Soon after, they found John's limbs, head, and internal organs strewn around the kitchen, some cooking, and some were even located in the backyard. The police speculate that the body parts found in the backyard were ones that Katherine attempted to eat, although she never admitted as much.

Pleading Guilty

It should go without saying that John Price's brutal murder not only shocked the small town of Scone but the entire nation of Australia. It was perhaps one of the most brutal murders the country had ever seen, and to make matters even worse, in many people's eyes, it was committed by a mother.

The case received immense media attention, not just in Australia, but throughout most of the Western world. Correspondents and journalists from British, French, German, and American media outlets were all in the courtroom to catch a glimpse of Australia's notorious female cannibal.

The salacious details of the case allowed the headlines and articles to write themselves.

While the media was busy picking apart the life and times of Katherine Knight, Katherine made a play to mitigate her bad situation. She attempted to enter a plea of guilty to manslaughter, which may have meant she would have done very little time in prison, but the judge rejected the plea.

Knight's attorneys pleaded with her to forgo a trial. They reasoned that the mountain of forensic evidence was just too much to overcome, and public opinion was clearly against her because of her past. Eventually, she agreed and allowed her lawyers to attempt to reach a plea bargain with the prosecutors. But the prosecutors weren't having it. They told Knight's attorneys that no deal would be given to the cannibal.

Then, on the eve of the trial, in October 2001, Katherine Knight inexplicably threw herself at the mercy of the court and pleaded guilty to John Price's murder. The sentencing judge, though, was not impressed with Katherine's sudden change of heart and sentenced her to life in prison with the added stipulation of "never to be released." The move by the judge was historic because even those convicted of murder in Australia are rarely given life without the chance of parole. The ruling was even more historic because it was the first case in modern Australian history where a woman was given a life sentence without the chance of parole.

Knight has kept a low profile since being in prison, but there are unconfirmed reports that she has been putting her meat-cutting skills to work in the prison's kitchen.

CHAPTER 10:

THE STRANGE LIFE OF THE LOBSTER BOY, GRADY STILES JUNIOR

For millions of Americans with disabilities, before the *Americans with Disabilities Act* became the law of the land in 1990, the difficulties of life were even worse. People with disabilities had few legal protections, which meant that it was actually legal to discriminate against them. They could be denied housing and other services, and of course, they were subject to harassment and bullying.

They also found it extremely difficult to find work.

Since there were no anti-discrimination laws on the books, disabled people were often the last to be hired and the first to be fired. For many with disabilities, the only option was to perform in circus and carnival sideshows.

With that said, not just any disabled person could become a "sideshow freak." Successful freaks needed to have a disability that was truly out of the ordinary and exotic to most people—simply being blind and/or deaf would not cut it. A good sideshow freak also had to have a gregarious, outgoing nature.

Obviously, it also helped to have thick skin.

By the first half of the twentieth century, a definite sideshow sub-culture emerged across the United States. The sideshow workers developed their own insular communities where their disabilities were barely noticed by each other. The freaks lived, worked, and married among their own kind, and even created entire neighborhoods composed totally of sideshow workers. Some sideshow freaks would even go on to become very wealthy.

For the most part, the freak community was peaceful. Outsiders rarely caused issues, and crime was very low within the community.

But it was not entirely absent.

When one notable freak committed a murder in 1978, it set in motion a chain of events that ultimately resulted in his own death. A close examination of the case reveals that sideshow freaks have the same hopes and dreams as everyone else.

They also have the same internal flaws as the rest of us.

A Family of Crustaceans

When Grady Stiles Junior was born in 1937, the deck of cards of life was stacked against him in many ways. He was born with the genetic disease known as ectrodactyly, an affliction in which those affected are missing digits on the hands and/or feet, creating the look of claws. Although the disease is not painful to those who suffer from it, it creates major mobility problems and can interfere with the ability to perform day-to-day functions, depending on the severity.

Grady Stiles Junior had a severe case of the disease.

The Stiles family had suffered from ectrodactyly from as far back as at least the early 1800s, and possibly earlier. Things were no doubt difficult for those in the Stiles family who were afflicted with the debilitating disease, but the emergence of the American circus and sideshow culture in the middle and late nineteenth century proved to be a benefit to the beleaguered family.

Grady Stiles Senior made a name for himself in the sideshow community and eventually made quite a good living. In fact, Stiles Senior was one of the first notable freaks who, through self-promotion and good investing, was able to build a nice life for himself and his family.

Although Stiles Senior's wife was not afflicted with ectrodactyly, his sons were. Stiles Senior knew that there were few options available to people with his disability, so he introduced his two sons to the sideshow business, and the three toured together as the "Lobster Family."

When they weren't touring around the country with circuses and sideshows, the Stiles family lived in Gibsonton, Florida, which became the de facto national headquarters of all American freaks. The community grew to a substantial size and was even featured on an episode of *The X-Files* in the 1990s.

When Stiles Senior died, he passed on the moniker to Stiles Junior.

One Tough Lobster

Most people would assume that, based on his disease, the Lobster Boy was not very formidable physically speaking.

They would be wrong.

Since the disease affected his hands and feet, Stiles Junior was forced to use a wheelchair most of the time to get around. If a wheelchair was not available, he would ambulate by crawling. Actually, Stiles Junior crawled as much as he used a wheelchair, which resulted in him developing exceptional upper body strength by the time he was a young adult.

And he wasn't afraid to use that strength against people.

Stiles Junior was known to use his impressive strength to beat those with whom he had disagreements, including his wife and children. The Lobster Boy was generally known to be a difficult person to deal with, but when he was drinking, things got even worse.

And Stiles Junior drank copious amounts of booze nearly every day.

The Lobster Boy's violent attitude and poor disposition earned him the enmity of many people in the freak community, so those who knew him usually gave the man a wide berth. They all knew that sooner or later, the combination of Stile Junior's temper, anger, and alcoholism would converge to create a fatality.

The fatality happened in 1978.

In 1978, the Lobster Boy's oldest daughter was getting married in Pittsburgh, Pennsylvania, and the entire Stiles family was expected to attend, even the Lobster Boy, whom many thought it was better not to invite. Despite the Lobster Boy's failings, every girl wants her father to be at her wedding, so Stiles Junior showed up days before, ready to give his daughter away in the ceremony.

Like with most American wedding parties, the night before the ceremony is a time to revel with old friends and family and to meet new ones. The Stiles wedding party began their celebrations in the afternoon, and by the evening, most in attendance had a good buzz.

The Lobster Boy was plastered.

After displaying his typical anger and bad attitude toward several guests, the groom stepped in and asked his future father-in-law to refrain himself or leave. Taking what the groom said as a slight, Stiles Junior pulled out a handgun and shot his would-be son-in-law dead.

The Lobster Boy's trial proved to be as bizarre as a carnival freak show. Since the county jail could not accommodate Stiles Junior's disability, he was allowed to be free on bail. He was eventually found guilty of third-degree murder but only sentenced to fifteen years of probation because the judge believed it would be cruel and unusual punishment to place him in a prison without proper facilities.

The Lobster Boy was glad to have essentially beaten the murder rap, but others in the Stiles family were growing weary of his antics.

The Lobster Hit

Not long after the 1978 murder, Stiles Junior remarried his first wife, Mary Theresa. He claimed that since she was a positive influence on his earlier adult life, he believed she would be again. The Lobster Boy promised to mend his ways and live a Christian life of sobriety.

For a few months, it seemed as though the Lobster Boy had truly turned over a new leaf, but before too long, he returned to his ways of heavy drinking and violence.

The violence soon became too much for Mary Theresa, who began plotting to kill her husband in late 1992.

Mary Theresa first enlisted her son from another marriage, Harry Glenn Newman Junior, who in turn hired a seventeen-year-old sideshow worker named Chris Wyant to do the deed. Wyant was paid $1,500 for the murder, which took place on the evening of November 29, 1992.

On the night in question, Stiles Junior was sitting in his favorite chair watching television with his wife in their Gibsonton home when she abruptly decided to leave and visit some friends who lived nearby. As soon as she left, Wyant emerged from a hiding spot in the back of the house, crept into the living room, and shot twice from a pistol, hitting Stiles Junior in the head and killing him instantly.

The police investigation quickly led back to Stiles Junior's own family, with the trio being rounded up and arrested for their roles in the murder. Theresa May used a battered wife defense, but the jury only partially bought it. She was acquitted of murder but found guilty of manslaughter and sentenced to twelve years in prison.

Interestingly, the sentences for the other two conspirators were also mixed. The triggerman, Wyant, was found guilty of murder and sentenced to twenty-seven years in prison, while Newman Junior was also convicted of murder but sentenced to life in prison.

In the aftermath of the Lobster Boy's murder, some still question that official version of events. Grady Stiles III claims that there was little premeditation and that it all was the result of his father's abusive nature and something his mother said.

"What actually happened was my mother and my dad had gotten in another fight as usual, and my mother had made the comment that something needed to be done," Stiles III said. "My brother had overheard that and went to the neighbor kid and told him that something had to be done."

The details of the Lobster Boy's murder are less important than how he lived. In many ways, Grady Stiles Junior rose above his disability, but in other ways, he let it drag him down into an abyss of alcoholism and violence. Those closest to him were generally fearful of his wrath, and few people considered him their friend.

The fact that there were no pallbearers at his funeral is a testament to the type of life the Lobster Boy lived.

CHAPTER 11:

THE MURDER OF
MARLENE WARREN

For Marlene Warren, life was pretty good in May 1990. The forty-year-old was married to a successful businessman named Michael, and the couple had a bright teenage son named John. The Warrens lived in exclusive Palm Beach County, Florida, a community that even had its own airstrip.

Michael ran a successful car sales business, and they also owned several rental properties throughout southern Florida. Both of the Warrens worked hard for what they had, however, their home and businesses were all in Marlene's name because she had brought a reasonable amount of money to the marriage. Still, both of the Warrens worked hard to make their businesses successful, and Michael in particular often put in extra hours at their car dealership.

However, he was doing more than work when he was putting in overtime.

In the months before Marlene was murdered, the Warrens began doing a lot of business with a repossession company that was owned by Sheila Keen and her ex-husband. Sheila was an attractive, vivacious twenty-seven-year-old who wasted no time when she saw something she liked.

Sheila liked Mike.

The affair between Mike and Sheila began with occasional innocent lunch dates, which then progressed into longer lunches, and then finally a full-blown romantic affair. Mike quickly fell head over heels for the younger woman and soon began treating her as his mistress by buying her expensive luxury items and even paying her rent.

The excessive amounts of money Mike was spending on Sheila soon came to the attention of Marlene.

Marlene was known for being sharp, and she often did the accounting for their businesses. She soon noticed mysterious regular monthly payments that had no discernible business functions. When she asked Mike about the discrepancies, he was evasive, which only escalated her suspicions.

Michael had to tread lightly. If she found out about his affair with Sheila, he stood to lose everything.

The Killer Clown

The morning of May 26, 1990, began like most others in the Warren home. Mike departed early for work at the car lot, which left John and Marlene at home alone. As Marlene was about to leave for work and John for school, the most curious of visitors stopped by the house.

When Marlene answered the door, she was surprised to be greeted by a clown with a bright red nose and orange hair. The clown was holding a bouquet of roses in one hand and two balloons, one printed with the words "You're the Greatest," in the other. Probably thinking that the gifts were a surprise from Mike, Marlene reached out to take the items from the clown, but when she did, the clown shot her in the face.

Marlene died instantly.

A number of neighbors heard the shot and witnessed a clown get into a white Chrysler LeBaron convertible and leave the area.

The Palm Beach County Sheriff's Department arrived at the Warren's home within a matter of minutes and began their investigation. Law enforcement officers are used to seeing strange things every day, especially in a larger, more urban county such as Palm Beach, but this case was perhaps the most bizarre of all. Everything from the clown to the shooting in broad daylight to the getaway all seemed so strange, but at the same time, it seemed to add up.

Palm Beach County homicide investigators immediately suspected Mike Warren was involved.

Whenever a person is murdered, investigators immediately focus on the spouse, if there is one, because statistically speaking, the odds are overwhelming in favor of the spouse being the perpetrator. So, the investigators had a logical place to start, and once they did some minimal digging, they uncovered that Mike was having an affair with Sheila Keen.

The affair established a clear motive.

Still, there was no real evidence to make an arrest, never mind a conviction in court. The investigation continued, and soon the getaway car was located not far from the Warrens' home. It turns out that the car was reported stolen from Mike's car lot.

Things were not looking good for Mike and Sheila.

The investigation next focused on the actual clown who committed the murder. At first glance, it may have seemed like the clown outfit was a good disguise because witnesses were unable to tell what race the clown was or even the person's gender, but the choice of disguise betrayed the killer's lack of criminal sophistication. Criminals who wear ski masks, balaclavas, and bandannas to commit their crimes do so not only to hide their identities, but also because those disguises are difficult to trace.

Clown outfits are not very common, and only specialty shops sold them in 1990.

The homicide detectives canvassed the county and questioned every employee in all of the area costume and specialty stores. It didn't take long for them to find the store where the outfit was sold, and the employee who sold the costume was able to pick Sheila Keen out of a photo lineup.

Finding the source of the flowers and balloons was also easy, since not many supermarkets sold specialty balloons with slogans on them. Sheila was picked out of another photo lineup by the person who sold her the flowers and balloons.

There was still no physical evidence that tied Sheila directly to the crime, although the circumstantial evidence was certainly damning, and some have been convicted with less. But the Palm Beach County authorities needed an airtight case against Sheila and Mike, and there was virtually no evidence that pointed toward Mike's guilt.

That is not to say that the detectives weren't looking.

Numerous search warrants were conducted on the Warrens' home and their businesses to find evidence that implicated Mike in his wife's death. They were not able to find anything that directly tied Mike to his wife's murder, but they did uncover numerous shady activities in which he had involved the Warrens' businesses. The Palm Beach County prosecutors were able to collect enough evidence to charge Mike with odometer tampering and grand theft. Mike pled guilty to the felonies and received a four-year sentence in the Florida Department of Corrections.

The Palm Beach County investigators were hoping that while Mike was cooling off in the state prison system, they would be able to drive a wedge between him and Sheila. The detectives approached Mike several times before he went to prison, and while he was incarcerated, in the hope that he would give Sheila up.

Yet while in prison, Mike stayed out of trouble and true to Sheila.

A Cold Clown Case

The Palm Beach County Sheriff's Department clearly failed in its efforts to drive a wedge between Mike and Sheila, and in fact, the investigation seemed to bring the couple closer. After Mike was released from prison in 1996, he and Sheila got married and left Florida. They moved to the Kingsport, Tennessee area in the Smoky Mountains and started new lives. They married in 2002 and opened a successful restaurant, which they later sold for a nice profit.

The couple was free and clear from the Palm Beach County authorities, or so they thought.

DNA profiling was in its infancy when Marlene Warren was murdered in 1990. Large amounts of blood and other biological elements were needed for forensic examiners to determine a definite DNA profile, and even when they could cull a profile from a sample, it could take months.

A lot has changed in the last twenty-seven years.

During their investigation in the early 1990s, the homicide investigators were able to retrieve a small amount of biological evidence from which they were unable to get a DNA profile at the time.

The investigators have not yet revealed how they obtained the evidence, but the original investigators in the 1990s were far-sighted enough to know that it could one day lead to an arrest.

The new DNA evidence led to Sheila Warren's arrest in September 2017.

"You basically get one shot, and if you roll the dice and take that chance and she is found not guilty, you never get that chance again," said Palm Beach County Sheriff's Detective Paige McCann. "Sometimes patience is the best."

Mike Warren has yet to be charged, but authorities were hopeful that after some time in jail, Sheila would be happy to tell them everything.

Sheila eventually pled guilty to second-degree murder and was sentenced to twelve years in prison. With a 2023 plea deal, time served, and good behavior, she was released in 2024.

CHAPTER 12:

THE PHOENIX CANAL MURDERS

You have no doubt heard the term "random crime" or "random murder" at some point in your life. At first, the term seems self-explanatory, but then you realize that the definition is very ambiguous and, for the most part, subjective. Many who claim to be experts define a random crime as one where the victim was seemingly picked at random.

But is that ever the case?

Experts particularly like to point out that many serial killers operate randomly, picking their targets as if they were picking numbers on a roulette wheel. The reality is that although serial killers may not target specific individuals, they nearly always target a certain demographic, or they choose particular locations from where to launch their attacks.

In the world of serial killers, nothing is random.

Even the most random of all serial killers are often captured when astute law enforcement officers notice a definite pattern in their behavior. Finding a pattern in seemingly random killers is partly how the Phoenix Canal murders were recently solved.

During the early 1990s, three young women were discovered murdered in locations around the Phoenix Canal in Phoenix, Arizona, in what appeared to be random acts. But the more investigators worked on the case, the more they began to suspect that the killer was committing his acts in a very logical pattern.

Once the investigators discovered the killer's patterns, modern science helped them identify and capture him.

A Spate of Murders

The string of murders known as the Phoenix Canal Murders began when twenty-two-year-old Angela Brosso left her apartment to go for a bike ride on an evening in November 1992, but never returned. Angela's friends and family were worried, so they filed a missing persons report with the Phoenix Police Department. After a few days of searching turned up nothing, the police believed they would probably never know what happened to Angela Brosso.

Then, eleven days after Angela disappeared, the headless corpse of a White female was discovered floating in the Phoenix Canal. Homicide investigators were called in to find Angela's killer, or killers, but after their investigation began to stall, they believed that the second young woman was the victim of a "random" crime.

Angela's heartbroken family thought there was little they could do and that her killer would probably never be found.

Then, about ten months later, in September 1993, another "random" murder took place in the same area under similar circumstances.

Melanie Bernas was a seventeen-year-old high school senior who was looking forward to her last year of high school. Like Angela Brosso, Melanie decided to go for a bike ride but never returned.

Her body was found near the Phoenix Canal several days later.

The authorities now knew that the seemingly random crimes were in fact connected. Besides the visible pattern related to the crimes, there were other ones that could be determined by professional profilers. Before the case was turned over to profilers, though, there was a small amount of biological evidence that was recovered from one of the victims.

In 1993, as noted in the previous chapter, DNA profiling was still in its infancy in the United States, but biological evidence was routinely taken from crime scenes. But to do anything with biological evidence taken from a crime scene, it has to be matched with an offender. The match can come from a known suspect, or, as is often the case today, the offender's DNA profile is in the national Combined DNA Index System, or CODIS.

The CODIS database was still a couple of years away in 1993.

The Investigation

After the second Phoenix Canal murder in 1993, the killer appeared to have gone into an extended "cooling off period." The case itself went cold, although profilers continued to work on the case to establish a pattern to catch the killer.

The profilers were not with the FBI or the Phoenix Police Department, though.

When the case went cold, it attracted the attention of members of the Vidocq Society. The Vidocq Society is a private organization of both retired and active law enforcement and legal professionals who work to solve cold cases in their free time. Members bring their diverse skill sets to the society: forensic analysis, investigative procedure, and criminal profiling. The Phoenix Canal murders particularly caught the attention of Vidocq members with profiling backgrounds, as they believed that the pattern they saw in the killer's two known murders could be used to determine specifics about his background.

The profilers concluded that the killer would have a history of violence, especially toward women, going back several years. They believed that the killer was living near the Phoenix Canal at the time and that he had probably moved several times since the murders. The profilers also thought the killer had probably killed again, although he changed his method of operation, so the newer murders might not be linked to the Phoenix Canal killings.

Still, like the DNA sample, a profile is only helpful if you have a suspect.

Identifying the Phoenix Canal killer became a top priority of many in the Vidocq Society, so when a couple of the group's members met Colleen Fitzpatrick at a conference, they thought she could lend her expertise to their quest.

Colleen Fitzpatrick is a professional genealogist based in California. Her work usually involves locating long-lost relatives for inheritances and helping people fill out their family trees, but by the 2010s, some in the Vidocq Society saw in her background a way to catch the Phoenix Canal killer.

Fitzpatrick was given a sample of the DNA profile taken from the crime scene in 1993 and simply asked what she could do with it. The Vidocq Society members didn't put any pressure on her and didn't know what to expect, and they were more than surprised when they heard back from Fitzpatrick.

Having completed her examination of the DNA, Fitzpatrick told her new friends that the sample probably came from a male with the surname "Miller."

With the profile of the killer completed, the investigators needed a suspect. Although the case had gone cold since 1993, new tips in the early 2010s led to it being reopened. Phoenix homicide detectives took the profile composite that was created by the Vidocq Society and cross-referenced it with all of the names they had received from their tips.

One name immediately stood out: Bryan Patrick Miller.

The investigators quickly ran a background check of Miller, who was forty-two years old in early 2015, and learned that his life eerily fit the pattern that the profilers had proposed. Miller moved around the West a bit, and most importantly, he had a history of violence.

Miller had a 1990 juvenile conviction for aggravated assault in the stabbing of a Phoenix-area woman. He was also charged with stabbing a person in 2002 in Washington State, but he was acquitted of that charge.

Miller was also living near the Phoenix Canal at the time of the murders in 1992 and 1993.

In the years after the Phoenix Canal killings, Miller married, fathered a daughter, and maintained stable employment in the Phoenix area. Homicide investigators believed they had their man, but an accurate criminal profile is not enough for an arrest warrant in any United States jurisdiction.

They needed to get some physical evidence.

Undercover officers began trailing Miller night and day until they were able to surreptitiously attain some of his DNA, which proved to be a match with the sample collected in 1993.

Miller was arrested in January 2015, convicted, and sentenced to death in June 2023, and currently sits on death row for the death of Melanie Bernas.

The authorities suspect Miller in several other assaults and murders of teenage girls in Arizona and Washington.

CONCLUSION

In this latest installment of the series, you were introduced to twelve new amazing crimes. Some of these crimes baffled the investigators, and nearly all of them shocked the public. They were certainly some of the more interesting true crime cases in history.

Crime is a phenomenon that we all fear but are also drawn to in some ways. We truly enjoy learning about the details of strange crime cases and the motives that drove dangerous criminals. We all fancy ourselves part detective and part psychologist, and even—sometimes—part criminal.

Despite living in a cynical society where not many things are taboo, the taboo of murder remains. Because of that taboo, there will always be shocking murder cases to read about.

TRUE CRIME
STORIES

BOOK 2

INTRODUCTION

In the following pages, you will be introduced to twelve amazing crime cases that sometimes stumped investigators and always shocked the public. Many of these cases are extremely violent and difficult to comprehend, and as much as you may be so disturbed that you feel like you should stop reading, you will be compelled to keep turning the pages.

These are twelve true crime cases that are truly as fascinating as they are brutal.

In every one of these true crime anthologies, there are always one or more themes, and this volume is no different. In fact, this volume contains cases that can be placed into three themes, although some of the cases overlap and can be categorized in two or all of the themes.

The most pervading theme in this volume is the scourge of youth violence and the devastation it brings to affected communities. Although most of the youth violence cases profiled in this volume took place in the United States, youth crime and violence are certainly a worldwide problem. Numerous juvenile murderers are profiled, with not only an emphasis on the details of their crimes, but a look at what drove them to commit their antisocial acts.

You will read about how a seventeen-year-old honor student and all-around good kid named Anthony Barbaro decided one day to turn his quiet upstate New York town into a war zone. The case of the triple murder of the Doss family is also profiled. As bad as any murder is, it is always worse when it involves multiple victims, but this case was particularly perplexing when it was finally determined that the killer was a sixteen-year-old girl who was a friend of the family. You will also read about the heart-wrenching story of Robbie Middleton, an eight-year-old boy who was attacked, set on fire, and left to die. Robbie showed incredible tenacity by surviving his horrendous wounds for several years, long enough to give a crucial piece of evidence that led to the arrest of his teen attacker. There are also the youth violence cases of young perpetrators James Franklin, Antonio Barbeau, and Cassie Jo Stoddart.

Although the phenomenon of teen violence may dominate this volume, there are plenty of other cases with different themes. Two notable cold cases are profiled— one from the United Kingdom and the other from the United States. In the case from the United Kingdom, the murder of a woman went unsolved for decades before advances in forensic science finally led to the capture of the killer. Other than it being a cold case, the case from the United States was markedly different. The case involved the death of a little boy and how the authorities tracked his own mother for nearly twenty-five years, collecting enough evidence so that they could finally make an arrest.

Finally, as with all volumes in this series, there is a fair share of cases profiled that can only be considered bizarre.

You will read about a pair of Canadian thrill killers who took their unnatural desires for extreme sex as far as they could go, ending with the brutal murder of an innocent woman. A young Canadian serial killer is also profiled, who effectively turned many people's ideas about serial killers upside down.

The tragic case of a schizophrenic who thought he was being chased by a cannibalistic cult is also discussed.

So take a deep breath, brace yourself, and open the pages of this book.

CHAPTER 1:

THE COLD MURDER
CASE OF NOVA WELSH

Fortunately, in most industrialized countries, your chances of becoming a murder victim are relatively low. True, murders happen every day, and in some countries, with higher crime rates they are more common, but the reality is that homicide remains among the ultimate taboos.

With that said, Hollywood and other forms of media have done their part to make it seem as if crazed killers are lurking around every corner, waiting to randomly take the life of any unsuspecting person who passes by. This mentality has led many people to arm themselves with whatever weapons are legal in their country and many more to invest in expensive home security systems.

But the statistics show that most murders are not committed by strangers.

Although murder is uncommon, murders committed by a spouse or significant other are the most common type. For most people, it is not the crazed killer lurking in the bushes that they should be afraid of, but the person sleeping next to them in bed.

The majority of these types of murders are committed in a fit of passion, and even the ones that are premeditated are done by people with little to no criminal background. Because of those factors, spousal killers are usually quickly apprehended.

Very few spousal murders become cold cases, and in the few cases that do, the detectives usually know that the perpetrator is the spouse. It is just a matter of them compiling enough evidence to make an arrest that will hold up in court.

The cold murder case of Nova Welsh is unique because it is one of the few crimes of passion that went cold for decades. When Nova was murdered in 1981, the police immediately suspected her long-term boyfriend and the father of her two children, but a lack of physical evidence prevented them from making an arrest.

As the decades rolled by, many people forgot about the case, but a few determined investigators familiar with advances in technology were finally able to solve it and bring closure to Nova's family.

Nova Welsh and Osmond Bell

Nova Welsh's tragic story began in the late 1950s and spans two continents and several decades. Nova Welsh was born in Jamaica to a middle-class family that wanted to find more opportunities elsewhere. Jamaica's high crime rates, corruption, and political instability were all factors that contributed to the Welsh family looking abroad for a new start. Although the United States was close and an English-speaking country, its immigration laws were fairly restrictive at the time, so the Welsh family took advantage of their status as citizens in the British Commonwealth and moved to the United Kingdom.

In the period immediately following World War II, the United Kingdom began opening its doors to its former colonial subjects, which meant that thousands of Indians, Pakistanis, and Caribbean people, among others, came to the country for a number of different reasons. The desire to escape poverty in their home countries was a strong factor for many. Jobs were more plentiful and paid more in Britain, and it had a generous safety net if one were to lose their job. Britain also became a safe haven for political dissidents who feared violent reprisals in their home countries.

Like most immigrants around the world, the Welsh family decided to move to a location where there were plenty of people from their old country to fall back on for support. They chose the Midlands City of Birmingham due to its sizable West Indian/Caribbean community.

Nova was ten years old when the Welshs moved to Birmingham, and, as difficult as the move was in some ways, it was exciting in other ways for the young Jamaican immigrant. She received a better education than she would have in Jamaica, and there were far more and better material goods and creature comforts available in the United Kingdom.

But there were also unseen temptations in the new land.

Because Nova's parents worked long hours to make ends meet in the significantly more expensive United Kingdom, their supervision of Nova was relaxed. Although Nova stayed out of trouble on Birmingham's sometimes mean streets, she came under the influence of a charismatic young Jamaican immigrant named Osmond Bell.

In the early 1970s, Osmond Bell was a familiar sight around Birmingham's Caribbean community. Bell was a smooth-talking teenager who attracted a following of other young men and boys, not to mention the attention of several girls. The young man often walked on the edge between the legal immigrant community and the underworld. Although he never accumulated a serious criminal record, he had several contacts with Caribbean organized crime groups, a fact he often liked to tell people as a threat.

One of the girls who was drawn to him was Nova Welsh.

Bell was one year older than Nova but considerably more street savvy when the two met. The young man had lived in the United Kingdom for most of his life and could move around the city of Birmingham with ease. Nova was impressed with the fact that Osmond knew people all over the city and felt safe whenever she was with him.

The two young Jamaican immigrants began a romance that quickly became serious. Nova moved into an apartment with Osmond, and by the late 1970s, the couple had two sons.

The hope and excitement that Osmond's and Nova's relationship began with was gone by the end of the decade. Bell rarely worked, was a problem drinker, and often cheated on Nova. He also refused to commit fully to the relationship by marrying Nova, but worst of all, he was physically abusive.

Bell was known to hit Nova when he got drunk or his whereabouts were questioned by her. He did his best to keep Nova isolated from her friends and family. For the first few years of their relationship, he was fairly successful at this, but by 1981, the young mother began making some major changes in her life that didn't involve Osmond Bell.

Drifting Apart

Throughout the 1970s, Nova's sisters and friends encouraged her to leave the shiftless Bell. Still, due to her traditional Caribbean roots, Nova continued to try to make the relationship work. She argued that her sons needed a father figure, but that became less and less of an issue the more Bell devolved into alcoholism and abuse.

Eventually, Nova realized that Osmond Bell would never marry her and would probably never be much of a father to their two sons, so she decided to move on with her life. She found full-time work, developed a new social network, and started dating.

In 1981, at the age of twenty-four, Nova Welsh appeared headed in the right direction and well on her way to building a new, successful life.

Nova could no longer bear Osmond's physical and psychological abuse, so she made the assertive move of kicking him out of their apartment in July 1981. Although he didn't like the situation, there was little he could do.

This was a new Nova Welsh.

But Osmond Bell was still in the picture.

While Osmond had neglected his fatherly duties by the middle of 1981, he still kept tabs on Nova. Osmond was an extremely jealous man who believed that Nova and their children were essentially his property. As he frequented the bars and shops in the Caribbean neighborhoods of Birmingham in the days after he was evicted, he learned that his children's mother was dating another man.

Osmond Bell would not stand for this.

A Crime of Passion

By early August 1981, Osmond Bell was positively outraged by the situation in which he found himself. Within a matter of weeks, he had been kicked out of his apartment, lost his long-term girlfriend, and had his access to his children limited. Worst of all, it appeared that his girlfriend had moved on from him by dating another man.

Bell was persistent, though, and kept trying to get back with Nova.

Finally, on August 18, 1981, Nova Welsh relented and allowed Bell to come to her apartment to discuss their sons.

The evidence shows that Bell probably didn't go to Welsh's apartment with the intent to kill her, but instead, things got out of hand when Nova told him that they would never get back together.

The discussion quickly turned into an argument, which in turn led to yelling, before Bell snapped, placing Nova in a choke hold, breaking her neck.

Bell was immediately faced with the reality of what he had done. If arrested, he could face a very long prison sentence.

He had to cover his crime.

Luckily for Bell, his method of murder was relatively clean. He didn't have to worry about cleaning up blood or other bodily fluids, and there was no weapon that could be tied to him. With that said, he knew that any suspicions of Nova's murder would be cast on him. Instead of leaving her body for his sons to find, he decided to hide Nova in a utility closet of the apartment complex. Bell was able to drag Nova's corpse down a flight of stairs without anyone seeing him. He got to the utility closet that he hoped would be his ex's final resting place, at least long enough to obfuscate the police investigation.

After Bell placed Nova's body in the closet, he realized that the door didn't have a lock or even a proper latch. The broken closet door kept swinging open every time he tried to close it.

Osmond Bell was never seen as a particularly intelligent person by those who knew him, but he was resourceful. Bell took the piece of gum he was chewing, placed it in the door jamb, and closed the closet door.

He then went on his way as if nothing had happened.

Nova's body wasn't discovered until several days later, when residents of the apartment complex complained about a rotten smell emanating from the little-used utility closet. When maintenance checked the source of the odor, they were shocked to find Nova Welsh's partially decomposed body.

Two Suspects

As with any homicide, the detectives immediately focused their attention on those closest to Nova who may have had reasons to kill her: Osmond Bell and her current boyfriend.

Bell and the current boyfriend were both cooperative with the police and both denied having anything to do with Nova's murder. The detectives dutifully collected all the evidence at the crime scene, but there was little they could do given the technology available at the time. The killer left no fingerprints in the utility closet, and although the prints of Bell and Nova's new boyfriend were found in her apartment, there were legitimate reasons for those being there.

The detectives next turned to investigating the backgrounds of Bell and Nova's new boyfriend. Nothing in Nova's new boyfriend's background suggested that he was violent, but the police quickly learned that Bell had a history of violence toward Nova.

Osmond Bell was looking more and more like the killer.

But then one of Nova's friends turned a letter over to the police that she had received.

The letter claimed to have been penned by a woman who witnessed Nova's new boyfriend commit the murder. It was unsigned, and the supposed writer stated that she was too afraid to come forward publicly at that point.

The actual author of the letter was Osmond Bell, who, although not especially intelligent, was clever enough to know that such a ruse could throw the police off his trail.

The detectives had a gut feeling that Bell was the killer, but the letter cast doubt on that theory. There was also no physical evidence that tied Bell or the other boyfriend to the murder, so the case went cold.

Scientific Advances

As the decades went by, Osmond Bell must have surely thought he'd gotten away with murder. There were no witnesses to his crime, and it seemed as though he had effectively cast enough suspicion on another person to bring the investigation to a standstill. Bell went on with his life, but as he did so, advances in science were catching up to criminal investigation procedures.

Today, the process of DNA profiling is an everyday part of police work, and most people know something about the procedure due to the numerous television shows, both documentary and fictional, which highlight its use in investigations. DNA profiling was first used successfully in a court case in the United Kingdom during the late 1980s. By 2016, it had been used to capture thousands of killers, rapists, and other criminals around the world.

Armed with this new technology, Birmingham homicide investigators reopened the Nova Welsh murder case by getting court orders for DNA samples from Osmond Bell and Nova Welsh's other boyfriend at the time. The samples were compared with the small amount they were able to take from the piece of gum Bell had used to keep the utility closet door closed.

Bell's DNA matched that on the gum.

Osmond Bell was charged with murder in 2016 and went to trial in early 2017. Although the DNA evidence was compelling enough to place Bell at the scene of the crime, the jury didn't think he killed Welsh with premeditation. Bell was acquitted of murder but found guilty of manslaughter.

But if the killer thought he would get off lightly, he was wrong.

When he went before the court for sentencing, he was given a verbal lashing by the judge, who found it particularly disturbing that Bell could commit such an act against the mother of his children.

"Having killed her, you concealed her body, doing nothing to assuage the pain and grief of your own children. When the police became involved, you thought it was getting a little hot. You wrote a letter intending to point suspicion away from yourself and towards someone else," said sentencing judge Patrick Thomas.

Judge Thomas then handed down a twelve-year prison sentence, half of which must be served behind bars. Because Bell is now over sixty years old, it could very well be a life sentence.

CHAPTER 2:

MICHAEL MACGREGOR AND TANYA BOGDANOVICH, THE CANADIAN "THRILL KILL" COUPLE

In the annals of crime history, there are more than a few cases of killer couples. The reasons why these murderous couples killed varied to some extent, but lust was often the driving force. Usually, the man was the dominant member of the relationship and was the one who introduced the woman to the vocation of serial killing. Oftentimes, the woman was used to lure hapless female victims, although in nearly every known case, the woman also actively participated in the sadistic torture sessions and murders.

Some of the more notable killer couples include the "Sunset Strip Killers," Doug Clark and Carol Bundy, who killed seven people in 1980 in southern California. Clark is believed to have been the mastermind behind the couple's reign of terror, but Bundy was a willing participant and even committed a murder on her own.

A few hundred miles to the north of southern California, in northern California and Nevada, married couple, Gerald and Charlene Gallego, killed ten people during the late 1970s and early 1980s. Like the Sunset Strip Killers, the Gallegos were led by the male half, who meticulously planned out the details of their rapes and murders.

Less well-known to Americans, but infamous household names in Canada, are Paul Bernardo and Karla Homolka. This couple was responsible for the murder of three girls and young women in Canada, including Homolka's own sister. Again, all evidence shows that it was Bernardo who planned the murders and manipulated Homolka to a certain extent.

In January 2013, another Canadian couple became almost as infamous as Bernardo and Homolka when they abducted, raped, and murdered an innocent woman. Although the couple was quickly caught, most in the law enforcement community believe that if they had not been, then they no doubt would have kept killing—like the three couples already mentioned in this chapter. Michael MacGregor and Tanya Bogdanovich displayed all of the anti-social hallmarks that any serial killing couple has, with one major difference: the female was the dominant one in this killer couple.

Two of a Kind

At first glance, there seem to have been very few things that Michael MacGregor and Tanya Bogdanovich had in common. There was a considerable age difference, and their backgrounds were dissimilar. Still, the two shared some dark desires that eventually brought them together and later, to commit murder.

Michael MacGregor was born in 1994 and grew up in the southwestern Ontario city of Sarnia. He lived in a modest, middle-class neighborhood that was very much like one you would find across North America. Sarnia may be in the same province as Toronto, but in many ways, it has a hometown feel that is more midwestern American. Crime is low, the schools are good, and people are neighborly in Sarnia, which has made it an attractive destination and a growing city.

As a child, MacGregor had no legal problems and by all accounts, was a well-adjusted kid: he got along with his neighbors and never caused problems in school. He had a good relationship with his parents and enjoyed going on trips with them.

Yet MacGregor never could really "find himself."

He had few interests in high school, was an average student at best, and didn't have many friends. After he graduated high school, MacGregor did what most of his fellow students did and entered college, but he just wasn't ready for the rigorous studying needed to be successful at that level.

MacGregor dropped out of college during his first semester. He lived in his parents' home, and for money, delivered food for a local pizzeria. For the most part, Michael MacGregor was not very different from many eighteen-year-olds, except he was missing a special someone with whom he could share his time and dreams.

But Michael MacGregor's dreams were not conventional, to say the least.

When he wasn't delivering pizzas, MacGregor spent most of his free time surfing the web and visiting various internet chat rooms. He found himself drawn to websites that catered to bondage fetishes, finding that the more violent ones were the biggest turn-ons. MacGregor began downloading thousands of images of violent pornography, but he was still not satisfied—he needed to make his violent sexual fantasies a reality.

The problem was that, in the world of sexual sadism and masochism, or "S&M," he was a "sub," which means "submissive." Michael MacGregor needed to find a "dom" or "dominant" partner who could show him the way. After trying to find his dominant half on several websites unsuccessfully, he finally struck gold at an obscure internet chatroom named "Fetlife."

In 2012, Tanya Bogdanovich was twenty-eight years old and very familiar with the world of sexual sadism. Although ten years MacGregor's senior, they were a perfect fit in many ways, as she was the dominant personality for which he was searching.

But they came from completely different worlds.

Where MacGregor's family life was stable and both of his parents were living at home, Bogdanovich, like many in her generation, was a child of divorce. Although countless children of divorce go on to live productive lives and some of the most notable people in modern society come from divorced families, there is no doubt that it can have a negative impact in some cases.

Divorce clearly had a negative impact on Bogdanovich's life.

She spent most of her youth with her mother and never really knew her father, so she never received the support of a second parent. Her mother never disciplined her much, and when she did, Tanya simply ignored her. From a young age, Tanya learned that she could do virtually whatever she wanted. Her mother never really seemed to care anyway.

Bogdanovich never really seemed to fit in anywhere as a child, going from one peer group to another until she finally started to run with rougher crowds that were into drugs and alcohol. By her teen years, Bogdanovich already had a substance abuse problem, and she later claimed that she was also raped as a teenager.

Like many children who are victims of sexual assault, Bogdanovich became extremely promiscuous, changing sexual partners quite frequently. Most of Bogdanovich's relationships were flawed from the beginning, and many were physically and psychologically abusive. Despite the chaos of her life, or possibly because of it, she had three children from her late teens until her mid-twenties.

Tanya Bogdanovich never came close to winning any Mother of the Year Awards.

She had no job skills to speak of, and since she wasn't particularly ambitious, Bogdanovich turned to the world's oldest profession to make money. Tanya Bogdonavich carved out a place for herself in the western Ontario sex work scene by offering her services as a dominatrix.

It was through her work as a professional dominatrix that Bogdonavich was able to earn enough money to pay her rent, and it also allowed her to indulge some of her more taboo desires that mixed sex and violence.

Still, she could only do so much as a professional dominatrix, and the reality was that she could only do what her clients wanted—there was always a safe word that could end the session.

Bogdanovich desired something more real and more violent. For that, she went to Fetlife, which is where she met MacGregor in late 2012.

Fetlife is a Canadian-based website that caters to people who enjoy non-normative sexual tastes. As it states on its welcome page: "Like Facebook, but run by kinksters like you and me. We think it is more fun that way. Don't you?"

The site offers a plethora of different chatrooms and a message board where "kinksters" can discuss their sexual fetishes with like-minded people or possibly find a sexual partner.

The site, though, has been the source of controversy.

Besides its explicit content that goes beyond mainstream norms for many, Fetlife users have been involved in more than one criminal investigation. Most recently, Illinoisan Brendt Christensen was charged with kidnapping a female Chinese scholar named Yingying Zhang in June 2017 near the University of Illinois campus in Urbana, Illinois. The investigation has revealed that Christensen had a kidnapping and rape fetish and that he was quite open about it on numerous message boards dedicated to similar fetishes on Fetlife.

Bogdanovich and MacGregor met on a message board dedicated to bondage and sadism fetishes.

Sexually speaking, the two were a perfect fit. MacGregor was a "sub" and Bogdanovich was a "dom."

The two spent several hours online discussing their sexual preferences and fantasies, which, besides S&M, also included rape fantasies. After simulating their fantasies in chatrooms and then on their phones, the two decided to take their relationship to the real world.

But when the couple did so, they both felt that they had to go as far as they could with it. The pair's idea of S&M was on the extreme side of what is considered typical by other aficionados of the fetish.

For instance, to Bogdanovich and MacGregor, simply tying each other up with bedsheets was not enough. Instead, they role-played violent rape scenarios where choking and cutting with knives was the norm. The two especially like to choke each other until the point of passing out. They found it thrilling to see their partner's eyes roll back into their head as they were about to lose consciousness. The knife play could also get serious, as there was more than one occasion where injuries were sustained.

For MacGregor, the transition of their relationship from the virtual to the real world was a dream come true. The socially awkward college dropout now had a girlfriend who shared his dark desires. He had a lot to look forward to in late 2012.

For Bogdanovich, it was just another notch in her belt of sexual conquests.

Tanya was actually involved in a long-term relationship with another man when she began her real-world sexual relationship with MacGregor, but that mattered little to the mother of three. Bogdanovich operated under the premise that everything and everyone in the world was there to fulfill her needs or entertain her in some way. Tanya was also attracted to weaker men, so her current boyfriend had little say in what she did with other men.

MacGregor, though, seemed perfect for Bogdanovich.

"I feel so lucky, I can't even believe it. I can feed every need. I can fulfill every urge, I feel no shame about what I like or who I am with you because U (sic) have the (sic) urges or at least ones that work so perfectly with mine," Bogdanovich said to MacGregor in an instant message.

Eventually, the two began to tire of the situation; MacGregor began seeing other women, and Bogdanovich also kept her revolving door of men working. But just when it seemed that their relationship would end, Bogdanovich posted an eerie message online to her favorite "sub."

"Rape brought us together, violence has kept us together, violence has kept us going and rape will be what holds us strong when our bond is challenged."

To keep her "sub" happy, Bogdanovich formulated some demented ideas that involved abduction, rape, and eventually murder.

A Diabolical Plot

The violent kidnapping, rape, and murder fantasies that MacGregor and Bogdanovich acted out and eventually turned into reality were disturbing enough on their own, but they are even more so when one considers that Bogdanovich was not only a mother of three children at the time but also a nurse.

While Tanya was working as a sex worker and dominatrix, she was also studying at nursing school in her spare time. It may seem strange that someone so broken and dysfunctional, who reveled in causing and receiving pain, would enter a profession where she would help alleviate people's pain. Perhaps she thought the work would be easy, or maybe she thought she could get her hands on some prescription drugs to use in one of her fantasies; whatever the reason, she took the Hippocratic Oath and went into nursing.

Although she was not the brightest student, Bogdanovich eventually completed her schooling and found work full-time as a nurse in the Sarnia area.

If only her employers knew what she was really like.

By early December 2012, Bogdanovich told her willing sexual acolyte that they needed to make their violent sexual fantasies a reality, and to do so, they obviously had to find a victim. Since neither of the two was a seasoned criminal, their early plans were full of holes, and the attempts to carry them out were awkward at best.

But they both knew that they wanted a young female victim.

The couple decided to go on "dry runs" at the local Sarnia mall. They would approach teenage girls and ask them if they would like to leave with them and go somewhere else. After a few dry runs, the pair thought better of the plan when they realized that malls are full of witnesses and security cameras.

The next evil idea came straight from the mind of Tanya Bogdanovich.

Bogdanovich decided to surprise her boyfriend with something original for his nineteenth birthday. Instead of giving him an electronic device or some clothes, Tanya gave MacGregor a collection of digital images of local teenage girls she took from Facebook profiles.

MacGregor was ecstatic.

The couple spent hours looking through the images and gathering information on their favorite girls in order to decide the best time and place to snatch their quarry. They stalked the local mall and area high schools looking for their favorite victim. The couple also practiced their roles in the kidnapping many times on each other.

But despite all the time the couple put into finding a victim for their twisted sexual fantasies, their crime ended up being one of opportunity.

New Year's Eve 2012 was a big night in Sarnia. The bars were filled with revelers, and just as many people were attending New Year's house parties, which is where twenty-seven-year-old Noelle Paquette found herself.

Paquette was an attractive school teacher who never had a problem making new friends. According to her friends and family, her smile was infectious, and she was the type of person who would give you the shirt off her back if needed. She was also extremely trusting of people.

Too trusting.

The night had not gone the way Paquette had planned. Instead of spending some quality time with her boyfriend, the two ended up at a loud party where both had drunk too much and then got into an argument. Noelle pleaded with her boyfriend to leave the party, but he said he was enjoying himself and wanted to stay. A couple of hours after the new year of 2013, Noelle had had enough and told her boyfriend that she was walking home.

The last text message that Noelle sent was around 2:30 a.m. on January 1, 2013, to her boyfriend.

New Year's Eve was a particularly boring night for Tanya Bogdanovich. She spent the night working until 11 p.m. and then ran some errands and drove around Sarnia extensively. Sometime after 2:30 a.m., she noticed the attractive Paquette walking alone down the cold streets of Sarnia underdressed.

Bogdanovich pulled up next to Paquette and offered her a ride. The school teacher at first declined the offer, but reconsidered when she thought about how long she had to walk in the cold. She was also reassured by Bogdanovich's demeanor. The sexual sadist could appear sweet and even charming if need be.

Once Paquette got into Bogdanovich's car, the two drove a short distance until they pulled over to let a man into the car.

It was Michael MacGregor.

Bogdanovich had texted her paramour to alert him of the situation and that it looked like they would finally be able to turn their violent fantasies into reality.

MacGregor got into the backseat behind Paquette and pulled out a knife. He put it to the young woman's neck. He told her that if she cooperated, then she'd live.

MacGregor and Bogdanovich had no intention of letting Paquette go, however. They had agreed ahead of time to leave no witnesses—and not only that, the act of murder would fuel their sexual highs.

Without saying a word, Bogdanovich drove to a location about fifteen miles outside of Sarnia that the couple had reconnoitered recently. MacGregor dragged the frightened, crying Paquette from the car and threw her to the cold, hard ground.

As Noelle begged for her life, the despicable duo merely laughed as MacGregor handed the knife to Bogdanovich. The young sadist then proceeded to rape the school teacher. But Noelle's torment had just begun—the duo then took turns stabbing her for a total of forty-nine times.

After killing Paquette, the two lovers shared a passionate embrace and then left the scene.

Not far from the murder scene, Bogdanovich and MacGregor were pulled over for a minor traffic violation. The police noticed that the duo was covered in blood and that blood was all over the car's interior. A further search revealed that MacGregor was bleeding from an injury. Perplexed at the situation, the police asked where all the blood came from, to which Bogdanovich answered that they were engaged in S&M in the woods and were celebrating the New Year "with kink."

The police were rightfully suspicious, but Paquette's body had yet to be found, so MacGregor was brought to the local hospital for his wounds, and Bogdanovich was able to leave.

No Way Out

As MacGregor was being put on a stretcher for the ambulance ride to the hospital, he made the curious remark, "Is this the strangest thing you ever had?" to one of the paramedics. The paramedic told the police officers at the scene about the question, who then gave their "accident" victim more scrutiny. MacGregor went into surgery for his wounds, which looked like self-inflicted stab wounds to the attending physicians.

The suspicions surrounding the circumstances of MacGregor's admittance to the hospital were aggravated by Tanya Bogdanovich, who spent most of January 1 and 2 lurking around the hospital's ER waiting room. Many of the hospital staff thought she was acting extremely strangely. Others believed that she was MacGregor's mother.

Bogdanovich's concern for MacGregor's condition probably had less to do with worries about his health and more to do with what he might say about their thrill kill of Noelle Paquette. Tanya may have enjoyed her twisted time with MacGregor, but it was becoming apparent that she didn't trust him.

Noelle Paquette's mangled body was finally found on January 2, and at that point, it was only a matter of time before the police determined that Bogdanovich and

MacGregor were the culprits. Less than thirty hours after the discovery of Noelle Paquette's body, Bogdanovich was arrested outside of the hospital, and MacGregor was taken at a nearby motel.

Once the two were in police custody, they spilled their guts. Neither offered much of a defense, which is why the people of the city of Sarnia and the province of Ontario were not surprised when the murderous duo pleaded guilty in February 2016 to Paquette's murder. MacGregor's lawyer later said that his client's plea was done to spare his and Paquette's family the pain of a trial, but the reality is that he was perhaps the most hated person in Canada at the time, and there was no way he could have beaten the charges.

There was no legal way out of the situation for either MacGregor or Bogdanovich.

When the two were sentenced, the judge gave an especially sharp rebuke of their choices and actions.

"You chose in the darkest and most violent way to satisfy your overpowering lust," said Superior Court Justice Bruce Thomas. "Your actions are vile and they are despicable and as a result, you will be removed from the society for what might perhaps be for the rest of your lives."

CHAPTER 3:

THE MURDER OF
TIMOTHY WILTSEY

It is said that murder is the ultimate taboo, so, therefore, the most taboo of all murders would be the killing of a child. The reason should be obvious to most: children are innocent. Children have yet to make the mistakes in life that often put adults in positions to be killed. While random murders such as the murder of Noelle Paquette do occur, they are the exception and not the rule. Most murder victims are acquainted with their killers, and the situation in which the murders take place are often more complicated and nuanced than what is reported on the local ten o'clock news.

But things are much different when a child is murdered.

The abduction and murder of a child is something that cannot be justified, and most find it impossible to forgive a person who does such a thing. Although many seem to believe that these types of murders are committed almost entirely by strangers, the reality is that vindictive parents are just as likely to commit such a heinous crime. The idea that a parent could somehow abduct and kill their own child is something that is truly difficult for most people to grasp—it becomes nearly impossible to do so when it is revealed that the killer is the child's mother.

The overwhelming number of mothers in the world have a maternal instinct to provide for and protect their children. Human mothers are often compared to female bears that would do anything to protect their cubs. Since the Paleolithic era, when humans still lived in caves, it was the mothers who spent most of the time with their children and who were the children's last line of defense if the men were not around or had been captured or killed. Even today, the instinct that mothers have to protect their children is still very much alive. One does not have to peruse the internet very long to find news stories of protective mothers who foiled home invasions or who helped capture a sex offender.

Unfortunately, some mothers have no maternal instinct.

Michelle Lodzinski is one such woman who was apparently born with no maternal instinct. In 1991, in a case that can only be described as bizarre, Lodzinski stood accused of abducting and murdering her own five-year-old son, Timothy Wiltsey. The struggle to bring Wiltsey's killer to justice spanned thousands of miles and numerous states over a period of nearly twenty-five years.

But when the judge's gavel finally came down, it seemed there were still more questions than answers surrounding the case.

Michelle Lodzinski

Lodzinski was born the youngest of six children in a strong Roman Catholic family in northern New Jersey in 1968. Although young Michelle may not have gotten all of the luxury items she wanted as a child due to the size of her family, her father was a good provider. The Lodzinski children always had enough food to eat, and they always had clean clothes.

The Lodzinski children were brought up in the Church, and they all were required to take the sacraments. However, as Michelle became a teenager…things changed.

Lodzinski's friends and family reported that the changes in Michelle were not drastic, but that she was more interested in hanging out with her older boyfriend, George Wiltsey, than she was in going to church or spending time with her family. Eventually, Wiltsey convinced Michelle to move with him to Iowa, where he had family who could help him find work. Although Michelle's parents were initially against the move, when they learned that Michelle was pregnant, they gave their blessing.

Michelle was depressed during her sojourn in Iowa, which is unsurprising when one considers all of the circumstances. She was still very young, a juvenile by legal standards, and therefore probably frightened and concerned about what the future held for her. Along with that, all of her friends and family, her support network, were over 1,000 miles away in New Jersey.

Then there was the weather.

Although New Jersey gets its fair share of snow and cold temperatures in the winter, it is nothing compared to Iowa, where, due to its location in the middle of the continent, the weather can change quite rapidly in a matter of hours. Not only that, but winter can last for six months in the Hawkeye state.

The separation from her family and the cold Iowa winter proved to be too much for Lodzinski.

One day, not long after Timothy was born, Lodzinski packed everything up and moved back to New Jersey with her newborn son. George later claimed that he was not happy about this, but he did little to fight the move. Michelle never filed for child support and sent back every present that George attempted to send to his son.

Michelle Lodzinski simply erased that part of her life.

Lodzinski seemed to have a talent for simply walking away from parts of her life that she didn't like. After leaving George Wiltsey, she would repeat the pattern with other men, jobs, and ultimately her own son.

After leaving her son's father behind in Iowa, Lodzinski had no problems meeting men in New Jersey. Michelle was a fairly attractive young woman, had a good personality, and was always looking for a man who could take care of her. She had no problem meeting men, but few usually called her back for a second date. She later claimed that none of the men she dated wanted a relationship with her when they learned about Timothy.

Lodzinski may have had relationship problems during the late 1980s and early 1990s, but she did have her immediate family to support her and Timothy. By all accounts, the Lodzinski family helped Michelle watch Timothy when she was at work and offered money when times were tough.

And times could get tough for Michelle.

Lodzinski had dropped out of high school to have Timothy, and although she later earned her General Equivalency Degree, it did little more than help her get entry-level jobs with few prospects for advancement. Lodzinski's good looks and personality were often enough to get her jobs in offices and banks, but she soon grew bored with these positions and routinely quit before finding another job.

Still, the money Lodzinski made in entry-level office jobs, combined with funds from her family, meant that she could send Timothy to a private Catholic school in South Amboy, New Jersey. By the middle of 1991, Lodzinski was working as a bank teller, and everything seemed to be going well for her. Timothy liked his school, and she seemed to be at peace with life.

But sometimes looks can be deceiving.

Timothy's Disappearance

Memorial Day weekend 1991 was a particularly warm one in northern New Jersey. Those who weren't indoors enjoying their air conditioning were either at the beach or at one of the many outdoor carnivals taking place around the state. Michelle Lodzinski told friends and family that she planned to take Timothy to a nearby carnival in Sayreville, New Jersey, that weekend to celebrate the end of the school year and the beginning of summer.

Lodzinski's neighbors reported seeing Timothy playing in his front yard on the afternoon of May 25, which happened to be the last day he was seen alive.

Later that evening, a distressed Lodzinski reported that Timothy had gone missing from the Sayreville carnival. She claimed that they were waiting in line for a ride, but that she left him for a few minutes to buy some soft drinks. When she returned to their place in line, Timothy was gone.

Although taking place more than ten years before the Amber Alert system was implemented in the United States, the disappearance of Timothy Wiltsey quickly grabbed headlines. The case was featured in local media, which included the nearby New York City market, before getting picked up by national news outlets. John Walsh featured the case on his *America's Most Wanted* television show, and Timothy's picture was displayed on milk cartons throughout the northeast. As the media attention picked up, more and more attention was being given to Michelle Lodzinski.

And Lodzinski was not afraid of the attention.

The story that she told to the police and the media began to be seen as strange and suspicious by most people. Reporters questioned why she would leave a five-year-old alone in line, which she answered by simply saying, "He doesn't like to wait in lines."

The general public was also surprised and disturbed to a certain extent by how little emotion Lodzinski seemed to show. She always answered questions about her son's disappearance matter-of-factly with a flat affect and never cried. When asked about this, she replied:

"Everyone is waiting to see a grieving mother on TV break down, crying, hysterical because the public, they thrive on that stuff," Lodzinski told reporters in 1991. "But I'm not going to do it."

As Lodzinski was giving her emotionless interviews to the press, the public wasn't the only ones watching. The local police were beginning to think that the young mother knew more than what she was saying about her son's disappearance.

Lodzinski was interviewed numerous times by the local police, and each time her story seemed to change. She told the investigators that before going to the carnival, she and Tim visited a local park. The investigators later learned that the park was closed that day.

She then told the detectives that Timothy was wearing a bright red shirt that day, which would have been memorable, but no one at the carnival remembered seeing him. In fact, the only people other than Lodzinski who remembered seeing Timothy on May 25 were the next-door neighbors.

Eventually, the detectives called Lodzinski on her obvious lies and duplicity, which caused her to change her story yet again. She then claimed that two men with a knife abducted Timothy, and in another interview, she said that two men and a stripper named "Ellen" took her son. Lodzinski offered no reason why someone she knew would take her son or why she failed to call the police immediately after it happened.

At this point, the police asked Lodzinski to take a polygraph test.

Although polygraph tests, often known as "lie detectors," are not admissible in any criminal court proceedings in the United States, police routinely use them to eliminate people from their suspect pools. Results from a polygraph examination can also be used to get search warrants.

For whatever reason, most likely arrogance, Lodzinski agreed to take the test.

She failed miserably.

After Lodzinski failed the polygraph test, the results were leaked to the press, and what little public support Michelle once had quickly evaporated. Out of desperation, she agreed to take another polygraph exam.

During the exam, Lodzinski even asked, "How am I doing?" The examiner didn't need to respond—she failed the second exam as badly as the first.

Despite everything seeming to point toward Michelle Lodzinski either being involved in her own son's disappearance or at least knowing much more about it than she was telling the police, there was not enough evidence to make an arrest. In fact, since there was no body, the police didn't even know what crime was committed, if in fact a crime was committed at all.

As the months after Timothy's disappearance rolled by, the case receded a bit from the public eye. Other stories were being covered in the local media, which led some to believe that Michelle Lodzinski was getting away with something awful.

Then the case took a major turn on October 26, 1991.

On that afternoon, a schoolteacher named Daniel O'Malley was indulging in his favorite pastime of birdwatching. The urban sprawl of New York City, which most of northern New Jersey is a part of, may not seem like a good place to watch birds, but the state is actually full of many swamps and sloughs that are located between and among office parks and housing developments. The wooded areas are great places to watch birds...and also to hide bodies.

On the day in question, as O'Malley was searching for birds, he found a children's "Teenage Mutant Ninja Turtles" themed tennis shoe. At first, he thought nothing of the discovery, but the more he thought about it, the more he realized that something just didn't fit.

Then he remembered the disappearance of Timothy Wiltsey.

O'Malley specifically remembered Michelle Lodzinski telling reporters that Timothy was wearing Teenage Mutant Ninja Turtles-themed shoes when he went missing. Knowing that the find could be important, O'Malley brought the shoe to the Sayreville Police Department.

With their suspicions already firmly fixed on Lodzinski, Sayreville investigators called Michelle to identify the shoe as Timothy's. Interestingly, or perhaps not so, Lodzinski was adamant that the shoe did *not* belong to her missing son.

After Lodzinski's denials, the police promptly sent the shoe to the lab for forensic testing. Unfortunately, forensic testing in 1991 was far from where it is today. DNA profiling was a new procedure that was not used in every case, and when it was, it was very expensive and time-consuming. Since Timothy was a minor, though, extra manpower and resources were dedicated to testing the shoe, with inconclusive results.

Despite the setback, the local police believed that the shoe's location was the key to finding Timothy. After the shoe was found, the FBI also began assisting local and state law enforcement in the investigation.

The winter months prohibited investigators from returning to the area where O'Malley found the children's shoe, but when spring arrived, FBI agents canvassed the area, eventually discovering Timothy Wiltsey's skeletal remains on April 23 and 24, 1992.

The investigators now knew that Timothy was murdered after he was abducted.

Gathering Evidence against Lodzinski

By the middle of 1992, the local police and FBI had only one suspect in Timothy Wiltsey's abduction and murder: Michelle Lodzinski. Homicide detectives and FBI agents combined their resources in a task force to compile as much evidence as they could find against Lodzinski and then make an arrest.

But they found making an arrest was not so easy.

The circumstantial evidence against Lodzinski seemed convincing enough to most in law enforcement. Lodzinski's story about the carnival just didn't add up, as no one remembered seeing Timothy there with his mother.

"I got a sick feeling," said Laura Mechkowski about her encounter with Lodzinski at the carnival. "I spoke with her and she did not have a child with her. I was very upset. There was a child missing and there was no child."

As damning as statements from eyewitnesses at the carnival may have been, the discovery of Timothy's body proved to be even harder for Lodzinski to explain. Not only had she once worked at a nearby office park, but she failed to disclose that information to the FBI.

Still, there was not enough for the authorities to make an arrest.

But that didn't mean that they couldn't apply pressure to Lodzinski.

Homicide detectives and FBI agents made routine calls and visits to nearly all of Lodzinski's friends and family, which started to take a toll on the former mother mentally. By late 1993, Lodzinski seemed obsessed with the FBI as she talked about their surveillance of her constantly and developed a paranoia of the law enforcement organization that was not totally without merit.

Then came January 21, 1994.

On that day, a family member of Lodzinski's found her car mysteriously idling outside of her home with no one inside it. More family members soon arrived at the house to look for Lodzinski, but she was nowhere to be found.

It seemed that Michelle Lodzinski had just vanished off the face of the earth.

To her friends and family who believed her innocence, the new turn of events seemed to validate her claims that Timothy was abducted by shady thugs. To them, it appeared that she had also met the same fate. The Lodzinskis sat by their phones and searched around northern New Jersey for three days. Then they received the call that Michelle had been found hundreds of miles away in downtown Detroit.

Lodzinski's family and friends were at a loss as to why she was in Detroit. She had no family or friends there, so they figured it must be connected to the people who abducted and murdered Timothy. But when Michelle returned to New Jersey, things got even more bizarre.

Lodzinski claimed that the FBI abducted her and, for whatever reason, dropped her off in Detroit three days later. She never gave a specific reason why the FBI would do such a thing and only talked vaguely about conspiracies against her.

Two weeks after the incident, Michelle's brother received a threatening message written on an FBI business card. It was at this point that Michelle Lodzinski began losing the few supporters she had left. People began to think that Lodzinski was either crazy, trying to shift the blame for her son's murder, or both.

No one believed that an FBI agent would send a threatening note on his own business card.

The FBI later located the print shop where the card was made and confirmed that Michelle Lodzinski was the person who ordered the custom-made card.

Although investigators were slowly amassing a pile of circumstantial evidence against Lodzinski, she remained free to live her life. By the late 1990s, it seemed as though Lodzinski had moved on and never expected to hear from investigators again.

At least regarding the murder of Timothy.

Lodzinski was arrested for stealing a computer from her place of employment in 1997, which led to her moving from New Jersey to Florida. After living in Florida briefly, she moved to Minnesota and then back to Florida in 2003. Lodzinski married and gave birth to another child: life seemed to be treating her fine by the early 2000s.

But the homicide investigators working on Timothy's case never gave up.

An Arrest

The primary reason why Michelle Lodzinski was not arrested in the 1990s, despite the immense amount of circumstantial evidence that pointed toward her guilt, was that there was a lack of physical evidence. The police could have arrested her at any time, but county prosecutors told the police that the charges probably would not stick even if a grand jury indicted Lodzinski. They were repeatedly told that the public was becoming more tech savvy and was aware of advances in forensic technology.

The police needed to find a forensic "smoking gun."

A smoking gun was never found, but enough circumstantial evidence was uncovered to make an arrest. Perhaps the best evidence the authorities had was a blue blanket in which Timothy's remains were wrapped. Numerous witnesses stated that it looked like the same blanket that Lodzinski tucked Timothy into bed with every night.

Finally, in 2014, Middlesex County New Jersey prosecutors believed that the investigators had collected enough evidence to not only charge Michelle Lodzinski with her son's murder, but also to convict her.

New Jersey authorities traveled to sunny Florida, where they arrested the unsuspecting Lodzinski and later formally extradited her to New Jersey. In a trial that most considered a foregone conclusion, but was no less heart-wrenching,

Lodzinski was found guilty of murder in May 2016. Michelle Lodzinski evaded justice for nearly a quarter of a century, but she was sentenced to a minimum of thirty years in prison in January 2017.

Yet there was more to come. On December 28, 2021, New Jersey's Supreme Court vacated Lodzinski's murder conviction. The majority held that the evidence was legally insufficient to prove beyond a reasonable doubt that Lodzinski "purposefully or knowingly caused" Timothy's death. Subsequently, Lodzinski was released from prison and returned to Florida.

CHAPTER 4:

THE JEFFREY FRANKLIN
MURDER SPREE

The phenomenon of family annihilation has been covered numerous times throughout the volumes of this true crime series. It is a special type of mass murder that seems much worse than other types of mass murders. Mass murders committed on the job are often barely thought about and have even become the source of macabre jokes—the term "going postal," which generally refers to someone losing their cool, is derived from a series of mass shootings at U.S. post offices during the 1980s and 1990s. Although the vast majority of us never consider homicide as a viable alternative to real-world problems, we've all had problems at work and can therefore understand, on some level, why a person would shoot up their workplace.

But it is nearly impossible to understand why someone would kill their entire family.

Although family annihilations are rare, they are the most common form of mass murder in the United States. Family annihilations affect the psyche of the general public so much that some of the more notable cases have made it into pop culture.

The 1974 annihilation of the DeFeo family in Long Island, New York, by Ronald DeFeo Junior left both parents and all four of Ronald Junior's siblings dead. Although the motives for the murders were probably financially- and drug-based, the sheer violence of the acts led to the creation of the *Amityville Horror* franchise of books and movies.

The 1988 Brom family murders near Rochester, Minnesota, are another example of a family annihilation that shocked the public so much that its details made it into pop culture. In that case, the Brom's sixteen-year-old son, David, killed both of his parents and two siblings with an axe. In the years since the Brom murders, the Chicago-based heavy metal band Macabre has retold the gory story in a song recorded on one of their albums and in live performances to their legions of fans.

On the night of March 10, 1998, a teenager named Jeffrey Franklin attempted to take his place alongside Ronald DeFeo Junior and David Brom as the most notorious, and youngest, of family annihilators. Franklin brought death and destruction to his quiet Huntsville, Alabama, neighborhood that night, but thankfully came up short in his kill count and his bid to become an official family annihilator

The Franklin Family

At first glance, the Franklins seemed like a quintessential all-American family. Father Gerald and mother Cynthia worked hard to build an upper-middle-class life for themselves and their four children. They were raised in traditional southern families themselves and wanted to pass on many of their beliefs and traditions to their children, especially their belief in Christianity. Gerald and Cynthia were involved in their children's school functions and promoted a Christian lifestyle at all times, which meant that swearing was not allowed in the home, attendance at church was required, and the children were closely monitored.

Of course, the way children turn out in these types of homes varies. Most end up like their parents, but in some ways, the heavy emphasis on rules makes these environments ripe for rebellion. By the time he reached his teens, the oldest son, Jeffrey, seemed to do whatever he could to test his parents' patience. To those who knew the Franklins, however, there was always something more to Jeffrey's rebellion. Something they just couldn't put their fingers on.

Something just wasn't right with Jeffrey.

Jeffrey's parents began noticing small things about their son at an early age that seemed a little "off." He would pull pranks on other kids and his family, which often landed him in trouble with his teachers and parents. It was mostly small things like talking back to teachers or moving desks around in the classroom. Although Jeffrey never did anything violent or too serious, his parents were concerned enough to bring him to a youth behavioral specialist.

After a plethora of examinations, doctors diagnosed Jeffrey with attention deficit hyperactivity disorder. The Franklins were a bit upset to learn this, but they were also thankful that it was fairly common and treatable. Jeffrey was prescribed the drug Ritalin, and everything seemed to be fine.

Then Jeffrey became a teenager.

When Jeffrey entered his teen years, he began hanging around what his parents thought was a tough crowd. They all wore black and identified with the "gothic" subculture that was popular during the 1990s. Jeffrey quickly adopted the look, music, and lingo, and began using words and phrases that his parents didn't quite understand.

Nor did they want to understand.

Still, Jeffrey continued to attend church with his parents and looked to be on his way to graduating high school on time and then going on to college. His parents hoped that the goth phase would pass once he went on to college and developed new interests and friends. But by early 1998, Jeffrey Franklin was digging himself into a very deep and dark hole.

The gothic clothing and music may have seemed disturbing to Jeffrey's parents and siblings, but the real problems were developing during his extracurricular activities. By early 1998, Jeffrey had quit all official extracurricular activities at his school and instead opted to spend most of his free time drinking and doing illicit drugs. There is evidence that his parents learned of his extensive partying and tried to put an end to it, but Jeffrey was not going to let anyone tell him what to do.

He would kill if necessary.

The Attacks

The precise reasons why Jeffrey Franklin turned his wrath on his own family are still unclear. Again, it is nearly impossible for most people to even consider such a thing, but it appears that Jeffrey had been arguing with his parents for some time over his alcohol and drug use before the events of March 10, 1998. Notably, Franklin was 17 years old at the time of the murders, not 19 as a later court document stated.

Based on Franklin's statements to the police and a handwritten note he wrote earlier detailing the plan, a chronology of the event can be made.

Apparently, no one in the Franklin family knew what Jeffrey had in store for them that evening. There were no arguments beforehand, nor did Jeffrey make any threats. He simply started attacking his family members.

Jeffrey attacked his mother first with an interesting weapon. Instead of starting the massacre out with a more traditional weapon, such as a knife, gun, or club, Jeffrey attacked his mother with a flat or rat-tail file. Although the tool's killing efficiency is probably questionable, Jeff got the jump on his mom and quickly killed her by hitting, stabbing, and gouging her with the file.

After committing the act of matricide, Jeffrey then searched for his fourteen-year-old sister, who he found in another part of the house. He struck his sister numerous times with a hatchet, but miraculously, she lived.

The next three members of the Franklin family were attacked in quick succession.

Once he realized his mother was dead, Jeffrey changed weapons to a sledgehammer. Although the sledgehammer was much heavier, Jeffrey used his stealth tactics once more, surprising his father when he came in the front door. Jeff bashed his dad in the head a few times with the hammer and then switched back to the hatchet.

It was time to kill his nine- and six-year-old brothers.

By the time he got to his brothers, they had heard enough of the commotion throughout the house to know they needed to get out. Jeffrey managed to inflict some wounds on the two kids, but they were aware enough to play dead.

Jeffrey's dad Gerald was still alive, though, and he managed to make it out of the back door of the home before he collapsed and eventually died. A neighbor saw Gerald fleeing from the back of his home, bleeding, and called the police.

When the police arrived at the Franklin home, Jeffrey made one last desperate attempt to stay free by fleeing in his car with the cops giving chase. Apparently knowing that his situation was untenable, Jeffrey pulled his car over and gave up. As he was driven away handcuffed by the Huntsville police, he turned in the backseat of the police car and stuck his tongue out for all the news cameras.

The Aftermath

When the final kill count was tallied, Jeffrey Franklin fell short of his infamous family annihilating peers. He managed to kill both his parents, but his three siblings survived with varying degrees of injuries. Generally speaking, three murders are needed for an incident to be considered a "mass murder," and since most of Franklin's family lived, his crime cannot be considered a true family annihilation.

Despite Jeffrey's failure to attain mass murdering infamy, the attacks left an indelible mark on the community of Huntsville.

The homicide investigators assigned to the case were surprised and appalled at the level of brutality that Jeff inflicted on his family. The city has its share of crime, but most of it was drug- or gang-related, and the domestic violence that happened never approached the levels Jeff Franklin dished out to his family that night.

Blood was sprayed on the walls and pooled on the floors.

As the investigators worked their way through the house, room by room, they made an interesting discovery in Jeff's room. Shoved far inside of a stereo speaker was a note that can only be described as Jeffrey's blueprint for murder.

"I know Dad will be home at this time and I'm going to be, I'll wait by the front door, behind the little hutch, and I'll hit him with a hammer. Mom will be out on a walk, when she comes back I'll have the radio playing loudly, I'll call Mom in the room and ask her what's on the agenda for today, then I'll kill her, and what about the brothers and sisters. Well, I'll take them, I'll strangle my little brother in this room and I'll lure my other little brother into this room and strangle him. Then my sister I will rape her then I will finish her off."

As graphic as the note was, it didn't explain *why* Jeffrey wanted to kill his family. Still, it proved intent, which is what prosecutors would need to secure a first-degree murder conviction against Jeffrey Franklin.

Alabama is considered a "law and order" state because it has the death penalty, which it regularly uses, and criminals are routinely given long sentences. The district attorney pushed hard to give Franklin the death penalty, and the conservative citizens of Madison County, Alabama, appeared willing to give it to the juvenile.

Seeing that he had no defense and that a guilty verdict might mean a trip to Alabama's death row, Franklin pleaded guilty to murder and was sentenced to three consecutive life sentences.

It appeared that Franklin would spend the rest of his life in prison.

For many serial killers and mass murderers who are captured, prison is a difficult experience. These people often seem scary to normal people—and they no doubt are scary when one considers their horrendous acts—but when they are placed in an environment of equity with other criminals, they tend to be viewed as the worst of the worst. They are routinely reviled and abused by the seasoned inmates, who are often career criminals and/or gang members.

When Jeffrey Franklin entered the Alabama Department of Corrections, he soon learned that he was at the bottom of the totem pole.

Since his incarceration, Franklin has received numerous misconduct reports, one for attempting to cut his wrists and another for slamming his head into a wall. From what little has leaked out of the prison system concerning Franklin's life there, it appears that he has been the target of abuse by other inmates and was once beaten severely by another inmate.

Still, prison is a place where inmates have a lot of time on their hands. They use their free time to better themselves, prey on other inmates, and devise ways to get out, both legal and illegal. Jeffrey Franklin has used much of his free time in prison trying to free himself legally. It turns out that Alabama inmates with life sentences can apply for parole after serving fifteen years.

Franklin argued that with time served in the county jail while he was awaiting trial, he was eligible to apply for parole in 2013. Although the courts did add the county jail time to his prison sentence, he was not given a parole hearing until the summer of 2016.

Franklin was denied.

Franklin's parole denial, though, is largely a moot point as Madison County prosecutor Rob Broussard explained.

"Number one, if you have three consecutive life sentences, I would think he's not eligible for a serious look to parole unless he's done three consecutive life sentences, 45 years," Broussard said. "I think when you look at the nature of the crime, him killing his parents in the way he killed them. And on top of that, an individual who tried to kill his three siblings, including a six-year-old with a butcher knife, this guy will always be inherently dangerous and I feel confident that a parole board will not let him see the light of day."

When Jeffrey Franklin is not being abused by the stronger inmates, he spends his time painting and drawing, which has finally given him a bit of notoriety. Thanks to the website deathmerchant.com (which is no longer active), Franklin was able to reach out to a host of serial killer and mass murderer groupies. He was also able to sell some of his artwork on the website. Because of the website, Franklin developed a modest following of his own groupies, so despite technically failing as a family annihilator, he finally achieved a certain level of infamy to put him on par with the likes of Defeo Junior and Brom.

Thanks to the computer age, it appears that we may not have heard the last of Jeffrey Franklin.

CHAPTER 5:

THE ANTHONY BARBARO
SCHOOL SHOOTING

Family annihilations may account for the most deaths in mass murders in the United States, but school shootings have received much more attention. The phenomenon of mass murders committed by civilians during peacetime is actually very new. There were few such cases reported before the 1960s, but after that time they have unfortunately become much more frequent.

Mass murders can happen anywhere—a mall, a workplace, on the street—but when they happen at a school, it is especially shocking. Most people value the concept of schools and view them with an almost reverent attitude. Schools are the institutions that teach our children and young people how to be good, productive citizens in society.

So, an assault on a school is an assault on all of us.

For most of American history, schools have been viewed as peaceful places devoid of violence for the most part. Yes, schoolyard fights are fairly common among boys, but those fights are usually minor and resolved very quickly. Americans traditionally felt safe in schools—until August 1, 1966.

That was the date when a University of Texas graduate student named Charles Whitman opened fire on students, faculty, and others from a tower on the University of Texas' main campus in Austin. Whitman's mass shooting left seventeen people dead, including himself, and rocked the United States.

From that point on, Americans looked at schools much differently.

A series of other school shootings followed Whitman's rampage. On January 17, 1989, a man named Patrick Purdy opened fire on a Stockton, California, elementary school, killing six. The most infamous mass murder of the 1990s took place on April 20, 1999, when teenagers Eric Harris and Dylan Klebold shot up their high school, killing fifteen people, including themselves. Finally, the worst school massacre in American history happened on the campus of Virginia Tech University when former student Seung-Hui Cho shot and killed thirty-two students and employees of the college on April 16, 2007.

There are, of course, other school shootings, but the above are the best known and worst in terms of kill counts.

But before Purdy shot up a playground full of pre-teens and after Whitman brought chaos to Austin, a teenager named Anthony Barbaro decided to shoot up his upstate New York high school on December 30, 1974. Barbaro's massacre is often overlooked because he did not deliver as much carnage as the others—he killed three and wounded eleven—and it took place nearly ten years after Whitman's massacre and more than ten years before the majority of the school shootings began in the late 1980s.

But the Anthony Barbaro school shooting was much different than the others due to Barbaro's background.

Unlike all of the other notorious school shooters mentioned above, Barbaro exhibited few if any of the warning signs of a potential mass murderer. If anything, Barbaro was very atypical in his profile: he got along with his fellow classmates and teachers, had no problems at home, and was a good student with a bright future.

Somehow, Anthony Barbaro fell through the cracks.

An Honor Student

Anthony Barbaro was born in 1958 to a middle-class family in Olean, New York. Although in the state of New York, Olean is located in the western part of the state on the Pennsylvania state line, far from New York City. The closest major city to Olean is Buffalo, but residents of the town like to see themselves as being far from big-city life

Olean has traditionally been a politically conservative town where guns and pickup trucks are more common than yoga studios and coffee shops. The town came to prominence in the late nineteenth century when it was part of the Pennsylvania oil boom. Immigrants from Europe and around the world flocked to Olean to work in nearby oil fields, which helped the population of the town peak at over 20,000 in the middle of the twentieth century.

The Barbaros were descended from hard-working Italian immigrants who came to the area during the oil boom. By the time Anthony was born, the Barbaro family was well respected in the community, playing a prominent role in their local Catholic parish and volunteering in various civic groups. Anthony's father had a well-paying position as an executive at an engineering firm, and his mother was a full-time mother and worked part-time at a local fast food restaurant. Anthony and his two younger siblings, a brother and sister, had everything they needed, and there was no abuse of any type in the Barbaro home.

Everything was fine in Anthony Barbaro's home life.

Barbaro's school and social life also appear to have been stable. Anthony had a circle of friends with whom he regularly spent time, none of whom ever stated that he made violent threats or even talked about violence in general. He also worked part-time with his mother at the fast food restaurant and was said to be a good employee with no problems.

In terms of academics, Anthony Barbaro was at the top of his class. School seemed to be easy for the teenager, who was a senior at Olean High School during the 1974-1975 school year. Although he spent a fair amount of time studying, homework came easily to Anthony, so he was able to dedicate his time to other pursuits.

When he wasn't studying, working at the fast food restaurant, or spending time with his friends or family, Anthony was taking part in extracurricular activities at his high school. He was on the bowling team for a short time but was cut. Those who knew him at the time said that he didn't seem very upset about getting cut from the team, and it is generally not considered to have played a role in his later actions.

The extracurricular activity that Anthony Barbaro excelled in was shooting.

It was once common for many high schools in rural America to have rifle teams, and it still is in many western states. So it was common in the 1970s to see high school students carrying rifles around town on their way to competitions or to practice at ranges, which could be anything from an official indoor range to a field in the middle of nowhere.

Anthony was the star on his team, which he achieved by regular practice with his own Remington .30-06-caliber rifle with telescopic sight.

Early in his senior year, Anthony learned that his grades, combined with his extracurricular activities, had earned him a scholarship to the prestigious New York University in New York City.

Most kids in his position would've been thrilled, but Anthony kept his feelings to himself. He told his parents that he was happy about the news, but that he didn't want to celebrate it. In fact, Anthony Barbaro was known to be quite reserved, almost brooding, when it came to his feelings.

Because of that, no one thought anything was amiss with the young scholar on the afternoon of December 30, 1974.

The Massacre

On December 30, Anthony and his siblings were enjoying the time off from school for Christmas break; at least, Anthony's brother and sister were. Anthony spent part of the morning watching television with his ten-year-old brother, Chris, and then at around noon told him that he was going to practice shooting.

Chris didn't think his brother was going to practice on humans.

Since Anthony was a star shooter on his school's team, his parents let him take his rifle out regularly without permission. They reasoned that Anthony was a bright, responsible young man who knew the dangerous capabilities of a loaded gun.

They were right about their son, but for the wrong reasons.

After he retrieved his gun, he apparently took a meandering route to the high school because he did not arrive there until about 2:50 p.m. No one knows what Anthony did in the time between when he left the Barbaro home and when he arrived at Olean High School, but it is probable that he took some time to consider what he was about to do. Unlike some other notorious school shooters, Anthony Barbaro didn't leave what can be considered a manifesto, so any statement about how long he had been planning his assault is conjecture.

With that said, the details of the massacre clearly show that Anthony Barbaro had been thinking about and had been planning the assault on the high school for some time.

When Barbaro arrived at Olean High School just before three, he entered the school through an unlocked door. Since classes were out for break, most of the school was locked, but there was still a skeleton crew of janitors and maintenance workers there, which is why one of the doors was unlocked.

Once Barbaro gained entry into the school, he headed for the student council room on the third floor. It was there that he set off a smoke bomb in front of the room, which was probably intended to obscure the origins of his gunfire. The smoke bomb comprised a coke bottle filled with gasoline and a wick.

The smoke bomb had the unintended effect of setting off the fire alarm. This brought the workers on duty to the source but also covered Barbaro's gunfire as he shot his way into the student council room. Once inside the student council room, Barbaro was ready to go to work.

Earl Metcaff was the first janitor to respond to the disturbance on the third floor. According to his co-workers who were also working at the school at the time, he thought it was some kids pulling a prank.

It was no prank.

As Barbaro was setting up in the student council room to begin his massacre, he saw Metcaff approaching the room from a window that faced the hallway. Without hesitation, Barbaro used his well-honed shooting skills to dispatch the unsuspecting janitor with one shot.

Things were just getting started.

Barbaro then moved to a window facing the street and began indiscriminately shooting at pedestrians on the street below, and then the first responders who showed up to help them.

The small town of Olean suddenly became more akin to a shoot 'em up-style video game.

The crazed teen shooter next shot and killed a twenty-five-year-old mother named Carmen Drayton, who happened to be driving by the school. He then spied meter reader Neal Pilon across the street and killed him with a single shot.

Barbaro then turned his wrath on the firefighters who were trying to rescue the wounded, injuring eight.

Besides the three lives he claimed, Barbaro wounded eleven others during the course of his shooting spree. The local police and sheriff's departments were unable to stop the assault, so the New York State Police and the National Guard were called.

Three hours after the massacre began, state police officers shot tear gas canisters into the room Barbaro was using as his gun turret. But the intelligent young man seemed to have thought of everything and was equipped with a gas mask.

Fortunately for the people of Olean, Barbaro's gas mask was defective.

The police found Barbaro unconscious in the student council room. He was quickly cuffed and whisked away to the county jail, where he was charged with murder.

Unanswered Questions

Although Barbaro was a juvenile at the time of the massacre, he was charged as an adult due to the severity of the crimes and because he was nearly eighteen. Barbaro was charged with a total of fourteen felonies, which included: three counts of second-degree murder, six counts of first-degree assault, and five counts of first-degree reckless endangerment. Although the murders were clearly planned, New York state statutes reserve the charge of first-degree murder for only a select few types of murders, such as the murder of a police officer.

Still, Anthony Barbaro was looking at spending the rest of his life in prison.

Barbaro was remanded to the adult section of the Cattaraugus County Jail, but was placed in an isolated cell block for his own protection. Not surprisingly, he was denied bail.

Barbaro pleaded not guilty by reason of insanity. If a jury or a judge had found in Barbaro's favor, it would have probably meant a lifetime in a secure mental hospital for the once-promising student.

Instead of going away to college in the fall of 1975, Anthony Barbaro sat in a cell in the Cattaraugus County Jail awaiting his fate. He had a lot of time to think about his actions and spent his time like many jail inmates do, writing letters to friends, family, and the occasional criminal groupie. Like many other high-profile criminals who came before and after him, Barbaro developed a relationship with a young woman through letter writing. Although his pen pal never visited him, they seem to have developed a deep bond, as evidenced by some of the letters they exchanged, especially the last letter Barbaro sent her.

As Barbaro's case slowly worked its way through the system, everyone in western New York repeatedly asked the same question: why?

A clear answer never came. On November 1, 1975, Anthony Barbaro was found hanging in his cell. Efforts to revive him were unsuccessful. A thorough search of his cell turned up three suicide notes that were similar in their overall context but differed in details. One was addressed to his family, one to the young woman he was writing to, and another "to whom it may concern."

The notes were articulate and introspective, which only created more mystery surrounding Barbaro's murderous motives. The note addressed "to whom it may concern" partially reads:

"I guess I just wanted to kill the person I hate most — myself, I just didn't have the courage. I wanted to die, but I couldn't do it, so I had to get someone to do it for me. It didn't work out."

It continued:

"People are not afraid to die; it's just how they die. I don't fear death, but rather the pain. But no more. I regret the foods I'll never taste, the music I'll never hear, the sites I'll never see, the accomplishments I'll never accomplish, in other words, I regret my life. Some will always ask, 'Why?' I don't know — no one will. What has been, can't be changed. I'm sorry. It ends like it began; in the middle of the night, someone might think it selfish or cowardly to take one's own life. Maybe so, but it's the only free choice I have. The way I figure, I lose either way. If I'm found not guilty, I won't survive the pain I've caused — my guilt. If I'm convicted, I won't survive the mental and physical punishment of my life in prison."

Perhaps the letters demonstrate just how tragic this case was. In some ways, Anthony Barbaro possessed a wisdom that few adults have, but unfortunately, for some reason, he couldn't reconcile whatever drove him to violence with his precocious mind.

Barbaro's case of suicidal ideation turned outward underscores the complexity of juvenile violence, showing that even seemingly well-sdjusted youth can be driven by overwhelming psychological crises distinct from the external factors we've seen in other cases throughout this anthology, such as neglect, poverty, and abuse.

Barbaro could have done much with his life and would've no doubt been a benefit to society.

Instead, Anthony Barbaro will always be remembered as a mass murderer and a school shooter.

CHAPTER 6:

THE MURDER OF
HAROLD SASKO

This volume of true crime cases includes many heinous crimes committed by young offenders. The reasons vary, but the results of the crime have all left people shaking their heads and wondering why young people would commit such horrific acts. Some cases, such as Anthony Barbaro's shooting spree, defy explanation and have no true motives, but maybe worse are the teen "thrill kills."

Unfortunately, human history is full of many thrill kills. Whether it is a sadistic military commander, a serial killer, or a young person, all thrill killers are driven by an unnatural desire to see other humans in pain and to watch them die.

Most cases of thrill kills, especially among serial killers, are stranger-on-stranger crimes. The killer usually picks his victim, or victims, out of convenience, although other factors also play a role.

But sometimes those closest to you are thrill killers, looking at you every day the way a cat does a mouse, waiting for the right time to pounce and sadistically play with you before ending your life.

This is exactly what happened to fifty-two-year-old Kansas entrepreneur Harold Sasko when he offered to share his home with a troubled young woman. When Sasko was found stabbed to death in his Lawrence, Kansas home in January 2014, suspicion immediately fell on his nineteen-year-old roommate, employee, and possible lover, Sarah Gonzalez McLinn.

When the local authorities finally revealed the details behind Sasko's murder, the public was surprised to learn of a bizarre plot that included plenty of drugs, booze, and a desire to kill for no other reason than to see how it felt.

Some say Sasko was killed for doing a good deed, while others believe that he was the victim of a May-September romance gone wrong.

A more complex narrative was revealed during the trial, but whatever the circumstances, to many it was clear that Gonzalez McLinn killed Sasko for her own satisfaction.

An Unlikely Pair

Harold Sasko and Sarah Gonzalez McLinn came from two completely different worlds. That was the partial result of them being from two different generations. Sasko, a late Baby Boomer, was thirty-three years Gonzalez McLinn's senior and officially two generations ahead of the young Millennial. It would not be an exaggeration to say that Sasko grew up in quite a different country than what Gonzalez McLinn knew as a child.

A native Kansan, Sasko was the tenth of twelve children in what can be described as a typical post-war, Midwestern family. The Saskos were church-going people who instilled those values in their children, along with a strong work ethic and the value of earning and saving money.

The values especially resonated with young Harold.

After graduating from high school, Harold worked a number of different jobs before realizing that he had a knack for numbers and business. He operated a number of successful businesses and eventually got married. Sasko and his wife had a daughter, but they eventually drifted apart and divorced.

But Sasko's ambition never diminished.

By the 1990s, Sasko became involved in the fairly new, Texas-based restaurant chain Cici's Pizza. Eventually, Sasko bought two Cici's franchises in Topeka, Kansas, and one in his hometown of Lawrence.

For the most part, Sasko lived a quiet, suburban lifestyle in a middle-class neighborhood of Lawrence. He got along well with his neighbors, and most who knew him described him as a "good guy."

Sasko's friends and family said that he often went out of his way to help people, even those he didn't know very well. They said that he particularly had a soft spot for his employees, many of whom were young with various problems. Sasko was willing to take a chance and hire anyone whom he thought would work hard, including people who were recently released from jail and/or a treatment center.

With his daughter living with his ex-wife full-time, Sasko seemed to find surrogate children among his many employees. He allowed one of his employees to use his car for a vacation and helped another one get a loan so that he could buy a car.

Harold Sasko's generosity toward his employees seemed to know no bounds.

Then, in 2013, he told the woman he was dating that he was allowing an eighteen-year-old female employee to move into his home. He explained that the employee had a difficult home life and that she was having a tough time finding a place to stay. The girlfriend didn't like the fact that such a young woman would be living in the same house with Sasko, but he was intent on helping the employee.

The employee was Sarah Gonzalez McLinn.

About the only thing that Gonzalez McLinn had in common with Sasko was that they were both born in the same state. Born nearly two generations after Sasko, in the mid-1990s, Gonzalez McLinn grew up in a very different Kansas. Gonzalez McLinn barely knew her father and was raised exclusively by her mother and her mother's family.

The McLinns learned at an early point that Sarah was going to have problems.

In her quest to connect with her Hispanic father, Sarah began running with kids of various Hispanic backgrounds on the streets of Topeka. The image she had of her father was, for the most part, negative—according to the McLinn family, Gonzalez had rightfully earned that reputation—but it was also "cool" to a teenager who wanted to be rebellious. Because of that, Sarah often sought out the criminal elements in the Hispanic community of Topeka. Although the McLinns tried to pull her away from the negative influences, she kept going back to find her missing father figure.

Sarah developed a drug habit in her early teens and was often associated with known gang members.

By the age of eighteen, Sarah Gonzalez McLinn's life was a mess.

As the young woman's life seemed to spiral out of control, she found employment at a Cici's Pizza owned by Harold Sasko. According to his friends, Harold soon learned about Sarah's difficult childhood and the fact that she was still having problems finding a place to live.

To Harold's friends and family, they believe he saw Sarah as a "project."

"To me, I think he saw it as a project to fix, to help make better," said Harold's brother, Glenn, about Gonzalez McLinn.

Gonzalez McLinn had been living at Harold's for just a few short months by January 14, 2014. By all accounts, the two got along fine, and the living arrangement seemed to be going well. Some of Harold's employees even thought that the situation was going so well that it was more than platonic.

Harold and Sarah usually went to work together, and on the days when Harold didn't work, or when he was at one of his other stores, he usually made it back to drive Sarah home. To this day, it is unknown if the pair developed a romantic relationship, but it is a possibility considering how much time they spent together.

Whether they were romantically involved or not, it was clear to all who knew them that they got along quite well, which is partially what made the events of January 14 so shocking.

The Murder

The exact circumstances that led to the tragic events on January 14 remain murky, but based on Gonzalez McLinn's later confession and the forensic evidence, a reasonable outline can be drawn. Both Sarah and Harold had the evening off and decided to spend it at the house drinking some beers. Harold apparently thought it was just going to be a quiet night in, but Sarah had other ideas.

At some point during the evening, Gonzalez McLinn put her devious plan into action when Harold wasn't looking. She crushed several Ambien sleeping pills into a powder and put it into Harold's beer. The bitter taste of the beer apparently masked the taste of the powdered pills because Sasko readily drank the concoction.

It didn't take long for him to pass out.

As Harold was lying on the floor of his house unconscious, Sarah bound his arms and legs with zip ties and gagged his mouth. The actions were entirely superfluous, though, since Sasko had enough alcohol and Ambien in his system to incapacitate him for several hours.

Gonzalez McLinn then proceeded to the next phase of her plan.

Making sure to hit the right spot, Sarah aimed a knife straight for Harold's neck, severing arteries and veins in the process. She stabbed him a few more times for good measure, but the defenseless pizzeria entrepreneur would've died from the first stab.

Apparently, Gonzalez McLinn never considered what she'd do after she killed Sasko. She was too small to move Sasko's body, and Sarah was determined not to involve anyone else.

She had few options at this point.

Some criminals would attempt to burn the house to cover up forensic evidence, but Gonzalez McLinn was not much of a criminal, nor very bright.

She decided to go on the run.

It is obvious that Gonzalez McLinn had no real plan to live on the lam, as evidenced by nearly every decision she made after killing Sasko. Sarah simply left the house, and all of the physical evidence, as it was, and fled in Sasko's 2008 Nissan Altima with his dog.

From Lawrence, Sarah drove hundreds of miles south to Bishop, Texas, near the U.S.-Mexican border, apparently in an attempt to evade justice by hiding out in Mexico. Something made Sarah change her mind, though, and she instead drove hundreds more miles to Florida. While in Florida, she slept in Sasko's car and camped out illegally in and around the Everglades.

Meanwhile, back in Kansas, Gonzalez McLinn's family reported her missing on January 17. When she never showed up for a family dinner on the 14th, which of course was the night she murdered Sasko, her family immediately thought nothing of it. They reasoned that lately Sarah had become more responsible and probably decided to pick up an extra shift at work. She would call them soon to let them know what happened.

But when Sarah never called, her family began to worry.

The McLinns worried that Sarah had drifted back into her old crowd and was using drugs again, or worse, some of her old associates had done something to her. They called the police, who went to Sasko's home to search for the missing young adult, but instead found the mutilated body of a middle-aged man.

A warrant was immediately issued for Sarah Gonzalez McLinn's arrest.

Not long after the warrant was issued in Kansas, local police arrested Gonzalez McLinn in Florida for camping in a park after hours. A search of her/Sasko's car turned up a small amount of marijuana and prescription pills that were not in her name.

The police also found an axe and two knives that are believed to have been used in Sasko's murder.

It didn't take long for Gonzalez McLinn's warrant to show up on the Florida police computers, so she was held without bond awaiting police from Douglass County, Kansas, to fly down to Florida. Douglass County detectives were surprised to learn that not only was Gonzalez McLinn not going to fight extradition to Kansas, but that she was also willing to give a complete confession to Sasko's murder.

In the long and rambling confession, Sarah told the detectives that she had been having violent thoughts and fantasies for some time and that she "wanted to know what it felt like" to kill someone.

The detectives were shocked to learn that the young, seemingly innocent-looking girl in front of them had taken a human life just for the thrill.

An Insanity Defense

When Gonzalez McLinn was finally brought back to Kansas and given court-appointed lawyers, it was time for them to create a legal defense. Sarah Gonzales McLinn's defense argued that the murder was an act of "delayed self-defense" due to years of alleged abuse and sex trafficking by Sasko.

But there was a mountain of evidence stacked against their client. Besides her lengthy confession, there were several other pieces of circumstantial and physical evidence that squarely pointed toward Gonzalez McLinn's guilt.

Sarah's flight after the killing showed signs of premeditation, or at least the recognition that she had done something wrong, which would work against any type of insanity defense. DNA taken from the weapons recovered from Sasko's car matched the murdered entrepreneur, and the toxicology report showed that he had ingested six Ambien tablets, further proof of premeditation. The final piece of evidence of premeditation was a series of Google searches someone in the home made using phrases such as "neck vulnerable spots."

After carefully reviewing all of the evidence, Gonzalez McLinn's attorneys knew that they would have a nearly impossible time getting a jury to convict their client of anything less than first-degree murder. In many such murder cases, lawyers often see convictions for lesser offenses, such as second-degree murder or manslaughter, as a victory when their clients are facing first-degree murder charges and a possible sentence of life without the possibility of parole, or even the death penalty.

Sarah's lawyers knew they had to take a different path, so they decided to try an insanity defense.

Insanity defenses are rarely successful in the United States, and even when they are, the defendant is usually placed in a secured mental hospital for an indeterminate period, often the rest of their life. Still, Gonzalez McLinn's lawyers argued it was better than the alternative of life in prison with no parole.

The defense brought in forensic psychiatrists who testified to her multiple diagnoses, including Dissociative Identity Disorder (DID) and PTSD, claiming an alternate personality was responsible for the act. DID is when the person afflicted believes they have multiple, distinct personalities. The experts said that a personality named "Alyssa" was Sarah's murderous alter-ego and that it was essentially uncontrollable.

The jury didn't buy the insanity defense.

On March 20, 2015, Sarah Gonzalez McLinn was found guilty of first-degree murder. Later that year, she was sentenced to what is known as the "hard fifty" in the state of Kansas, or a fifty-year minimum behind bars.

Gonzalex McLinn has since alleged that Sako raped her, controlled her finances, held her captive in his Lawrence home, and she has sought clemency for her crime.

Due to her young age, there is a possibility that Sarah will be released from prison one day, but due to the minimum sentence imposed, she will be a much older woman by then.

CHAPTER 7:

THE MURDER OF
THE DOSS FAMILY

As evidenced by several of the chapters in this volume, youth violence is a scourge that doesn't appear to be going away anytime soon. Youth violence has been recorded throughout history, but the especially heinous cases are, for the most part, a modern phenomenon and relegated to the last four decades. Although the crime rate in the United States dropped in the early 1980s, youth crime increased.

Gang violence has plagued America's inner cities, but a new breed of seemingly conscienceless youth criminals emerged from the suburbs and rural areas beginning in the 1970s. Sociologists argue that this group of youth criminals is often spurred by a lack of direction, which leads to thrill-seeking in the forms of illicit drug use and other criminal activity.

But that doesn't explain the sheer brutality of many of these crimes.

Many of these youth murders are extremely sadistic when compared to other murder cases, and, as the case of Anthony Barbaro demonstrates, sometimes there is no apparent motive.

The next case, like Barbaro's, involves a juvenile killer who took innocent people's lives for no known reason. After that fact, though, this case diverges significantly.

On May 11, 2011, the bodies of thirty-four-year-old Amanda Prewett Doss and her two children, eleven-year-old Guinevere Doss and eight-year-old Texas Johnson, were discovered in their burned-up Redwater, Texas home. The subsequent investigation revealed that the family had been murdered, and the fire was set to cover the crimes.

The news sent the Texarkana, Texas and Arkansas area into a panic.

The initial investigation eventually went cold, but when it was eventually solved, residents of the area were shocked to learn that the perpetrator was a juvenile girl.

It set many people's notions about crime upside down but reaffirmed the ideas of those who knew about the ever-increasing problem of youth violence in the United States.

A Bizarre Case

As soon as the investigation into the murders of the Doss family began, it was immediately shrouded in mystery. The case began when Amanda Doss' parents received a frantic phone call on the night of May 11 from Guinevere, who was screaming into the phone for her grandparents to come help. The disturbed grandparents phoned 911 and then raced over to their daughter's home, only to find it engulfed in flames.

First responders arrived shortly after Amanda's family, but they were unable to rescue anyone from the inferno.

The investigators were interested to know about the phone call that Guinevere made to her grandparents, but unfortunately, she gave no details about her plight. With the phone call being an apparent dead end, the investigators turned to the burned home and the bodies recovered from it for answers.

An autopsy revealed that Amanda and her two children had been stabbed to death. It remained unknown if sexual assault had occurred, but fire investigators were able to prove that the fire was deliberate and was no doubt set to eliminate any physical evidence left at the scene.

The homicide investigators immediately thought they were dealing with a sophisticated, possibly career criminal. To them, it seemed to have all the hallmarks of a pro: there were no witnesses left, and the arson was clearly done to destroy any physical evidence. Of course, anyone could do those things, but their experience told them that the chances were that the murders were done by someone well-acquainted with the criminal underworld.

The fathers of Amanda's children were questioned first, along with all of the other men in her life, but their alibis were all rock solid. The detectives then widened their net to include known sex offenders in the area, as well as other career criminals who had burglary, kidnapping, and/or arson on their rap sheets.

Although a few interesting leads turned up, no viable suspects emerged.

Eventually, in what was perhaps somewhat of a desperate move, a $145,000 reward was offered for information leading to the arrest of the Doss family's killer or killers.

As the months went by, leads about the case began to evaporate until there were none.

The Doss Family

As no viable leads concerning the identity of the Doss family's killer, or killers, ever panned out, residents of Redwater repeatedly asked, who would want to kill Amanda and her children?

No one could come up with an answer.

Amanda was a single mother who garnered significant attention from potential suitors but was more interested in the welfare of her children. She worked full-time, but like many single mothers, found it difficult to juggle work and her children. Her parents weren't always available to watch them, and she got little help from her children's fathers.

Luckily, Rachael Pittman lived nearby.

Rachael Pittman was a sixteen-year-old girl who lived a few miles away from the Doss family in 2011. Like most kids her age, Rachael wanted to have her own money and the independence that goes with it, so she started babysitting in her early teens. Amanda Doss was introduced to Rachael through a mutual acquaintance as a potential babysitter who would work at a reduced fee.

Amanda was pleased with Rachael's work, as she appeared to get along well with her children and was reliable.

But Rachael lived in her own world. It was a world that she kept most people, including her own family, out of, and it was indeed a dark world. She had few friends, and unlike many kids without friends her age, she seemed not to want any friends. In the days immediately after the murders of the Doss family, Rachael Pittman's mother said she didn't seem very disturbed by the events but rationalized that everyone grieves differently.

Rachael's behavior seemed to get stranger, until one day, about three months after the Doss murders, she gave her mom some disturbing news—she was the person who killed Amanda and her family. At first, Rachael's mom didn't believe what she had just heard and told her to quit joking. She had become accustomed to Rachael's sometimes strange behavior and macabre sense of humor, but deep down she knew that this was different.

After Rachael insisted that she was telling the truth, her mother immediately reported the confession to the police.

Rachael Pittman was arrested on three counts of capital murder as a juvenile.

Arrest and Trial

Although a capital murder charge in the state of Texas means that the defendant could face the death penalty, Rachael was not eligible as a juvenile, and even if certified as an adult, she could still not be executed due to federal law.

Still, many of the residents of metro Texarkana wanted to see Rachael on death row.

Texas is a "law and order" state where most of the residents are more than willing to "throw the book" at an offender, no matter the person's gender or age.

But it was precisely Rachael Pittman's gender and age that had so many people scratching their heads. Robbery was not apparently the motive, and since Rachael was said to have gotten along so well with Amanda's children, revenge doesn't appear to have been a factor.

And as much as the local and state media were trying to get a story, the judge placed a gag order on the case, so Rachel's statement to the police was never released to the public.

Despite the death penalty being off the table due to Pittman's age when she committed the crimes, the prosecutor still pushed to charge her as an adult, which meant that she faced the possibility of spending the rest of her life in a tough Texas prison.

On February 9, 2012, the judge agreed with the prosecutor and ruled that Rachael Pittman would be tried as an adult.

Besides Rachael's confession to her mother, there was little evidence that pointed toward Pittman committing the triple murder. Because of this, she was initially confident of her chances in court and planned to take the case to trial. But as both sides prepared for a potentially long trial, the prosecutors presented Rachel with crime scene photos of her victims. According to her lawyers, the photos deeply troubled their young client, who then decided to change her plea to guilty and throw herself at the mercy of the court.

In January 2013, Rachael Pittman was given two life sentences for first-degree murder. She will be eligible for parole on August 12, 2041, when she is in her mid-forties.

Most of the people involved with the case and the majority of the people of Redwater were pleased with its resolution. They believed justice had been served, and now the community could move forward.

But not everyone shared those sentiments.

Conspiracy Theories

Almost as soon as Pittman was taken into the custody of the Texas Department of Corrections, many people in the Texarkana area began asking questions that never came up at trial. Many thought that there was much more to the case than the public was being told, which led to many different conspiracy theories being propagated.

The judge's gag ruling did little to quell many of the questions and only seemed to add to the paranoia. People argued that they could understand why the judge thought it was prudent to impose a gag order during the trial, but they didn't understand why the ruling was kept in place even after Pittman was sent to prison.

Because of the gag ruling, it will remain unknown if Pittman related a motive for the triple murder to the police.

The average person around Texarkana, though, was more interested in Rachael Pittman's ability to kill three people than her motive. Many people thought it was nearly impossible for a sixteen-year-old, especially a girl, to kill three people and get away with it for months.

Rumors began to swirl around Texarkana that Pittman was merely helping some mysterious woman. The rumor/conspiracy theory held that the mysterious woman who was really the brains behind the murders became a suspect in the investigation at one point, and she even failed a polygraph test. The local police, though, were unable to make a case against the woman, so they had to let her go. The authorities then bowed to local pressure to close the case, so they arrested Pittman, who was involved in the murders according to the theory, and then quickly closed the case.

There is no evidence to support this version of events, but until the documents pertaining to the case are released to the public, conspiracy theories will no doubt continue to flourish.

CHAPTER 8:

THE TEEN HATCHET KILLERS, ANTONIO BARBEAU AND NATHAN PAAPE

All of the many youth crimes profiled in this volume are truly terrible and shocking. The obvious question asked in the course of most of these cases is, how could a seemingly innocent kid be so violent and emotionally damaged? Did something happen to make them that way, or were they just born "bad?"

These are, of course, questions that have been asked repeatedly and, in most cases, will probably never be answered. Sometimes it is important to look at the victim.

With the exception of Jeffrey Franklin, the other examples of youth violence profiled in this volume were non-familial assaults and murders. Excuses and self-defense arguments can always be made, whether legitimate or not, when someone kills a stranger or non-family member.

Justification gets infinitely more difficult when family members are involved, and people in general see such crimes as inherently worse. For example, Lyle and Erik Menendez argued that they killed their father in retaliation for years of physical, sexual, and emotional abuse, which many people were willing to consider, but the murder of their mother was a bridge too far for most.

Probably even worse than patricide or matricide would be the killing of a grandparent.

Grandparents are traditionally the family members who give one the most unconditional love, even more than parents. Most grandparents who are involved in the lives of their grandchildren offer an extra shoulder to cry on and usually spoil their grandkids with money, food, and other items.

Why would anyone want to kill a grandparent like that?

On September 17, 2012, the small town of Sheboygan Falls, Wisconsin, was riveted when it was learned that one of its elderly residents had been brutally beaten to death in her own home. Most thought that a drug addict drifter would be the culprit and were perplexed to learn that the killers were the woman's thirteen-year-old grandson and his friend.

Murders rarely happened in Sheboygan Falls, and they were never perpetrated by thirteen-year-old boys on their grandmothers.

Quiet Sheboygan Falls

Located less than an hour's drive north of Milwaukee off Interstate 43, Sheboygan Falls, Wisconsin, is a small town that eventually became a bedroom community exurb of Milwaukee. For the most part, crime is an extremely rare phenomenon in Sheboygan Falls, and murder is almost unheard of; before 2012, the last murder in the town happened in 1996.

It is truly the type of town that people like because it is somewhat far removed from the problems of big-city Milwaukee, but still close enough to drive there for work, shopping, or other things. By 2012, Sheboygan Falls' residents were a mix of two groups. Many were younger families who had moved there to escape the crime, congestion, and higher taxes of Milwaukee. Many of these people commuted back and forth from Milwaukee and saw the town more as a place to sleep at night than a community of which to be part. The other group consisted of the residents whose families had lived in the town for generations. These people were generally more invested in the town and took the extra step to know their neighbors and to take part in civic activities and events.

Barbara Olson was in the latter category.

Olson had called Sheboygan Falls home for her entire life. The seventy-eight-year-old great-grandmother had raised a family in the quiet town that she loved so much. When many of her retired and elderly friends began moving to Florida, Texas, and Arizona to beat the long Wisconsin winters, Olson remained steadfast in her love of the area. She was the typical upper Midwesterner who may complain about the heavy snow and sub-zero temperatures in the middle of the winter, but actually would never have traded it in for life in Florida.

Barbara Olson had everything she needed in Sheboygan Falls: her friends, children, and grandchildren, including Antonio Barbeau.

In September 2012, Antonio Barbeau and Nathan Paape had just started the eighth grade. Simply put, there was nothing extraordinary about either of the two boys. They didn't participate in any extracurricular activities at their junior high school, and neither did well in their coursework.

Neither boy was ever accused of being very bright.

Antonio's family would later claim that a serious car accident he was in at the age of ten left him mentally disabled. Nathan also showed signs of being developmentally delayed.

Although it looked like neither of the two boys would ever go on to do great things, they never showed signs of problematic behavior, either. Besides some minor infractions, neither of the two was ever in serious trouble at school, and most adults who knew them said they were fairly respectful.

The boys showed particular respect and affection toward Barbara Olson. Barbara was Antonio's maternal grandmother, and in true grandmotherly nature, she often doted on Antonio, whom she saw as an underdog. Antonio and Nathan would spend hours on end at Barbara's, watching television, playing in the backyard, and trading sports cards. Barbara was always happy to have her grandkids stop by for visits, but Antonio began to change during the summer of 2012—to the point where she became leery of him.

Antonio and Nathan were living in their own world at that point.

The two boys spent their free time almost exclusively together—they really didn't have other friends or girlfriends. Their parents were involved in their lives but gave them a certain amount of freedom.

They rarely asked the boys what they were doing and never pried.

The events of September 17 made them wish they had.

A Ridiculous Plot

The authorities later learned that Barbeau's and Paape's attack was premeditated and had been planned for some time. However, it is important to remember that the two perpetrators were thirteen-year-old boys who were not exactly at the top of their class.

Their complete lack of understanding of consequences was manifested when they decided to kill Barbara Olson for monetary gain.

In the months before the murder, the two boys learned that they liked marijuana. Despite living in a small town and being quite young, they had no problem getting access to marijuana, but had problems raising funds. They were both too young to work legally at stores or restaurants, and neither had the gumption to make money mowing lawns and/or shoveling driveways and sidewalks.

Antonio suggested robbing his grandmother.

The two boys were under the assumption that the retired grandmother who lived on a fixed income was wealthy. They floated different ideas to get Olson's money, such as burglary, but came to the conclusion that murder would be the best option for them to get some weed.

When school got out on the afternoon of September 17, Barbeau went over to Paape's house as he often did. But on this day, instead of hanging out, the two boys were doing their final preparations for murder. Antonio pulled out a hatchet and showed it to Nathan, who was impressed with the weapon. For his part, Nathan grabbed a hammer from the garage.

The two boys were ready to kill a grandma for some weed money.

About an hour after meeting up at Paape's house, Nathan's mother gave the two boys a ride to Barbara Olson's. After saying goodbye to Nathan's mom, the two boys told her that they would find their own way back home later.

Barbeau and Paape then went to the side of the garage that was connected to the house to put their nefarious plan into action. Once in the garage, they planned to stealthily enter the house and surprise Barbara, but she heard sounds in the garage and opened the door to greet them.

The details of what happened next are a bit murky because, although both boys confessed to the crime, they pointed the finger at each other in court, so it is difficult to say which one attacked first. The autopsy revealed that Barbara was struck at least twenty-seven times with the axe and hammer. After the duo hit the defenseless old woman several times, she collapsed in the doorway.

The two criminal masterminds planned to drag the small woman's body to her car, where they planned to put her in the trunk and then dispose of her in a rural area. It seemed so easy as they both had seen it done so many times on television.

But the two thirteen-year-olds quickly learned that TV is not reality.

After having problems trying to move Barbara's body to the car, they decided to give up the endeavor and leave her in the garage for someone to find, probably one of Antonio's relatives. The pair then pillaged the house for anything of value and came up with $150 in cash and some jewelry.

Score!

The two boys then put the final phase of their plan into action: to place the blame for the murder on someone else. They drove Barbara's car to a local bowling alley known to be frequented by some of the local toughs and left the keys in the ignition with the jewelry they had stolen on the front seat.

Feeling that all of a sudden life was good, the boys then bought a bag of pot and a large pepperoni pizza.

The Discovery

As ridiculous as Barbeau's and Paape's murder plot was, it was two days before any suspicion was cast their way. In the two days after killing Barbara Olson, Barbeau and Paape spent their time smoking pot and watching television.

They didn't have a care in the world.

On September 19, one of Barbara's daughters came by the house for a routine visit. She didn't think anything was wrong with her mother, but the children liked to take turns checking up on her. As soon as she entered the garage, she was horrified to find her mother dead in a pool of blood.

The police were immediately called, and within hours, Barbara's car was located in the bowling alley parking lot. The police recognized that the car's placement and the jewelry on the front seat were meant to throw them off and to possibly entice someone to steal the car, the jewelry, or both.

They also recognized that everything looked like the work of an amateur.

Once the police determined that there was no forced entry into Barbara's house and that it actually looked like she had opened the door for her killer, they began to focus on those closest to the pensioner.

Barbeau's and Paape's names came up as possibly the last two people to see her alive. However, no one could see how two thirteen-year-olds could do such a thing, especially since Antonio was Barbara's grandson.

Still, police officers generally have good intuition, which was sending them more and more in the boys' direction.

A search of Antonio's locker at school turned up bloody clothing, which led to a search warrant for both of their homes. A search of the Paape home turned up more bloody clothing.

Antonio Barbeau and Nathan Paape were charged with the first-degree murder of Barbara Olson as adults.

But things were just getting started.

Pointing the Finger

Although Barbeau and Paape were only thirteen when they killed Barbara, the county prosecutors thought that the crime was heinous enough to get the two charged as adults. After a hearing to decide the matter, a judge agreed and certified the duo as adults.

If convicted, the boys faced the prospect of spending the rest of their lives in a maximum security prison for adult men.

Needless to say, the two boys were frightened and immediately set about to defend themselves in court. But the reality was that they had little defense. Although they pointed the finger at each other almost immediately, they both gave statements implicating themselves in the plot, and both placed themselves at the crime scene. Still, their attorneys were bound to put up credible defenses.

The boys' attorneys succeeded in their first battle—severing the two cases into separate trials. By doing that, they could more logically point the finger at one another. It would only take one juror to believe the story, thereby getting a mistrial.

Despite severing the cases, both boys' lawyers put up similar defenses: "He made me do it!"

Before going to trial, though, Barbeau's lawyers decided to play one final card that could keep their client from spending the remainder of his life in prison. They had Antonio plead not guilty by reason of mental disease or defect, arguing that the injuries he sustained in the car accident several years prior left him unable to process right and wrong like a normal person.

As Barbeau's lawyers were preparing his defense, the influence of the boy's family, combined with possibly a guilty conscience, began to take hold. The extended Olson family didn't want to see a lengthy trial, so some began urging Barbeau's parents to convince him to take a plea bargain.

The prosecutor didn't offer Barbeau a plea bargain, but the teenager still changed his original not guilty plea to no contest in June 2013. He essentially threw himself at the mercy of the court. On August 12, 2013, Antonio Barbeau was given the very adult sentence of life in prison with the possibility of parole after thirty-six years.

Around the time that Antonio pleaded no contest, Nathan went on trial. Paape made the rare move in a criminal trial of testifying in his own defense. His lawyers believed that doing so would help humanize their client and that it would be difficult for a jury to convict a fourteen-year-old boy of murder.

Paape's testimony was unconvincing.

In testimony that many thought looked well-rehearsed, Paape stated that he only hit Olson a couple of times and only did so because he was scared of Barbeau. Although the prosecutor treated Paape with kid gloves as he did the cross-examination, he did get the teen to admit that they took turns hitting Olson with the different weapons.

The jury didn't find Paape particularly convincing, convicting him of first-degree murder. The presiding judge later handed down a sentence of life in prison with the possibility of parole after thirty-one years.

"In my 24 years on the bench, I've not seen anything of this nature. Not even close," Circuit Court Judge Timothy Van Akkeren said in issuing his sentence. "It gives me great sadness to see someone of your age going into the system."

Despite the long sentences, since both were thirteen when they entered the system, they will probably be released one day. Will quiet Sheboygan Falls be ready for them?

CHAPTER 9:

CODY ALAN LEGEBOKOFF, THE CANADIAN COUNTRY BOY KILLER

A cursory examination of modern serial killers reveals that they come in all shapes and sizes. Thanks to the modern media, though, there are many misconceptions throughout society pertaining to serial killers. There seem to be two common serial killer archetypes portrayed in fictional movies, television shows, and books. The first is a middle-aged white male who is not very bright and is an unemployed drifter.

The second archetype is also usually a middle-aged white male, but in contrast, he is often depicted as highly intelligent; a genius, even. The Hannibal Lecter character is perhaps most emblematic of this archetype, but one does not have to look long to find other serial killers portrayed as geniuses across a variety of media.

Although both of these archetypes have elements of reality, they are far from the truth.

The Radford University serial killer database, which is considered the definitive source of serial killer demographic information, has thrown a wrench into many misconceptions about serial killers. For instance, whites only make up over 50% of all serial killers in the United States, while Black males make up close to 40%. It is true that women are far underrepresented in serial killing, with only 10% of all known serial killers being women. Most serial killers are in their thirties or older, affirming the middle age stereotype.

There is a great range in IQ levels among serial killers, but the average comes out to be about average IQ. Contrary to the unemployed drifter stereotype, most serial killers work—although not always steady jobs—and many have families and social networks.

Part of the reason why it is difficult to pigeonhole serial killers is that they are so diverse in their motives.

Most people commonly think of serial killers being driven by lust, such as Ted Bundy and Jeffrey Dahmer, and although that is a common motive, it is only one among many. Many serial killers care little about the act and are instead driven by financial rewards. Black widows, who are usually women, and hitmen, such as Richard Kuklinski, kill repeatedly for the comfort of financial rewards. Still, other serial killers operate under the idea that they are in the middle of a political war, such as Joseph Paul Franklin, which to them justifies all murders they commit.

Finally, there are serial killers who are driven by a combination of motives. These are the most difficult for the authorities to track because they often change their method of operation.

These are the serial killers who defy categorization.

In many ways, Cody Legebokoff also defied categorization and truly never fit the standard serial killer stereotype in looks or behavior. Legebokoff has been described by many as an "all-Canadian boy." Coming from a decent family, Legebokoff was the quintessential western Canadian, who played hockey and enjoyed country music. He had a large network of friends, was charming and good-looking, and never displayed any violence around those who knew him.

It turns out that he was also one of Canada's youngest serial killers.

In his somewhat brief run as a serial killer, Legebokoff not only fooled everyone who knew him by being a good friend, family member, and employee on the one hand, while killing on the other, but he also displayed a startling amount of criminal sophistication for a young man with no criminal background. He learned the vocation of serial killing quickly and was able to adapt his method of operation to avoid detection.

If it weren't for a chance encounter with law enforcement on a lonely road, Cody Legebokoff might still be killing in the Great White North.

Just Another Canadian?

Cody Legebokoff was born in 1990 to a middle-class family in northern British Columbia. When most people think of British Columbia, the cosmopolitan Vancouver comes to mind, but that was not the world where Legebokoff was raised.

Northern British Columbia, like Alberta, Saskatchewan, and Manitoba, is very different from Vancouver or Toronto. In many ways, those areas are more like the western or even southern United States than they are the rest of Canada. The people of the western provinces, outside of Vancouver, tend to be much more conservative politically and live similar lifestyles to their American counterparts.

Farming and ranching are a major part of the region's economy, and the people have developed a hardy, self-sufficient attitude. Guns and pickup trucks are fairly common, and country music is the most popular form of music.

Truly, many Canadians view the western provinces as their version of the American South.

Legebokoff appeared perfectly happy and well-adjusted in this environment as a child. He learned how to hunt and fish and excelled in the truly Canadian sport of hockey. Cody also discovered that he had an aptitude for mechanical work at a young age and loved to tinker with boat and lawnmower motors. He eventually turned that love into a career as a mechanic.

Not long after Legebokoff graduated from high school, he did what many young men do and left his home to see the world. For Legebokoff, that meant moving to Lethbridge, Alberta, where he lived for a short time. But eventually, he became homesick and moved back to northern British Columbia to build a life.

And a career as a budding serial killer.

Legebokoff ended up settling in Prince George, British Columbia, which, at 75,000 people, is the largest city in the northern part of the province. It is also one of the fastest-growing cities in Canada, so Legebokoff had no problem getting a job and a place to live. He quickly found work as a mechanic at a local Ford dealership, and he used his extensive social connections from high school to find an apartment. His roommates were three young women who all claimed they felt safe around Legebokoff.

In late 2008 and early 2009, Cody Legebokoff looked far from being a future serial killer. His laid-back, country-boy persona made him a hit with the ladies, and his life seemed to be going in the right direction. He was doing better financially than most people his age and had no problems to speak of.

But Cody Legebokoff had a dark side.

Many of Cody's friends knew that he liked to party heavily sometimes. He had quite a tolerance for alcohol and was known to do cocaine from time to time, but most of his friends never thought it was a problem—he never let his partying get out of hand.

Or so they thought.

By early 2009, Legebokoff's chemical use had gone from occasional all-night partying to daily cocaine use. It was also around that time that he began frequenting sex workers in Prince George, both for sex and to acquire cocaine. Legebokoff's life was quickly spiraling out of control, but he was able to keep his problems concealed from his friends and family.

Concealment of their crimes is perhaps the main trait that all serial killers share.

A Teenage Killer

At some point during Legebokoff's months-long drug binges, he decided to start killing. No doubt he'd had murderous fantasies for some time before doing his first kill, possibly since childhood, but it's a big step to go from thinking about murder to actually doing it.

Cody Legebokoff started his killing spree on the evening of October 9, 2009, at just the age of nineteen.

On the night in question, Legebokoff drove to Prince George's skid row and picked up some cocaine and a sex worker named Jill Stacey Stuchenko. Stuchenko was a thirty-five-year-old mother of five who was down on her luck, fighting a severe cocaine addiction. Unable to care for her children due to her addiction, Stuchenko took to sex work to feed her expensive cocaine habit.

It is unknown if Stuchenko and Legebokoff knew each other before October 9, but it was certainly the last time the two met. After picking up Stuchenko, they went to a remote location on the edge of town near a gravel pit and did cocaine in Legebokoff's truck before having sex. It's not known if Legebokoff planned to kill Stuchenko, or if he snapped for some reason, but at some point during the encounter, he began beating her.

Legebokoff beat Stuchenko until she stopped breathing, and her face was a collapsed mess.

The police found Stuchenko's body in the gravel on October 20. Besides the massive trauma sustained on her body, especially the face, there were signs she had been sexually assaulted. Prince George has a relatively low crime rate, so the murder in itself was news, but since Stuchenko was a sex worker and drug user, her death quickly fell out of the headlines.

For his part, Legebokoff spent the first few days after the murder paranoid, but after the body was found and the police never showed up, his paranoia began to recede.

Cody went about his daily routine: working, partying, dating, and hanging out with his friends. To those who knew Legebokoff, he didn't seem any different in the period after October 9, 2009.

As much as Legebokoff may have enjoyed the act of killing, the whole situation scared him. He had never been in trouble with the law before and was not very familiar with law enforcement techniques. Despite becoming less paranoid about getting caught as time went by, he was still reluctant to kill again.

He didn't want to get caught.

It was at this point that the cowboy killer went into his "cooling off" period. The FBI's classification of a serial killer is contingent upon two major factors: the killer has to have murdered three or more people in a period where each is separated by time (in a series), and there has to be at least one "cooling off" period between murders. For many notorious serial killers, the cooling-off period takes place after their first kill. For most serial killers, the cooling-off period takes place not over any moral conflicts, but because the killer in question is afraid of capture.

But like with most serial killers, Legebokoff's urge, or reasons to kill, were stronger than his desire not to get caught. Legebokoff even reasoned, how would he get caught for killing sex workers?

The urge to kill manifested itself once more in Legebokoff's soul nearly a year later. On the evening of August 31, 2010, he met another drug addict and sex worker named Natasha Lynn Montgomery.

Legebokoff is believed to have dispatched Montgomery by beating her to death in much the same way as he did Stuchenko, but he changed his method of operation a bit by disposing of her at some, as of yet unknown, location. The authorities believe that Lebegokoff dismembered Montgomery's corpse in some remote, forested location and then scattered her remains for the animals to eat.

After killing Montgomery, Legebokoff appeared to have hit his murderous groove.

Less than two weeks later, on September 10, the cowboy killer struck again.

The victim this time was another known sex worker with a drug problem—thirty-five-year-old Cynthia Frances Maas. The cowboy killer approached Maas like all of his other victims—as a potential john and drug user—and after winning her confidence, he raped and beat her to death.

Maas was reported missing by her family, but because she was a known sex worker and drug user, they were told she was probably intentionally trying to avoid them. Cynthia's family continued to pressure the local police until about a month after she went missing, her body was discovered in a local Prince George park.

An autopsy revealed that Maas had been raped and beaten to death, with the fatal injuries coming from what appeared to be stomps to her head. The examination also showed that she had been dead for about a month.

The discovery led to immediate panic and controversy in the northern British Columbia city.

Maas' family believed that as an American Indian, she was the victim of racism. They argued that if she had been White, then the police would have done more to find her. The local police denied the accusations and pointed out that she lived a risky lifestyle and that they had no reason to believe she had been abducted or murdered when she was reported missing.

As the Maas family publicly sparred with the local police over their treatment of the case, many local residents believed that Cynthia was a victim of the enigmatic "Highway of Tears" serial killer.

The Highway of Tears refers to British Columbia Highway 16, which goes east to west across the northern part of the province, running through Prince George. There have been at least twenty-one murders committed along, or with the victim was taken from, Highway 16 since 1969. Most Canadians are familiar with the macabre history of the highway, but there is no evidence to suggest that all, or even most, of the murders are connected. Still, many people in northern British Columbia were convinced that Maas was the killer's, or killers', most recent victim.

The local, provincial, and federal law enforcement officials all looked into the theory, but few believed that Maas' death was the result of a Highway 16 serial killer. In fact, the local police seemed to rule out any serial killer, and they never considered whether Maas' murder was connected to Stuchenko's or Natasha Montgomery's disappearance.

Meanwhile, the Country Boy killer was living the good life, attending parties and dating young women. It seemed as though Legebokoff would never be caught, but then he made a critical mistake by deviating from his M.O. and victimology.

Up until late November 2010, Legebokoff had focused most of his murderous desires on sex workers. Homeless people, drug addicts, and sex workers are often the favored victims of serial killers because they are, in effect, invisible to polite society, and it can take time for their disappearance to be noticed. Although the discovery of Legebokoff's third victim garnered media attention because her family got involved, when a suspect was not quickly found, the case receded in importance to law enforcement and the local media.

Why the cowboy killer changed his M.O. and victimology remains a mystery, but there is a good chance that hubris played a role. Since he had gotten away with three murders without anyone even vaguely thinking he was the perpetrator, there is a good chance that Legebokoff decided to up the ante by committing a more daring murder.

For his next victim, the cowboy killer went to the internet.

Legebokoff began trolling for his next victim on the Canadian social networking website Nexopia. After searching some profiles, he decided to focus on fifteen-year-old Loren Leslie. Although Leslie was different from Legebokoff's other victims, in that she wasn't a sex worker and was a juvenile, she did have a host of problems. Leslie was on bad terms with her parents and often skipped school to hang out with her friends, drinking alcohol and smoking marijuana. The more her parents tried to discipline her, the more she rebelled.

In November of 2010, she met an attractive twenty-year-old guy on Nexopia who described himself as a country boy with a big heart. Of course, the country boy was Cody Legebokoff, and about the only things truthful on his profile were his picture and his professed love of country music.

But a fifteen-year-old girl can be easily influenced by an older guy, an adult, who listens to her. After talking online and via text message for a few weeks, the two decided to take the relationship to the next level and meet in person on November 27, 2010.

It is unknown if Legebokoff immediately pounced on Loren, but it is certain that he planned to kill her. After raping and murdering the teenager, the cowboy killer took her corpse to a remote location off a logging road several miles outside of Prince George. Legebokoff must not have thought much about the digital trail he left when luring Loren into his trap, but in the end, it didn't matter anyway.

The cowboy killer took his time dismembering Leslie, as the act was all part of what drove the serial killer. Like Dahmer before him, Legebokoff was aroused, not just by the act of murder, but also when he eviscerated his victims' corpses. Once he was done cutting up the body, he spread the parts around the forest for the animals to eat.

Nature would eliminate all evidence.

But the cowboy killer was young, unsophisticated as a criminal, and a bit arrogant. Although he obviously brought Loren Leslie to the remote location to dispose of her body in a most messy way, he didn't think to bring a clean change of clothing.

As he pulled out from the logging road onto the main highway, he did so in an erratic manner that piqued the interest of a Royal Canadian Mounted Police officer who just happened to be patrolling the relatively deserted road. The officer pulled Legebokoff's truck over, thinking he had a drunk driver on his hands.

A quick look at Legebokoff and the interior of the truck revealed a large amount of blood. Based on Legebokoff's demographic and the region, the officer thought that he had busted a poacher, which Legebokoff seemed to confirm. When the officer asked the cowboy killer where the carcass of the game was, though, he suddenly became less talkative.

The officer also didn't notice any meat in the back of Legebokoff's truck.

Within an hour, conservation officers arrived to check the wooded area around the logging trail, but instead of finding deer carcasses, they found human limbs and a female torso.

Through a chance traffic stop, the police had just arrested a notorious serial killer.

The Cowboy Killer Goes on Trial

When Legebokoff was placed in jail and charged with first-degree murder in the death of Loren Leslie, the local detectives were not only shocked at the depravity of the crime but also by the seemingly wholesome exterior of the killer. Legebokoff did not jibe with their stereotype of a serial killer: he was young, handsome, charming, and successful.

But then the detectives were reminded of Ted Bundy.

Once the detectives realized that Legebokoff was a genuine sociopath, they took another look at some unsolved murders and disappearances around Prince George. The more they looked, the more Legobokoff looked good for the murders of Jill Stuchenko, Natasha Montgomery, and Cynthia Maas, in addition to Loren Leslie.

As the pre-trial maneuvering was taking place by both sides, Legebokoff tried to plead guilty to second-degree murder by admitting to being at the scene of every murder but not actually taking part in any of the violence.

Of course, the argument is ridiculous at face value. The odds that someone will ever witness a murder are fairly remote, but for times is nearly impossible. No one believed Legebokoff's story, and he was squarely rebuked by the prosecutor.

"If you choose to assist that person to complete his plan, you have made yourself a party to a planned and deliberate murder," prosecutor Joseph Temple said.

With no plea bargain offered, the Country Boy Killer was forced to go to trial, where he was found guilty on four counts of first-degree murder on September 11, 2014.

The judge handed Legebokoff a sentence of twenty-five years to life and the requirement that he be registered as a sex offender for the remainder of his life. Before sending the Country Boy Killer to serve his sentence, though, the judge had harsh words for the teen killer.

"He lacks any shred of empathy or remorse," British Columbia Supreme Court Justice Glen Parrett said of Cody Legebokoff. "He should never be allowed to walk among us again."

CHAPTER 10:

THE MURDER OF
ROBBIE MIDDLETON

The problem of youth violence has been profiled throughout this book and is in many ways this volume's theme. As discussed throughout the book, the motivations for youth violence cover a wide spectrum, with the most notorious cases being driven either by unknown reasons or a thrill kill. Although the details of these cases diverge, most share a commonality in that the crimes that made these young people famous, or infamous, were usually single events. Yes, many of these kids had problems that led up to their extreme acts of violence, but their infamous acts were usually the culmination of whatever was going wrong inside their heads.

There may have been warning signs, but nothing was very apparent, and none had histories of committing extreme acts of violence on other kids.

The case of Robbie Middleton is different in that respect.

On the afternoon of June 28, 1998, Robbie Middleton was enjoying his eighth birthday in the woods near his family's home when he was set upon by a predator, beaten, tied to a tree, and then set on fire. Although Robbie lived through the ordeal, he suffered third-degree burns to 99% of his body, leaving him permanently disfigured. Ultimately, at the age of twenty-one, Robbie died from a rare form of cancer that was the result of the many operations and skin grafts he had to endure.

The case was truly tragic on those facts alone, but it became even more so when it was revealed that the assailant was a thirteen-year-old neighborhood boy. But unlike some of the cases profiled in this book, the assault of Robbie Middleton was not this teen's first rodeo with the law. By the time Robbie's attacker reached the age of eighteen, he had committed dozens of major crimes ranging from property theft to sexual assault.

The case of Robbie Middleton has brought up the age-old question once more: are some people born evil? After reading about this case, you will probably answer yes.

The Assault

When Robbie Middleton woke up on June 28, 1998, he was all smiles. The sun was shining, school was out of session, and it was his eighth birthday: what could be better for a kid? The plan was for Robbie to spend time with his mother later that afternoon when she got home from work, but the morning and afternoon were his to do as he liked, as long as he stayed around the neighborhood.

Although Robbie was young, the Middletons lived in a quiet, safe neighborhood in the quiet, safe town of Splendora, Texas, so letting him go out alone was no issue. Besides, there were always other kids in the neighborhood to play with, and the adults always looked out for any trouble.

But unfortunately, the trouble they usually looked for was in the form of other adults.

As Robbie was running about the woods near his house, he was suddenly grabbed and beaten. Before he had a chance to scream or run away, his attacker tied him to a tree and tormented him for a few minutes before spraying gasoline on him.

Robbie pleaded for his tormentor to let him go, but the evil person just laughed and set Robbie on fire.

Somehow, as Robbie was engulfed in flames, he was able to wiggle free from the rope and roll on the ground to put out the fire. He then ran for blocks until he nearly made it home, collapsing on the sidewalk.

A neighbor noticed Robbie and called the ambulance.

A Long Recovery

When Robbie was brought into the emergency room, the attending physicians didn't give him much chance of living. They told Robbie's mother that most adults wouldn't live after having 90% of their body burned, and so they didn't think an eight-year-old could last very long. They told Robbie's mother to prepare for the worst.

But Robbie had a will to live that may have surprised the doctors and nurses, but it wasn't a surprise to his family.

Robbie survived the initial operations and the first few weeks in critical condition, but he faced the daunting task of years of therapy and recovery. Ultimately, he needed over 150 operations, many of which were painful skin grafts. Still, Robbie faced the future with a good attitude and rarely complained about the chronic pain.

When Robbie's condition stabilized, the local police visited him to find out what exactly had happened. Since he was so young and playing unattended, the police thought that he could have accidentally burned himself, or possibly he was burned playing with fire with some other kids.

The police were shocked to learn that it was no accident.

Robbie named thirteen-year-old neighborhood boy Don Wilburn Collins as his attacker but offered no motive.

And the police refused to press the disfigured eight-year-old for further information.

The police arrested Collins for felony aggravated assault and placed him in a juvenile facility to await trial. After sitting in the facility for several months, a judge decided to release Collins, stating that beyond Middleton's hospital room accusation, there was no evidence tying the boy to the assault.

The police knew that Robbie wasn't lying, but there was little they could do. They had to fall back on good old-fashioned detective work in order to bring the teen to justice.

Meanwhile, Robbie tried to move on with his life. Despite the countless operations and skin grafts that he had to endure and the fact that his face was permanently disfigured, Robbie wanted to attend normal schools. Although he had to deal with plenty of stares and some cruel jokes, Robbie persisted and eventually developed a network of friends who were loyal to him throughout his high school years.

Robbie did well in his classes and by his senior year was one of the most popular kids in his class. But his medical problems continued to be an albatross around his neck. Just when things would seem to be going well for Robbie in school or socially, he would have to leave school temporarily for another series of operations. Most of Robbie's operations were done in various Shriners' hospitals around the country, which is where he met other kids in situations similar to his, some worse.

Robbie used his time spent in hospitals constructively, by making contacts with doctors and others who specialized in helping burn victims. He learned about the medical procedures, the costs, and how indigent people can or cannot afford to pay for the treatments.

Eventually, Robbie took his knowledge and experience as a burn victim and became an advocate for others in his situation. He gave talks about the subject at hospitals around the country and became the face of a movement that advocated for more funds to research burn treatments and procedures.

Truly, Robbie had turned the awful circumstances of his life into a testament to human resiliency, helping others in the process.

Still, something was missing: justice.

Years had gone by, and the only suspect in Robbie's assault, Don Collins, had yet to receive any justice for his heinous act. And as time went by, it became painfully clear that Don Collins was the type of person born to do bad things and would continue to do so until he was put away for a long time.

Don Collins

The term "bully" has been thrown around quite frequently in recent years, and some would say overused. Bullies come in all shapes and sizes but share one thing in common: they get pleasure from seeing fear in others. The average schoolyard bully may use violence, or the threat of violence, to intimidate victims, but often enough, many bullies turn out to be more bark than bite.

There was definitely bite behind Don Collins' bark.

By the age of thirteen, Don Collins had already made a reputation for himself in Splendora as a budding thug and bully. But Collins took his bullying beyond just teasing, words, or even threats.

Collins routinely beat neighborhood kids younger and smaller than him, and when there wasn't a kid around for him to abuse, he turned his wrath on animals.

"Everyone was afraid of him. He was the big bully that stomped kittens to death," said Robbie's mom, Colleen.

And by "everyone," Colleen even meant the adults in the area. Collins had no guidance at home, and the other adults in the neighborhood were afraid to say anything for fear of what he might do. He was frequently seen carrying knives, clubs, and other weapons and was known to have an unnatural attraction to fire.

Robbie Middleton, unfortunately, learned about Collins' love of fire the hard way.

After Collins was released from the juvenile hall due to a lack of evidence in the fire-borne assault on Robbie Middleton, the adults of the neighborhood grew even more afraid of the dangerous child living among them. Parents kept their eyes on their children more, but they weren't able to keep an eye on them or Collins all the time.

Don Collins struck again in 2001.

About three years after he attacked Robbie, at the age of sixteen, Collins attacked another eight-year-old boy in Splendora. The attack was eerily similar to the one on Robbie in many ways. He singled out an unsuspecting boy who appeared to be alone, pulled a gun, and then sexually assaulted the boy. Unlike the attack on Middleton, though, justice caught up to Collins the second time.

Collins was arrested and charged with felony assault, battery, and felony sexual assault. He was remanded to a juvenile facility to await trial. Although the details of the case are sealed because of privacy laws regarding juvenile defendants in the United States, it is known that Collins served four years in a Texas juvenile facility for the crime.

Texas is known for its tough adult prisons, but the juvenile facilities also have acquired somewhat of a violent reputation. Many of the same gangs present in the adult facilities have a presence in the juvenile camps, and assaults are not uncommon in some of the tougher units. Generally speaking, the bigger kids, known gang members, and bullies, such as Collins, are separated from the younger and weaker kids, but that still doesn't stop all the violence.

Despite the sometimes rough nature of Texas' juvenile corrections system, the officials do emphasize rehabilitation, as every kid in the system will be released into society one day. Vocational and treatment programs were available for Collins to take part in while he was incarcerated, but instead of working to better himself and atone for the pain he had caused others, Collins appeared to have been merely counting the days until he was released.

Once he was released, although convicted of the crime as a juvenile, Collins was required to register as a sex offender as an adult. But instead of following the rules, Collins quickly disappeared and decided to do things his own way, doing drugs and committing more crimes.

Eventually, Collins was arrested, charged, and convicted of failing to register as a sex offender. He was sent to the adult department of corrections and released in 2011.

While Collins was serving time in an adult prison, the authorities of Splendora and Montgomery County began looking at him as a potential suspect in some unsolved cases. The cases included burglaries, sexual assaults, and arsons, but one case kept surfacing to the top: the assault of Robbie Middleton.

The Montgomery County prosecutors wanted to get justice for Robbie and his mother and wanted to make sure that Collins would never be able to victimize another child.

Charges Filed

As Collins spent the 2000s partying and victimizing people, Robbie Middleton was fighting for his life. Although he was brave and strong for his age, the injuries he suffered in the 1998 attack were just too much for a human, especially one so young, to handle. Finally, after fighting most of his life, Robbie Middleton died of a rare form of cancer in 2011, just months before his twenty-first birthday.

The news was, of course, devastating to those who knew Robbie, but something positive came out of it—a way to finally arrest Collins. Two weeks before he died, Robbie gave a videotaped statement where he said that Collins had raped him two weeks before the fire attack.

"He pulled my clothes down and started raping me," Middleton said on his deathbed.

The Montgomery County prosecutors thought that Robbie's confession, along with Collins' M.O. of sexually assaulting young boys, was enough to bring charges. But the prosecutors were not content to charge Collins with assault; they charged him with murder based on the testimony of Middleton's doctors, who said the cancer was the result of operations, which only happened because he was so thoroughly burned.

Don Collins was arrested and charged with first-degree murder as an adult in the death of Robbie Middleton in 2013.

When Collins finally went to trial in 2015, he denied having anything to do with the 1998 assault. His lawyers argued that since no one saw him commit the crime, there was not enough evidence to convict. The defense may have worked for a less odious individual, but the judge allowed witnesses from the neighborhood to testify about Collins' egregious behavior toward other children, animals, and even adults.

Needless to say, the jury did not find Collins sympathetic.

Collins was convicted of first-degree murder and sentenced to forty years in the Texas Department of Corrections. Based on the nature of Texas' correctional system, it is very unlikely that Collins will serve all of that time behind bars.

Despite the long sentence and a conviction for killing a child, Collins was unperturbed by the entire affair.

"The bright side of this is I'll come out with an education," Collins was heard saying to one of his attorneys.

Collins is correct; he does have a good chance of getting educated in one of Texas' tougher prisons, where he will no doubt be sent. Since his case was well-publicized, all of the seasoned convicts and gang members will know just how sick Collins' crimes are, and many will likely want to teach him a thing or two.

Don Collins' education may end up being about how child predators are treated in American prisons.

CHAPTER 11:

THE PORTLAND
MACHETE MURDER

One of the major problems that modern, industrialized criminal justice systems face is how to deal with mentally ill criminals. The reality is that a sizable amount of any population is afflicted with varying forms of mental illness at any time, and although most of those people lead productive, normal lives, for some, the illness proves too much.

For those with the worst forms of mental illness, round-the-clock care and a very specific medicine regimen are needed to keep the diseases in check. Sometimes it is all too much, which leads to the afflicted person living on the streets. Statistics vary concerning what percentage of the homeless suffer from mental illness, but all studies show it is several times higher than the rest of the population. On the streets, the mentally ill are forced to live on the charity of others, and if that is not enough, they turn to crime.

Although rare, sometimes the crimes they commit are quite violent.

Erik Meiser

Erik Meiser was born in the mid-1970s, and as soon as he could talk, people knew there was something wrong with him. He suffered from hallucinations and delusions at an early age, which resulted in him being hospitalized and diagnosed with schizophrenia.

Although Meiser's childhood was difficult, he lived a pretty normal life in his early adulthood thanks to a regular antipsychotic medicine regimen. Eventually, he was able to find steady employment and even started a family, but the problems of schizophrenia were never far away. By the late 1990s, Meiser quit taking his meds for long periods of time, which resulted in him having hallucinations and paranoid episodes. Because of that, he was unable to keep steady employment and began drifting from job to job and town to town.

When Meiser was off his prescribed meds, he would try to substitute by self-medicating with alcohol or illicit drugs, particularly cocaine and methamphetamine. The latter two drugs proved to be especially harmful, as they raised his paranoia to an extremely high level. When he did visit his family, it was to tell them about a shadowy conspiracy against him. Since Meiser's family was well-acquainted with his condition, they tried not to indulge his ideas, but things only got worse.

Meiser believed that there was not only a shadowy conspiracy of people out to get him, but that they were trying to turn his son into a cannibal.

By the late 2000s, Meiser's family heard little from him. The schizophrenic father spent most of his time hiding from the shadowy conspiracy, and to make ends meet, he would burglarize homes throughout the state of Oregon.

Erik Meiser had an uncanny aptitude for burglary.

The Machete Attack

In September 2012, Erik Meiser was having a difficult time. He had been homeless again for several months and was off his antipsychotic medication, so he was feeling especially paranoid. He thought that a cannibal cult was following him throughout the state of Oregon and that at any moment they could capture him and eat him alive.

During this period, Meiser spent most of his time on the streets of Portland, burglarizing homes to get money for his next meth fix. On one pleasant late summer evening, Meiser was scoping out a Portland neighborhood and ended up at the home of Fritz Hayes Junior and his wife, Margaret.

Meiser noticed that most of the lights were off, so he crept up slowly to the back of the house.

After looking in a number of the windows and not seeing any movement, Meiser reached into his trusty bag and pulled out a crowbar and hammer, which he used to gain entry into the home through the back door.

Like a career burglar, Meiser went past the expensive electronic items and went straight to the bedrooms. He could always grab whatever electronic items he could fit into his bag on the way out, but first, he needed to locate the more valuable items, such as cash and jewelry. As Meiser was rifling through the couple's bedroom, he heard something in the front of the house.

Did the cannibal cult find him?

Fritz and Margaret were a young couple who liked to spend their money on each other whenever possible. On the night in question, Fritz surprised his wife with a dinner date at an expensive local restaurant. After their meal, the couple drove back to their home and immediately noticed that a light was on in their bedroom.

Fritz told Margaret to wait in the driveway.

As soon as Fritz entered the home, he was attacked by Meiser, who had a machete.

Meiser hacked away at Fritz, who managed to fight off the crazed attacker to a certain extent. The attack ended up on the Hayes' front lawn, which is where Meiser finally got the upper hand. The crazed impulses of the schizophrenic, combined with the machete, were just too much for Hayes, who died on his front lawn from multiple machete hacks.

Immediately after killing Hayes, Meiser fled the neighborhood. He knew that he had just killed someone, but he wasn't sure who the person was. Meiser began to think that Hayes was actually part of the cannibal cult and that it would only be a matter of time before they found him among the sizable homeless population of Portland.

Meiser had to flee the area.

When the police showed up at the Hayes home to investigate the attack, they had little to go on. They knew the attacker was a White male, but they didn't have much else. Since the crime happened in an otherwise quiet neighborhood, it garnered considerable local media attention, which is where the first tip came to the police.

A random tip to the police said that the assailant was probably a man named Erik Meiser and that he was hiding in the southern Oregon town of Corvallis.

Within days, the Corvallis Police arrested Meiser, and he was brought back to Portland to stand trial in Multnomah County for the first-degree murder of Fritz Hayes Junior.

It turned out to be a case that proves sometimes the wheels of justice turn slowly.

Years of Legal Proceedings

When Erik Meiser was brought before a judge for his initial bond hearing, it was apparent that he suffered from mental illness. A review of his medical and criminal records revealed that, in fact, Meiser had spent a good part of his life in mental institutions and correctional facilities.

Meiser's attorneys decided to present an insanity defense.

However, while Meiser had a history of mental illness, his decision to stop taking his prescribed medication and self-medicate with illicit drugs was a key factor in the prosecution's ability to demonstrate his capacity at the time of the crime.

And it is not like he would necessarily beat the case that way, anyway. If found not guilty by reason of insanity, he would probably be confined to a secure mental hospital for the rest of his life.

Still, his attorneys fought on and on in what seemed like endless hearings to determine Meiser's mental ability to stand trial. The defense argued that his condition made him unable to conform to the law's requirements.

Meiser was declared unfit to stand trial three times, but was eventually cleared by a judge and stood trial in 2017, more than five years after Hayes was murdered. Meiser was convicted of first-degree murder and sentenced to twenty-five years to life in prison.

Hopefully, for the sake of the staff and inmates at the state prison, Meiser no longer thinks that a cannibal cult is after him.

CHAPTER 12:

THE MURDER OF
CASSIE JO STODDART

The final case profiled in this volume is yet another brutal example of youth crime. Although the details of this crime are certainly shocking, the legal repercussions are far more important.

We all know that youth crime is a problem in the United States and that it causes tremendous damage to society. The victims of youth crime are, of course, the ones most obviously affected. Youth property crimes cost millions of dollars a year, and as costly as that is, it is nearly impossible to put a price tag on the amount of damage that youth violence has brought to countless innocent victims. No one will argue that youth crime has been extremely costly to the United States.

What people will argue about, though, is how to deal with youth offenders. Correctional philosophies, like many things, tend to be cyclical. Youth criminals were once treated fairly lightly in this country: as an example, until the 1980s, it was extremely rare for juvenile offenders, even those charged with murder, to be charged as adults. Since the 1980s, it has become a regular practice in many states to charge juveniles above the age of fifteen, especially repeat offenders, with felonies in the adult court system for a variety of different crimes. Rehabilitation is still stressed to a certain degree, but the philosophy is now that it must be accompanied by stiff repercussions.

But what about juvenile murderers?

After the crime rate peaked in the United States in the early 1980s, juvenile crime actually went up, which included the taboo crime of homicide.

The courts were left to figure out what to do with a vast increase in homicidal teenagers. The reality is that juvenile killers, like killers in general, had little sympathy from the American public in general. Most Americans were fine with giving juvenile killers life sentences or even the death penalty. By the late 2000s, there were up to 1,800 men and women serving life sentences in American prisons who committed their crimes as juveniles.

State and federal legislatures followed the public sentiment concerning this specific class of killers by giving them little attention. But the courts are a separate government branch in the United States and quite capable of changing things in their own right.

The next case is one in which an example of brutal teen violence became famous, not so much for the details of the case, but more so for the legal challenges that followed.

Unexpected Violence

Pocatello, Idaho, is a small but growing city in the state's southeastern agricultural region. The city is home to Idaho State University and is within a short drive of the more scenic and mountainous areas of the state. Unemployment and crime are low, and the air is clean, which has made Pocatello a magnet for migrants seeking to escape the crime, high taxes, and overcrowding of California.

Cassie Jo Stoddart's family was among those who left California to escape its problems, but unfortunately, they learned that the phenomenon of youth violence can happen anywhere, at any time.

On the evening of September 22, 2006, sixteen-year-old Cassie was housesitting with her boyfriend in a quiet Pocatello neighborhood. As they began the evening by watching some movies, the doorbell rang. Standing on the porch were their two sixteen-year-old friends, Brian Lee Draper and Torey Michael Adamick. Cassie invited the two boys inside, and the four sat down to watch some movies.

Draper and Adamick hadn't known Cassie very long at that point, but the three shared a mutual friend in Cassie's boyfriend. Cassie liked Draper and Adamick, although she admitted to other friends that the two could be weird at times and liked to talk about violence. Writing it off as typical testosterone teenage talk, Cassie often invited the two along when she was with her boyfriend.

Adamik and Draper were not the type of boys who stood out in the crowd. They both looked fairly average, and neither did anything to attract attention. They were just two anonymous kids in Pocatello.

But Draper and Adamick didn't want to be anonymous. They wanted everyone to know their names.

After the four watched television for a while, Draper and Adamick told Cassie and her boyfriend that they had changed their minds and decided to go to a movie theater. They said their goodbyes and left. Shortly after Draper and Adamick left, Cassie's boyfriend also left in time to make his curfew.

Minutes after Cassie's boyfriend left the house, the power went out. Before Cassie could even check the circuit breaker, she was set upon by Draper and Adamick. The two boys took turns, with one holding Cassie down while the other stabbed her.

The coroner's report indicated that Cassie was stabbed a total of twenty-nine times.

The news horrified the quiet Idaho city, and a manhunt ensued to find the killer of the innocent teenager. At first, the local police believed that the perpetrator was probably a well-seasoned criminal, such as a burglar or sex offender.

But their theory quickly changed when they put together a chronology of Cassie's last hours.

Since Cassie's boyfriend, Brian Draper, and Torey Adamick were the last ones to see Cassie alive, they were all brought in for questioning as suspects. Cassie's boyfriend was quickly cleared, but once the police put a little pressure on the other two, they quickly cracked. The boys both admitted to taking part in the murder, but they also tried to mitigate their guilt by pointing the finger at the other. When the investigators asked why they killed someone who was supposed to be their friend, they answered in vague terms about being influenced by horror movies and the 1999 Columbine massacre.

It was an open and shut case against the two. They were both found guilty of first-degree murder and sentenced to life without the chance of parole in 2007.

But in many ways, the case was just getting started.

Miller v. Alabama

As stated above, the movement to treat juvenile criminals more lightly, or as their advocates would say, "more humanely," had shifted from the legislative branch to the judicial branch. Attorneys in the prison reform movement believed that they could successfully challenge life sentences without the possibility of parole for juveniles under the Eighth Amendment of the United States Constitution, which forbids the use of "cruel and unusual punishment."

Although the strategy had been tried unsuccessfully, a case involving a fourteen-year-old boy who had been convicted of murder in Alabama and given a life sentence came before the United States Supreme Court in 2012.

In a five-to-four ruling, the Supreme Court ruled in *Miller v. Alabama* that it was unconstitutional to impose a mandatory life sentence on a juvenile, even those convicted of murder. It does not mean that a juvenile *cannot* be given a life sentence, only that the judge must consider the defendant's age before passing the sentence.

As big as this ruling was, it initially did little to help Draper and Adamick. They were stuck in the Idaho Department of Corrections doing their mandatory life sentences, as the ruling was not retroactive.

However, four years later, the U.S. Supreme Court's 2016 ruling in *Montgomery v. Louisiana* made the *Miller v. Alabama* decision retroactive, allowing both Draper and Adamcik to file petitions for resentencing.

The ruling immediately applied to over 2,000 people in American prisons, including Draper and Adamick.

After he filed for resentencing in 2018, Adamick's sentence was upheld.

CONCLUSION

After reading this book, you may view crime a bit differently. Instead of seeing crime as something that happens to other people on the other side of town, it is evident that violent crimes come in many different forms and are perpetrated by a wide range of people.

Many of them are children.

The problem of youth violence, like all crime generally, will probably never be totally eradicated, but perhaps someday soon, our society will learn more about what drives this phenomenon. Unfortunately, when viewing the many examples of youth crime profiled in this book, the prognosis does not look good. Until society completely understands what drives youth violence, it can not be alleviated, and as this book has shown, there are many reasons why kids kill

Sometimes kids kill for no reason at all.

This volume also sheds light on many bizarre crimes, some of them perpetrated by juveniles. As difficult as it is for any well-adjusted, law-abiding person to contemplate crime in general, some of the crimes profiled in this book would make a career criminal sick.

Crime is certainly a sickness that afflicts society, and like biological diseases, it will be impossible to eradicate it all, but perhaps trying to understand the worst cases will be a start.

TRUE CRIME
STORIES

BOOK 3

INTRODUCTION

When you open the pages of this book, you'll be transported into a world where criminals believe they rule, but where they also usually receive their just rewards. The nature of some of these crimes is hard for most normal people to understand and most are truly disturbing, yet you will no doubt be compelled to keep reading.

These are twelve of the most perplexing and bizarre crime cases from around the world that have occurred in the last forty years.

Although none of these crimes are directly connected to each other, there are some common threads that make some of these cases eerily similar.

Vacation travel and going on road trips is a favorite pastime for millions of people around the world. Although there are inherent dangers associated with travel, for most, especially in industrialized countries, road tripping is as safe as it is enjoyable.

In this volume, you will learn about two cases where road tripping went terribly wrong. First there is the case of the retired couple, Lyle and Marie McCann, who spent their golden years in a recreational vehicle traveling across Canada and the United States. They never had any problems until a chance encounter with a career criminal. Meanwhile, across the Atlantic Ocean in Spain, an American hiker met with a similar demise along a path that is used by religious pilgrims, but also by violent criminals from time to time.

The case of Lyle and Marie McCann is also significant in the annals of crime history because someone was charged with their murders even though their bodies have yet to be discovered. Thousands of miles away and about fifteen years earlier, a similar case played out in New Zealand. You will read about how two young New Year's revelers accepted a ride from a stranger and were never seen again.

You will also read about two examples of mass murder that share some disturbing similarities. The perpetrators of both cases attempted to wipe out an entire family, but the details of each were extremely bizarre. You will have to read it to believe it!

Similar to all the volumes in this series, some cases can only be classified as strange and creepy.

You will read about the possible existence of a cult in Australia composed of well-connected men that operated during the 1970s and 1980s. Instead of going out in the woods and conducting arcane rituals, this cult is alleged to have abducted, raped, and murdered at least five young men, with many more victims suspected.

Finally, you will learn about a case where social media helped catch an unlikely killer. Like many young people today, the killer was a social media junky, who tried to use social media as an alibi. The scheme worked for a while, but the more investigators looked at this suspect, the killer's own social media pages helped lead to an arrest.

The criminal world is a dark and dangerous place, but this book will give you a glimpse of it from the safety of your home. Keep an open mind—and remember that evil can strike anywhere and at any time!

CHAPTER 1:

THE ABDUCTION AND MURDER OF SAMANTHA KNIGHT

Crime comes in all shapes and colors, and no matter what category a crime may fall into, whether it is burglary or murder, it can do irreparable harm to those affected. Professional criminologists, psychiatrists, and psychologists often state that crime victims continue to be victimized long after a crime. Victims of violent crimes are often left with visible scars and even those who suffer from theft or other property crimes often feel violated for days, months, and even years after the crime.

Post-traumatic stress is a serious problem that crime victims, especially those who are victims of violent and sexual crimes, have to deal with every day. Even when crime victims get professional help, the emotional scars are permanent and often very deep.

There is no doubt that any crime is demoralizing to the victims.

Beyond the individual victims, crime eats at the very fabric of a society in a plethora of different ways. There are the monetary costs that society pays to the victims and to provide housing in jails and prisons when offenders are captured. There are also the intangible costs, such as the erosion of public trust that the citizens have toward their government and their neighbors when crime rates soar

Crime in general can certainly plague a community, city, or nation, but when looked at as a whole, there are definitely some crimes that do more damage than others.

Of course, murder is rightfully called the ultimate taboo because it can never be taken back. No matter how much a killer may show remorse toward his victim or his victim's family, the victim can never be brought back. With that said, there are often mitigating circumstances in murder cases.

Murders are often committed in the heat of the moment and what constitutes self-defense is certainly a gray area in most jurisdictions. One could even argue this with many other crimes. For instance, the argument that drug crimes and sex work are "victimless" is often made and many convicted of property crimes claim they had no other recourse to make ends meet.

But there are times when crime, especially murder, can never be justified.

The victimization of children, especially when it ends in murder, is a class of crime that not even most career criminals attempt to justify. Children are essentially defenseless and always innocent, which makes their victimization the most heinous of acts in the eyes of the vast majority of people, no matter their backgrounds. Child predators erode the social fabric more than any other class of criminal, and because of that, most countries have special laws that give extra prison time for their acts.

Unfortunately, most child predators know their victims and are often trusted by their victims' families.

This was the case in the particularly heart-wrenching abduction and murder case of eight-year-old Australian Samantha Knight in 1986.

Samantha's killer used the trust of her family to gain access and then disposed of her body, creating a mystery that spanned more than twenty years. As the police slowly but surely began to unravel the puzzle of the missing girl, many shocking details were revealed, including the fact that a friend of Samantha's mother knew that a pedophile was lurking in their neighborhood.

Samantha Knight

Samantha Knight was born on March 25, 1977 to Peter O'Meagher and Tess Knight-O'Meagher. Not long after getting married, Peter and Tess discovered that they didn't have much in common and spent more time arguing with each other than anything else. They hoped that the addition of a child would help their marriage. But as it often is the case, the arrival of Samantha only seemed to make things worse.

Not long after Samantha was born, the fighting got to be too much, so Tess moved out. She took back her maiden name and decided to raise Samantha as a single mother.

Tess soon learned that being a single mother is not an easy thing, especially in the expensive Sydney, New South Wales metropolitan area. Getting minimal financial support from Peter, Tess was forced to move around the Sydney area a lot to find apartments that were within her price range. Despite the constant upheaval, Samantha was a well-adjusted girl.

By August 1986, Tess and Samantha were living in an apartment complex in Bondi, an affordable suburb of Sydney. At first the complex seemed like an ideal location. It was located in a low-crime neighborhood, and there were plenty of other children in the neighborhood for Samantha to play with, but Tess still needed to work long hours to make ends meet.

For the most part, Tess felt that the neighborhood was safe enough to let her daughter play, go to the local store, and do other things around the area without adult supervision. It was a neighborhood where everyone knew each other and were willing to look out for anyone in trouble, especially a child. Still, since she did often work long hours, Tess needed an affordable babysitter from time to time.

After asking some of the local mothers if they knew a good, yet affordable babysitter, one of the women suggested she call a man named Michael Guider. Tess was told that Guider was great with children and that he often charged little to nothing.

Guider proved to be the ultimate wolf in sheep's clothing.

An Inconspicuous Predator

The problem with most child predators, at least when viewed in hindsight, is that they rarely come across as a pedophile. Sure, after a notorious child molester is arrested and his picture is plastered on the local news, people always make comments to the effect that the guy certainly looks like a pedophile.

But the reality is often quite different.

Unfortunately, child molesters are among the craftiest and most manipulative of all criminals as they often have a keen ability to not only tell their victims what they want to hear, but also to essentially *be* whatever society expects them to be. Because of that, child predators come from all walks of life and often operate for years before anyone even suspects them of their twisted crimes.

Child predators may be the most despicable of all criminals, but they are also among the most adaptable—chameleons in the truest sense of the word.

Michael Guider was one such chameleon.

Guider was born in Melbourne, Victoria in 1950 to what can only be described as a truly dysfunctional family. He never knew his father, and his mother was a raging alcoholic. When she was drunk and at home she would often verbally berate and abuse Michael and his younger brother, but most nights she wasn't home.

Michael's mother preferred hanging out in bars to her home and she was known to bring men back to the Guider home from time to time.

Clearly motherhood wasn't for her.

As Guider's mother continued with her alcoholic ways, she decided that Michael and his brother were too much of a hindrance to her lifestyle, so she sent them to live in state institutions for much of their adolescence. It was while he was housed in institutions that Michael Guider claimed he was first molested by older children and that he, in turn, later molested other children.

Guider would even claim that he sexually assaulted his own brother and mother.

There is no doubt that Guider had an incredibly difficult childhood that contributed to his life as a pedophile, but there were also other factors at work beneath the surface. Guider's brother suffered through much of the same abuse, even more so because he was victimized by Michael, but never went on to be a child molester.

It seems clear that Michael Guider was sick from an early age, if not born that way. The difficult early life was a trigger that led him to act on his impulses. Many of the professionals who worked with young Michael Guider in the child welfare institutions of the state of Victoria knew that he was a monster and would one day harm one or more children. Once he became an adult, though, there was nothing they could do—Michael Guider would be released into Australian society.

After he turned eighteen, Guider moved from Melbourne to Sydney, which was a big change for him. Melbourne and Sydney are Australia's two largest and most important cities, but they have significant cultural differences. Historically, Melbourne was more blue-collar and working class and a bit more politically and socially conservative than the cosmopolitan Sydney.

Sydney, on the other hand, was ground zero for Australia's version of the counter-culture movement of the 1960s and when gay rights became an issue in Australia, Sydney was where most of the activists lived.

Guider thought that he could get lost in Sydney's bustle in the 1970s and for a time it seemed he was right. It appears that he made an attempt at normalcy by finding full-time employment and developing a social network of law-abiding friends.

Beginning in the 1970s, Guider developed an interest in Australia's Aboriginal culture and made several trips to the Outback to study their sacred grounds and to interview tribal members. He eventually went on to publish a number of works on the subject and made many contacts with academics in the field, who respected both his works and him as a person.

Little did they know.

When he wasn't studying Aboriginal culture or committing crimes, Guider worked as a gardener at a Sydney hospital. He even had a girlfriend for a while in the early 1970s.

But it didn't take long for Guider to show his true colors to his girlfriend.

Apparently Guider tried to hide his predilection for small children from his girlfriend and his other associates, but things like that are difficult to keep from a significant other. The girlfriend saw something that didn't look right and ended the relationship. Guider responded by burning down her place of business.

The former girlfriend was apparently too scared to carry the matter further with the local police. Even if she wanted to, there was little evidence that tied Guider to the crime. It was simply her word against his, and at that point, they were both respected members of the community.

Guider was able to stay free to victimize the children of Sydney.

When Guider was finally arrested in 1996, it was revealed that he had been molesting children for most of his life. Unlike many child molesters, Guider had no particular preference in terms of gender—he victimized boys and girls, picking his victims based more on availability than anything else.

The precise number of his victims is unknown, but some estimates place it well into the hundreds.

Guider's method of operation was as devious as it was sick. He would first befriend a single mother, usually in his neighborhood, gaining her trust and would then offer cheap or free babysitting services. Once the child or children were in his grasp, he would give them sleeping pills and molest and photograph them when they were passed out. The M.O. allowed him to operate with seeming impunity because, unfortunately, most of his victims never knew that anything had happened.

Eventually, as his host of victims continued to grow, more and more rumors circulated about the creepy hospital gardener. The rumors finally led to allegations, which in turn led to the arrest of Guider. He was caught red handed with numerous pictures of his victims, and as it turned out, some of his victims *did* remember his awful acts. Guider was charged with several counts of child molestation in 1996, and among the evidence the police discovered were thousands of pictures of nine girls and two boys.

Michael Guider was sentenced to a minimum of sixteen years in prison with a non-parole period of ten years on sixty charges against eleven children.

But that would certainly not be the last time that Australia heard from Michael Guider.

Almost immediately, reports came out that Guider was having a hard go of it in some of New South Wales' toughest prisons. He was forced to spend most of his time in isolation because whenever he was released into the general population he would be promptly beaten by the other inmates.

Even the most hardened criminals have a moral code.

The decision by the prison officials to keep Guider in isolation was partly for his own protection, but it was also because local, state, and federal investigators believed he could help clear the books on several open investigations—some of them murders.

Authorities were particularly interested in Guider's possible involvement in the 1986 disappearance of Samantha Knight.

The Search for Samantha

In the early evening hours of August 19, 1986, Tess Knight came home from a long day at work to an empty house. She didn't immediately think anything was amiss—she thought that Samantha was probably out with some kids in the neighborhood playing. After making some calls and asking around in the neighborhood, Tess learned that Samantha came home from school just after 4 p.m. and was last seen playing with some local kids about an hour and a half later.

After a couple hours of calling and searching, Tess Knight knew that something was wrong, so she called the local police. The police canvassed the neighborhood and found nothing, so Tess went to the local media.

Every television station and newspaper in the Sydney metro area covered the case, flashing the police tip line on the bottom of the screen so anyone could make an anonymous call if they saw anything. Eventually, the news coverage of the case spread throughout all of Australia and was a major story for several weeks, but unfortunately, the police received no credible leads.

It was as if little Samantha Knight had just vanished off the face of the earth.

She stayed missing for seventeen years.

As the case slowly receded from the minds of most Australians and went into the "cold" file of Sydney detectives, new leads and a new name started surfacing.

Denise Hofman is a freelance journalist with an interest in Australian Aboriginal history and culture. Her work brought her to a number of different Aboriginal sites during the 1980s, which is when and how she met Michael Guider.

Guider was seen among journalists and academics as a fairly bright and articulate guy, but there was just something "off" about him. When Guider was arrested on a slew of child molestation charges in 1996, many of his journalist and academic associates were surprised but not that much. Besides his not-so-normal personality, he was known to say some strange things from time to time. Hofman remembered one such conversation that haunted her enough to go to the police in the late 1990s.

Hofman informed the Sydney police that she was told about a particularly strange conversation one of her journalist colleagues had with Guider during the early 1990s. She said that Guider talked about the Samantha Knight disappearance in a peculiar way, particularly that he seemed a bit enthused about the crime and apparently knew some details.

Hofman said her friend didn't want to get involved in the case, but she thought it was her duty to do so.

The police agreed and thanked Hofman for her cooperation and opened an active investigation into Guider.

The Samantha Knight case was officially reopened.

Unfortunately, as the police began working on the case again in the late 1990s, they were left with the realization that as good as Guider looked for the crime, there was little evidence tying him to it. Hofman's statement was hearsay and couldn't be used to get an arrest warrant, and although Guider was a convicted child molester who lived in Samantha's neighborhood at the time of her disappearance, it was all circumstantial evidence.

Getting a conviction would be difficult but not impossible.

Since Guider was safely tucked away in a protective custody unit in a New South Wales prison, Sydney homicide investigators had time on their side. With that said, they were eager to close the case and desperately wanted to locate Samantha's body for her family.

The investigators decided to approach the case from a different angle.

They paid Guider a visit in prison in 2000 hoping to elicit a confession, or at least something that could lead them to Samantha's body. After four years of beatings at the hands of the other inmates and spending most of his time in isolation, Guider was clearly a broken man. His hair was disheveled and his greying, long beard looked like it could have housed a family of birds. He was eager to talk to the police.

He was probably eager to talk to anyone who wouldn't beat him up.

Guider readily admitted to molesting Samantha and her friend—which the friend's mother actually knew about—a number of times in 1984 and 1985. Despite the confession to molestation, he refused to admit he killed Samantha.

At that point, the investigators knew that they had their man and it was only a matter of time until they compiled enough evidence that would lead to Guider's murder conviction.

The next break the police received came in the form of a jailhouse informant. Although jailhouse informants are commonly used in trials around the world, their testimony is often viewed skeptically by jurors, so prosecutors only use them along with other more solid pieces of evidence. In the Samantha Knight case, the informant was a career criminal named Frank Soonius.

Soonius told the police and later testified in court that while he was in an isolation cell next to Guider, the latter was quite candid about what he did to Samantha Knight. Soonius' testimony was convincing because it detailed how Guider used the same demented M.O. on Samantha as he did on countless other children.

Soonius claimed that Samantha woke up from her drugged state and asked Guider, "What are you doing?" and since she could identify him he, "...gave her another drink with another tablet and she fell asleep again," this time forever.

Guider would later claim that he accidentally gave her the fatal dose.

With no real reasonable legal defense possible, Guider pleaded guilty to manslaughter in 2001 and was sentenced to an additional seventeen years in 2002. Due to the high-profile nature of the case, there was little chance that Guider would ever be released.

Closure and More Victims?

It's unlikely that Guider ever felt remorse for what he did to his victims. He steadfastly refused to disclose where he disposed of Samantha's body until, for whatever reason, in 2003 he told investigators he had buried her on the grounds of the Royal Sydney Yacht Club. Forensic teams were dispatched to the location with cadaver dogs and although the dogs hit on a location and excavators were called in, Samantha's remains were never found.

In the years since the Samantha Knight case was solved, Guider's name has come up in relation to a number of missing children cases throughout Australia. For most of the cases there is little to link the pedophile to the missing children, but one case has investigators believing that the former gardener may have killed another child after Samantha.

A young girl named Renee Aitken was abducted from her suburban Canberra home in 1994. Her body has never been found, and there has never been an arrest in the case. Guider became a suspect when investigators found several articles about the abduction in a macabre scrapbook he kept, and a man fitting his description was seen lurking in the area around the time of Renee's abduction. The investigators' interest in Guider was further piqued when they learned that he was living in the Canberra area when Renee was abducted.

At this point no charges have been laid and Michael Guider died in prison in 2024.

CHAPTER 2:

THE MURDER OF
ZOE HASTINGS

Although crime can happen anywhere, you have a much higher statistical chance of becoming a crime victim in an urban area. Of course, the statistics vary from country to country, but the axiom that crime is more of an urban phenomenon is generally true, especially in the United States.

Thousands of crimes happen everyday in urban areas across the United States and much of it is often reported as "random," especially when it comes to murder.

But is there really such a thing as "random crime?"

Besides crime being more common in urban areas, statistics also show that murder victims are more likely to be killed by someone they know than a stranger. Seemingly, this statistic leads many to believe that if a murder victim doesn't know their killer, then the crime was simply random.

The reality is that criminals, especially killers, always have a reason for committing their crimes. Their targets may not be personal, but they are rarely random. Even serial killers have a method to their madness.

The unfortunate reality is that stranger-on-stranger murders, which may appear random, are committed for several reasons: to silence a potential witness, in the commission of another crime that "goes too far," or just for pleasure.

Perhaps the term "unsuspected killing" or "chance killing" makes more sense.

On a warm Texas evening in October 2015, an attractive eighteen-year-old woman named Zoe Hastings became the victim of a chance killing. The police and community believed it was a random murder, but once the case unfolded and the perpetrator was caught, it was revealed to be far from random. Although Zoe didn't know her killer, in the murderer's twisted mind, he had plenty of reasons to kill her.

The case also made headlines because it was one where nothing was as it initially seemed.

No matter if you call the crime "random," "chance," or "unsuspected," it shook a quiet suburban community and devastated a tight-knit, law-abiding family.

Zoe Hastings

Zoe Hastings was the eldest child in a large family that included three other girls and one boy. The father, Jim, is an elementary school teacher at a suburban Dallas, Texas school and mother Cheryl works as a nurse. The Hastings family are ardent members of The Church of Jesus Christ of Latter-day Saints (LDS), whose followers are often referred to as Mormons. The Mormons very much believe in the biblical tenet that people should be fruitful and multiply, which is why they usually have very large families.

The Hastings were no exception in that regard.

But more than being just a large family, the Hastings were very close. Although Jim and Cheryl worked hard to provide a nice home in a good neighborhood for their children, they always made sure to spend quality time with their children. They went on many family vacations and Zoe often worked with Jim on art projects.

Zoe was a well-adjusted young woman and a devout member of the LDS church, which can often be difficult for a young person today. The Mormons have some fairly strict rules that they expect their members to follow, such as abstinence from pre-marital sex, alcohol, illicit drugs, tobacco, and even caffeine, so followers tend to be a bit more conservative.

With that said, by all appearances Zoe was a true believer.

The attractive blonde had several potential suitors, but instead dedicated most of her time to family and church instead of dating. Zoe lived at home and took part in local LDS activities, which was what she was on her way to do on the evening of October 11, 2015, when she by chance crossed paths with Antonio Lamar Cochran.

As much as Zoe Hastings was the personification of the all-American girl with a bright future who would be a benefit to society, Antonio Cochran was an American monster who in his thirty-four years was nothing but a drain and detriment to the community. He spent most of his adult life in jails and prisons and had amassed a rap sheet that included drug, property, violent, and sexual offenses.

There was nothing random about the way Cochran chose his victims—anyone, especially women, had the potential to be one of his unfortunate casualties.

A Fateful Encounter

On the evening of October 11, 2015, two lives couldn't have been going in more completely different directions than those of Zoe Hastings and Antonio Cochran. Zoe was on her way to a church function, around 5 p.m., when she pulled into the parking lot of a Dallas Walgreen's to drop off a DVD at a Redbox kiosk.

Cohran was looking for another victim.

The attractive blonde woman, who happened to be alone, was too much for the career criminal to resist. He made his move and she was never seen alive again.

The evidence would later show that Cochran rushed Zoe as she was getting back into her car and then carjacked her. After driving to a location near a creek, he then brutally raped the young woman and cut her throat, leaving her to bleed to death. To cover his tracks—at least so he thought—he then put Zoe into the driver's seat, placed something on the gas pedal, and put the car into drive, sending it into the creek.

The car and Zoe's body were discovered later that night by the police, who originally thought it was a horrible car accident.

But it didn't take long for them to realize that Zoe was the victim of a brutal murder.

When Zoe didn't show up at the church her parents were a bit worried. Unlike many people her age, Zoe was very punctual and if she were running late for any reason, she would usually call. Still, her parents thought that she probably met up with some friends and lost track of the time.

They started to worry, though, when the hands on the clock moved past ten.

Zoe's cellphone was on her parents' plan and all of the phones in the Hastings home could be tracked by an app. Jim thought that the app would be useful because Zoe had a tendency to misplace her phone, but he never thought it would be used to locate his missing daughter.

The Hastings parents opened the app on their phones and followed their devices to the creek bed where Zoe's body was.

The police were already there.

The Hastings' worst fears were realized when a homicide detective told them that their daughter had been murdered.

Too Dumb to Execute

The medical examiner determined that Zoe died a particularly painful death. Dallas homicide detectives traced the girl's steps and quickly determined that the abduction took place at the Walgreens. Witnesses reported seeing a Black man "rush" up on her in the parking lot, and the store's surveillance videos showed a Black man loitering around the front of the store before the carjacking.

Still, none of the witnesses or any of the store employees recognized the man.

But sometimes the criminals do the cops' work for them. Some criminals really are plain dumb.

DNA profiling has been around since the late 1980s and has helped put countless criminals in prison for their crimes. It has also set more than a fair share of innocent people free. The Combined DNA Index System, or CODIS, is a DNA database that was established by the federal government in late 1998. DNA profiles are placed into the database when they are convicted of crimes, and in some jurisdictions when they are arrested. Today, every state in the United States enters the DNA of convicted felons into the database.

Since he had such a lengthy felony record, which included convictions from the 2000s, Antonio Cochran was in the CODIS database and was a match for semen taken from the crime scene.

It seemed to be an open and shut case for capital murder, which in Texas usually means the death penalty.

Since the death penalty is used regularly in Texas, it looked as though Cochran would have a needle put in his arm.

But when it comes to the death penalty in the United States, it pays to be dumb.

Based on his actions and some of his past convictions alone, it was clear that Cochran was no scholar, but when court appointed experts tested him, it was revealed that he had an extremely low IQ. In fact, Cochran's tested at borderline "mentally deficient," but the experts also added that he still knew right from wrong.

At that point in the proceedings, the prosecutors were faced with a tough decision. They wanted to give Cochran the death penalty, but believed that there was a good chance that any possible conviction could be overturned on appeal due to his mental deficiencies.

The prosecution decided to rescind the death penalty but kept the "capital" charges, which in Texas means that, if convicted, Cochrane would be given an automatic sentence of life in prison without the chance of parole.

No deal was offered to Cochran, so he took the case to trial.

His lawyers did not put up much of a defense. In fairness to them, there was little they could do. Eye witness and video evidence placed Cochran at the scene of the abduction, and his DNA was found on the victim. The career criminal was also not a sympathetic defendant.

The jury found Antonio Cochran guilty of the lesser charge of murder, not capital murder, which would have resulted in an automatic life sentence without parole. He was sentenced to life in prison, with eligibility for parole after thirty years and a $10,000 fine. The prosecution did not seek the death penalty due to his diagnosed intellectual disability.

Being dumb saved Cochran's life, and it also gave him a chance to get out of prison one day.

The Hastings family issued a statement to the press after the verdict. Instead of focusing their attention on Zoe's killer, they discussed what she meant to them.

"Today, we express our gratitude to local law enforcement, officials, and loved ones helping our family. Our Zoe was full of life and love and light. She was full of talent. She was happy and joyful. She is loved by her parents and her siblings. She loved the Lord, Jesus Christ, and loved serving others. She was planning to serve a mission to share this message of the Savior's love with others. It pains us to know that her life has been taken, yet we feel comfort in knowing that our family is forever and we will be together again someday. We are grateful for the privacy and respect given to us during this extremely difficult time. Please continue to pray for our family. We appreciate and need your support."

CHAPTER 3:

MAYHEM ON THE CAMINO DE SANTIAGO

Most Americans and many people from outside the United States are familiar with the Appalachian Trial. The Trail stretches for over 2,000 miles from northern Maine to northern Georgia—or the other way around, depending on which way one is hiking—and is hiked by thousands of people every year.

"Hiking through" the entire stretch takes several months, but those who do it claim that the experience is as spiritually rewarding as it is a physical challenge.

There are several similar trails scattered throughout the United States and around the world, which have in recent years become much more popular with the advent of the internet.

Europe's equivalent is the Camino de Santiago, which is translated as "Road of Santiago."

Although the Camino de Santiago is similar to the Appalachian Trail in that both are popular hiking trails in their respective parts of the world, the former is as much of a religious pilgrimage as it is a test of individual endurance for those who decide to hike it.

The Camino de Santiago is an approximately 500-mile path that runs from the French-Spanish border in the Pyrenees Mountains to the Cathedral of Santiago de Compostela in the city of Galicia, Spain. Unlike on the Appalachian Trail, hikers on the Camino Santiago always go in one direction: westerly to Galicia.

The Cathedral of Santiago de Compostela is dedicated to the apostle Saint James the Great, who lived in the ninth century. The cathedral is believed to house the remains of Saint James, which makes the site a holy place in the Roman Catholic Church. Not long after Saint James' death, religious pilgrims began using the Camino de Santiago to visit the cathedral in efforts to find spiritual enlightenment or hopefully to see propitious signs from God. During the Middle Ages, it would have been common to see people from all walks of life hiking the trail, from monks to crusader knights to sex workers.

Today, people from all over the world hike the trail everyday for much the same reasons the knights and monks did in the Middle Ages. The only difference is that most people have to take a month off from work to do the trail!

For the most part, hiking the Camino de Santiago is a safe endeavor. Over 200,000 people from around the world walk the path every year with few reported incidents. Because most of the hikers are on a spiritual quest and feel a sense of community with each other, crimes that happen to hikers are usually perpetrated by non-hikers.

Unfortunately, the number of crimes committed against hikers has increased in recent years and most of the victims have been women.

Arizona resident Denise Pikka Thiem became a victim on the Camino de Santiago when she went missing from the trail in April 2015. Her bloody corpse was later discovered not far from the trail, which led to an investigation that nearly became an international incident. The murder of Thiem raised many questions about travel and safety on the Camino de Santiago, which for many stripped the trail of its veneer of innocence.

The 2010 Martin Sheen produced and directed film, *The Way*, tells the story of a man, played by Sheen, whose son recently died. In a desire to come to terms with their fractured relationship and things he regretted never telling his son, Sheen's character takes time off from his job to hike the Camino de Santiago. Along the way he meets a variety of different characters who all have their own personal demons to overcome, and together they all find solace and meaning on the trail.

The Way has introduced many people around the world to the Camino de Santiago, including forty-one-year-old Denise Pikka Thiem.

Pikka Thiem was a native of Hong Kong who immigrated to the United States in her adulthood for more opportunities and out of a sense of adventure. She was physically attractive and intelligent and all of her friends and coworkers described her as friendly and helpful.

Denise was also very ambitious and successful.

For most of her adult life, Denise put her career above anything else. Although she had many friends and an extended family on multiple continents, she decided to focus on her career instead of having her own family. By 2015 her ambition had paid off as she had a high-paying job at Pet Smart's corporate headquarters in Phoenix. It seemed as though Pikka Thiem had the world at her fingertips.

But something was missing.

As is the case with many ambitious, successful people, Denise had a void in her life that no amount of money, or a dog or a cat, could fill. She yearned for a legitimate spiritual experience that could define her life and her place in the world. After she watched *The Way*, she believed she knew what that experience was.

Denise told her friends and anyone who would listen about the film. After talking about it for a while, she decided that she would take the big step and actually commit to hiking the Camino de Santiago, hoping to find meaning as Martin Sheen's character did in the movie.

As Denise planned her trip, it began to evolve into a world trip that would take most of 2015, which meant she had to quit her job. Although some of her friends were a bit worried, Denise assured them that she'd be alright; after all, she was already a seasoned world traveler who had friends and family on nearly every continent.

When Denise left on her world trip in early 2015, the first leg brought her through Asia where she visited several friends and family members and toured some of the continents' most well-known sites.

In March, she had arrived in Europe and was ready for her hike on the Camino de Santiago.

Miguel Angel Munoz was the same age as Denise Pikka Thiem in 2015, but that was about all the two had in common. Munoz was born and raised in Madrid, Spain, but grew tired of city life and eventually moved to the countryside in northern Spain. He bought a small parcel of land with a run-down cottage near the Camino de Santiago. Essentially, he lived a minimalist existence on his land, not unlike what people lived like hundreds of years ago along the trail.

But Munoz was not interested in the spiritual aspects of the trail and by all accounts did not appreciate those who did.

Munoz can best be described as a recluse, but little else is known about him since he rarely left his land. He eked out an existence with the resources available to him on the farm and had very little contact with people in the nearby villages.

It would not be unfair to say that Munoz was a strange man.

The Trip

Denise began her trip on March 6, 2015, and the first month was for the most part uneventful. To get into the spirit of the trip as much as possible, Denise decided to leave her cellphone behind. Like many people today, Daphne found cellphones distracting, and she wanted to concentrate as much as possible on the trip. The problems of the modern world were no longer her concern.

Still, she wanted to document as much of her trip as possible, so she brought along a digital camera and her laptop. She used the laptop to post updates of her hike to her social media accounts every day, sometimes multiple times a day.

Like the Appalachian Trail, there are many things to see along the Camino de Santiago that often lead to hikers taking detours for several days. The trail runs through Pamplona, which is, of course, where the famous "Running of the Bulls" is held every year and there are several scenic vistas and villages that hikers find especially alluring.

Denise was smiling in every one of her updates and seemed enthused about completing the journey. On April 5, when she was about halfway through the trail, she posted her last update to social media.

For the first couple of days after that post, none of Denise's friends and family were very worried. They thought that she just got sidetracked in some interesting town that either had no internet access or she just forgot to post updates.

But deep down most knew there was a problem.

Denise was a reliable person, so when a couple of days turned into a week, her friends and family began making calls.

Easter Sunday

April 5, 2015 was Easter Sunday, which in Spain is a major holiday. Although Western Europe is very secular in regards to religion, Spain still holds strongly to Catholic tradition. On Easter Sunday, the Camino de Santiago was alive: church bells could be heard and hikers were making their way to and from mass.

Denise's update for that day showed that she had an enjoyable day with some fellow hikers, but it was her last post. Unfortunately, her final hours had to be reconstructed by homicide detectives.

As night began to fall, Denise found herself alone and a bit disorientated. She had wandered off the trail, probably to take some pictures, and relied on the many signs on the trail to find her way. She was probably on her way to an inn for the night, but the signs she followed led her away from any inns—and the Camino de Santiago completely, for that matter.

The signs were a ruse that led directly to Miguel Munoz's farm.

The details of what happened next are a bit murky because they are based onMunoz's statements in court, and he was not always very forthcoming.

According to Munoz, once Denise ended up at his farm, things got out of hand very quickly.

"I offered to show her the way, but she got nervous and I hit her on the head with a stick. I don't know why," said Munoz.

After killing Denise, Munoz then buried her body a few yards from his house.

A few days later, in what can only be described as a strange move, Munoz dug up the corpse and reburied it in a more remote location frequented by wild hogs. Apparently he thought that the body being so close to his house would make him look more guilty if it was ever discovered.

Or perhaps he was plagued by a guilty conscience.

But Munoz can't have been affected too much by a guilty conscience because he robbed Denise after killing her. Her electronic devices were never recovered, so they may still be floating around somewhere in Europe, or he may have destroyed them to cover his tracks, which would certainly make sense from a criminal perspective.

But then he made an amateur mistake.

Since many of the towns and villages along the Camino de Santiago are quite small, they are not up to modern financial standards, which means that credit cards are often not accepted and ATM/PIN machines are rare. Because of that, hikers often carry large amounts of cash.

Denise Pikka Thiem was no exception in this regard.

When Denise began her trip on the French-Spanish border, she had around $2,000 American. Since most of the inns and cafes along the trail accept most of the world's major currencies, including the US dollar, Denise did not have to exchange her currency for euros.

But any *locals* with a large amount of dollars would have to exchange for euros.

Not long after Denise disappeared, Munoz exchanged $1,100 he stole from her for euros. He probably thought that since no one at the currency exchange office knew him, he wouldn't arouse any suspicion.

But little did he know there was already an international search underway to find Denise.

An International Incident

When Denise quit posting updates of her trip to social media, her friends and family immediately got involved. Trying to find a missing loved one thousands of miles away in another country, across an ocean, is a difficult endeavor, but Denise Pikka Thiem's friends and family were up to the task. Since she was a successful person, Denise had connections to people in powerful positions.

Within weeks of her disappearance, Denise's loved ones put pressure on Arizona politicians until United States Senator John McCain responded by making statements to the Spanish Prime Minister about the case. How much that played a role in the case is unknown, but other members of Denise's family tried to play a more active role in the investigation.

Denise's brother, Cedric Thiem, packed up his belongings and moved to Spain in late April 2015. He hired local investigators and did some of his own detective work in the towns along the Camino de Santiago.

As the Spanish government was being pressured by American politicians, local investigators were already zeroing in on Munoz.

The currency exchange he made immediately after he murdered Thiem was suspicious because it was a large amount. All currency exchanges above a certain amount require an identification and signature, which is easily checked by the police.

As the police investigation focused on Munoz, other female hikers came forward to say that he had harassed them, and most importantly, lured them to his house with the fake signs.

Finally, after several months of investigation, Munoz led the police to Denise's body.

A jury found Miguel Ángel Muñoz guilty of murdering Denise Pikka Thiem. He had initially confessed, but then later recanted, claiming he was pressured by police. He was sentenced to 25 years in prison, which included an additional two years for robbery.

CHAPTER 4:

THE UNICORN KILLER

Today many Americans, especially Baby Boomers, view the 1960s with nostalgia, seeing it as a forward-thinking period led by young idealists. To people who remember the 1960s this way, it was an invigorating and exciting decade for the most part. Sure, the Vietnam War was raging and thousands of young American men were being killed there, but young Americans back home were peacefully standing up to the "man" and opposing it. Enthusiasts of the 1960s will also argue that those same hippies who opposed the war did a lot to change the social mores of the United States, transforming it from the uptight country that it was to the free and open society it is today.

But as with anything, idealized perceptions are often different from reality.

The Vietnam War dragged on well into the 1970s and only ended when middle America, which was firmly opposed to the hippies, grew weary of seeing their sons, brothers, and husbands coming back in body bags from a war that had no obvious benefits for the average American.

In fact, in many ways, 1960s America is much like it is today: it was a country polarized, sometimes violently, over politics, race, and culture.

Sure, the majority of the hippies were more interested in music, smoking pot, and free love than they were in anything else. There was, however, a small yet highly-visible strain of the New Left that was extremely violent. Many, if not most, of the 1960s violent leftists came from privileged backgrounds who in ferocious bouts of self-righteousness embarked on terrorist campaigns across the country.

The Weather Underground and the Black Panthers are perhaps the two best known of the 1960s leftist terrorist groups. Their members carried out bombings, assassinations, and instigated riots in numerous locations before their members were all either killed, arrested, fled the country, or gave up their violent tactics. Those two groups later influenced and/or spawned even more violent groups during the 1970s, such as the Black Liberation Army, the Symbionese Liberation Army, the United Freedom Front, and the Boricua Popular Army.

Truly, the 1960s was an extremely turbulent period in American history.

It was during the 1960s that a naïve but attractive young woman from Texas named Holly Maddux met a leftist counter-culture guru named Ira Einhorn who swept her off her feet. She was intrigued with the man's apparent in-depth knowledge of social issues and his charisma, which attracted many people to him, men and women. Einhorn was a true 1960s icon, who often rubbed shoulders with even more renowned figures of the period and had many important connections.

Although Einhorn preached free love and outwardly supported women's rights and feminism, beneath the surface he was an ogre who could not take rejection.

After a tumultuous relationship of five years, Maddux's body was discovered in Einhorn's apartment and murder charges soon followed.

But the hippy guru would do everything in his power to avoid justice, which led to a twenty-year manhunt that spanned two continents and several countries.

The Unicorn

Ira Einhorn was born in 1940 to a middle-class Jewish family in Philadelphia, Pennsylvania. From a young age, Ira showed considerable promise as a student. Although he never excelled in athletics, he was an excellent student academically and was usually at the top of his class. His teachers generally liked him, but Ira was known to be more outspoken than most kids were at the time, which sometimes earned him the ire of his teachers and led to disciplinary problems.

With that said, Einhorn never found himself in trouble with the law as a youth or young adult.

Einhorn applied to several different universities around the United States before he graduated from high school and finally settled on the prestigious University of Pennsylvania. When Einhorn entered college, he was just like any other kid his age at the time, but by the time he graduated, he was a leading character in Philadelphia's nascent counter-culture scene.

Einhorn, like many young Jewish people of his generation, jumped headfirst into the counter-culture movement. He ingested copious amounts of left-wing politics and illicit drugs to challenge societal norms and to push himself beyond his limits. He also was an ardent proponent of free love, attempting to bed nearly every woman he met.

By the mid-1960s, Einhorn had carefully crafted a persona as a hippy guru and gave himself the nickname "the Unicorn," based on the English translation of his German name—"one horn."

Most people who graduate from college immediately begin looking for work, but to the Unicorn, work was for "squares."

Einhorn developed a wide ranging and intricate network of financial benefactors who were more than happy to give him money for any number of "projects" that he developed.

By the late 1960s, Einhorn's social network included members of the influential Canadian-Jewish Bronfman family, activist Abbie Hoffman, and Grateful Dead lead man Jerry Garcia.

Perhaps the highlight of Einhorn's "career" was his role in organizing the world's first Earth Day celebration in 1970. He was the emcee of the event and took credit as the event's primary organizer, although others would later claim that he played a minimal role and only worked his way into the program once it was already organized.

If one were to look at Einhorn, though, it seemed incredible that he could make so many high-level contacts.

The Unicorn's appearance was usually unkempt; he wore a beard that looked like it housed a family of rats and rarely combed his hair. Einhorn was also overweight, average looking, and was known to have incredibly bad body odor because he rarely bathed or showered. He was the stereotypical "dirty hippy."

Einhorn was also known for being lazy, and as mentioned above, he rarely worked and usually lived off the generosity of his benefactors. And most of his "projects" were usually gimmicks that he rarely finished.

Still, to those who knew Ira Einhorn, he possessed an incredible amount of charisma.

"He was a fast talker and always fascinating," said Claude Lewis, a former writer for the *Philadelphia Enquirer* who interviewed Einhorn on numerous occasions in the 1960s and '70s concerning his counter-culture projects. Others that knew Einhorn said that he had an uncanny knack of being able to share common ground with any individual, no matter their background. The scruffy Einhorn was known to walk into a room and within minutes everyone was hanging on his every word, especially the women.

Although most of the men in the counter-culture movement claimed to support women's rights and Second-wave feminism, the reality is that they usually didn't practice what they preached in their personal lives. Neither did Einhorn, for the most part: he could be as misogynistic as any cave man, but he knew how to "play the game." While other men in the counter-culture rarely asked their girlfriends and wives for input on issues, Einhorn would go out of his way to ask for the female opinion, which appealed to many of the young feminists he was around.

Apparently, women were able to get past Einhorn's smell and arrogance because he had no shortage of girlfriends and one night stands.

The Unicorn could not be faithful to one woman, but there was one woman he expected to be faithful to him.

Helen Holly Maddux

Helen Maddux, who went by the nickname "Holly," couldn't have been from a more different world than Einhorn. Born in 1948 to a World War II veteran and a homemaker Holly was raised in Tyler, Texas. Even today, Tyler is a world away from the cosmopolitan metropolitan areas of Dallas and Houston, and in the 1950s, it was even more so. Like many of the people in that part of the country, Holly's parents worked to instill Christian and middle American values in her and her siblings. They went to church regularly and were taught to value education and hard work.

Although their upbringings were very different, Holly and Ira both excelled in school. Holly graduated at the top of her class and earned a scholarship to study at the exclusive private women's college, Bryn Mawr, in Pennsylvania.

It was the late 1960s when Holly arrived in Philadelphia, which was like another planet to the young Texan. Although the transition to life in the big city was difficult for Holly at first, she eventually adapted and found herself in the middle of the local counter-culture scene. Despite all of the distractions, Holly did well in school and graduated in 1971.

Instead of returning to Texas, she decided to stay in her adopted city. Holly told her family that there were simply more opportunities in Philadelphia, so she was going to stay there to see what she could find.

Less than a year later, in 1972, she found the Unicorn.

Einhorn was immediately smitten by the blonde-haired blue-eyed Texan when he met her at a popular counter-culture bar. Although Holly was put off by Einhorn's hygiene, he worked his verbal magic and talked her into a date. Friends later said that she was attracted to Jewish men and for his part, Einhorn only dated *shiksa* women. The date turned into several and within a short period Holly moved into Einhorn's trashy apartment near the Penn campus.

Almost immediately there were signs of trouble in the relationship.

Einhorn made it clear to Holly that he was not a one woman man and that he didn't care if she had sex with other men, which he never tried to hide from his friends and associates. George Keegan, one of Einhorn's former friends and benefactors, said that he remembered a party where the Unicorn "came over and said, 'Would you take Holly home? I'm going home with someone else.' Holly just sat there, silent. She put up with it, and unfortunately, so did we."

He repeatedly told Holly that it was natural to have an open relationship and that was how free people lived.

Holly was not so sure, but she went along with it to please Einhorn. She finally gave in and agreed to have sex with other men and to participate in group sex.

"I think Ira convinced her that she had to do these things to realize her full potential," said Maddux's childhood friend Toni Ferrell.

Einhorn was clearly in Holly Maddux's head, but things began to change when she brought her hippy guru boyfriend home to Texas to meet her family. Although Einhorn was generally a disgusting slob, he apparently went over the top with his antics to bother Holly's parents and her three younger sisters and younger brother.

He started eating when the Madduxs said grace, ate with his hands, picked his toe nails at the dinner table, and treated Holly like dirt in front of her family. Holly's parents bit their tongues and said nothing because they thought Einhorn wanted conflict.

"We concluded that he basically came down there to try and promote a rift between Holly and my father," said one of Holly's sisters, Elisabeth Hall.

The trip to Texas was the turning point in Ira and Holly's relationship. It made her finally see what Einhorn really was.

Moving On

After Einhorn and Holly got back to Philadelphia, Maddux began spending much less time at the apartment they shared. Einhorn didn't seem to mind much—it allowed him to pursue other women and interests he had. For Holly, it meant a chance to break away. She began spending time in New York City and eventually met a man she wanted to have a serious relationship with in late 1977.

She moved out of Einhorn's apartment, but had left many of her personal effects there, so she returned to collect them on September 9, 1977.

That was the last day anyone saw Holly Maddux alive.

Based on the forensic evidence and statements later made in court, when Holly returned to the apartment, Einhorn was there waiting. He probably wasn't too upset that she was with another man, but was angry that she was leaving him. Einhorn was a true control freak who had to have the last say, so in a fit of rage while the couple was arguing, he grabbed Holly by the neck and strangled her to death.

What Einhorn did next made what would already have been a high-profile case truly bizarre.

Instead of dumping Holly's body or burying it somewhere, he simply placed it into a moving trunk he had and packed it with Styrofoam and air fresheners. As strange as the Unicorn's concealment of his crime was, it did make sense on some level. Since Einhorn was known for such incredibly bad body odor and his apartment was just as unsanitary, the odor of a decaying body could've been theoretically masked by the other smells.

Still, when Holly went missing, people began to worry.

When Christmas 1977 came and went and Holly's family didn't hear from her, they contacted the Philadelphia Police Department. Investigators contacted Einhorn, who claimed he last saw Holly on September 8 when she left his apartment to go to the store but never returned.

The police were suspicious, but at that point, there was nothing they could do.

The Discovery

For the next two years, Ira Einhorn went about with his life as if nothing had happened. It was 1979 and although only ten years removed from the 1960s, for many it seemed like a lifetime. The Vietnam War was over, and Americans were more concerned about the economic recession and fuel crisis than they were with Einhorn's latest "projects." Most of Einhorn's more ambitious friends had long since abandoned their tie-dye shirts for pinstripe suits and either entered the halls of government, or gasp, the corporate world.

But Ira Einhorn continued with his antics and lifestyle.

Einhorn continued to seduce women and never bothered changing his hygiene habits as the country moved into a new decade and a considerably more conservative outlook on the world. To many, Einhorn was a bit of a relic, a living anachronism of the bygone past that many Baby Boomers had come to remember fondly. Because of that, Einhorn was able to continue to elicit money from his wealthy patrons.

But on March 28, 1979, about a year and a half after Einhorn killed Holly Maddux, things were about to change.

The Unicorn's look and hygiene habits always resembled that of a nineteenth century mountain man, so his neighbors had grown accustomed to foul stenches emanating from his apartment. The smells, though, were usually somewhat discernable: they were a combination of body odor, marijuana, and rotten food. By the summer of 1978, a new smell began to waft from Einhorn's apartment that his neighbors could not place because few had ever smelled it. By the winter of that year, it was impossible to ignore.

Einhorn's neighbors knew that saying something to him about the odor was out of the question. The arrogant hippie would simply ignore their pleas and probably do so in a rude manner, so they took their complaints to the apartment manager.

When the apartment manager finally investigated the smell, he knew right away that it was not body odor or rotten food—it was the scent of death.

The apartment manager called the police, and on March 28, 1979, they made their second and final visit to see Ira Einhorn. For whatever reason, Einhorn let the police into his apartment without a warrant, and they immediately went to the closet that was the source of the smell. They opened the trunk and discovered the desiccated body of what appeared to be a female. They weren't sure at first, though, because the body only weighed thirty-seven pounds when it was discovered.

Einhorn was immediately placed in handcuffs and brought to jail. He was later officially charged with the first-degree murder of Holly Maddux.

Almost immediately, Einhorn's friends and associates rallied around him.

Since he was charged with first-degree murder and the evidence against him looked fairly convincing—the victim's body was discovered in his apartment—he was denied bail. But Einhorn's supporters, which included community leaders and Barbara Bronfman of the Bronfman family, hired high-profile defense attorney Arlen Specter, who would later go on to be a US Senator from Pennsylvania as a Republican and then a Democrat.

Specter was able to get Einhorn a bail reduction hearing where numerous respectable community leaders were called as character witnesses for the stinky guru. They all testified that they believed Einhorn was innocent and assumed part of the responsibility for his bail.

The arguments were convincing. The judge agreed to give Einhorn a $40,000 bail.

Murder trials usually move especially slow in the United States and even more so when the defendant is out on bail. In the two years that Einhorn was free on bail, he met with his legal team to plan a defense, but there was little they could do. The most he could argue was that Holly died in some sort of accident and that he placed her body in the trunk because he felt the prosecutor would be after him due to his high-profile counter-culture activities.

Einhorn knew that it was a weak defense.

For the most part, while he was free on bail, he continued with his carefree lifestyle. Einhorn continued to see women and partied, drinking and doing drugs, but he was also planning.

He was not planning for his trial, though.

Einhorn was planning to leave the United States and all of his problems behind. Just days before his trial began in 1981, Ira Einhorn fled to Europe, which began a manhunt for him that lasted more than twenty years.

The Unicorn on the Run

Although the evidence against Einhorn certainly looked very convincing, it did not stop his patrons from donating money to his flight fund. Bronfman and others knowingly helped Einhorn find safe passage out of the United States, along with his new girlfriend, to the United Kingdom. Since he left the country before his trial started, and there was at that point no warrant for his arrest, he flew into London under his real name and even lived there for some time semi-openly.

He wasn't flaunting the fact that he was a fugitive from American justice, but he really wasn't hiding it either.

Einhorn and his new girlfriend wined and dined with wealthy British limousine liberals and spent time in London's pubs.

Life must have seemed easy once more for the Unicorn, until he received word that the American authorities were onto him and that the British were cooperating and would likely have no problems turning him over to the Americans if captured.

In the middle of the night, Einhorn fled to the small country of Wales, which is part of the United Kingdom, and therefore subject to most of the same laws concerning extradition. From Wales, Einhorn skipped across the Irish Sea and landed in the Republic of Ireland, where he lived for some time.

But Einhorn quickly learned how difficult it is to be a fugitive.

He received a tip that the Irish and American authorities had found where he was living and were on their way to arrest him. He quickly left his home, evading the authorities by minutes.

The Unicorn was learning that, to be a successful fugitive, he had to keep moving and could not be tied down. He eventually left his girlfriend for a Swedish woman named Annika Flodin.

Flodin bore a strong resemblance to Maddux as both were tall blondes and she also had an unnatural fixation with the one-time hippy guru. The two married and lived in Sweden for a while where they lived off Flordin's family money.

Eventually, Einhorn and Flodin moved to France where he went by the alias "Eugene Mallon."

By the early 1990s, the Unicorn must have thought that the authorities in Pennsylvania had forgotten about him, but that was the furthest thing from the truth.

The state of Pennsylvania convicted Ira Einhorn of murder *in absentia* in 1996. He was sentenced to life without parole.

But the Pennsylvania authorities would have to find him if they ever wanted to see that sentence carried out.

The Capture

In 1997, Einhorn and his wife were living in a quaint village in southwestern France. He had no reason to believe that the authorities were on to him, but over the years some of his former benefactors had second thoughts about the former hippy guru. The 1993 trial opened the eyes of many of his friends and associations, who for the first time saw the mountain of evidence stacked against Einhorn and what he had done to Holly Maddux.

Finally, multiple tips were made to the American, French, and INTERPOL authorities that the Unicorn killer was living in the village of Champagne-Mouton.

On a quiet morning, the French authorities swept in and arrested Einhorn, who was asleep naked in his bed.

Almost immediately, the arrest caused a media sensation in both the US and Europe. At fifty-eight, Einhorn had notably aged as he was by then grey and his hair was thinning, but the scruffy hippy was still quite recognizable. Since France and the United States have a mutual extradition policy, it appeared as though Einhorn would be sent back to Pennsylvania in short order.

But the Unicorn had other plans.

Although the two countries have an extradition agreement, it is rather complex, and from France's perspective, there are several exceptions. Einhorn's wealthy wife hired some of the best criminal defense attorneys in France to defend him. The first victory they won was getting bail for Einhorn.

Prosecutors in Philadelphia and the family and friends of Holly Maddux were perplexed that a judge would actually allow an international fugitive bail, but there were many conditions and the cameras of the international media were watching every move the Unicorn made, so the likelihood of him absconding was low.

His lawyers brought up numerous arguments that kept the case in the French courts for about four years. First they argued that Einhorn shouldn't be extradited because he may face the death penalty in the United States, but American officials argued that he was already sentenced to life in prison.

Einhorn's extradition was also prevented initially as French authorities needed to follow the European Court of Human Rights' requirement that defendants convicted of crimes *in absentia* be given a new trial. This was a possible sticking point, but wanting to bring Einhorn to justice, the Pennsylvania state legislature passed a new law in 1998, often referred to as the "Einhorn Law" that would allow for the Unicorn to get a new trial.

Finally, in 2001, the French courts agreed that there was no reason why they shouldn't allow Einhorn to be extradited. He was sent back to Philadelphia in shackles and given a new trial in 2002.

By the time Einhorn went to trial, he looked worn down and broken. He was no longer a popular guru and had few supporters in the court room. Most people would have pleaded guilty in the face of overwhelming circumstantial and physical evidence, but Einhorn's pride wouldn't let him do such a thing.

His defense was that the CIA set him up because he was a threat to their plans and those of the military industrial complex.

Needless to say, the jury rejected the defense and found him guilty of Holly Maddux's murder in October 2002. He was sentenced to life in prison without the possibility of parole.

To the inmates Einhorn lives with, his status as a former hippy guru meant little to them.

He was just another woman killer. He died in prison in 2020.

CHAPTER 5:

THE LYLE AND
MARIE MCCANN MURDER CASE

The idea of "work" as a concept has been debated and theorized in the West for centuries by thinkers ranging from Karl Marx to Adam Smith. For most of us, though, work is simply a responsibility to pay for the things we need to support ourselves and our families. If we are lucky, we have jobs that we truly enjoy and are actually careers, while we all strive to find jobs that allow us to save money for retirement.

Retirement is what most people work for in Western countries and for many what makes an often dreary job bearable.

But the way people enjoy their retirements varies from individual to individual.

Some dedicate their time to hobbies, while others find purpose and comfort in volunteering.

A large percentage of retirees enjoy spending their time traveling in North America in recreational vehicles (RVs). Many seniors spend months at a time in RVs that have all the amenities of home and are often nicer than some apartments. Some retirees even live in their RVs year round, spending the winter months in the southern states and then heading back up north during the summer.

For the most part, RVing in North America is a safe endeavor. Tens of thousands of RVers make trips every year with few incidents and the campgrounds located across the United States and Canada are usually very safe.

But of course, there are always outlying incidents where violence happens to unsuspecting RVers.

The bizarre murder case of retirees Lyle and Marie McCann is one such case. The McCann's were a retired Edmonton, Alberta couple who spent most of their free time traveling across Canada and the United States in their RV. They enjoyed the company of each other and would often go out of their way to visit their children and grandchildren, which is what they planned to do when they left their home in Alberta on July 3, 2010. The McCanns planned to pick their daughter up from the Abbotsford International Airport outside of Vancouver, British Columbia on July 10, which gave them plenty of time to sight-see along the way.

But the McCanns never arrived.

The McCanns' burned-out RV was discovered less than 200 miles from Edmonton, and although their bodies were never discovered, the authorities believed they were murdered.

The ensuing investigation had more twists and turns than an Alberta highway mountain pass, and in the end, although a person was convicted of their deaths, there are still unanswered questions.

The McCanns

To all their friends and family, Lyle and Marie were the textbook example of what a marriage should be. It probably helped that they were born and raised in a different time—Lyle was born in 1931 and Marie was born in 1932—but there is little doubt that they truly loved each other and their family. Both were natives of Alberta, having grown up during World War II when food rationing and sacrifice were common.

During the early 1950s, Lyle became an over-the-road truck driver, making runs all across Canada and into the United States. Lyle loved his job as it gave him a chance to meet interesting people and to see North America and get paid for it.

Trucking also gave Lyle the ability to raise a family in a nice neighborhood.

Lyle met Marie around the time he began his trucking career and the two married in 1952. They made their home in the quiet Edmonton suburb of St. Albert, which is where they lived most of their married lives.

The McCanns would have three children and by most accounts they were a picture-perfect family: there were no marital problems, drug use, or violence in the McCann home.

When Lyle retired from trucking in the 1990s, he looked forward to spending even more time with Marie doing something they both enjoyed—traveling. While Lyle was still working, the couple enjoyed traveling and also the outdoors, so they decided to combine the two pastimes by buying a RV.

There are many different routes one can go when buying a RV. There are trailers of varying lengths, fifth wheels, and motorhomes. They all have benefits and disadvantages, with varying price tags, so a proper purchase really depends on one's needs.

The McCanns decided to buy a Gulfstream Coach motorhome. It certainly has an advantage over trailers and fifth wheels in that you don't have to worry about having a truck to pull the RV. The downside is you will need a car if you want to leave your motorhome hooked up while you leave the campground.

The McCanns solved this problem by buying a Hyundai Tucson to pull behind their RV.

Throughout the late 1990s and 2000s, the McCanns made several trips across Canada and the United States. The McCanns stayed away from urban areas for the most part and instead visited most of the remarkable natural sites across North America, seeing many beautiful things and meeting many interesting people along the way.

The McCanns' children warned them to be wary of strangers, especially in the United States, but Lyle and Marie assured them that problems were few and far between on the road.

Although Lyle and Marie were right, it only takes one encounter for things to end badly.

The Fatal Trip

After Lyle and Marie celebrated Canada Day (July 1) at their home in Alberta, they planned to drive through the Rocky Mountains to pick their daughter up at the airport in British Columbia and then camp in Chilliwack near the Canada-United States border. It was a trip that the couple had made plenty of times before and was for the most part pretty easy. Most of the trip would be on a four lane and although some of the two-lane portions were on winding mountain roads, Lyle had driven those same roads countless times in an eighteen wheeler.

Lyle had also done the drive in heavy snow, rain, and sleet with deadlines, so a lazy drive in an RV was no problem.

The couple planned to take an entire week to get there, which meant that they had to camp along the way.

After talking with their daughter on the phone, they left on the morning of July 3, but were never heard from again.

It was as if the McCanns had vanished off the face of the earth.

While the McCanns were enjoying their retirement, a young man named Travis Vader was finding life most difficult. In 2010, Vader was thirty eight years old with no permanent address, a history of hard drug abuse, and an extensive criminal record that included convictions for burglary and theft.

About the time the McCanns were beginning their lives in retirement, Vader was plunging headfirst into the criminal underworld. Like many criminals, Vader began his descent with alcohol, but before too long, he began doing cocaine, methamphetamines, and any other hard drug he could get. Like most drug addicts, Vader resorted to crime to fuel his addiction. He began burglarizing homes and businesses in the Edmonton area until he was caught and sent to jail.

But for many drug addicts, jail is only a time to temporarily sober up. When they get out, the cycle begins anew.

By the summer of 2010, Vader was in a tough spot. He was broke and homeless and hadn't talked with most of his family in some time. It was while he was in this desperate state that he fatefully came across the McCanns.

At this point, the authorities are unsure of the details concerning what happened next, but they believe they know what happened based on the available circumstantial and forensic evidence.

The McCanns' burned-out camper was discovered near Edson, Alberta on July 5, but their Hyundai was missing. It appears that most likely the McCanns stopped to camp for the night and were surprised by Vader, who was tweaking for his next fix. Believing that the McCanns had money in their camper, or that he could sell or trade some of their belongings, Vader surprised them with a gun.

Lyle and Marie were probably compliant, believing that Vader would leave after he got some money. But Vader had other ideas and dispatched the McCanns. The police, though, are divided over how the murders took place.

One theory is that things got out of control quickly, and the McCanns were murdered near their campsite. If this is what happened, then either Lyle tried to fight Vader off or drug-induced paranoia caused Vader to start shooting.

The other theory is much darker. It is possible that after Vader got the jump on the McCanns, he ordered them into the Hyundai at gun point, drove to a second location, and then shot them and disposed of their bodies somewhere in the Canadian Rockies. The Hyundai was located on July 16 about thirty miles off the route the McCanns were taking to British Columbia.

The Investigation

Although the McCanns' bodies had not been found, law enforcement officers with the province of Alberta, the city of Edmonton, and the Royal Canadian Mounted Police believed that they had a homicide on their hands. The various agencies combined their resources to compile a list of probable suspects, and at the top of the list was Travis Vader.

Vader was well-known to the Edmonton police in particular because that was where he had amassed most of his rap sheet. There was little that initially tied Vader to the disappearance of Lyle and Marie McCann, other than a hunch and some anonymous tips to law enforcement. But career criminals usually have warrants out for their arrests.

This time the police were in luck—Vader was wanted on drug charges.

The police only had to find the itinerant drug addict. After chasing down some leads and turning over some rocks, the Edmonton police finally located and arrested Vader on July 19. Although Vader was not cooperative with the investigators, many of his friends and family were. One of Vader's friends told the police that he spent some time on his rural property during the first week in July, which led to the investigators getting a warrant and searching the property. Although the McCanns were not found at the property, several pieces of circumstantial evidence were discovered that tied Vader to the missing retired couple.

After the first couple of months that the McCanns were missing, the investigation slowed down to a crawl. The investigators were receiving fewer tips, but Vader wasn't going anywhere anytime soon, so they could afford to take their time.

Then on July 27, 2011, just over a year after they disappeared, the McCanns were officially declared dead by the Canadian government. Travis Vader was now being investigated for his role in their homicides.

It would not be until April 2012 that Vader was charged with the McCanns murders. Besides the first-degree murder charges, Vader also faced a number of theft, drug, and weapons charges. He was first found guilty of drug and weapons charges in October 2012, but those charges would only keep him locked up for a few years. If he were convicted of murder in the McCann case, Vader would likely spend the rest of his life in prison.

Two Crazy Trials

The criminal court systems in most Western countries tend to be very similar due to the fact that they give the defendant a number of rights and some would say "privileges." For instance, in nearly every Western country, indigent defendants are given court-appointed, publicly-funded attorneys. Criminal defendants are also allowed numerous appeals if they are convicted.

With that said, the limits of a criminal defendants' rights vary from country to country.

In Canada, which is officially part of the British Commonwealth, the "Crown," which is the prosecution, can stay charges on a criminal defendant. Stayed charges are similar to dropped charges but differ in that they can be brought back up after a certain period. It is a legal maneuver used by the Crown prosecutors when they think they don't have enough evidence, but they feel they have the right defendant.

In Vader's case, the Crown decided to stay the original murder charges against him in March 2014 and just try him on the drug and weapons charges. They theorized that Vader would most likely be convicted, and based on his lengthy criminal record, he would be sentenced to considerable prison time. While Vader was cooling his heels in an Alberta provincial prison, they figured, the Crown could gather more evidence in the McCann case.

But sometimes things don't go as planned.

Travis Vader was found not guilty of the drug and weapons charges on October 8, 2014. After the acquittal, a defiant Vader spoke to the press, saying the Crown "Put me in jail for four years to investigate me when there was nothing there to begin with."

The Crown was not too happy, which led to them bringing back the stayed murder charges. Vader was rearrested and put back in jail, but a judge allowed the career criminal bail in a bizarre case that kept getting stranger.

Although Vader was allowed bail, which is nearly unheard of for first-degree murder charges, he was given several restrictions. He was required to wear a monitoring device on his ankle, had to check in with a probation officer for drug tests, and was required to be gainfully employed. Vader was also prohibited from associating with known criminals and drug users.

Those requirements were simply too much for Travis Vader.

In May 2016, Vader failed a drug test, so the police went to arrest him at the address he had given to the courts, but when they arrived he was nowhere to be found. The setback was only minor, though, because Vader was still wearing his monitoring device. The police simply went to the address where he was and arrested him. Vader was surprised to see the police pull into the convenience store parking lot where he was attempting to score some drugs.

The police, on the other hand, were a bit surprised to learn that he was driving a stolen vehicle.

The turn of events allowed the authorities to once more put Vader in jail while he awaited his murder trial in late 2016.

The Crown prosecutors believed they had enough evidence to convict Vader of murder.

The closest thing to direct physical evidence the prosecutors had was a baseball cap recovered from the McCann's Hyundai that had a trace of Vader's DNA. It didn't prove he killed the couple, or that he even had anything to do with their disappearance, but it did show that he was probably in their car around the time they went missing.

There was also the discovery of Lyle's ballcap with a bullet hole through it. Again, it didn't prove that Vader fired the shot, but it did go to show that more than likely Lyle and Marie were killed before their car was stolen. Finally, and perhaps the most incriminating, were a series of text messages sent from the McCann's cell phone to Travis Vader's girlfriend.

Vader had no explanation for this.

Vader faced a judge instead of a jury for his murder trial, which ended up being a fortunate circumstance for him. Justice Denny Thomas found Vader not guilty of first-degree murder but guilty of second-degree murder on September 15, 2016.

But almost as soon as the judge announced his verdict, he also announced to the press that he had made a mistake.

He stated that the two second-degree murder convictions were based on his understanding of Section 230 of the Canadian Criminal Code, which essentially states that a defendant can be convicted of murder, even if he did not intend to kill the victim, if the murder was committed in the commission of another crime.

It turns out that Section 230 was declared unconstitutional in 1990, but for whatever reason, it still remains on the books.

Justice Thomas then simply substituted the murder convictions for manslaughter and then sentenced Vader to life in prison with the possibility of parole in January 2017. The sentence is equivalent to what he more than likely would have received if the second-degree murder convictions stood.

Needless to say, Vader and his attorneys were not happy and promptly filed appeals.

"This court cannot proceed to impose a life sentence upon Mr. Vader for an offence that does not exist," his lawyers wrote in an appellate brief.

The children of the McCanns, though, were happy with the results and look forward to moving on with their lives.

"We are very pleased with the decision today, and are comfortable that justice is being served here," said the McCann's son Bret. "I hope that any sentence or parole eligibility recognizes his total lack of remorse and his lies."

CHAPTER 6:

MESAC DAMAS, THE VOODOO FAMILY ANNIHILATOR

Family annihilations are an especially disturbing category of the already-disturbing phenomenon of mass murder. Instead of the killer focusing his wrath on a crowd of strangers, the family annihilator targets his family members, attempting to kill as many as possible before either making a getaway or killing himself.

When one looks at some of the most infamous family annihilators, there seems to be a variety of different motives that drove the killers. Ronald DeFeo Junior and David Brom were young men who didn't get along with their fathers and used drugs before they snapped one day and killed their entire families.

John List was apparently driven to kill his family by an intense hatred of his wife, a desire to start over, and strange religious philosophies.

Others, such as James Ruppert, were inspired by jealousy.

Mesac Damas is a lesser known, but no less deadly, family annihilator who killed his wife and five children in 2009. Besides the kill count, Damas' case grabbed headlines due to the killer's unique background and strange behavior before, during, and after his trial. Like Ronald DeFeo Junior more than thirty years before, Damas argued in court that he was driven to kill his family by demons, which he first became acquainted with in his native country of Haiti.

A Strange Background

Mesac Damas was born in 1976 in the francophone Caribbean nation of Haiti. Damas quickly learned how difficult life in Haiti can be: nearly everyone is poor, crime is rampant, most of the country is without indoor plumbing, and political coups are common.

Damas' family, like most Haitians, was poor. Still, his parents worked whenever they could find jobs to support him and his siblings. They also tried to instill religious values in their children by bringing them up in an evangelical Christian church.

Although the majority of Haitians officially identify themselves as Roman Catholics, various non-denominational Christian and evangelical Christian groups have made inroads in the country over the last three decades. Damas' family was impressed with the message of personal salvation, but they also wanted to find comfort in this world, so they applied for visas to the United States.

After waiting several years for their visas, Mesac's parents were finally awarded travel and work visas to the United States in the mid-1980s. But the visas didn't include Mesac, so his parents were faced with a dilemma. Thinking that they might not have another chance, they decided to go on without Mesac and left him to be raised by their extended family in Haiti.

Mesac's new family clearly had different spiritual philosophies than his parents.

Although most Haitians are Catholics, it is certainly a very different form of Catholicism than what one would find in Ireland, Italy, or even most of Latin America. Haitian Catholicism is heavily influenced by and some would say subordinate to Voodoo.

The Voodoo religion is essentially an animist faith that was taken with slaves from west Africa across the Atlantic Ocean during the centuries of the trans-Atlantic slave trade (1500s until the early 1800s). Unlike some other places in the New World where there were much higher numbers of European colonists and many Protestants, the country that would become known as Haiti was settled by very few French colonials, who for the most part allowed the slaves to practice any religion they wanted. Voodoo then developed as a New World version of African animism combined with some elements of Roman Catholicism.

Voodoo is a highly ritualized religion and also polytheistic—where demons and angels can influence the course of human events if prompted to do so by a priest or priestess who knows the right spells and incantations.

Not long after his parents immigrated to the United States, Mesac Damas forgot all about the evangelical type of Christianity his parents followed and instead fully embraced the Voodoo theology of his extended family.

He would bring that theology with him to the United States.

Coming to America

Having no real opportunities in Haiti, Damas longed to immigrate to either Canada or the United States where he had family and friends who were doing much better than anyone he knew in Haiti. Because his parents became permanent resident aliens in the United States and later citizens, they were allowed to sponsor Damas. At the age of nineteen, Damas finally got his wish and was issued a visa to work and live in the United States.

Damas first arrived in the Miami area, which is home to the largest Haitian expatriate community in the world. After spending some time there and getting acquainted with the state of Florida, Damas moved to the Gulf coast city of Naples in the late 1990s.

By all accounts, this was a stable and productive period in Damas' life.

Damas was a cook at various restaurants and bars in the Naples area and he had a reputation as a good worker. He was a skilled cook, worked well with others, and was always prompt. Not long after Damas established himself in the Naples area, he met another Haitian immigrant named Guerline Dieu.

Dieu was immediately enraptured by Damas' smooth talking. To her, it seemed as though he had goals and was going to go somewhere in life. The two also shared a similar background, so to Dieu, Damas seemed like a real catch.

The couple married in 1999 and would later have five children.

But as the 2000s went by, it was apparent to all who knew the couple that there was trouble in paradise.

Although Damas was never known as an adulterer, he was extremely paranoid and often thought Guerline was cheating on him. Damas' paranoia led to him being extremely possessive of his wife, to the point where if he saw Guerline simply ask a man for directions, he accused her of cheating on him. The paranoia quickly turned into emotional and psychological abuse, which then evolved into physical abuse.

If Damas didn't get his way, he would beat Guerliene up until she acquiesced.

If Damas wanted sex, he was going to get it, no matter what Guerline had to say about it.

By the late 2000s, the situation was becoming untenable for Guerline and her children. Not only was Damas becoming much more violent and volatile, he was acting unpredictably and bizarrely.

Guerline had enough.

The Murder

In September 2009, Guerline planned to leave Damas. She knew that he wouldn't be happy with the situation, but she thought that being straightforward with him would be the best course of action.

After all, they had five children together, so he would no doubt agree to part ways amicably, Guerline thought.

She couldn't have been more wrong.

"Divorce me? I'll fucking kill you!" Damas said when Guerline approached him about the divorce.

Thinking that he just needed to cool down, Guerline didn't press the issue, planning to talk with him some other time. A day of silence passed between the two until the evening of September 17, 2009.

Damas went to work his scheduled shift at a local restaurant that evening, but was clearly distracted according to his coworkers. After only working a couple of hours, Damas punched out early and went to a local department store to pick up some supplies.

These were no ordinary supplies Damas purchased.

Damas bought a large fillet knife and some duct tape.

He had some voodoo inspired gifts for his wife and children.

Damas then went home where it is believed he had one final argument with his wife. He probably tried to talk her out of the divorce, but Guerline would not relent. As the argument got more heated, it moved to the apartment's bathroom where it became physical. He started by beating Guerline, but at some point he remembered the knife he had just bought and so began using it on her, over and over.

Damas later said that a voodoo demon materialized in the apartment that helped him kill his wife. The demon then told him to finish the act.

Facing a life sentence for murdering his wife, Damas decided to go all the way with his bloodbath by killing all of his children. He stabbed each child as they slept. There were no signs of struggle, which means that if the children even heard Damas killing Guerline., they probably thought it was just another night in their home.

After killing his family, Damas made no effort to conceal his crimes. Instead, he drove to Miami and bought a one-way ticket to Haiti.

He was going to hide out in his native land.

Damas probably thought that he could evade the long arm of American justice in Haiti for a number of reasons. Since he was a native and knew the language, he could blend into the population and move about freely. He also probably thought that he could recognize most American authorities from a mile away because most are White and the Black agents don't speak the French Creole language of Haiti.

But Damas was never known for being a particularly smart guy.

Haiti is actually probably one of the worst places an American fugitive can go, even a fugitive with Haitian roots. Haiti is close to the United States, so it is easy for federal agents to go back and forth and to establish contacts and sources in the country, of which they have plenty. Most importantly, Haiti also has an extradition treaty with the United States, and since it is heavily reliant on American aid, it rarely fights extradition requests.

And few countries in the world would give shelter to a family annihilator.

Damas was in Haiti for less than a week before one of the US Marshalls' many informants in that country called in a tip on the mass murderer's location. On September 23, the US Marshalls arrested Damas at the home of one of his family members. The extradition process happened quickly, and in no time, Damas was in the Collier County jail in Florida. When investigators from the Collier County Sheriff's Department and the Naples Police Department put Damas in the interrogation room for the obligatory interview, they thought he would invoke his right to remain silent.

The investigators were dead wrong.

In his lengthy confession, Damas not only related the grisly details of the six murders he committed, but also his motive. He told the investigators that he was cursed by voodoo priests when he was a child and that spirit or demon physically manifested itself on September 17 and made him carry out the heinous acts.

After his confession, Damas was charged with five counts of first-degree murder in a Collier County, Florida courtroom.

It was pretty clear that he murdered his family, but it was equally unclear if he was sane when he did it.

Crazy Courtroom Antics

The first and most pertinent question surrounding Mesac Damas' case was his sanity. There was no doubt that he committed the murders—he had admitted to the crimes in a complete statement—so the primary issue concerning Damas' trial is if he would be found not guilty by reason of insanity.

Surely a sane man wouldn't brutally kill his entire family, right?

The reality is that, in the United States, insanity defenses are frequently used but are rarely successful. There are also many nuances to an insanity defense, which vary from state to state. A successful insanity defense essentially proves that the defendant did not know the difference between right and wrong when they committed the crime. If found not guilty by reason of insanity, the defendant is usually confined to a mental hospital, possibly for the remainder of their life.

A defendant can be found sane at the time of the crime in question, but not presently sane, or sane enough, to stand trial, which is what took place in Damas' case.

Many believe that Damas was aware of the legalities surrounding an insanity defense, so he purposefully acted as "crazy" as he could.

And he certainly did plenty of things to make it appear that way.

Damas frequently refused to cooperate with his attorneys, and when he did, he referred to himself as COG, which was an abbreviation for "child of god." When he was in the courtroom, Damas asked the judge to refer to him as COG and would often do other bizarre things, such as having conversations with himself while the attorneys were making motions.

He would also make pronouncements about God in the courtroom and threatened to kill himself on more than one occasion. Because of his courtroom antics, Damas was often forcefully ejected from the proceedings and banned from the courtroom for days at a time.

Then there were times when he refused to enter the courtroom. For those occasions, the Collier County deputies created a special wheelchair just for Damas that was complete with restraints and a hood to keep the family annihilator from spitting.

Because of the high-profile nature of his case and due to the fact that he was a child killer, Damas had to be isolated from the general population in the Collier County Jail while he was awaiting trial. There is no doubt that most of the inmates in the jail were probably happy with the decision because he refused to shower, which created a strong odor that could be smelled throughout the cellblock.

Damas also seemed to be self-destructive. He refused to take his diabetes and blood pressure medications and would often refuse food for several days in a row.

All of this seemed like the behavior of an insane person, but was it just an act?

A judge initially ruled in 2011 that Damas was competent to stand trial, but after some more courtroom antics, the ruling was changed in 2014.

The judge ruled that Damas was *currently* not competent to stand trial. The ruling had nothing to do with Damas' competency when he committed the murders—he was never declared not competent in that matter.

After a brief stay at a mental hospital, Damas was declared competent to stand trial in October 2014.

Final Resolution

Once Mesac Damas was declared competent to stand trial, his lawyers continued to argue that he was unfit, and he did his best to prove them right by continuing his antics.

But it was to no avail.

Damas' lawyers tried to put together a reasonable defense, but the insanity defense was no longer an option and the classic "the voodoo devil made me do it" had not been tried in decades. Still, they planned to take the case to trial because he was facing the death penalty, and death row inmates are routinely executed in Florida.

Then, when the trial was nearing, Damas made the bold move of throwing himself at the mercy of the court by pleading guilty to all six counts of first-degree murder. Perhaps he thought that the move would elicit a degree of sympathy.

If so, he was sorely mistaken.

On October 27, 2017, Mesac Damas was sentenced to death. At his sentencing, Damas gave the judge a note that read: "Go ahead, continue your work, may blood be upon your shoulders." It was signed COG.

As Damas awaits his date with the needle, he will have plenty of time on his hands.

No doubt, we have not heard the last of Mesac Damas.

CHAPTER 7:

THE DISAPPEARANCE OF
BEN SMART AND OLIVIA HOPE

World history is full of many intriguing cases of notable disappearances. In 1021, the Islamic caliph al-Hakim went to the hills outside of Cairo, Egypt to pray and never returned. An exhaustive search only turned up his donkey and some bloodstained clothes. Al-Hakim's friends and foes alike were perplexed by his disappearance and today it is one of the great mysteries of the pre-modern world.

Closer to our own time, American female aviator Amelia Earhart went missing somewhere in the South Pacific in 1937, which also spawned an intensive search but turned up nothing. Numerous theories, some of which border on the preposterous, have been advanced to explain Earhart's disappearance, but more than likely, as with al-Hakim's disappearance, it will forever remain a mystery.

Conspiracy theories have been forwarded concerning the disappearances of both Earhart and al-Hakim, but the reality is that people disappear every day.

The majority of those who disappear actually turn back up at some point. Many of these people leave on their own accord for any number of reasons: teenagers escaping a terrible home life, individuals in heavy debt or facing criminal charges, and people who are just tired of their lives but don't want to commit suicide. There are also people who are abducted but later return to their homes.

Then there are those who have been murdered, but their bodies have not been found.

In cases where the disappeared are believed to have been murdered, law enforcement agencies treat the case as a homicide instead of a disappearance. Historically, getting a murder conviction without a body is extremely difficult, and in some jurisdictions, impossible.

But in recent years, many jurisdictions have changed their laws to make it easier to prosecute someone without the presence of a body. One particular case where this very concept was put on trial was the disappearance of Ben Smart and Olivia Hope in New Zealand.

Ben and Olivia were two happy-go-lucky kids spending the 1998 New Year with each other and some friends on the Marlborough Sounds, which is located on the northeast coast of the South Island of New Zealand. The pair disappeared that night and were never seen again, but after months of investigation, a man was arrested, tried, and convicted of their murders.

The case continues to garner much media attention and polarize those who follow it in the tiny southern-hemisphere nation.

A New Year to Remember

In the weeks leading up to the 1998 New Year, Ben Smart, Olivia Hope, and all their friends began planning a celebration that they would remember for the rest of their lives. Unfortunately for them, at least those still here today, the memories ended up being based on tragedy.

But tragedy was the furthest thing from their minds on December 31, 1997.

Ben and Olivia grew up on the northern tip of New Zealand's South Island. The area resembles locations in Scandinavia in many ways, with hundreds of fjords, islands, isthmuses, and peninsulas seemingly inviting visitors to explore them. In fact, the scenic beauty of New Zealand's South Island is what attracts thousands of tourists from all over the world to the country every year.

Since the region is so unique, even when compared to the rest of New Zealand, a distinct subculture exists in the small towns that dot the shores. Most people in the region are at least somewhat familiar with boating and many own their own seaworthy vessels. The locals have had a deep connection with the sea from ancient times: the Maori natives traversed the straits in their large canoes and later European settlers made a living by fishing in its waters. Today, locals still live off the ocean but mainly do so by renting out their vessels to tourists and recreational fishermen and as "water taxis" to shuttle people around the many islands.

Overall, the people of the area are friendly and helpful, and the crime rate is among the lowest in the country, which made the events of New Year 1998 that much more disturbing.

Ben and Olivia began their night early by having drinks with some friends at the Furneaux Lodge. The Furneaux Lodge is a 100-year-old bar and restaurant that is a popular night spot in the area. Located in the Marlborough Sounds, lodge patrons can take in the scenic view of the many islands and peninsulas from the back patio. For New Year, the owners of the lodge had several live bands playing for a far above capacity crowd that had spilled out on the lodge's front lawn.

Ben and Olivia stayed at the lodge for the official start of the New Year and then planned to go to a boat that Olivia's sister rented named the *Tamarack* where they planned to sleep off their alcohol binge.

When the pair finally made it to the *Tamarack* in the early morning hours, they found out that they had lost their bunk to some other revelers.

Ben and Olivia were still in high spirits and didn't want to cause problems. Actually, according to their friends and family, neither were the type to make a big deal about small things, so it was no surprise they both decided just to catch a water taxi back to the mainland and go home.

Around 4 a.m., the couple caught a water taxi commandeered by Guy Wallace. Besides the pilot, there were two other men in the water taxi—one was twenty-seven-year-old Scott Watson.

As Wallace piloted his vessel back to the mainland, Watson struck up a conversation with Ben and Oliva. After talking for a bit, Wallace overheard Watson offer the couple a bed on his boat, the *Blade.*

To Wallace, though, something wasn't right.

"[It was like] When you know there's something wrong and you can't put your finger on it," Wallace later said about Watson.

Still, he must not have been too disturbed because he dropped the trio off at Watson's boat and went on to pick up more fares.

Ben and Olivia were never seen again.

The Investigation

When neither Ben nor Olivia showed up at their respective homes on January 1, their parents were a bit worried, but not yet frightened. Both were fairly independent and since it was the New Year, they expected them to party a bit.

Perhaps they were somewhere "sleeping it off."

By late evening on January 1, both sets of parents began calling all of Ben's and Olivia's friends, finding out that they were last seen around 4 a.m. leaving the *Tamarack* on a water taxi. The information didn't seem to mean much at the time, but when Ben and Olivia failed to show up on January 2, both sets of parents called the police.

The police launched an investigation immediately, which brought them to the last people who saw the couple.

After interviewing Olivia's sisters and friends who were aboard the *Tamarack*, the police then widened their net and tracked down the owner of the water taxi that Ben and Oliva were seen boarding.

They interviewed Guy Wallace first, since he was one of the last persons to see the couple alive. He told the police about Scott Watson and how he dropped Ben and Olivia off at the *Blade*. He said the boat was a ketch and that the owner had wavy hair and an unkept appearance.

Most of that turned out not to be true.

The case led to intense media scrutiny in New Zealand, and it was even featured on newscasts in nearby Australia. The police reacted to the attention by devoting more resources to the case and naming it "Operation TAM."

The first thing they did was to bring Wallace, along with another witness, in for another interview.

Wallace drew a sketch for police of a boat he thought was a "38-40 foot ketch?" The prosecution's case argued that Wallace was mistaken about the number of masts and that the boat was, in fact, the one-masted Blade. Wallace later expressed his belief that he may have contributed to the incarceration of an innocent man by misidentifying the boat.

Wallace and the other witness picked Watson out of a photo lineup as being the man who was dropped off with Ben and Olivia at the *Blade*, but some say it was a flawed lineup. Watson's lineup picture looked more like the man that Wallace initially described to the police, but photos of him partying on New Year's Eve show him clean cut with a short haircut.

Despite the apparent inconsistencies, the police focused their investigation on Watson as their prime and only suspect. The police obtained a warrant to search Watson's boat, which initially didn't turn up anything. After the police received a second search warrant, they discovered blonde hairs on a blanket.

The hairs were tested for a DNA profile, which proved they belonged to Olivia.

The fact that the hairs were only found after the second search seemed suspect to many following the case. Cynical people asked why the hairs were not found on the first search and pointed out that Olivia's comb had been in the forensic lab and it therefore may have been the result of an incidental transfer.

Others went even further and suggested that the hairs could have been planted.

The small bit of circumstantial evidence that pointed the finger at Scott Watson was enough for the police, who then arrested him in June 1998 for the murders of Ben Smart and Olivia Hope.

Scott Watson was what law enforcement professionals call a "good suspect."

Most people familiar with the case, even those who believe Watson is guilty, agree that he probably wouldn't have been charged if he were a "regular" family-type guy. The reality is that Watson was a bit of a loner and known in the area as a guy who could be volatile. Although he had no criminal record as an adult, he had a lengthy juvenile record, which included arrests and convictions for crimes ranging from theft to assault.

When he finally went to trial in early 1999, Watson's only supporters were his father and a few family members. Most of New Zealand wanted to see Watson hang, and if the country still had the death penalty, there would've been no shortage of volunteer executioners.

In May 1999, after a short deliberation, a jury found Watson guilty of murder. He was sentenced to life in prison with the possibility of parole after seventeen years.

Appeals

New Zealand is like many Western countries in regards to a convicted criminal's right to appeals. As soon as he was convicted and sent to prison to serve his life sentence, Watson began working on his appeal. His first appeal was denied in 2000 and the next two were as well in 2003 and 2004.

Despite his failures in the appeals courts, Watson's family has continued to support him and at least publicly profess his innocence.

"Of course, the system doesn't want to listen, so that's the end of it," said Scott Watson's dad Chris Watson concerning the appeals process.

But as the initial tragedy of the disappearance and presumed murders of Ben Smart and Olivia Hope faded a bit in most New Zealanders' minds, many began to take a more critical look at the case. Many now find it hard to believe that a man could be convicted with such little physical evidence, while others think that Watson was outright set up by the police who needed to make an arrest because they were under such intense media scrutiny.

Some of the arguments in Watson's favor were put forward in a recent documentary titled, *Doubt: The Scott Watson Case*, which aired on New Zealand television.

Apparently, he has been trying to make the best of his situation in prison.

He married a woman in 2004 but has since divorced. Watson was also convicted of assaulting another inmate in 2007 and is said to be a bit of a tough guy behind bars.

Watson went before the parole board in 2015 and 2016, but was unanimously denied both times. Since he claims his innocence, the board said he showed no remorse towards his victims, which is a key indicator of rehabilitation. Besides his lack of remorse shown, or because of it, the board stated that they believed he is a violent risk to the public.

As of 2025, Watson has exhausted most of his appeals options. Unless another killer is discovered, there is a real possibility that Watson will be an old man when he is finally released from prison.

It appears that what happened in the final hours of Ben and Olivia's lives will probably never be known.

CHAPTER 8:

THE MURDER OF
SUSAN MORRIS

Although crime has always existed, it is a much bigger burden for modern societies. No longer do governments simply "lock up criminals and throw away the keys," but they attempt to rehabilitate the vast majority of offenders. Even offenders serving the remainder of their lives in prison live in much better conditions than they would have 100 or even fifty years ago. This applies to death row inmates in the United States as well because they are entitled to numerous appeals, and if they are executed, it will more than likely be through a lethal drug cocktail instead of at the end of a hangman's noose.

The current systems in most industrialized nations are not perfect, but they are also a far cry from the medieval dungeons of yesterday.

Most people agree that the emphasis on rehabilitation instead of punishment seems logical because the majority of all offenders, even most killers, will return to society one day.

But there is one penological dilemma that continues to confound most politicians, criminologists, and greater society—how to treat sex offenders.

The core of the dilemma concerns the fact that sex offenders are not driven by the same motivations as the other class of criminals. Greed, revenge, and even hate are not what drives the average sex offender. In fact, there is not even a professional or academic consensus of what drives sex offenders.

As academics continue to study the motivations of sex offenders, governments around the world have taken measures to limit the damage they do to society. The idea of chemical castration has become more popular in some countries, namely in Europe, because it is proven that it significantly reduces the libido and the ability to have sex in the offender. But critics of chemical castration point out that the method does nothing to change the thinking of sex offenders.

A chemically castrated sex offender can still hurt others.

Sex offender registries have been cited as another way to reduce the ability of sex offenders to reoffend. Beginning in the 1990s, individual states in the United States began to enact laws that make it mandatory for those convicted of sex offenses to be on a list. Every state now has a sex offender registry, which includes some convicted of misdemeanor offenses as well as those with felony sex offense convictions. The worst offenders are placed on a list for their entire lives.

The lists have proved to be a good way to track offenders, but they do little to stop a sex offender from reoffending. In response, some states, such as Minnesota, have even enacted laws whereby a repeat sex offender can be "committed" in much the same way as someone deemed mentally ill. Once committed, the sex offender can then be sent to an institution for an indefinite period.

On a warm night in Florida, an unsuspecting twenty-one-year-old woman was abducted from a parking lot at the University of West Florida, raped, and murdered by a man who had raped another woman days earlier and was on parole for sex offenses in another state.

A Promising Future

Susan Morris was a regular, down-to-earth girl who grew up in Florida and was extremely close to her family. She never caused her parents any problems growing up and did well in her high school classes. Besides getting good grades, she was active in the community and scored well on her college entrance exams, which was good enough for her to gain acceptance to most of the major universities in the state of Florida.

But Susan wanted to stay close to her family, so she chose to go to the University of West Florida in Pensacola.

Along with the proximity to her family, the University of West Florida has one of the top television production programs in the region, which was what Susan wanted to study.

While she was in school, Susan got good grades and also maintained an active social life. She was a member of a sorority, but shied away from the party scene. Susan's goal of working in the news business was more important to her than going to keg parties.

School was Susan's life and her future, but unfortunately, it also played a large role in her murder.

Eric Scott Branch

Most career criminals begin their life of crime at an early age with petty offenses and progress into more serious crimes as they approach adulthood. If they don't catch a life sentence, many career criminals reach a point of "criminal burnout" by their late forties or early fifties and then often entirely give up the lifestyle.

This pattern does not necessarily apply to sex offenders, though.

Most sex offenders, like non-sex offender career criminals, begin their criminal lifestyle early, but many, if not most, commit extremely serious crimes throughout their lives. There are few sex offenses considered "petty," so there is therefore no progression as there is with theft, drug offenses, and other non-sex crimes.

Also, sex offenders rarely stop on their own, and age does not seem to slow them down.

From a young age until the day they die, sex offenders are driven by an urge to sexually abuse others.

Eric Scott Branch clearly fits this profile of a sex offender.

About the only thing that Branch and Susan Morris had in common when their paths crossed in 1993 was that they were both twenty-one.

Unlike Susan, Branch was a directionless individual who took far more out of society than he contributed. From a young age he was constantly in trouble in school for truancy and fighting and was often in the juvenile court system. He committed petty crimes such as theft at an early age but also began sexually assaulting younger girls when he was a teenager.

When he wasn't victimizing people, Branch liked to drink and do drugs. Work was a concept that meant nothing to Eric Branch.

To those who knew Eric Branch in the late 1980s, he clearly seemed destined to spend considerable time in prison.

Branch's destiny was realized when at the age of eighteen, he sexually assaulted a fourteen-year-old girl in Indiana. His lawyers argued that the sex was consensual, which ultimately helped to mitigate the time he spent in prison. In 1991, Branch was convicted of felony sexual assault and sent to prison in Indiana.

The American prison systems were much different when Branch was released in late 1992 than they are now. At that time, inmates were often simply given a gate fee and told to report to a parole officer within a certain period of time, no matter their offense. They were often prohibited from leaving the state of their conviction and sometimes even a particular county, but there was little that could be done to stop an ex-con who wanted to leave the state. Monitoring devices were rarely used for parolees in the early 1990s.

Sex offender registries were also extremely rare in the United States before 1994 and even when they were used, if an offender were on a list in a particular state, he could simply move to another state with no registry to avoid the associated scrutiny.

Branch took full advantage of this state of affairs by simply leaving the state of Indiana for Florida late in 1992. When Branch absconded from his parole, a warrant was issued for his arrest in Indiana, but he was always one step ahead of the police.

Branch spent New Year's 1993 in the resort town of Panama Beach, Florida. After consuming copious amounts of alcohol at a nightclub on New Year's Eve night and striking out with every woman he tried to pick up, he decided to take what he couldn't get through conventional means. He lurked outside of the nightclub until he caught an unsuspecting woman walking alone and raped her.

Knowing that there was probably a warrant for his arrest in Indiana and if caught he could be tied to the rape in Panama City, Branch drove the short distance to Pensacola to get a different car.

Once he got there, he decided to take another victim.

January 11, 1993

Susan had a full day of classes on January 11, so she slept as late as she could and made it to campus in the late morning. Instead of coming home that day for lunch, she decided to eat in the campus food court before heading to another class. Her last class of the day was an evening class that usually got done around 9 p.m.

Since Susan arrived on campus early in the day, she had to park toward the back of a parking lot that was far from the building where she had her last class. Later in the afternoon, after many of the students had left for the day, she was able to move her car closer to the building where she had her last class. She thought the walk would be easier and it would be much safer.

Unfortunately, sometimes things don't work out that way.

Eric Branch was also in Pensacola on January 11, but he was up to no good. He had dropped his car off at the Pensacola Airport and was trawling the city looking for a new car and whatever other trouble he could find

Sometime after 8 p.m., he made his way to the University of West Florida campus to find another car. He was planning on going back to Indiana, possibly to turn himself in to the authorities.

He noticed that the parking lots were largely empty, but there was one with a number of cars closer to a building. Branch was no car thief, though. He didn't know how to hotwire a car and didn't have any tools that he could use to steal one.

He planned to wait for an unwitting victim.

As Branch waited, Susan got out of class and walked to her car. Susan's friends and family said she was normally very cautious at night, but on this particular night she was tired and anxious to get home.

She didn't see Branch until it was too late.

Branch nabbed Susan and dragged her into a nearby wooded area where he beat and raped her before strangling her to death. After he was done, he took her Toyota and drove off as if he had just swatted a fly.

For some reason, Branch decided to stay in Pensacola for a couple more days where he was spotted by witnesses and on security cameras driving Susan's Toyota around campus.

Some of his friends also noticed that he had a deep cut on one of his hands, and when asked about it, he said that he had been in a bar fight.

They were immediately suspicious.

Perhaps sensing that his friends and acquaintances were suspicious of his activities following the New Year's rape and the murder of Susan Morris, Branch decided to head back up to Indiana.

After driving several hundred miles north, Branch ditched Susan's car in a Bowling Green, Kentucky parking lot and then stole another car. He proceeded on to Indiana where he was arrested for parole violations within a few days.

More charges would follow.

Murder Charges

Susan Morris' brutal murder grabbed headlines across the state of Florida and into the neighboring states of Georgia, Alabama, and Mississippi. Susan's family made heart-wrenching pleas in press conferences for anyone with information to come forward, galvanizing the area residents to catch her killer.

As the events were unfolding in Florida, Eric Branch was sitting in an Indiana jail waiting to see how long he would be sent back to prison for his parole violation.

But not long after he was captured in Indiana, tips began pouring in to the Escambia County, Florida Sheriff's Department that investigators should take a look at Eric Branch.

It didn't take long for homicide investigators to compile a plethora of physical and circumstantial evidence that implicated Branch in Susan's murder.

Once Branch's car was recovered from the Pensacola airport, a forensic examination revealed that Susan's DNA was inside the car. Branch's DNA was recovered from Susan's car and most damning was that Branch's DNA was recovered from Susan's body.

It was a textbook "slam dunk" case for the prosecution.

When the Escambia County prosecutors learned that Branch had raped another woman days earlier and that he was on parole for sexual assault, they didn't hesitate to move forward with the death penalty.

There was little that Branch could do, so he decided to stall.

Branch had his lawyers file numerous pre-trial motions, and if they refused, he would fire them. To the Morris family, it seemed as though Branch's trial would never happen, but finally in 1997 it got underway.

The verdict was a foregone conclusion—guilty.

The only question remaining was if the jury would give Branch the death penalty.

Branch's lawyers did what they could in the penalty phase of the trial. They argued that his terrible upbringing and family life should mitigate the sentence to life in prison without the possibility of parole instead of the death penalty.

Either way, the remainder of Branch's life would be bleak.

If the jury somehow decided to give Branch life in prison, then he would have to spend that time in one of Florida's tough maximum security prisons, such as the aptly named Starke, with the "jacket" of a sex offender.

He would no doubt be the constant victim of seasoned convicts and prison gangs.

If the jury sentenced Branch to death, then he would certainly be executed at some point in the future. The state of Florida doesn't allow death row inmates endless appeals and regularly carries out executions.

The jury voted for the death penalty.

Branch immediately went to work filing numerous appeals, which were all denied. His last chance was an appeal to the Florida Supreme Court in early 2018.

"After reviewing Branch's response to the order to show cause, as well as the State's arguments in reply, we conclude that Branch is not entitled to relief," the Supreme Court opinion said.

On February 22, 2018, Mark Branch was executed by lethal injection. As the execution was carried out, he repeatedly yelled "Murderers!" at the prison staff.

No one was moved by his antics.

Many people were moved, though, by a statement Susan's sister, Wendy Hill, read on behalf of the Morris family:

"We have mourned her longer than she was with us."

CHAPTER 9:

CHEYENNE ROSE ANTOINE, THE SOCIAL MEDIA MURDERESS

Social media has transformed over the last two decades from something that only techies who frequented the furthest corners of the internet were familiar with, to something grandmas use on a daily basis.

Truly, social media has become an ubiquitous part of modern society.

Sites like Facebook, X, and LinkedIn are a part of everyday life and as the number of users has dramatically increased, so have the uses.

Many people use sites such as LinkedIn for business purposes: to post their resumes and to search for new jobs. Sites like X and Gab have become the virtual clearing house for the average person's political opinions and, of course, Facebook is where people stay connected with friends and family.

Although most people in industrialized countries use some form of social media, at least a couple of times a month, many young people are seemingly obsessed with it. Taking selfies and updating profiles seems to be a full-time job for some people.

People take pictures of their food and post it on social media.

Some take photos of alcoholic drinks and post them to Facebook.

Some have even posted more nefarious activities on social media.

There is an alarming trend that is developing where social media plays a role in high-profile crimes. One of the more recent examples of this was a 2017 assault in Chicago that was livestreamed on Facebook. In that case, a group of Black youths assaulted and held a "friend" with an intellectual disability against his will because he was White. As bad as the case was, the fact that it was livestreamed helped make the police's job that much easier.

There have also been a number of recent cases where threats were made on Facebook and X that resulted in violent retaliation by the threatened parties.

Although social media played a role in all of these crimes, it was also used by law enforcement officers to catch the criminals. In that respect, social media is like a double-edged sword.

There is another recent crime case where social media was used to solve a murder.

In March 2015, eighteen-year-old Brittany Gargol was found strangled to death in a landfill near Saskatoon, Saskatchewan, Canada. At first, the homicide investigators working the case had few leads and little evidence to work with, but after an extensive search of the victim's social media accounts, they were led to a most unlikely killer.

Life in Saskatoon

Most non-Canadians, and even many Canadians, know little about Saskatoon, Saskatchewan other than it is mentioned in the 1975 song "A Little Bit South of Saskatoon" by American Country Western crooner Sony James. Truly, the location of the city seems as foreign and exotic as its name.

The reality is that Saskatoon is a fairly important regional city in Canada.

Located on the northern Great Plains, Saskatoon is known for its extremely cold winters yet pleasant summers. Because it is in the middle of Canada's bread basket, it quickly became the economic hub of the region after its founding in the late nineteenth century. Railroads and major highways connect the city to the rest of the country, making it easier for grain to go to the more populated areas of Canada and beyond. Saskatoon is also the largest city in the province of Saskatchewan with a metropolitan area of nearly 300,000 people.

Saskatoon also has many museums and other cultural attractions and an active nightlife scene. But few people familiar with the city will argue that it is another version of Vancouver or Toronto.

Saskatoon's culture reflects that of Saskatchewan's and the western Canadian region in general, which includes Manitoba and Alberta. It is much more politically conservative than the rest of the country and ethnically more representative of Canada 100 years ago—the majority of its inhabitants are White with a significant minority community of First Nations peoples.

Another detail that separates Saskatoon from other Canadian cities is its higher than the national average homicide rate. Violence in general is endemic to many neighborhoods in Saskatoon and unlike in the United States where violence is often driven by gang and drug activity, in Saskatoon alcoholism and heavy drinking is more than often the culprit.

First Nations peoples in particular are involved in many alcohol related violent crimes, but the people of the area generally are known for heavy drinking and fighting.

Although women are often the victims of alcohol fueled violence in Saskatoon, they are also sometimes the perpetrators.

Cheyenne Antoine and Brittany Gargol

In 2015, Cheyenne Antoine and Brittany Gargol were much like any two eighteen-year-old "besties" one would find in many locations. When they weren't working, the pair would spend most of their free time with each other shopping, taking selfies and posting them on social media, and drinking, which was probably their favorite pastime.

The two began drinking while they were still in high school and once they turned eighteen, they took their partying to the next level. They developed contacts around the city that allowed them to attend house parties nearly every night. And although the legal drinking age in the province of Saskatchewan is nineteen, the two women knew enough bartenders and doormen that they were also able to drink at many of the city's bars.

The two young women also liked to smoke marijuana and flirt with guys at bars and parties.

Neither of the two were doing much more in life, but most eighteen-year-olds aren't planning for retirement.

Personality wise, Cheyenne and Brittany were both gregarious and out-going and had no problem meeting people. They were also both attractive brunettes and seemed to compliment each other's looks, according to many of their friends.

Cheyenne and Brittany genuinely had an affection for each other, but beneath Cheyenne's generally ebullient nature were a host of demons waiting to be unleashed.

Cheyenne was born to a family of alcoholics who didn't instill much discipline or direction in her. She constantly had problems in grade school, often acting out violently if things didn't go her way. Because she was so incredibly difficult to handle, Cheyenne was made a ward of the province of Saskatchewan and spent most of her youth in foster homes and provincial care facilities.

Brittany knew about Cheyenne's background and was also aware that she was still prone to violence—she witnessed Cheyenne violently attack people, both men and women, on more than one occasion while they were drinking.

Still, Brittany never believed that her best friend for life would ever turn her wrath on her: why would she?

The Murder

On the afternoon of March 25, 2015, Cheyenne and Brittany met up and began their evening early with a few beers and some marijuana. After taking some selfies and updating their social media profiles, the two women headed out to have a rowdy night in Saskatoon. They decided to check a few different house parties and then to possibly head to a bar or two toward the end of the night.

Both girls had quite a high alcohol tolerance for eighteen-year-olds.

The night started out fine, but as the evening went on it was clear that something was bothering Cheyenne. She kept making snide remarks to and about Brittany until finally Brittany asked her what her problem was. Cheyenne never really told her but instead started yelling and accusing her of something that wasn't quite clear.

All of the witnesses were under the influence of drugs and alcohol so their recollection of the details of the fight are hazy.

At some point, Cheyenne suggested that the two should leave and Brittany agreed. Although she was clearly in no condition to drive, Cheyenne took charge of the situation, telling Brittany that she was driving them to another location.

Brittany thought she meant another party or a bar.

After driving for about twenty minutes, Brittany was probably curious and possibly a bit nervous that they ended up outside of the city's limits at a landfill. Cheyenne somehow lured Brittany outside of the car, possibly by offering a drink or to smoke some marijuana, and quickly took control.

Cheyenne quickly took off the belt she was wearing, pushed her bestie to the ground, and then began strangling her with it. It didn't take long for the larger Cheyenne to choke the life out of the petite Brittany.

When she didn't feel her friend struggling anymore, Cheyenne dropped the belt, got back into her car, and drove back to Saskatoon.

She had just made her first and biggest mistake.

When Brittany failed to come home for several days, her friends and family grew worried. They knew that she lived a wild lifestyle and would often spend days or weekends away from home at a time, but she usually called and always posted updates on her social media accounts.

Brittany Gargol's social media accounts had not been updated since March 25. The last entry showed her and Cheyenne smiling for a selfie. The only post after that was one by Cheyenne that said: "Where are you? Haven't heard from you. Hope you made it home safe."

Cheyenne was apparently not too drunk to create an alibi for herself on social media.

Brittany's family finally called the police and filed a missing persons report. They told the police that Cheyenne Antoine was her best friend and was also presumably one of the last people to see her alive.

When the Saskatoon Police contacted Cheyenne, she was apparently ready. She told the investigators that she spent most of the afternoon and evening with Brittany, going to house parties and that they ended up at a bar toward closing time. Cheyenne then said that Brittany left with a man they just met that night.

Cheyenne was not immediately a suspect, but when the investigators looked into her story there appeared to be some important details she left out and others that she added. When the police tracked down some of the people from the last party that the girls attended, they learned that the two had a heated argument. The investigators then tried to verify their presence at the bar near closing time but couldn't.

No one had seen either woman on March 25 at the bar in question.

None of that made Cheyenne a suspect immediately. Since she was a heavy drinker, the police reasoned that the inconsistencies in her story were probably the result of being under the influence of drugs and alcohol. It was just the case of a young woman who partied too much, causing her to get her days confused.

As the months went by after the murder, Cheyenne continued to play the role of grieving best friend by leaving comments and posts on her social media accounts about Brittany. One post that was replete with grammatical errors and typos, dated September 10, 2015, seemed to betray Cheyenne's guilty conscience.

"Aweh , i miss you soo much bert! wish heaven had visiting hours so i could come see you, but i'm so glad you came & visited me in my dream last night. Woke up with tears in my eyes, i'm blessed to have met you & have you be apart of my life, still can't believe those last two days were going to be the last 2 days i got to be able to hug you, talk to you & laugh with you, i will cherish && hold all our good memories we've had over the years since grade 9 until we meet again. Looking forward to that day i see you again, say hello to my mommy up there for me!! That dream felt so damn real, & you were all bubbly & happy like you always were. i love you so muc brittney [sic] jane & miss you sooo much </3 You were way to young to go, gone but never forgotten. You were truely an angel on earth but i guess God needed you up there. You always believed in me, & i will make you proud my girl."

It was Cheyenne's heavy drug and alcohol use that made it easy for her to kill her best friend, and it would also prove to be what eventually led to her arrest. After a night of heavy drinking with a friend, Cheyenne admitted to killing Brittany. According to the friend, Cheyenne said that because of how much she had drank that day she didn't remember much of the act, but said it was done in the heat of the moment and that she was sorry.

The revelation disturbed the friend, who promptly called the police with the information. The information wasn't enough for an arrest, but it proved to jump start a stalled investigation that was at risk of becoming a cold case. The police began to look closer at Cheyenne, especially her social media posts.

One particular post dated March 25, 2015, caught their attention.

In the selfie of the two women they noticed that Cheyenne was wearing a distinct belt. It just so happened to be the exact same type of belt that was found at the murder scene.

Charges Filed

The social media posted selfie was enough for the Saskatoon Police to file first-degree murder charges against Cheyenne Antoine almost exactly two years after Brittany was killed, in March 2017.

The evidence was certainly damning, but it was still circumstantial—Cheyenne's DNA was not on the murder weapon and she was certainly not the only woman to own such a belt in Saskatoon.

But along with her confession and her phony alibis, there was a good chance that the jury would convict her of murder.

Cheyenne offered to plead guilty to the lesser charge of manslaughter, which was accepted by the Crown Prosecutor in January 2018. She was sentenced to seven years in prison.

Antoine was given statutory release in May 2024 and sent to a drug treatment facility for women. However, soon after Antoine was found with drug supplies in her possession and amphetamine in her system, and then absconded. She faces new charges for robbery, flight from police, dangerous driving and resisting arrest.

Cheyenne will likely have more years in prison to think about the course her life has taken.

Maybe she'll realize that Brittany was a far better friend than the bottle ever was.

CHAPTER 10:

BEVAN SPENCER VON EINEM AND "THE FAMILY" MURDERS

The 2016 United States presidential election was one of the most unique in American history. Of course, there was the outsider candidate, Donald Trump, who ultimately went on to win the presidency over Hillary Clinton, who most believed was a lock due to her immense influence in American politics and her support from mainstream media outlets.

But the decline in the influence of the mainstream media on the American public was perhaps the biggest story of the election.

Alternative news sources, mainly from the right-wing of the political spectrum, but also on the left-wing, drove scandalous stories, in some cases showing that the emperor truly has no clothes.

One of the stories picked up by the alternative media involved an alleged pedophile ring that was led by some of Washington, D.C.'s elites. Numerous politicians, mainly Democrats, were said to be part of the ring, which came to be known as "Pizza Gate."

There was no one single version of Pizza Gate, but most argued that there was a widespread child sex abuse taking place by wealthy and politically connected elites that was protected by well-placed ring members in law enforcement. Some versions of Pizza Gate alleged that the ring members were part of a world-wide Satanic cult conspiracy, while others suggested that the abusers are simply pedophiles who have managed to use their privilege for the sake of their own twisted desires.

It is impossible to say for sure if it had an effect on the election results, but it surely struck a nerve with many Americans.

Despite the initial interest in Pizza Gate, no "smoking gun" was ever found so it was soon relegated to conspiracy theory status and sent to the deepest corners of the internet.

But the idea of wealthy elites engaging in ritual sexual abuse of children is not entirely new in the West.

During the 1980s, a number of high-profile child abuse cases in the United States that were peripherally linked to Satanism led to the so-called "Satanic Panic." Many cases of child sex abuse during that period were treated as part of a greater cult conspiracy that involved some of the wealthiest and most influential people in society. A number of victims were put under hypnosis where it was revealed that they were sexually abused during bizarre Satanic rituals.

More and more victims came forward and before long the phenomenon spread to Europe, Australia, New Zealand, and South Africa.

By the time the Satanic Panic ended in the early 1990s, many of the allegations were proved to have been false and no hard evidence of a world-wide Satanic conspiracy was ever uncovered.

Long before Pizza Gate and the Satanic Panic, a conspiracy of well-connected child abusers was revealed in the state of South Australia, Australia.

During the late 1970s and early 1980s, a group of professional men in South Australia are believed to have abducted and murdered at least five young men and raped many more. Unlike other similar conspiracy theories, the local authorities are convinced that this one was real and even gave the conspirators a collective name—"The Family."

The members of The Family have been careful and since they are well-connected they have been able to avoid capture; all except one—Bevan Spencer von Einem.

Spencer von Einem was convicted of abducting and murdering a boy in 1983 and sent to prison, presumably for the rest of his life.

But now that Spencer von Einem is near the end of his life many are wondering if he'll finally blow the lid off of The Family or if he will take his secrets to the grave.

Bevan Spencer von Einem

Spencer von Einem was born in 1945 in Australia to German immigrants. Little is known about his childhood or even his adulthood until around the time he was arrested, but a few facts are known that connect him to individuals possibly connected to The Family conspiracy.

Einem was good with numbers, which he used to build a successful career as an accountant in South Australia. During the 1970s, Einem did work for some of the state's wealthiest and best connected individuals, which is probably how he met his later conspirators.

He used the money he made as an accountant to buy and sell different properties. Which netted him more money, though he was living with his mother at the time of his arrest.

Einem was never much of a partier and presented himself as a conservative, well-spoken individual who anyone would want as a neighbor.

Beneath his controlled exterior, Einem had interests that would not be considered normative, especially in 1970s Australia. Although Einem never hid his homosexuality, he was also never very open about it. He never came off as stereotypically gay, or at least what was considered to be in the 1970s, and rarely discussed his or anyone else's sexuality around most people.

But by the late 1970s Einem became involved with a close-knit group of professional men who shared his proclivity for boys and young men.

The South Australia police believe this group was none other than The Family.

The Murder of Richard Dallas Kelvin

In early 1983, the South Australia and Adelaide police knew nothing about The Family or Bevan Spencer von Einem. Although murders that were later attributed to the group had already happened, Einem's arrest in 1983 exposed a possibly wider ranging conspiracy.

The murder in question took place on June 5, 1983.

On that afternoon, a fifteen-year-old boy named Richard Dallas Kelvin was playing ball in an Adelaide park with some of his friends. After the sun went down, Kelvin said goodbye to his friends and took a city bus to his neighborhood. When he got off at the stop near his family's home, Kelvin began the less than one block walk but was nabbed off the sidewalk by Einem and thrown into a car.

When Richard never returned home, his parents were confused and worried. They called all of his friends and learned that he was last seen getting on a bus headed for their home. The police were called and quickly categorized the case as a possible abduction.

It turned out that Richard Kelvin's father was a popular news anchor in Adelaide, which brought the case to an entirely different level. The Kelvin family used their influence in the media to keep the case in the public eye and to keep pressure on the police. Within a week, the entire city of Adelaide was looking for Richard Kelvin.

While Richard's parents were doing whatever they could to find him, he was enduring excruciating pain at the hands of the sadistic Einem.

After abducting Richard, Einem brought him to a secret location that functioned as torture chamber. Einem bound Richard and forced him to take sedatives so he would be a more pliable victim. He then proceeded to beat and rape Richard for five weeks. Einem only gave Richard enough food and water to keep him alive, but it wasn't enough to overcome the shock that Richard's body had endured.

After Richard died, Einem discarded his body like garbage about ten miles outside of the city.

Needless to say, the Kelvin family was heartbroken when they learned Richard had been brutally murdered, but they were determined to help the police catch his killer or killers.

The investigation began with the autopsy of Richard's body. The examination determined that his body had suffered massive trauma and that he was dehydrated and malnourished at the time of death. The coroner ruled that the cause of death was due to massive bleeding from the anus, which was caused by repeated trauma from some type of weapon or instrument.

The publicity the case drew due to Richard's father immediately paid off with a number of tips. Witnesses who claimed to have witnessed the abduction said they heard screaming and then saw more than one man and a woman push Richard into a car.

The revelation that a group may have been behind Richard's murder was not new to the Adelaide Police in 1983. They had already received tips that a group of well-connected men were abducting and murdering area men, so the idea that Richard was a possible victim of this group was not totally surprising to them.

Still, they had to look at every possible theory and go where the evidence led them.

All of the evidence was leading them to Bevan Spencer von Einem.

The Arrest and Trial of Einem

When the police began compiling a pool of suspects for Richard Kelvin's murder, Bevan Spencer von Einem's name was on every list. His name was linked to other sexual assault investigations in the area, but he was the type of guy that seemed untouchable.

Despite receiving several anonymous tips about Einem, the police could never find any physical evidence that tied him to any crimes.

They couldn't even discover any circumstantial evidence that would be enough for an arrest.

Just when they thought that Einem would walk, a couple of astute investigators decided to check the accountant's prescription drug records.

The autopsy of Richard Kelvin determined that he had been drugged with the powerful sedatives Mandrax (Quaalude in the United States) and Noctec and a records check revealed that Einem had prescriptions for both drugs. It was enough for the police to obtain a search warrant for Einem's home.

Although Einem admitted to having the prescriptions for Mandrax and Noctec, he said that he no longer used the drugs and that there were none in his home. A search of Einem's home uncovered both drugs.

Samples of carpet fibers were also taken that were later matched to those found on Richard Kelvin's body.

The last piece of evidence collected against Einem was the testimony of an informant who said that he had abducted and raped, but not murdered, several young men with Einem throughout the 1970s.

All of the evidence was enough to bring murder charges against Einem on November 3, 1983.

When Einem went to trial, he was probably the most hated man in Australia. Details of his crime led to efforts to bring back the death penalty and numerous threats were made on his and his mother's lives. Before Einem's trial started, it looked as though it would be nearly impossible to seat a truly unbiased jury anywhere in the country.

In the end, it really didn't matter.

Although the evidence against Einem was mainly circumstantial, it was more than enough to win a conviction and he didn't do himself any favors with a weak defense.

He claimed that he knew Richard Kelvin, but never explained how. Einem's lawyers argued he couldn't have killed Kelvin because he was at home with the flu the night of the abduction.

The jury saw through Einem's weak defense and found him guilty of first-degree murder on November 5, 1984. He was sentenced to life in prison with a minimum of twenty-four years before he would be eligible for parole. Due to misconduct in prison, Einem's minimum stay behind bars was later increased to thirty-six years.But in many ways, Einem's conviction was only the beginning of the story.

Among the anonymous tips that the police received connecting Einem to Richard Kelvin's murder, a number detailed a well-organized group of influential men in the Adelaide area who tortured and murdered young men for pleasure.

Einem's Connection to The Family Murders

When Einem was sent to prison for what would more than likely be the rest of his life, many Australians thought they had heard the last of the sexual predator. But tips kept pouring in to the Adelaide Police Department that appeared to establish a nexus between Einem and an organized group of Adelaide professional men.

Adelaide homicide detectives took the claims seriously and opened an investigation into Einem's possible involvement in other murders and the existence of an organized group of sexual predators they named "The Family" after one of the detectives told a reporter that they were working to "break up the happy family" of sex offenders.

After reviewing all of the cold case murders of young men in the Adelaide area—along with those of missing young men—during the 1970s and early 1980s, the homicide investigators identified four unsolved murders, as well as the murder of Richard Kelvin, which they believed were the work of The Family.

The earliest known case was the abduction and murder of sixteen-year-old Arthur Barnes on June 17, 1979.

On that day, Barnes was hitchhiking to his suburban Adelaide home when witnesses reported he was picked up by a group of men in a single car. He was then given a sedative and driven to another location where he was repeatedly raped and beaten before he died from blood loss from his anus.

Arthur Barnes' body was found a week later floating in a reservoir northeast of Adelaide.

The next grisly discovery of The Family's nefarious activities came when the mutilated remains of twenty-five-year-old Neil Muir were discovered on the seashore northeast of Adelaide on August 28, 1979. Muir had gone missing two days prior.

The autopsy of Muir's corpse revealed he was murdered in almost the same manner as Barnes: he had been drugged with a sedative and died from an anal perforation.

After the discovery of Muir's body, the Adelaide Police responded by sending more officers into the streets, focusing on the city's many gay "cruising" spots. But the reality is that most of the victims of The Family weren't gay; they were just young men and kids looking for rides.

Although the investigation may not have been focused in the right direction, the sheer number of police officers involved, and the increased media attention that came with it, led to more tips from the public.

It was during this period that Bevan Spencer von Einem's name first surfaced in an investigation.

The police learned that Einem was one of the last people to see Muir alive, which meant that he had some questions to answer. Einem admitted to the police that he knew Muir and saw him around the time of the young man's disappearance, but denied killing him. The police were rightfully suspicious of Einem, but at the time they didn't have enough evidence to make an arrest.

While the police were investigating Einem, The Family struck again.

In February 1982, nineteen-year-old Mark Langley disappeared from a friend's birthday party. Langley and his friends were drinking alcohol throughout the evening, which eventually led to an argument. After some harsh words were exchanged, Langley had enough and left the party, deciding to walk across the city to his home.

Mark was offered a ride by a strange man, given a beer laced with sedatives, and then brought to another location where he was raped and tortured for two days.

He died from internal injuries, much like the other victims.

Mark Langley's case was a bit different than the other ones.

When Mark's body was discovered in the hills east of Adelaide nine days after his abduction, the homicide investigators immediately noticed that his body had been mutilated in a manner unlike the others.

The autopsy revealed that Langley's body had been surgically opened post-mortem, which indicated to investigators that at least one of the killers had advanced medical knowledge. Since the incision didn't appear related to the actual sexual abuse, investigators postulated that it was probably done to remove an item that had the killer's, or killers', fingerprints on it.

The final known victim of The Family was actually killed a few months before Mark Langley, but his body was discovered a few months later.

Fourteen-year-old Peter Stogneff spent the day of August 27, 1981 skipping school. When he never returned home that day his family frantically searched for him and eventually the police were called.

Peter's battered and partially decayed remains were discovered ten months later on farmland about forty miles north of Adelaide.

The police later stated that they believed Peter Stogneff was the fourth murder victim of The Family.

The Adelaide Police received countless tips about The Family, but tips aren't enough to make arrests, especially when the suspects are wealthy and connected. With that said, the Adelaide Police were able to compile a list of potential Family members, which included at least two doctors, lawyers, and the brother of a former Olympian.

The investigation led to charges being filed in 1980 against Adelaide doctor Peter Leslie Millhouse in the murder of Neil Muir. Millhouse hired one of South Australia's top criminal defense lawyers and was able to win a "not guilty" verdict in late 1980.

Another doctor named Stephen George Woodwards was charged with various sex offenses in 2011 when it was revealed that he too was an alleged member of the notorious Family. The charges against Woodwards were later dropped and he has never been charged with any of the suspected Family murders.

By the late 1980s, the Adelaide and South Australia authorities went back to the drawing board, focusing their attention on the one Family member they had in custody—Bevan Spencer von Einem.

Einem was charged with the murders of Mark Langley and Arthur Barnes in early 1990, although there was no physical evidence linking him to either murder. Of course, the circumstantial evidence linking Einem to the murders is great: both victims were drugged and murdered in almost the same way that Richard Kelvin was killed. The police knew that there was little hope in appealing to Einem's conscience because he probably doesn't have one. Instead, they hoped that once he was faced with the stark reality of spending the rest of his life in prison he would roll on the other Family members.

They were wrong.

Einem kept his mouth shut, forcing the Crown Prosecutors to drop the charges against him in late 1990.

Based on his actions behind bars, it is clear that Einem has changed little during his more than three decades behind bars.

He was accused of raping a younger inmate during his first few years inside and has had numerous write-ups and reports in the years since. More recently, Einem pleaded guilty to possessing child pornography in 2009.

Since most of The Family members are now dead and it doesn't appear Einem will give up his co-conspirators, it seems likely that the exact number of their victims will remain a mystery.

CHAPTER 11:

THE COVINA MASSACRE

At first glance, most, if not all mass murders appear to be impulsive acts that happen on the spur of the moment. The reality is that many mass murderers often devote a lot of time and planning their carnage. Many of these events involved multiple weapons and sometimes even explosives, which often takes time to collect.

There are also logistical issues to resolve.

If the mass murderer has targeted a specific location, then they will need to plan how to get their weapons to the location and how they will ensure a maximum kill count.

Sure there are mass murders that do happen in the heat of the moment, but most involve a certain level of planning. With that said, the day of the event usually doesn't seem to hold much significance for mass murderers.

But there are some notable exceptions where holiday celebrations were targeted by mass murderers.

On Easter Day, 1975, which also happened to be a day after his forty-first birthday, James Ruppert opened fire on his extended family, killing eleven men, women, and children in the process. It is believed that Ruppert's low self-esteem, lack of success in life, and envy of his brother are what drove him to kill and his choice of Easter for his attack made it that much worse.

Holidays, especially the religious ones, are supposed to be sacred times when families get together to share their love.

Ruppert forever ruined that idea in many people's minds.

Similar to Ruppert's Easter massacre, a more recent mass murder in Covina, California made the headlines across the United States for its kill count and more importantly for the fact that it happened on Christmas Eve.

In the Covina massacre, the killer showed up at a Christmas party in 2008 to extract revenge against the happy, idyllic family that he lost.

Bruce Jeffrey Pardo and Sylvia Orza

Bruce Pardo, who was known by most of his friends and family as "Jeff," was born in 1963 in Los Angeles. Growing up in southern California, Pardo enjoyed the benefits of the region, such as the weather and opportunities, and took the drawbacks like the traffic, smog, and crime in stride.

Pardo was a smart guy who never had any legal problems in his life. He made good money as an electrical engineer and because of his background he never had a problem finding a good paying job.

Still, like most successful people, Pardo wanted someone with whom he could share his wealth. Pardo never married, but he did have a child from a long-term relationship. The child was permanently disabled in a swimming accident, which Pardo responded to by cutting off all ties to his child and the child's mother.

This was an early sign of Pardo's egocentric attitude.

In the mid-2000s, Pardo was looking for a new woman to share his wealth with and who could possibly give him a child. His search brought him to Sylvia Orza in 2004.

Like Pardo, Orza was a life-long Los Angeles area resident who was also looking for a new partner. Orza came from a large Mexican-American family who were very close and trusting of anyone within their family orbit, which by 2005 included Jeff Pardo.

Sylvia was impressed by how well Pardo got along with her extended family and quickly fell in love.

Although Sylvia had children from a previous marriage, she believed that Pardo would step in and be an excellent father for them when they married. Pardo finally asked Sylvia to marry him in late 2005 and the two were married in January 2006.

The honeymoon didn't last long.

Almost immediately, everything that Sylvia believed and hoped Pardo would be, turned out to be the opposite. Most successful couples share household responsibilities, but Pardo refused, expecting Sylvia to cook and clean even after she worked a full day.

Pardo also refused to open a joint bank account with his new wife and wouldn't even consider helping Sylvia's children, even for the smallest things.

All of this had the effect of souring Sylvia on her new marriage, but things took a definite change for the worse when she learned Pardo had a child. Sylvia wasn't upset that he had a child, but that he had lied to her. When they began dating, Pardo told Sylvia that he had never been married and had no children. Besides exposing Pardo as a liar, the situation also uncovered his cold and selfish attitude toward the world.

Sylvia thought, if Pardo could coldly ignore and write off his disabled child, what else was he capable of?

She was clearly right to ask such a question, which led her to file for divorce. About a year after the couple married, the divorce was finalized. Pardo had to pay Sylvia nearly $2000 a month in spousal support.

The alimony payments quickly became a financial burden to Pardo, who found living in pricey southern California suddenly less interesting and enjoyable with $2000 less in his pockets every month.

Pardo seethed with rage. "How could she do this?" he asked himself and anyone who would listen.

Pardo's friends and family tried to take his mind off his ex-wife by inviting him on trips and to parties and by trying to fix him up with other women.

Nothing worked. Pardo only seemed to get worse by the middle of 2008, which began to become more apparent with his job. After failing to come to work numerous times and after racking up several write ups, Pardo was fired from his job in July 2008.

Jeff Pardo would not let these indignities go unpunished.

Killer Claus

On every Christmas Eve, Sylvia's parents would host a Christmas party in their Covina, California home. All of the extended family and many friends were invited, which would often bring the total of revelers up to nearly thirty people.

On Christmas Eve night 2008, there were twenty-five people in attendance, including several children.

One of the features of the Christmas parties was the arrival of a neighbor dressed like Santa Claus who would hand out presents. Although the neighbor had moved, another Santa showed up in 2008 to take his place.

The new Santa was Jeff Pardo.

Pardo showed up at the residence around 11:30 p.m. and rang the doorbell. He was allowed in with no questions; everyone was happy to see Santa and gathered around to see what he had.

Instead of pulling out presents, Pardo took out a nine millimeter pistol and began shooting into the crowd of revelers. After unloading a clip of ammo, he reached down and opened a gift-wrapped box he brought along. Inside the box was a homemade flame thrower that he used to wreak even more havoc on the house.

The house caught fire in multiple locations and burned to the ground.

After the fire department finally put the fire out, first responders were able to pull bodies out of the rubble. Pardo's final body count was nine dead and three wounded, making it one of the worst holiday mass murders in American history. Among the dead were Sylvia and both her parents.

After massacring his former in-laws, Pardo drove thirty miles to his brother's house.

It may be that Pardo planned to flee after committing the murders. He had $17,000 in cash strapped to his body and had purchased a one way plane ticket to Moline, Illinois.

But Pardo's plans were apparently dashed when he burned himself with the flamethrower.

Pardo's burns were not minor, either—his Santa suit had melted into his skin.

In immense physical pain and knowing that it was only a matter of time before he was captured, Pardo killed himself with a single gunshot to the head.

When the investigators cleaned up the mess in Covina and at Pardo's brother's home, they were left with more questions than answers. How long had he been planning the massacre and did he intend to flee the country?

Although those questions will never be answered, Pardo left the authorities with a final parting shot. The police discovered his car parked on a side street rigged with explosives. Luckily for the investigators, they noticed the explosives, but Pardo no doubt intended to increase his kill count, even from the grave.

CHAPTER 12:

THE MURDER OF
KRISTY MANZANARES

Every day around the world, thousands of people step onto ships to go on luxury cruises. Cruising on the high seas is a popular way to travel for many people because the cruise company handles most aspects of the trip, from meals to shore-bound excursions.

Although cruising is also a very safe method of travel, it is not without hazards.

Murder on the high seas has been a popular plot element in many different books, movies, and television shows, perhaps reflecting an element of danger that people recognize in relation to cruising.

There have been several recent incidents that illustrate the real hazards of sea travel. The 2005 disappearance of George Smith IV from a cruise ship is one of the more high-profile cases of cruising danger, but there are also numerous other cases where cruise customers were the victims of theft, fraud, and even sexual assault.

The 2017 murder of Kristy Manzanares is a real-life murder on the high seas, although the case seemed to be much more open and shut than an early twentieth century novel.

A Tragic Vacation

Kristy and Kenneth Manzanares were two Utah natives who met in high school and quickly became sweethearts. Like many young people in the conservative-dominated state, the couple married a couple of years after graduation.

The couple followed the biblical command of "being fruitful and multiplying" by having three children and building a respectable middle-class life in Utah. They were close to both sides of their extended family and maintained a large and dependable social network. Neither Ken nor Kristy used drugs or alcohol, and there were no signs of infidelity or abuse in the marriage.

By all accounts, the Manzanares family was as happy as could be.

The two thirty-nine-year-olds decided to celebrate their eighteenth wedding anniversary with their children and extended family on an Alaskan cruise.

The family flew to Seattle where they boarded the *Emerald Princess* cruise ship bound for Anchorage, Alaska.

For the first half of the trip, everything seemed to be going well. Ken and Kristy looked happy and spent considerable time alone together, but also with their children and parents. They were all one big happy family.

But about halfway through the trip, something went tragically wrong.

On the afternoon of July 25, a family member went to Ken and Kristy's cabin to see if they wanted to meet for supper, but was horrified by what he saw.

Ken was standing over a bloody and lifeless Kristy. When he was asked what happened, Ken responded, "She would not stop laughing at me." Ken then tried dragging Kristy's body to the cabin's balcony but was stopped by the family member who then called the ship's security.

Suddenly the ship was in the midst of a real-life murder mystery.

Life Imitating Art

Ken was immediately placed in a holding cell, and the ship was forced to divert its route to Juneau so that the FBI could take custody of the accused murderer.

Since a major crime had apparently happened, the captain was forced to place the ship on lockdown—all guests would have to stay in their cabins until the ship docked in Juneau. The ship's staff never announced why the ship was in lockdown, which left some of the guests perturbed, but many took it in stride.

It turns out that, as part of the ship's activities that day, there was a ship-wide murder mystery game taking place. Many of the guests simply thought the lockdown was part of the game.

"We just thought this was part of the dramatic effects they were using for the murder mystery," Ship guest Vic Simpson said. "And then two more times they came on and asked for more security and medical teams, but again it just fit in so well with the murder mystery because it was about a murder on a cruise ship. So really that night I didn't think anything about it."

The guests were rightfully shocked when they learned that a real-life murder had taken place right under their noses. Kenneth Manzanares pleaded guilty to second-degree murder and was sentenced to thirty years in prison in June 2021. The sentencing judge noted the "violent and brutal" nature of the crime and disputed the defense's claims of brain abnormalities and bipolar disorder as mitigating factors. Manzanares later died in prison in 2021.

CONCLUSION

No one can deny that the phenomenon of crime is truly intriguing. A glimpse into some of the most scandalous and high-profile crimes in recent decades reveal that crime comes in many different forms and is perpetuated by a variety of different people with many different results.

Most of the results are tragic and bad for society.

Criminologists say that one of the first steps toward alleviating crime in modern society is not only recognizing that it exists, but also understanding that it has many complexities.

This volume revealed that passion is a driver in many crimes just as much as greed or revenge. Some people let their passions for others go unchecked and eventually that passion turns into raw violence.

A type of violence that is capable of killing many people in a single instance.

Of course, although crime can happen at any time, and there is a good chance that you will be the victim of a crime at some point in your life, you can't live your life wondering when it will happen to you.

The cases profiled in this volume should serve as a warning of the potential dangers that can await us all and possibly as a guidebook to avoid becoming a victim, but you should never alter your life because of crime.

Live your life; after all, that's what these criminals are trying to take from you.

TRUE CRIME STORIES

STORIES

BOOK 4

INTRODUCTION

The criminal mind is a perplexing thing for most of us to understand. Scholars and mental health professionals have dedicated their lives to understanding and trying to solve what drives criminals. However, even after decades of research, numerous studies, and hundreds of books written on the subject, it seems we are no closer to understanding the criminal mind.

Part of the problem is that criminals are driven by different reasons and urges. The traditional thinking is that most crimes are committed out of necessity; to feed one's family, for instance. A closer examination reveals that most crimes are not committed due to economic desperation, especially in modern, industrialized countries that have social safety nets.

Unfortunately, criminals are driven by complex motives, some of which are truly very dark, and are nearly impossible for most people to understand.

In the pages of this true crime volume, you will be introduced to twelve of the worst crimes that emanated from some of the darkest souls in modern times. You will read about callous acts of rape, torture, and murder that were often done for no other reason than to appease some twisted fantasy.

The cases span nearly 100 years of history and took place in several different countries, but there are some themes that many share in common.

One of the primary themes of this volume is the unfortunate phenomenon of child murder. You will read about two serial predators—Donald Smith and Ian Huntley—and how they slipped through the system numerous times after victimizing people, only to commit one final fatal act that shook their respective communities.

The murder cases of Shanda Sharer, Kiaya Campbell, Ame Deal, and Shayla O'Brien/Elsie Scully-Hicks demonstrate that, in most cases, children are murdered by those close to them.

And in the Campbell and Sharer cases, the perpetrators were actually children themselves.

Crimes against another vulnerable group, the elderly, are also profiled in this book.

You will read about how a serial killer known as the "Granny Killer" curiously targeted elderly instead of younger women in his reign of terror that ended with the same results—death, destruction, and ruined families. We also cover the Thomas Grasso case. Thomas Grasso was a young man who preyed on the elderly because he thought they were easy marks, but in the end, he finally received his just dues.

As with all of the books in this series, there are also some crimes profiled that can only be described as strange or bizarre. The murder of a man with no identity is profiled, demonstrating just how difficult it can be for the police to solve a murder—even when they have a body, and know the method and time of death—if they don't know the identity of the victim.

Another case profiled shows how a dispute between two normally peaceful farmers over a dog bite quickly degenerated into a bloody family annihilation. The Grasso case also falls into this category because it was a rare instance where a criminal stoically accepted his death sentence, but it was a politician who actually fought to keep him alive.

Finally, you will read about Matthew Scully-Hicks and David Deal. Instead of protecting their children, these men were responsible for their deaths, making them perhaps two of the worst parents profiled in these volumes, which is saying a lot.

There is no doubt that the world can be a dark and foreboding place, as this book demonstrates. Although the answers to what drives criminals will not be answered in these pages, you will be better informed after reading it. Criminals can strike at any time, for any reason, and just knowing that will give you an advantage.

CHAPTER 1:

THE MURDER OF
SHANDA SHARER

Crime has many faces, some of which are extremely brutal. But even when one considers some of the most brutal crimes from the annals of crime history, many of those crimes have perpetrators and victims who might not fit the common stereotype of a brutal killer.

Statistically speaking, the most brutal crimes are perpetrated by adult males. The majority of serial killers and the overwhelming majority of mass murderers are also men. Perhaps this goes without saying since many of the most brutal crimes on record often have a sexual assault component. Adult men are also physically stronger on average and statistically more prone to violence than other demographics.

With that said, there are always exceptions.

Worldwide, there have been some shocking instances of violent youth crime in recent decades.

In the United States, the crime rate in general declined from the early 1980s, and while statistics can be complicated, the general trend for youth crimes has also trended downward. However, the twenty-four-hour news cycle and extensive coverage of some particularly heinous youth crimes mean that many perceive youth crime as having spiked. One only has to watch the local nightly news in any major American city to hear about cases where juvenile offenders have committed violent assaults and even murders.

The senselessness of some of these crimes defies explanation, and there seems to be no quick-fix answers or solutions on the horizon.

Some youth crimes stand out more than others due to their extreme brutality.

In 1983, two California teenagers named Cindy Collier and Shirley Wolf brutally murdered an elderly woman in her home for no other reason than it was "fun."

The shocking case terrified people across the United States as they asked themselves if this would become the standard of youth crime in the future.

Ten years later, the world was shocked by horrific youth crime once again when two ten-year-old boys named Jon Venables and Robert Thompson abducted two-year-old James Bulger from a shopping center in the United Kingdom and then tortured and murdered him.

Psychologists, psychiatrists, and criminologists have attempted to identify the source of these acts of teen brutality, but it seems that for every academic professional who asks the question, there are almost as many answers. An examination of most of these cases reveals that there is, in fact, never one single factor that leads to such brutality. Most of these cases stem from a combination of elements, a deadly cocktail of factors if you will, which often include abusive homes and underdeveloped minds that don't know how to handle such adversity.

In January 1992, another one of these brutal situations played out in southern Indiana.

In this case, all of the perpetrators were girls, all of them under the age of eighteen, who conspired to mercilessly torture and kill a twelve-year-old girl named Shanda Sharer. The crime was one that was brewing for several months before it happened and was driven by a lethal mixture of teenage jealousy, abusive homes, peer pressure, drug and alcohol abuse, and a lack of social development on the part of the killers.

The crime shocked the nation and continues to periodically make headlines.

Shanda Sharer

Shanda Sharer was born into a working-class family in Kentucky coal country in 1979. Not long after she was born, Shanda's parents divorced, with Shanda going to live with her mother, Jacqueline, on the other side of the state in Louisville. Jacqueline would eventually remarry, divorce, and remarry again in the late 1980s.

Needless to say, Shanda's early life was unstable.

Jacqueline moved the family frequently to find work, to live with boyfriends, or to find apartments that were more affordable. The frequent moves meant that Shanda had difficulties making lasting friendships during her youth, and she was often willing to go out of her way to make friends, which later proved to be her demise.

By the late 1980s, the familial situation had stabilized somewhat for Shanda, though, as her mother remarried for the third time and they settled down in the Indiana suburbs of the Louisville metropolitan area.

Shanda was doing well in terms of her grades and school work by the summer of 1991 and seemed to be well-adjusted and developing a large circle of friends.

All of that would forever change within a year.

Hazelwood Junior High School

Since Shanda was born in June, it was up to her parents when she would be enrolled in school: they could have either held her back to be one of the oldest in her class or sent her ahead, where she would be one of the youngest.

Jacqueline decided to enroll Shanda early.

There are, of course, benefits to enrolling a child early. Theoretically, they will graduate high school at the age of seventeen, giving them a head start on the professional world.

For the most part, it would seem as if it wouldn't matter either way. Yet a one-year difference in age can be a major factor in emotional maturity in the teen years. When Shanda began classes at Hazelwood Junior High School in New Albany, Indiana, in the fall of 1991, friends and family felt that she was overwhelmed by the fast pace and the more emotionally mature and sophisticated kids in her class.

Shanda's problems fitting in led to her having numerous conflicts with her teachers and other kids.

The problem was at least a bit exacerbated by Shanda's resolute nature and the fact that she was often unwilling to let minor offenses slide. Shanda found herself at the wrong end of teen bullying until she'd had enough and punched one of her bullies in the face.

The fight earned Shanda time in after-school detention alongside her bully, Amanda Heavrin.

Like most kids their age, the two girls quickly forgot their conflict when they had to spend their time with each other in detention. In fact, the two girls realized that they had a lot in common, namely their unstable home lives, and they quickly became best friends.

Within a couple of weeks, their friendship became romantic.

Shanda and Amanda decided to take their new relationship to the next level by going to the school dance as a couple in October 1991. Although American society was generally less tolerant of gay couples in 1991, especially concerning teens, the two girls didn't have any problems at the dance because of their sexual orientation.

They did run into a problem, though, that ruined their night and ultimately ended Shanda's life.

Among the scores of kids at the dance was a fourteen-year-old girl named Melinda Loveless. Melinda was an extremely troubled girl with little positive happening in her life at the time. Loveless thought that Amanda was her girlfriend, so when she saw her with Shanda, she exploded.

Although there wasn't a physical confrontation that night, Melinda let Shanda know in no uncertain terms that she was stepping into her territory.

The confrontation at the school dance was followed by other public confrontations, including one where Melinda threatened to kill Shanda if she didn't break up with Amanda.

Eventually, Shanda's mother and stepfather found out about their daughter's sexuality and her ongoing conflict with Melinda Loveless. They were not pleased that Shanda appeared to be a lesbian, but they wrote it off as a phase that a lot of girls her age were experimenting with—they were much more concerned with Melinda Loveless.

Shanda's mother heard that Melinda had quite the reputation in the area for engaging in promiscuous sex, using copious amounts of illicit drugs, and using violence when she didn't get things her way. Clearly, Melinda Loveless was the type of kid that instils fear in the hearts of most parents. Shanda's parents saw Amanda Hearvin as the source of their daughter's problems, so they took her out of the public school and enrolled her at Our Lady of Perpetual Help High School in New Albany.

They hoped that the change would do their daughter good and that she would make new friends who were more stable and "normal."

Shanda's first couple of months at Our Lady seemed to confirm that she just needed a change of scenery. She was in cheerleading, volleyball, and basketball, and seemed to have made a new group of friends.

But she kept seeing Amanda in secret.

Amanda's and Shana's secret love affair became even more intense until it finally erupted into a night of unmitigated violence.

Melinda Loveless and Her Crew

By their nature, teenagers are social creatures. Teens form kinship groups in high school based on factors such as similar tastes in music or clothes, interest in sports, or participation in academic clubs. Melinda Loveless and her friends were united by their generally anti-social attitude and their desire for drugs and alcohol.

And there is no doubt that Loveless was their leader.

In many ways, Melinda Loveless was the poster child for the general problem of youth crime in America. She was born into a terrible situation, which was only made worse by the decisions she made during her teen years.

Loveless was born in 1975 to a blue-collar family in New Albany, Indiana. In January 1992, she was seventeen but had probably seen more pain and misery in her short life than most people will in a lifetime.

Melinda's father, Larry, was a Vietnam veteran who washed out of the local police department after he returned stateside in the 1970s. Throughout all of Melinda's life, her mother, Marjorie, was the breadwinner in the Loveless family.

Larry rarely worked and, for the most part, didn't show much ambition.

But Larry was very enthused about sex.

Larry repeatedly cheated on Marjorie with other women, and he didn't care if his wife did the same. In fact, Larry intimidated Marjorie into engaging in group sex, and she claimed that he once had her gang-raped when she upset him.

According to eye-witness reports, Melinda and her two older sisters were not spared from their dad's demented sexual desires.

When Larry wasn't sexually abusing his wife and daughters, he was physically beating Marjorie. The repeated sexual and physical abuse led Marjorie to attempt suicide twice and to attack Larry with a knife on one occasion.

Melinda rarely heard from her father after he left.

The oldest member of Melinda Loveless' crew and right-hand woman was a girl named Laurie Tackett.

Tackett was born in 1974 to an equally dysfunctional family. Her father was a convicted felon, and her mother was a fundamental Pentecostal Christian. From an early point in her life, Tackett had a difficult time conforming to her mother's strict house rules. Laurie had to observe a strict curfew and wasn't allowed to have any toys or games that her mother believed were "Satanic."

Despite the strict Christian upbringing, Tackett would later claim that she was molested by adults close to her on more than one occasion.

By the age of twelve, Laurie began to rebel against her mother's rules, first in passive ways and then more directly. The squabbles and arguments between Laurie and her mother eventually led to a physical confrontation, which resulted in visits by county child protective services officials.

The visit didn't slow down Laurie's rebellious streak.

By the age of fifteen, Laurie had shaved her head and adopted the Goth look, wearing black clothing most of the time. Laurie also told her friends and whoever would listen that she was adept at black magic and other arcane forms of knowledge. She enjoyed playing with Ouija boards until her mother took hers away, and would offer to read people's fortunes using either Tarot cards or Norse runes.

Tackett also began cutting herself in her early teens. The cutting probably started as a means to gain attention and as a cry for help, but as with many kids who engage in that type of self-destructive behavior, it became somewhat habit-forming and addictive. It was even reported that Tackett showed other kids how to cut themselves to get the maximum amount of blood without hitting any veins or arteries.

Around the same time, Laurie Tacket also learned that she liked booze, drugs, and other girls.

Although she was Loveless' loyal henchwoman, the two had only met in November 1991, about two months before Shanda was murdered.

One of Laurie Tackett's friends from earlier in her childhood was Hope Rippey. Hope was a bit younger than Tackett—she was born in 1976 and fifteen in January 1992—which played a role in their relationship as she was clearly the follower of the two. Although Rippey had been born in the area, she had moved with her family to Michigan for a number of years. Before moving, Rippey and Tackett were innocent childhood friends, riding bikes and playing hide-and-seek, and engaging in other youthful games. When Rippey returned to the Louisville area in 1991, she noticed big changes in her older friend, but thought little of it. To Hope Rippey, Laurie Tackett was her older, cooler friend, and anything she said and did was what the cool kids did.

Rippey met Melinda Loveless for the first time on the night of January 10, 1992.

The final girl that filled out the frightful foursome was fifteen-year-old Toni Lawrence. Rippey was Lawrence's connection to Loveless, whom she had also just met on the night of January 10.

Lawrence, like the other girls, also grew up in a home filled with abuse and neglect. She was sexually abused at the age of nine and then again at the age of fourteen.

Since the abusers were those close to her, Lawrence refused to go to the authorities and instead decided to deal with the abuse on her own.

One of the ways in which Toni Lawrence dealt with the pain of the abuse was through self-harm and cutting, which she learned from Rippey.

Lawrence also began to self-medicate through binge drinking and drug use.

Finally, in a pattern that is often familiar with victims of sexual abuse, Lawrence became sexually promiscuous at a young age. By January 10, 1992, Toni Lawrence already had dozens of sexual partners, both male and female.

Loveless, Tackett, Rippey, and Lawrence were truly four broken souls who had been dealt bad hands in life and were no doubt worthy of sympathy, but that would all change after they committed one of the most brutal and senseless crimes of the decade.

The Murder

On the afternoon of January 10, Rippey and Lawrence met up with Tackett and the three girls, then drove to Loveless' house. The four girls spent some time in Loveless' bedroom listening to music, smoking marijuana, and engaging in small talk before Loveless decided to step things up a level.

Melinda produced a large knife and began talking about committing violent acts. She was probably trying to gauge the interest of Rippey and Lawrence, whom she had just met, to see if they would be open to hurting someone.

The ploy worked.

The more Loveless talked about violence, the more the other three girls giggled, as if she were discussing boys or some new clothes. Finally, Loveless told the other girls that she had a specific target for her wrath—Shanda Sharer.

Loveless explained to Rippey and Lawrence how Sharer "stole her girl" and that she needed to pay somehow for wronging her. Perhaps sensing that her two new friends were not on board with murder, or even a violent assault, Loveless said that she wanted to use the knife to scare her romantic rival. She would simply show the knife to Sharer and tell her to back off Heavrin. Having the other three girls would also help raise the intimidation factor, she argued.

Loveless then assigned each of the girls a role to play in the intimidation plot. Since Tackett was the only one with a car, she would be the driver. Rippey and Lawrence were delegated with luring Sharer from her family's home because they were unknown to her.

Tackett, Rippey, and Lawrence agreed to go along with Loveless' plan. None of them would even question any part of the plot, nor did they stop to consider how easily something like that could spiral out of control.

Teen peer pressure is a powerful force.

Early in the evening, the four girls drove to the house where Shanda Sharer's family lived to retrieve the unsuspecting girl. Rippey and Lawrence rang the front doorbell and were greeted by Shanda. Since they had never met before, Rippey and Lawrence explained to the somewhat confused Shanda that they were Amanda Heavrin's friends and that she wanted to see her.

Shanda was a bit skeptical and asked them why she didn't just call. The girls replied that her phone privileges had been revoked and that she would have to sneak out of her parents' house for the two to see each other.

Feeling eased by their answer, Shanda agreed to leave with the duo but said that she was grounded and couldn't leave while her parents were awake. She told the two to come back around midnight and to wait outside her bedroom window.

Rippey and Lawrence agreed.

In the meantime, the four girls drove to Louisville and attended a rock concert. While the show was happening, Rippey and Lawrence had sex with two boys in the parking lot. All four were drinking alcohol and smoking marijuana.

Life was just one big party for the girls.

Around 11:30 p.m., the four made the trek back to the Indiana suburbs, where they drove around for a while before stopping at Shanda's home just after midnight.

As Shanda walked with Rippey and Lawrence to Tackett's car, they told her that Heavrin was waiting at an abandoned building near the banks of the Ohio River that the local kids referred to as the "Witch's Castle." The Witch's Castle is much like other similar places dotted across rural America: it is a place where teens and young people gather at night to drink alcohol, do drugs, and engage in sexual activity. Also, like many of these places, many origin legends were ascribed to the place in question, some involving witchcraft and the occult, which is how it earned the nickname the "Witch's Castle."

When Shanda heard that she was being brought to the Witch's Castle, she had no reason to be worried. She knew that it was where the local kids did mischievous things, far away from the watchful eyes of their parents.

Unfortunately for Shanda Sharer, her trip to the Witch's Castle would be her last.

Shanda got into the passenger side of the car. As soon as it pulled away, Loveless emerged from her hiding spot under a blanket in the back seat. She quickly reached over and put her prized knife around Shanda's neck.

Loveless began threatening and berating Shanda as they drove to the Witch's Castle. When they arrived, though, it became clear that the four girls really had no plan. Loveless and Tackett berated and threatened Shanda while Rippey and Lawrence looked on, equally confused and exhilarated by the situation.

Shanda asked the girls to stop, but they refused. She asked why they were hurting her, to which Loveless allegedly replied, "You know why!"

After beating and threatening Shanda for several minutes, Loveless ordered the other three girls to hold their victim down so they could tie her up with some ropes. They then put her in the trunk of Tackett's car and left.

At this point in the evening, the girls had committed kidnapping and felony-level assault, but they were still far from crossing over to the point of no return. They could have let Shanda go and probably received probation in the juvenile criminal justice system—if Shanda had even gone to the police. Testimony given by the four girls at their subsequent trials revealed that Rippey and Lawrence never planned to go as far as they did and that even early in the abduction, they had misgivings.

Still, neither girl said so much as a word of dissent to Loveless.

The four girls then drove around rural areas of southern Indiana for a couple of hours. Eventually, Tackett drove down an isolated logging road and stopped the car. Loveless and Tackett were apparently thinking the same thing because without saying anything, they both went to the trunk of the car and pulled Shanda out to the ground.

It was a cold January night, but the adrenaline derived from their orgy of violence kept the girls warm.

Loveless and Tackett stripped Shanda's clothes off her body and brutally beat her until she was barely conscious. Loveless then pulled out her favorite knife and tried to cut Shanda's throat, but it was too dull.

The two girls then decided to strangle Shanda, but the athletic twelve-year-old proved to be tougher than they thought. Shanda fought the girls off successfully for a few minutes until Rippey came running from the car and held her legs down so that Loveless and Tackett could finish her.

After strangling Shanda for a couple of minutes, they loaded her back into the trunk and drove to Tackett's home to smoke some marijuana.

The girls miscalculated a couple of things, though. First, they didn't consider how strong their young victim was. Although Shanda was smaller and younger than the other girls, she was in good shape and athletic. She didn't spend her time drinking and doing drugs like the other girls. Loveless and Tackett also didn't consider how difficult it is to strangle someone. Perhaps they thought that killing a person via strangulation is as easy as it is portrayed in movies, with it only taking a minute or two to kill someone.

In real life, it takes several minutes for someone to die from strangulation.

As the girls sat around laughing and smoking pot at Tackett's home, they heard some strange noises coming from the garage.

Tackett went outside to check and was horrified by what she found—Shanda was still alive, fighting for her life in the trunk of the car.

Tackett went back into the house and grabbed a paring knife from the kitchen. She wasn't going to let Shanda live.

After stabbing Shanda several times, Tackett shut the trunk and rejoined the other girls. The four smoked some more pot before Loveless came up with the idea to dispose of Shanda's body. Once more, Tackett proved to be Loveless' loyal henchwoman.

Loveless and Tackett left the other two girls at the house around 2:30 a.m. and went for another drive in the backwoods. Incredibly, Shanda was still alive. The two girls heard Shanda beating on the trunk as they drove, presumably trying to get out of her hellish prison.

But there would be no mercy for Shanda Sharer on this night.

The two girls pulled the car over, opened the trunk, and beat Shanda repeatedly with a tire iron. They then drove to a convenience store where they bought some gasoline, which they put in an empty Pepsi bottle. After driving around for a while longer, they finally stopped on what they thought was a fairly deserted road. They pulled Shanda out from the trunk of the car, dragged her to a grassy area, poured the gas on her, and lit her on fire.

The autopsy would later show that Shanda was still alive when she was immolated.

Loveless and Tackett then drove back to the house, where they met the other two girls. The four had a few laughs about the whole affair, and Tackett proposed that they have a séance to ask Shanda's ghost how it felt to be burned alive.

The crew decided instead to have breakfast at a local McDonald's, where they laughed some more about their heinous crime and made a pact to never tell anyone.

Loveless broke the pact as soon as they left when she called Hearvin to tell her what she had done for her.

Arrests and Trials

The lack of planning and criminal sophistication on the part of the girls led to their quick capture.

As soon as Loveless told Heavrin about the murder, she, in turn, told others.

On the morning of January 11, two passing motorists noticed what they thought was a strange-looking pile of burning debris on the side of the road. When they got out for a closer look, they were horrified to see that it was the remains of a person.

They immediately called the local police.

The police didn't immediately connect the discovery of the burned body to the murder of Shanda Sharer. Although Sharer's parents reported her missing, it would still be a few hours until the connection was made, due to a confession by one of the killers.

Toni Lawrence participated the least in Shanda's murder. When she went home on the morning of January 11, her conscience began to bother her. The more she tried to forget about the screams and the blood, the louder those screams got. Finally, Lawrence went to her parents and told them about her role in the murder.

Toni's parents brought her to the New Albany Police Department that night, where she gave a full confession of the crime.

The other three girls were arrested the next day.

The crime, of course, became a major news story throughout the United States and brought to the forefront the issues of youth crime and violence. Residents of the Louisville area were shocked and horrified that such a heinous crime could happen outside of the inner city.

One of the detectives working the case, Steve Henry of the Indiana State Police, perhaps summed up the sentiments that many in the region shared.

"If I said I hadn't lost sleep over this, I'd be lying," said Henry. "The hardest part is the age of the people we're dealing with."

But the young age of the girls would not be enough to spare them from doing time in an adult prison, or from even possibly getting the death penalty.

There was little defense that the four girls could put up in court. The physical, circumstantial, and eye-witness evidence against them was overwhelming. The only questions were: would they be tried as adults and, if so, would they be sentenced to death?

The first question was answered fairly quickly when a judge ruled that, due to the barbarity of the crime and the fact that all of the girls were at least fifteen at the time, they would be charged as adults.

Melinda Loveless and her crew were looking at doing some hard time care of the Indiana Department of Corrections.

The prosecutor kept dangling the prospect of the death penalty, which was enough to entice all four girls to plead guilty to various charges. Since Toni Lawrence was one of the youngest and the least criminally culpable of the group, the prosecutor allowed her to plead guilty to one count of criminal confinement (kidnapping), and she was sentenced to a maximum of twenty years in prison.

Lawrence was released from prison in 2000 and remained on parole until 2002.

Hope Rippey pled guilty to first-degree murder and was sentenced to sixty years in prison, which was later reduced on appeal to thirty-five years. Rippey was released from prison in 2006 and supervised parole in 2011.

Loveless and Tacket were both given sixty-year sentences for leading the attack and being the primary participants. Tackett was paroled in 2018, and Loveless was paroled in September 2019.

The case still periodically makes headlines as the girls, now women in their early forties, have been released. The case was even profiled on one episode of the *Dr. Phil* show that attempted to understand why kids commit such heinous acts. It has also been featured on more than one true crime television show.

The case has also been included in academic studies by professional criminologists, psychiatrists, and psychologists. It remains one of the worst cases of child-on-child murder in the United States.

To the people of southern Indiana, it will be a case that will forever haunt their once-quiet country roads.

CHAPTER 2:

THE MYSTERIOUS MURDER CASE OF ROLAND T. OWEN

Most of the cases profiled in this volume involve police investigations of one type or another. In the simplest terms, investigations are conducted to identify and arrest a suspect in a crime. Often when the police begin an investigation, they know—or think they know—who the culprit is but need to compile evidence that will lead to an arrest and conviction.

In real life, murder investigations and trials can be quite complex and often endure over the course of several months or even years. The investigations themselves can often be problematic.

The most apparent problems that arise in any murder case concern the evidence. Sometimes there appears to be an abundance of physical evidence, but upon further examination, it is revealed that the evidence has been degraded due to time or the elements. Even with the phenomenal advances that have been made in forensic science over the last thirty years, science does have limits.

Other investigations are hampered due to a lack of physical evidence. Crafty criminals who are versed in police procedures have shown an amazing ability to circumvent forensic examinations of their deeds, and in some cases, there is simply no evidence left at the scene.

But physical or forensic evidence is not the only type of evidence investigators use.

Long before forensic science, investigators often had to rely on eye-witness testimony to make arrests. Of course, there are many inherent problems with eye-witness evidence. For instance, many crimes are committed with no eye-witnesses around, and studies have shown that eye-witness testimony is often flawed.

Also, many times eyewitnesses are simply too afraid to come forward with their accounts.

All of these factors create nightmares for homicide investigators, but perhaps the most frustrating obstacle a detective faces is a victim with no name.

Unfortunately, there are millions of people who live on the fringes of society in the United States without proper identification. When these people become murder victims, the investigating detectives are often faced with their most difficult investigations. The investigators may quickly learn how the victim died, or even when they died, but the lack of a positive identity often prevents the investigation from progressing.

Who would've had a motive to kill this person? Who were this person's enemies? Was this person involved in a love triangle or shady business dealings?

When questions such as these cannot be answered, the case often turns cold.

This was the situation in one of the strangest murder cases profiled in this series.

On January 2, 1935, a mysterious young man checked into the Hotel President in downtown Kansas City, MO.

He never checked out.

It was later determined that the young man was beaten and stabbed to death during his stay, but it was the details surrounding the cases, or the lack thereof, which makes this crime truly mysterious.

No killer, or killers, were ever caught in connection to the crime, and in fact, no suspects were ever publicly identified, which all stemmed from the initial mystery about the identity of the victim.

Roland T. Owen Checks into Room 1046

On the afternoon of New Year's Day, 1935, a tall, husky young man walked into the lobby of the Hotel President in Kansas City and asked for a room. Although the young man was later described as decent-looking, he had a somewhat intimidating demeanor. He spoke in concise, matter-of-fact sentences, and his eye contact never wavered from those to whom he was speaking.

His intimidating façade was also at least partially due to the fact that he had cauliflower ear and a long scar on the side of his head.

He signed the guest registry as "Roland T. Owen" from Los Angeles, but never showed a driver's license. Hotel guests were rarely asked to provide identification back then, as hotels and motels were often viewed as places where a person could "get away" from their normal life.

To those who met Owen, it seemed as though he, too, was running from something.

Owen told the bellboy on duty that he would rather have stayed at another hotel downtown, but he didn't want to pay five dollars a night. Hotel rooms were much cheaper then, like everything else was in 1935 during the Great Depression.

When asked if he had a preference as to which floor, Owen replied that he wanted a room that faced the inner courtyard of the hotel instead of the street. The concierge didn't think much of the request at the time: he had seen and heard much more outlandish requests, so he simply fulfilled it without question.

The bellboy was a bit surprised that Owen had no bags; however, he had seen plenty of guests with no luggage, so he brought him to the room.

After the bellboy showed Owen the room and gave him the key, Owen took a comb, toothbrush, and brush from his overcoat pockets and put the items on the bathroom sink. He then told the bellboy that he wanted some clean towels.

Mysterious Visitors

Later that day, a maid came to room 1046 with some towels and to see if the guest needed anything else. The maid thought it was strange that the guest had all of the lights turned off, except for a lamp on a table. The guest said little to the maid other than that he needed the door to the room to remain unlocked.

Owen was adamant that the door stay unlocked, but he never said why.

When the maid was dropping off the towels to Owen's room, she noticed a handwritten note illuminated by the lamp that said, "Don, I will be back in fifteen minutes, wait."

During the next day, there was plenty of activity in and around room 1046.

Another bellboy who was working on the floor happened to overhear Owen on the telephone saying, "No, Don. I don't want to eat. I am not hungry. I just had breakfast."

Normally, the conversation would not have been something that caught the bellboy's attention, but he thought it was odd since he didn't see any food in Mr. Owen's room, and he hadn't left the room yet that day. Later in the day, while he was walking down the hallway, the bellboy heard two men having a conversation in room 1046.

Room 1046 was then quiet until the evening.

A woman who was staying in the room next to Owen's later reported to the police that she heard a man and a woman arguing in room 1046 that night, but paid little attention to it at the time.

There was also a report of a loud party on the floor that night, and another report of a sex worker wandering the floor looking for a client. It is unknown if these two events were related at all to the enigmatic Mr. Owen's stay at the hotel.

Owen was last seen that evening around 11 p.m., a few blocks from the hotel, when he flagged down a car he thought was a taxi. The man let Owen into his car and was immediately struck by the young man's appearance—he was wearing no overcoat during a Missouri winter and was bleeding from his arm. When asked about the wound, Owen only said that he was going to kill the person who did it.

The driver dropped Owen off at the Hotel President and never saw him again.

Phone off the Hook

Around 7 a.m. the next day, the hotel's switchboard operator noticed that the phone in room 1046 was off the hook. Bellboy Randal Propst was sent to the room to see what the problem was, but when he arrived, the room was locked with a "do not disturb" sign posted on the door handle. Propst yelled for the guest to put the phone back on the hook and left to do other work.

A couple of hours later, the switchboard operator noticed that the phone in room 1046 was still off the hook. Another bellboy was sent to the room, but it was still locked, so he used a passkey to enter. The bellboy noticed that the room was a bit messy and that Mr. Owen appeared to be naked and passed out drunk on his bed. He put the phone back on the hook and left.

Around 11 a.m., the switchboard operator noticed that the phone in room 1046 was once more off the hook. Propst was sent back to the room to rectify the situation, but oddly, the room door was now unlocked. He went inside to put the phone on the hook and immediately noticed a bloody Owen lying on the floor with his hands on his head. Owen told Propst that he "fell against the bathtub" and required medical attention.

Owen was brought to the nearest hospital, where he died later that evening.

The Investigation

As strange as the murder case of Roland T. Owen began, it only got much more bizarre during the course of the investigation. At first, the police were unsure if they had an accident on their hands as Owen claimed, or if it was something much more nefarious.

The initial investigation quickly determined that it was the latter.

In 1935, homicide investigators didn't have the luxury of advanced forensic science to help them solve cases, but they did have other tools at their disposal.

Homicide investigators employed the same tried-and-true investigation methods that have been successful throughout time. Plus, they were unhampered by civilian oversight and Supreme Court rulings on the rights of suspects, such as *Miranda v. Arizona* (1966).

But finding a suspect in Roland Owen's murder would prove to be elusive.

Upon entering room 1046, it quickly became apparent that Owen had been murdered. There was blood on the walls and ceilings, most of it dry, which led the investigators to conclude that the fatal attack had happened hours before Propst found Owen in a stupor.

Owen was attacked and left for dead before he apparently tried to call someone for help. It is believed that he knew his attacker, or attackers, and for whatever reason, he refused to reveal their identities to the police.

It also became apparent that the killer (or killers) may have been in Owen's room longer than the hotel staff had originally believed. The phone was probably knocked off the hook in the early morning hours during the assault. The attacker (or attackers) then left the room and placed the "do not disturb" sign on the door to give themselves time to get away.

After the phone was put back on the hook, Owen may have tried calling a doctor for help, but was unable to complete the call, passed out from blood loss, and left the phone off the hook once more.

Before he passed out, Owen either unlocked the door for some reason that will remain a mystery, or the bellboy who was there the second time that morning didn't lock the door on the way out.

Or the killer (or killers) were hiding in the room somewhere, and he didn't see them.

Furthermore, the chronology of the discovery raises subtle yet significant questions about the crime scene. At 8:30 am, the bellboy found the door to Room 1046 "locked—from the outside." This detail is important because a door locked externally typically implies the occupant is not inside, yet Owen was found nude and passed out on the bed. The bellboy used a passkey to enter. At 11:15 a.m., the room was found to be unlocked, and Owen was discovered conscious but injured.

The sequence—locked from the outside, then later unlocked—suggests the killer initially secured the room after the assault to delay discovery, or Owen unlocked it before collapsing from his injuries. These perplexing details contributed to the ambiguity that defined the original police investigation.

A number of other small clues were discovered in the hotel room that helped investigators piece together Owen's last few hours of life.

A hairpin was found on the floor, which indicated that a woman was in the room at some point during the two days. There were also four unidentified fingerprints on the lamp Owen used. Due to the small size of the fingerprints, the investigators believed they were left by a woman.

Finally, there was a label from a tie on the floor and an unsmoked cigarette. It did not appear that Owen was a smoker, and the label didn't belong to the tie he was wearing, so it is believed that there was another man, as well as a woman, in the room, which would fit the eye-witness accounts of hearing both male and female voices in room 1046.

The police actually had a fair amount of physical evidence at their disposal, but their investigation was stymied by the fact that they couldn't identify their victim. He had no identification on him, nor any personal effects that could point toward a possible identity.

Who Was Roland T. Owen?

Within days, the police found themselves at an impasse in the Roland T. Owen murder investigation. The murder took place before televisions were common and decades before television shows such as *Unsolved Mysteries* and *America's Most Wanted* helped investigators solve cases through nationwide tip lines.

The only forms of mass media available at the time were radio and newspapers.

The Kansas City Police put Owen's body on display at a local funeral home, hoping that some locals would recognize the murder victim. A sketch artist was also hired to draw a portrait of Owen that was published in the Kansas City daily newspaper.

A number of tips were generated.

It turned out that Owen had used several different aliases around Kansas City and that he was often seen in the company of young, attractive women. The police began thinking that Owen was the victim of a love triangle gone wrong. Just when they were about to move on that theory, they received a number of other tips that sent the investigation into several different directions.

One of the stranger tips that was made during the months immediately after the murder was publicized was from a local professional wrestling promoter. The promoter claimed that Owen was a former wrestler named "Cecil Warner." The Kansas City Police followed up on the wrestling tip but determined that Warner and Owen were not the same man.

In March 1935, a man called the Kansas City Police Department switchboard claiming that the murder victim found in room 1046 was his brother-in-law and that his name actually was Roland T. Owen. The caller told the police that he wanted to remain anonymous and offered few details other than to say that Owen had been in trouble with some people in the criminal underworld. He added that the investigators were on "the wrong track" concerning the love triangle theory.

Another major twist in the investigation came when money was sent to the Kansas City Police Department for Owen's burial with no return address.

The police honored the wish of whoever sent the money by arranging for the burial and even having a short funeral ceremony. The ceremony was conducted not so much for the deceased, but more so with the hope that Owen's killer, or someone who may have known about his murder, would attend.

Before the ceremony was conducted, a bouquet of roses was sent to the funeral home conducting the burial for Owen with the note, "Love forever – Louise."

Only the investigators attended Owen's funeral.

As Roland T. Owen's murder investigation limped along throughout 1935, it seemed clear to many that the case would probably never be solved, largely due to the fact that Owen, or whatever his name was, could not be positively identified. In 1936, though, the police received what seemed to be their most credible tip concerning Owen's true identity.

A middle-aged woman named Ruby Ogletree contacted the Kansas City Police and told them that Owen was really her son, Artemus Ogletree. According to Ruby, Artemus left their Birmingham, Alabama home in 1934 at the age of seventeen to find adventure and make a life for himself in the midst of the Great Depression.

Ruby Ogletree was adamant that her son was the man shown in the pictures in the newspapers as Roland T. Owen.

Although many people believed Ruby's story and considered the identity of Owen solved, a number of "loose ends" remained.

Ruby received three typewritten letters from someone claiming to be Artemus Ogletree in the months after Owen's murder. At first glance, it seemed as though Ogletree and Owen were two different men, but Ruby pointed out that her son didn't know how to type. Of course, Ogletree could have had someone type the letter for him, but why? Ruby also received a phone call from a man who claimed Ogletree had saved his life and was now living in Egypt.

Ruby Ogletree never again heard from her son.

279

Many now believe that Owen and Ogletree were the same man and that the letters and phone call were hoaxed by his killer, or killers.

The reality was that Artemus Ogletree was like many young men his age during the Great Depression. Due to the lack of work and money in the country, young men often had to travel just to get by, and some found it convenient to use aliases for whatever reason.

With so many red herrings and dead ends, the Roland T. Owen murder mystery gradually sank from the headlines and became a cold case, long before the term "cold case" was part of the standard police lexicon.

But the case was not forgotten.

The Owen murder case briefly re-emerged in the Kansas City headlines in 1937 when it was revealed that a similar murder had occurred in New York City that year. In the New York case, similar to the Owen case, a mysterious man with no known identity was killed in a hotel. Despite the outward similarities of the two cases, however, investigators couldn't find any conclusive evidence that linked the murders, so the New York murder was believed to have been a macabre coincidence.

The Kansas City investigators received another red herring in 2003 when an anonymous call was made to the Kansas City Library by a man claiming to have important information regarding the Owen murder case. The caller said that he had been going through the possessions of a recently deceased family member when he discovered a box full of news articles and press clippings related to the Owen case.

The tip was followed up on, but the person in question was determined to be unrelated to the case.

Today, even with the immense amount of advanced forensic technology at investigators' disposal, it seems doubtful that the mystery of the murder at the Hotel President will ever be solved.

CHAPTER 3:

THE WOLF FAMILY MURDERS

Generally speaking, crime is a phenomenon that is primarily urban, and the worst aspects of it tend to be modern, or at least that's what most people think. Crime rates are traditionally much lower in rural areas of the United States, even in some of the most economically depressed regions such as Appalachia, and this was even more true in the early twentieth century.

The sub-category of mass murder was especially rare before the 1960s.

Charles Whitman's assault on the University of Texas campus in Austin, Texas, in 1965 is generally thought of by scholars as the first case of mass murder in the modern era. Whitman's massacre was the first in a line of many mass murders that have included family annihilations, school shootings, and workplace massacres.

But crime still takes place in small towns and did well before 1965.

Occasionally, some small towns were even rocked by mass murder.

On a cold spring day in 1920, eight people were found shot and hacked to death on a farm outside the small farming town of Turtle Lake, North Dakota. The predominantly immigrant community of the area was shocked by the discovery, with many of the residents wondering if they had made the right decision by coming to America. An understaffed and underfunded sheriff's department poured all of its resources into catching the killer of the family, but in the end, the killer led the police right to him through a mile-long trail of circumstantial yet incriminating evidence.

The Wolf Family

The road that brought farmer Jakob Wolf and his family to their violent demise on April 22, 1920, was certainly a circuitous one that was full of many twists and turns. Jakob and his wife Beata were born in the Volga region of Russia and raised in a community of German-Russians known as Volga Germans.

The Volga Germans were first invited to Russia by the Empress Catherine II—more commonly known as Catherine "the Great"—to tame the wild lands of the Volga region. Despite the substandard soils of the region, the Volga Germans applied their work ethic and farming experience to make the region productive, and their numbers grew.

But the Volga Germans soon learned how difficult life in Russia could be.

They suffered raids by Tatar bandits and were subjected to the capricious nature of the tsars and then the Bolsheviks. As a result, the Volga Germans began immigrating to the United States, Canada, and Argentina in the late 1890s, looking for greener pastures.

Many of the Volga Germans settled in the US Plains States, which they found to be very similar to the Volga region in terms of climate and soil. Many of the men worked on the railroads until they saved enough to buy land and then sent for their families. As they did in Russia, the Volga Germans developed tight-knit communities that were high in social trust and religious convictions yet low in crime. The Volga German communities in the United States were somewhat insular and clannish, but not near to the same level as they were in Russia.

The Volga German immigrants learned quickly that their American neighbors were friendly and helpful if given a chance.

Jakob Wolf was drawn to a rural stretch of land about forty-five miles north of Bismarck through some of his friends and relatives from the Volga German colonies in Russia. He was told about how cheap land was and that it was much more fertile than what they were used to farming in Russia.

Wolf was particularly intrigued by how little the government interfered with farmers in America.

Wolf moved his family to North Dakota, bought the stretch of land he had been told about, and promptly set about to grow his family and build a successful farming business.

Like most of the Volga German immigrants, no matter their sectarian affiliation, the Wolf family was large and always growing. On April 22, 1920, the Wolf family consisted of Jakob, the forty-one-year-old father; Beata, the thirty-six-year-old mother; and daughters Bertha (twelve), Maria (nine), Edna (seven), Liddia (five), Martha (three), and Emma (eight months).

The large size of Jakob's family was a symbol of success among the Volga Germans, but so too was his success as a farmer.

Jakob Wolf possessed the lucrative combination of a green thumb and financial acumen. He knew when to plant his crops, where to plant them, and when to harvest, in order to maximize the yield and therefore the profits. Wolf also seemed to know when to expand his business and was eventually able to hire a thirteen-year-old boy named Jacob Hofer as a full-time hand.

Most in the community came to respect Wolf as a good father and husband and an excellent farmer and businessman. But despite the strong community bonds and pious nature of the Volga Germans, they were also susceptible to the human emotion of envy.

Not all of Jakob Wolf's neighbors respected his success.

Dispute with a Neighbor

Jakob Wolf got along with nearly all of his neighbors and was well-liked in town by both Volga German immigrants and generational Americans. He was seen as a good family man and an excellent farmer who would be willing to help most anyone.

But some people seemed to harbor resentment toward Wolf.

One man who truly had an axe to grind with Wolf was another Volga German immigrant named Henry Layer. Layer was angry because Wolf's dog bit one of his cows. Although this incident might seem easily resolved, Layer escalated the conflict over the course of several days.

A few days before April 22, Layer confronted Wolf on Mainstreet in Turtle Lake about the dog biting incident. According to witnesses, Wolf apologized for the attack and offered to work something out, but Layer was too irate to listen to reason. Some other men had to diffuse the situation, and both men went their separate ways.

But Henry Layer was the type of person who couldn't let things go. It also didn't help that he was clearly envious of Wolf's farming success.

The details of the events that transpired at the Wolf farm on the morning of April 22, 1920, will forever remain in question, but the local police were able to reconstruct the chronology based on available forensic evidence and statements given by Layer.

That fateful morning, Henry Layer drove to the Wolf farm to confront Jakob about the dog attack. Wolf allowed Layer into the house but immediately regretted his decision as the two men became engaged in a heated argument. Sensing that the situation was about to get out of hand, Wolf grabbed his double-barrel shotgun from a corner of the kitchen.

Layer made a move to grab the gun from Wolf, and a struggle ensued. As the two men fought for control of the gun, both shells were fired, killing Beata Wolf and Jacob Hofer, who were in the kitchen at the time.

Jakob Wolf then made a dash for the door, and Layer scrambled about the kitchen looking for more shells. After a brief yet frenzied search, Layer found the shells, reloaded, and ran outside, shooting Jakob Wolf dead.

At this point, Layer was in a killing frenzy and couldn't be stopped.

He noticed two of the Wolf girls run to the barn, so he followed them in and shot and killed both.

Layer saved his most heinous acts for last when he went back into the Wolf house. He found three more of the Wolf girls hiding throughout the house and mercilessly shot and hacked each one with an axe. He then dragged all of the bodies in the house into the basement.

After surveying the carnage he'd left in the house, Layer went back outside and dragged Jakob's body into the barn. He then covered all three bodies in the barn with dirt and hay.

Although Layer's massacre of the Wolf family was certainly methodical, he missed baby Emma sleeping in her crib. When news of the crime was first reported by the press, many people thought that the killer had a pang of conscience and refused to kill the baby, but it was later revealed that Layer simply missed her.

He would have killed her if he had seen her.

The farmhouses in southwestern North Dakota are far enough apart that one would have to be listening specifically for gunshots to hear them. Also, a few gunshots would not be out of the norm in rural North Dakota, especially in 1920, so nothing was reported until the next day.

When the next day came, some of the Wolf's neighbors noticed that their laundry was still on the clothesline from the previous day. The neighbors thought it was strange because Beata Wolf was an immaculate housekeeper who would never leave her family's laundry on the line.

There was also no visible activity around the Wolf's farm, which was strange since there were so many family members, and there was a lot of preparation to be done for the beginning of the planting season.

Neighbor John Kraft decided to drive over to the Wolf house later in the day. He was horrified when he found all of the bodies—and surprised to find baby Emma, hungry and cold but otherwise alright.

The McLean County Sheriff's Department suddenly found themselves confronted with a case of mass murder.

The Investigation

When McLean County Sheriff Ole Stefferud learned of the massacre just outside Turtle Lake, he knew that he had to work quickly to solve the crime. Stefferud didn't have the luxury of modern forensic technology nor the big budget of a major city's police department, but the Scandinavian-American investigator did possess the straightforward, pragmatic nature that was, and still is, so common in that part of the country.

Stefferud knew that he could solve the case through good old-fashioned police work.

The sheriff's police intuition told him that the perpetrator was not your average run-of-the-mill criminal—nothing of value appeared to be missing from the home, and the level of violence didn't fit the M.O. of any criminals he knew in the area.

Stefferud deduced that the killer was someone who knew the Wolfs and had some type of personal grudge against one or more members of the family. He also believed that the killer was not a seasoned criminal and probably made, or would make, a number of mistakes, such as returning to the scene of the crime.

To test his theory, Stefferud decided to stake out the Wolf farm. Early in the day, Stefferud drove to the Wolf house and parked his car around the back, where it wouldn't be seen from the road or if a car drove up the driveway. He then went into the house and waited there in total darkness.

After a few hours of waiting, a tired Stefferud noticed a car coming down the driveway to the house. A male driver got out of the car and began looking in the ground-floor windows.

The sheriff crept quietly out of the house and snuck up behind the peeping Tom.

"I'm the sheriff," said Stefferud in a flat yet firm voice. "My name's Stefferud. Who are you?"

"Layer," the window peeker replied. "Henry Layer, I live not far from here. My, isn't this a terrible thing!"

The sheriff said little more to Layer, but immediately put him at the top of the suspect list.

Layer's visit to the crime scene may have been written off by the investigators as a macabre field trip, but a number of other things he said and did in the weeks after the murders made him look even more guilty.

Almost immediately after the massacre, Henry Layer inserted himself into the investigation. Layer routinely visited the sheriff's department office to ask about progress on the case and to offer his insight, no doubt to put the investigators on the wrong track.

As Layer was attempting a campaign of subterfuge, the police learned of his conflict with Wolf. He told Stefferud that the disagreement between him and Wolf was a minor, everyday type of conflict that farmers often have and that he harbored no ill will toward Wolf. The investigators may have normally believed Layer's version of the events, but more and more pieces of evidence were falling into place that made Layer look like the killer.

Besides inserting himself into the investigation and having a known conflict with Jakob Wolf, Layer acted bizarrely at the Wolf family's funeral. All of the members of the family were put to rest together, with most of the town attending the funeral. Layer was there as well and was noted for his overly emotional histrionics that many thought appeared more theatrical than genuine.

Finally, Layer had no credible alibi for the time of the murders. He initially told the investigators that he was with his daughter at the time, but she failed to corroborate his alibi.

To the McLean County investigators, it clearly looked like Henry Layer was their man, but even in 1920, they needed more than just a hunch to make an arrest and get a conviction.

A possible break in the case came when a gun was found in a nearby swamp. The gun was the same gauge as the one used in the murders, and it had only recently been dumped at the location, which led the investigators to believe that it was the murder weapon. Unfortunately, no fingerprints could be lifted from the gun, and it was unregistered, so it couldn't be traced to an owner.

Sheriff Stefferud had to resort again to more traditional law enforcement methods to catch the killer.

On May 13, despite a lack of evidence, Henry Layer was arrested for the murders of the Wolf family. Stefferud knew that there was not enough evidence for the charges to stand up in court, so he put all of his effort into exacting a confession from Layer.

Fortunately for Stefferud, 1920 was long before the landmark Supreme Court ruling, *Miranda v. Arizona*.

There is no evidence that Layer was physically assaulted during his interrogation, but he was denied food and sleep for several hours. Despite the constant badgering by the investigators, Layer continued to deny his involvement in the murders. Stefferud saw that playing "bad cop" wasn't working, so he decided to use a different tactic—he appealed to Layer's conscience.

Stefferud placed a number of photographs of the Wolf family's bodies on the desk in front of Layer in the interrogation room and said nothing. He simply let Layer look at the pictures, hoping to invoke a response.

The tactic worked.

Layer confessed to all of the murders in detail and admitted that indeed the killings were the result of the conflict over Wolf's dog biting one of his cows.

In 1920, the justice system moved extremely quickly. Layer pleaded guilty to the murders the next day in court and was sent to the state prison with a life sentence two days later.

It seemed as though Sheriff Stefferud had brought some peace back to Turtle Lake, but there were still some loose ends that were never completely addressed.

Post Script

As with most high-profile murder cases and certainly one of this magnitude, not everything was resolved when Layer was sent to prison. Not long after he arrived at the state prison, Layer recanted his confession, claiming that he only did so under duress. Although there is certainly some truth to his being under duress, Layer never offered an alternative theory or explained why he acted so strangely after the murders.

Layer died five years into his life sentence.

The Layer family was hit hard by the case. Layer's wife and children became pariahs in the tight-knit Volga German community, and they had no source of income after Henry was sent to prison. Four of his children became wards of the state, and one died two years later in a farm accident.

Emma, the lone survivor of Layer's massacre, was sent to live with relatives and by all accounts went on to have a stable, fulfilling life. She married, had a family of her own, and died at the age of eighty-four in 2003.

The Volga German community around Turtle Lake has mostly assimilated into the larger community. No one is alive today who could remember the Wolf family massacre, which has helped to heal the wounds.

The town of Turtle Lake itself has received a bit of a financial and population boost recently due to the discovery of oil in the Bakken Formation and the subsequent rush. Few people who have moved to the area to work in the oil fields know about the Wolf family massacre, which is probably fine by the area's generational residents.

CHAPTER 4:

THE GRANNY MURDERS

Along with children, the elderly are the most vulnerable demographic group in any society. Unfortunately, their vulnerabilities often make them the victims of crime.

There are several factors that lead predators to prey on the elderly. Most obvious is the fact that the elderly are often not strong enough to fight off robberies and physical attacks. The average criminal looks for easy marks and victims who will give minimal resistance, so the elderly are often preferred over younger, stronger victims.

The fact that many senior citizens live alone also contributes to their becoming crime victims. Criminals prefer to operate in the shadows and to leave as few witnesses to their crimes as possible, so an elderly person living alone is an optimal target in many ways.

Finally, the numerous medical maladies that come with old age play a role in the victimhood of senior citizens. Elderly people afflicted with ailments such as dementia and Alzheimer's disease often find filing a police report difficult, and if a case goes to trial, their testimony is questionable. Also, physical diseases can limit an elderly person's ability to even call for help.

Despite the sobering statistics that show that elderly people often have a greater chance of being crime victims in general, there is one category of crime that they are less likely to face—serial killing.

The average serial killer prefers to hunt victims who are often considered society's "throwaways"—sex workers, homeless people, drug users, and alcoholics. When serial killers target vulnerable demographics, it tends to be children instead of the elderly. The reasons for this preference aren't known: perhaps it's because most serial killers are younger to middle age when they start, or it could have to do with access to victims.

Whatever the reasons, serial killers who target senior citizens are extremely rare, which makes the next case that much more interesting.

In 1989 and 1990, a serial killer stalked elderly women in suburban Sydney, Australia. Most of the victims were well-off to wealthy, and many of the murders took place in broad daylight near many witnesses.

The case became known as the "Granny Murders" due to the victims' ages, and it presented law enforcement officers with a quandary because they were faced with an entirely new type of serial killer profile.

But once John Wayne Glover was arrested for the murders, a closer look at his background revealed that although he may not have fit the standard serial killer profile in terms of victimology, he possessed many of the other attributes of a typical sociopath.

John Wayne Glover

John Wayne Glover was born in 1932 in Wolverhampton, United Kingdom. As a child, Glover was often hungry and had few luxuries due to rationing during World War II. He was said to have taken the situation in stride, but he also began running with a tougher crowd of older kids. While hanging out with these older kids, Glover learned how to steal food and money to avoid hunger.

Glover had no moral compunctions about stealing, with the War being an excuse instead of a reason to commit criminal acts. He rarely shared his ill-gotten gains with his family, often stealing from those closest to him.

Glover's petty thefts continued until he was arrested numerous times in his teens. He spent considerable time in state juvenile detention facilities.

Having no direction or academic ambitions, Glover joined the military in the mid-1950s. He thought that the military would give him some job and life skills, but he was promptly discharged when military officials learned that he had lied about his juvenile criminal record on his application.

Dejected, Glover went back home to live with his mother, Freda.

Most serial killers express traits in their childhoods that point toward their murderous potential. One of these traits, which Glover clearly exhibited, is a fractured and perhaps unnatural relationship with one's parents.

Glover never knew his father, and his mother was an overbearing and pushy woman. As Glover aged, he grew to resent, and eventually hate, his mother. For her part, Freda didn't seem to care what her son thought of her. She never tried to hide her alcohol abuse from John, nor did she seem to have any shame about the constant line of men who came and went from their home.

Freda married and divorced several times during her lifetime, but none of the men she was with ever took an interest in providing John with a positive male role model.

In reality, most of the men Freda Glover associated with were far from being role models, as most were alcoholics, drifters, and criminals.

John Wayne Glover had to learn how to be a man on the streets.

As Glover went from one low-paying job to another, he grew tired of life in England but had nowhere to go. He spent most of his free time dreaming about making it big until he heard a commercial on the radio about immigration to Australia.

During the early part of the twentieth century, the Australian government embarked on an official program known as the "White Australia Policy." The program barred or severely limited immigrants from traditionally non-White countries, while promoting immigration from White countries, especially English-speaking countries such as the United Kingdom, Ireland, Canada, and the United States.

Since Australia was still in the Commonwealth of Nations, immigration from another Commonwealth country, such as the United Kingdom, was much easier.

John Wayne Glover applied for and was granted a residence and work permit for Australia in 1956. Once he moved Down Under, he never returned to the UK.

Glover's move to Australia did little to mitigate his propensity and penchant for crime. He racked up several convictions in the states of Victoria and New South Wales for theft and fraud, but more ominously, the types of crimes he engaged in began to escalate.

While Glover kept committing crimes for financial motives, he was also arrested for a number of minor sex offenses in the early 1960s. Actually, some of those crimes would be considered major by today's standards—attempted sexual assault and exposure will certainly get one placed on any sex offender registry today—but they were reduced through plea bargains.

Although he was caught on several occasions, John Wayne Glover was learning important lessons about the system and how to get away with satisfying his dark desires. As he committed lesser sex crimes on the streets of Melbourne and Sydney, he learned that stealth was his ally. Glover was arrested for a number of his crimes because he spent too much time at the crime scene, so his M.O. evolved to include quick strikes, where he would either break into a place or commit a sex act and then leave quickly.

Glover also learned that, in a big city, anonymity could be a criminal's best friend.

He preferred to prowl in areas that he knew but where he didn't necessarily have a connection in terms of work or family.

Glover was also helped by the fact that he was a rather nondescript-looking guy. He could blend in relatively well with a crowd, and despite his abnormal sexuality, he was intelligent enough to keep that hidden from most people. He was also articulate enough to be able to strike up a good conversation with most people.

By his late twenties, John Wayne Glover had developed all the tools a successful serial killer needs.

With that said, Glover had also built up a respectable public persona by the late 1960s. He married in 1968 and later had two daughters. By this time, his last run-in with law enforcement was several years prior. He became a successful salesman for the Four'N Twenty meat pie company and eventually bought a nice home in the Sydney suburbs.

To everyone who knew Glover well, it looked like he had turned the page on his criminal past by 1970.

That couldn't have been further from the truth.

The Façade Slowly Crumbles

In fact, by the mid-1970s, Glover's hatred of his mother was compounded by an equally negative feeling toward his mother-in-law. Glover rarely confronted either woman, instead letting his feelings for them fester and brew into a bizarre fetish for all elderly women.

"We can only assume, but a lot of it goes back to his own life," said one of the detectives who worked on the Granny Murders. "He did have a very serious dislike of his own mother and mother-in-law, what could have amounted to hatred."

But like nearly every successful serial killer, Glover was able to hide his true feelings from those closest to him.

Unable to suppress his unnatural feelings toward elderly women any longer, Glover decided to instead feed his impulses in a gradual way. He began volunteering at nursing homes in the 1970s, where he was able to spy on vulnerable, elderly women. Eventually, Glover became bolder and more confident and started entering women's rooms without permission, often fondling them before quickly leaving.

Glover got away with these crimes because, just like a true predator, he sized his victims up before making a move. He usually targeted women with dementia or some other disability that limited their ability to either call for help or later give a statement.

In 1976, Glover's mother immigrated to Australia, which actually led to an increase in his serial molester activities. Although by all accounts he hated his mother and probably would've rather not seen her again after he left England, she developed breast cancer not long after moving to Australia and was forced to live in a nursing home.

Not long after, Glover's mother-in-law was also admitted to a nursing home.

By the late 1980s, Glover was a regular visitor to several of Sydney's nursing homes, always with a legitimate reason. If he wasn't volunteering in a nursing home, he was visiting his mother or mother-in-law, or he was making a sales call with the meat pie company.

Still, some of the staff at the nursing homes began to think it was strange that a middle-aged man would want to spend so much time in these places. Then, in December 1988, the curious staff members' suspicions were verified when he was accused of fondling a resident at a nursing home.

The police were called, but the victim was in no real condition to give a statement to the police, never mind testify in court if it were to go that far. The victim's family also wanted the case to go away, so charges were never filed against Glover.

The predator's victimology paid off, which would give him added impetus to attack more elderly women in the future.

John Wayne Glover was free to roam the streets of Sydney to find more victims.

The Series Begins

It remains unknown why John Wayne Glover made the drastic step from fondling to murder or why he did so at the age of fifty-six, which is considerably older than when most serial killers begin their killing careers.

Before he began killing, though, Glover took the next step by physically assaulting an elderly woman.

On the afternoon of January 11, 1989, Glover was walking around the affluent North Shore neighborhood of Sydney when he was gripped by his compulsion to victimize an elderly woman. Prior to this point, fondling his victims was enough to sate his desires, but on this day, he felt the urge to physically hurt someone.

Glover spotted eighty-four-year-old Margaret Todhunter walking down the street and quickly went in for an attack. He punched the senior citizen in the face and took her purse. Glover then took the more than $200 that he got from Todhunter and went drinking and gambling at the local RSL (Returned and Services League of Australia club; roughly the equivalent of VFW clubs in the United States.

John Glover had committed his first known act of violence against an elderly woman, but it was just the beginning of what would become known as the "Granny Murders."

The police investigated the assault on Todhunter, but they listed it as an average mugging, and the case was quickly forgotten. For his part, Glover was extremely worried about getting caught at first, although those fears quickly subsided when he never heard about the case on the news.

The pleasure that Glover received from assaulting Todhunter was quickly replaced by an even stronger desire to do more violence. Glover began thinking about violence and murder nearly every waking moment of the day and began planning his next move. The more he thought about it, the more he realized that the mugging of Todhunter provided him with a template for future crimes.

Glover decided that the North Shore would be his hunting grounds. He knew the area well, wouldn't stand out among the residents, and it was full of his favorite victim demographic—vulnerable elderly women.

Although Glover planned his crimes in terms of general location, he was a "disorganized" type of serial killer. He would often strike his victims unplanned and sometimes in daylight with witnesses nearby.

Alcohol also appeared to have played a role in Glover's murders.

After spending the afternoon of March 1, 1989, drinking at a local RSL club, Glover began walking home when he noticed eighty-two-year-old Gwendoline Mitchelhill walking the other way to her apartment.

The opportunity was just too good to pass up for Glover.

He turned around and began following the oblivious Mitchelhill and reached into his jacket pocket to pull out a hammer he had been carrying since the January 11 attack.

Glover waited until Mitchelhill was about to enter her apartment when he attacked. After striking her over a dozen times with the hammer, Glover grabbed his helpless victim's purse and took all the cash. He then quickly but calmly made his way home.

Gwendoline Mitchelhill was an incredibly strong woman for her age. Although barely conscious, she somehow crawled away from where Glover left her, apparently trying to get help, but unfortunately died a short time later.

When the police arrived, they found the crime scene literally "washed." Gwendoline's neighbors found her bloody and broken body, and after calling the police and paramedics, they decided to clean the blood from the apartment's entryway.

It was the first time, but not the last, that fate and circumstances would facilitate Glover's murderous rampage.

John Wayne Glover had finally gotten a taste of murder, and he liked it.

Just over a week later, on May 9, Glover once more felt the inexorable drive to kill. To sate his sick desire, Glover went back to the same neighborhood where he had claimed his first life and found eighty-four-year-old Winfreda Isabel Ashton walking home from the store.

Glover followed his quarry for a few minutes until he didn't see anyone else around, and then he pounced. He pulled Winfreda into some bushes, where he beat the helpless elderly woman and then pulled off her pantyhose and strangled her to death with them.

As with the previous murder, Glover took his victim's purse and used the money to drink and gamble at a bar.

Winfreda's body was discovered later in the day, and when the police arrived to investigate, they were immediately struck by the similarities between this murder and the Mitchelhill murder. A forensic examination of Winfreda's body detected no semen, but the placement of her body suggested that it was a sexual crime.

The Sydney police believed that they had a potential serial killer who hunted elderly women on their hands. Despite their initial theory, the police never related this idea to the public. Winfreda's murder was reported as just another random murder on the streets of Sydney.

Glover had gotten away with murder once more.

Cooling Off

The Federal Bureau of Investigation's definition of a serial killer is a person who kills at least three people in separate events, with at least one "cooling off" period between murders.

There are many reasons why a serial killer goes into a cooling-off period: they may fear getting caught or simply be unable to continue at the current pace due to work or familial obligations. It is unknown why John Glover entered a cooling-off period, although it is important to note that he did not shun his anti-social activities altogether.

After killing Winfreda Ashton, Glover returned to his old pathology of molesting women in nursing homes. The police believe that Glover committed at least five sexual assaults, mostly at nursing homes, between June and October 1989. At the time, Glover was not suspected of any crimes at the nursing homes, probably because he returned to his M.O. of either volunteering in or making sales calls to area nursing homes. He had legitimate reasons to be in nursing homes, and he always presented himself in a professional, comforting manner.

But simply molesting elderly women was no longer enough for John Wayne Glover—he needed to kill.

Unable to fight the urge to kill, Glover returned to his old hunting grounds of the North Shore on November 2, 1989, to claim another victim.

Eighty-five-year-old Margaret Pahud was walking home from grocery shopping on a seldom-used backstreet when Glover leaped into action, beating her to death and taking her purse.

Glover then spent Pahud's money at the local RSL club.

At this point, Glover had hit his serial killer stride. He knew when, where, and how to hit his victims and showed no signs of slowing down.

Glover was about to get much bolder and more brazen with his crimes.

The day after killing Pahud, Glover returned to his favorite hunting grounds at the North Shore. The Granny Killer didn't have to wait long before he spotted his next victim, eighty-one-year-old Olive Cleveland, walking to her apartment with groceries in her hands. Just as Cleveland was about to go through the doorway of her retirement community, Glover pulled her down a ramp and into some bushes where he beat and then strangled the senior citizen with her own pantyhose.

Glover then took the cash from her purse and went out drinking.

Cleveland's body was found a short time later by staff of the retirement home, and despite her pantyhose being wrapped around her neck, they thought that she had died from a fall down the ramp.

The staff cleaned the scene, wiping away any potential forensic evidence.

Glover would strike again on November 23 when he spotted ninety-three-year-old North Shore resident Muriel Falconer walking home from a supermarket, while he was driving through his hunting grounds. Despite it being the middle of the day with plenty of people around, the opportunity was too much for Glover. He parked his car—across from a police station—and followed Falconer until he could strike.

Glover dispatched Falconer following his standard M.O., but he was seen by a witness leaving the scene.

Would this be the end for the Granny Killer?

Panic in Sydney

Once the police deduced that Muriel Falconer was a murder victim, and in all likelihood the victim of a serial killer, they released their findings to the press. The Australian media had a field day with the story, which was in print every day and headlined on every television news report.

Although serial killings were not unknown in Australia in the late 1980s, Glover was one of the first in Sydney, and his reign of terror was unique because it was reported by the media and followed by the public as it happened.

Special news reports warned elderly women to travel in groups. They were told to be on alert for any suspicious-acting man because he could be what they were now calling "the Granny Killer."

Glover was also watching the news reports from the safety of his suburban home. The intense media and police pressure forced the Granny Killer to go into another cooling-off period, but like his first one, he did not stop committing crimes altogether.

Exactly a year after he began killing, on January 11, 1990, Glover made a costly mistake that would ultimately lead to his arrest.

On the day in question, Glover was making his rounds as a salesman to various institutions around Sydney when he decided to stop at a nursing home he had visited in the past. After lurking around the halls looking for a victim, he spotted a vulnerable eighty-two-year-old woman alone in a room. Glover crept into the room and began molesting the woman, but she tried to fight him off and made enough of a commotion that the Granny Killer got scared and fled.

Although staff members were unable to stop Glover from leaving, one of them was able to write down his license plate number.

When the police first received the report of Glover's latest sexual assault, they didn't think that it was anything more than a molestation case. They tracked down Glover through the license plate number and asked him to come into the nearest police station for an interview, but he refused.

The police then decided to pay a visit to Glover's home, but when they got there, they were told by his wife that he was in the hospital, recovering from a suicide attempt the previous night.

He had apparently taken an overdose of sleeping pills.

Detectives next visited the hospital, where they first talked to workers who gave the investigators a piece of paper with some cryptic messages scrawled on it. The police were immediately struck by the phrase "No more grannies," which made them think of the recent Granny Killer case.

At this point, the investigators believed that Glover was the Granny Killer, but they decided not to show their hand. Instead, they only questioned him about the plethora of nursing home assaults he had committed.

The investigators were positive that Glover was their man, but they didn't think they had enough evidence to make the case stick in court. Instead of arresting him, they decided to keep him under around-the-clock surveillance.

The Sydney police, though, learned that it is impossible to watch a person every second of the day.

After Glover was released from the hospital, he quickly noticed that wherever he went, the police followed. It was no doubt unsettling for the serial killer and temporarily put an end to his nefarious activities, but Glover's urge to kill was too great.

He would not let the police keep him from taking one last life.

Glover's final victim was a bit of a change from his normal M.O. and signature. In all of his previous murders, Glover hunted down women over the age of eighty who were unknown to him, murdered and robbed them, and left their bodies at the scene. The M.O. helped him avoid capture, but on March 19, 1990, Glover may very well have been trying to get captured when he claimed his last victim.

On the morning in question, the police watched as Glover left his home and drove a few miles to another house. They didn't know it at the time, but the house belonged to sixty-year-old Joan Sinclair, who was a long-time friend of Glover and his family.

The police had to make a decision: blow their cover but possibly stop a crime in the process, or let things develop so that they could build a better case.

They chose to follow the second course.

When a few hours passed and Glover had still not emerged from the house, the police started regretting their decision. Finally, at about 5 p.m., they decided to enter the house without a warrant.

They found Sinclair in a pool of blood, dead from a combination of being bludgeoned and strangled. A further search of the house led to the discovery of Glover unconscious in a bathtub, overdosed on Valium, with his wrists slit.

Glover was rushed to a hospital, where it was determined that his wounds were superficial. He would live to face a jury for the Granny Murders.

Trial and Aftermath

Although most of the evidence linking Glover to the Granny Murders was circumstantial, there was plenty of it, and the manner in which he was discovered at Joan Sinclair's house was tantamount to a smoking gun.

His lawyers offered the only defense they could—diminished capacity.

The prosecution countered that Glover was totally sane and that only a person with complete mental capacity could plan the murders as he did. They also argued that his crimes had a strong financial incentive because he robbed most of his victims and used the money to gamble and drink. Finally, the prosecution stated that he made the crimes look sexual in nature just to throw the investigators off his trail.

It didn't take long for a jury to come back with a guilty verdict.

Glover was given six life sentences in 1991, and in 2005, he committed suicide in prison.

Before he killed himself, Glover met with a friend in prison and gave the person a sketch with the number "nine" written on it. Some believe that nine represents the number of unknown murder victims Glover claimed.

Investigators are taking a look at a number of unsolved murders that possibly fit Glover's signature and M.O., but without his cooperation, it will be difficult to say for certain how many, if any, other elderly women the Granny Murderer killed.

CHAPTER 5:

THE MONSTER OF
WALMART, DONALD SMITH

In recent years, Walmart stores have attracted a negative reputation for a number of reasons.

Walmart's business model has been a constant source of criticism due to many of their cheap, yet low-quality products being produced in China and developing countries. Walmart employees are also often underpaid when compared to similar positions at other companies. The company's ability to offer the lowest prices in town has also led to an enormous number of traditional "mom and pop" stores closing, causing many people to lament that Walmart has destroyed the "American Mainstreet."

The merits of Walmart's business model will no doubt continue to be debated in American bars, classrooms, and even the halls of government for the foreseeable future.

But Walmart has also attracted negative attention due to its customers.

One doesn't have to peruse the internet very long to find entire webpages dedicated to the strange behavior of the people who frequent Walmart stores. The fact that most Walmarts are open twenty-four hours certainly plays a role in this; some people like to use Walmart stores as an after-hours club.

There have also been numerous cases where violent assaults and brawls have happened in the aisles of Walmarts, and in 2015, riots nearly broke out in a number of stores across the United States when EBT card machines quit working.

Most of these examples, though, are somewhat humorous and not necessarily indicative that Walmart is a place that evil or depraved people frequent.

Unfortunately, in June 2013, a predator named Donald Smith decided to make a Jacksonville, Florida-area Walmart his hunting grounds. Smith presented himself as a kind and helpful person to a woman named Rayne Perrywinkle and then abducted, raped, and murdered her eight-year-old daughter.

Smith's shocking crime caused revulsion across the state of Florida, earning him the moniker "The Monster of Walmart."

Donald Smith

In June 2013, Donald Smith was a fifty-five-year-old ex-con with a mile-long rap sheet behind him and no real future. He had long since backstabbed and double-crossed most of his family and friends and was only three weeks out of prison.

Smith was the definition of a career criminal and a predator, having spent most of his adult life in prisons and jails. His rap sheet included arrests and convictions for everything from theft to aggravated assault and a plethora of sexual assaults.

He had been on Florida's sex offender registry since 1993, which made him one of the earliest and longest-serving people on the list in 2013.

To those who knew Smith, it seemed as though his only purpose in life was to victimize and prey on others. It wasn't that he was necessarily a good criminal—as stated above, he spent most of his life in prison—but he was compelled to commit crime after crime.

The Crime

For single mother Rayne Perrywinkle, things could get pretty difficult from time to time. She not only had to stretch every penny she made to care for her three daughters, but she also had to work her hectic schedule around her children. On the night in question, Rayne was clothes shopping with her three daughters at a Jacksonville clothing store, but she found that the store was too expensive for her budget.

Donald Smith was also at the same store, but he wasn't shopping for clothes—he was shopping for a new victim.

Smith noticed that Rayne was having a difficult time, so he approached the mother and asked if he could help. Rayne initially rebuffed Smith, but he persisted and said that he could buy them some clothes at Walmart.

Rayne was leery of the offer but let down her guard when Smith told her that his wife would meet them there.

Donald Smith didn't have a wife.

"He looked into my face and told me I was safe," Rayne later recalled.

The single mother finally relented, and the group all piled into Smith's truck.

After shopping in Walmart for a while, Rayne grew suspicious when Smith's wife hadn't yet arrived. Smith assured her that she was on her way and then offered to buy the group some hamburgers from the McDonald's in the store.

Rayne agreed and, for some reason, also allowed her eight-year-old daughter, Cherish, to go with the stranger.

Cherish was never seen alive again.

When Cherish and Smith didn't return after a few minutes, Rayne went to the McDonalds, to see what was taking them so long, but was horrified to see that it was closed.

Three Minutes of Anguish

The evidence revealed that Smith quickly whisked Cherish out of the store and into his truck. He then drove a short distance to a wooded area where he raped, beat, and suffocated the helpless girl.

The forensic examiner estimated that it took Cherish three minutes to die.

Meanwhile, back in the store, Rayne realized what a colossal mistake she had made letting her daughter leave with a stranger. She called 911 to report the possible abduction, admitting several times during the call that she had made a mistake.

An Amber Alert was broadcast, but unfortunately, Cherish was already dead.

Cherish's body was found the next day, where Smith had left her. Thanks to the ubiquitous presence of security cameras in most Walmart parking lots, the police were able to track down Smith through the identification of his truck's license plates.

Smith was charged with capital murder and faced the death penalty for Cherish's murder.

When the trial finally got underway, there was little defense that Smith could offer a jury. His DNA was found on Cherish, the security camera footage showed him leaving the parking lot with Cherish, and his background as a sex offender also worked against him.

Essentially, it was an open and shut case.

As the court proceedings progressed, Smith seemed to know that he had little chance to beat the case, but it didn't seem to bother him. He appeared more interested in smiling for the cameras than saving his own life.

In their closing arguments, the prosecution appealed to the jury's raw emotion to send Smith to death row.

"From the grave she's crying out to you: 'Donald Smith raped me. ... Donald Smith strangled me until every last breath left my body,'" Prosecutor Mark Caliel said. "In the final moments of her life, this defendant took from that little girl everything that was innocent and pure. And then he took her life. Now it's time to hold him accountable for what he did."

In February 2018, the jury finally decided Smith's fate, taking only fifteen minutes to find him guilty, recommending the death penalty.

Smith smiled for the cameras after the verdict was read, like he had so many other times during his trial.

There are few positives to be taken from cases like this, but if Cherish's family can find solace in one thing, it is that Florida regularly executes its death row inmates.

It might be ten or fifteen years, but Donald Smith will one day have the needle of death put into his arm.

CHAPTER 6:

THE AUSSIE FEMME FATALES, JEMMA LILLEY AND TRUDI LENON

In terms of entertainment, there is no denying that violence plays a major role in modern society. Most hit movies and many television shows are laden with violence, and the overwhelming majority of video games are based on how many kills the player can get.

This trend doesn't just apply to fictional stories either. As most of you reading this probably know, true crime media, which is overwhelmingly violence-based, has become an extremely popular form of entertainment over the last twenty years.

Of course, many people argue that the trend has gone too far, insisting that life has begun to imitate art. They further argue that modern media has even gone so far as to glamorize criminals, especially serial killers.

Although the argument may seem outlandish at face value, a closer look shows that, in fact, there has been considerable glamorization, or even fetishization, of serial killers in the last twenty years.

One only has to look at films such as *Natural Born Killers* or the Hannibal Lecter franchise to see serial killers portrayed as misunderstood and wronged people, or as sophisticated geniuses who happen to be sociopaths.

There is no doubt that some people watch these movies wishing to be Mickey and Mallory or Hannibal Lecter.

In 2017, two Australian women named Jemma Lilley and Trudi Lenon made their bid to be a successful serial killer duo. The women lived in their own fantasy worlds where serial killers were revered and everyone else was reviled. Lilley and Lenon dreamed of committing numerous murders, but when they finally put their fantasies into action, they realized that while killing may be easy, getting away with murder is an entirely different story.

Birds of a Feather

To an outsider, it would seem at first glance that Jemma Lilley and Trudi Lenon had little in common. At twenty-five, Lilley was much younger than forty-two-year-old Lenon, who was a mother of three, but the two shared a similar outlook on life.

Essentially, Lilley and Lenon were two lost souls living on the edges of society.

It is quite possible that either of the women could have gone on to lead productive lives if they had never met. However, their dark personalities and deviant desires seemed to play on and feed off of each other.

To the greater society, Lenon in particular presented a carefully-crafted façade of a normal, law-abiding person. She was the mother of three children and in 2017 was attending university at Kwinana College in the metropolitan area of Perth, Australia. She was not necessarily known for being a great scholar, but she was helpful to the other students and her professors.

But when Lenon was not in school and her motherly duties were done for the day, she became "Corvina."

Covina was the alias Lenon developed for her nighttime romps in Perth's underground bondage and sadomasochism, or BDSM, scene. She made contacts in the scene through friends and on the internet in the late 1990s and early 2000s, and by 2017, she was a regular in many of the clubs and local hook-up spots.

People in the BDSM scene play different roles, with most choosing to either be a dominant, or "dom," or a submissive, or "sub" during their activities. Lenon played the role of a sub in the bedroom, and as it turned out, she was also quite submissive in other aspects of her life, especially when it came to her relationship with Lilley.

Like Lenon, Lilley preferred to live in her own ultra-violent fantasy world. As a child, Lilley showed little ambition or interest in anything pursuits like sports or academics, but she did develop a love for fiction, especially stories that involved serial killers.

After graduating from high school, Lilley went on to work full-time at a department store in Perth, but she spent most of her spare time writing and editing a book she began during her teen years.

The book didn't have much of a plot and instead followed the exploits of the main character, named SOS, who went around killing people. Lilley fashioned her serial killer character into an anti-hero, and according to her friends, she began to take on the persona of the character.

Similar to her older friend, Lilley assumed a nickname, going by the moniker "SOS." She created an alternate world for herself and began to obsess on social media about murder. After meeting Lenon, the two women became very close, possibly romantic. One text from Lenon, later retrieved by the police, stated that she would be Lilley's "sub" and do whatever she wanted.

Jemma Lilley wanted to kill.

As the women's relationship developed deeper, the talk of murder and serial killings became commonplace on their Facebook accounts. In one message, Lilley said that she wanted to record her first kill before the age of twenty-five and that at some point she wanted to go on a "slaughterfest."

SOS enjoyed the attention Corvina gave her, but was always quick to point out exactly how dangerous she was.

"My mind is the darkest being you will ever be laying your life in the hands of," Lilley once texted Lenon.

Eventually, Lenon moved into Lilly's house, and the two began planning their momentous first kill. After carefully researching different serial killers and their tactics, SOS determined that an organized murder would be best; it would probably take place at her house, where she could control the environment. She also knew that since she and Corvina were women, they would have to use subterfuge to kill their possibly physically stronger quarry.

They went on several outings to buy supplies for their diabolical plot. They bought 100 liters of hydrochloric acid in case they wanted to eliminate any trace of their victim and some concrete tiles in case they chose to bury him.

The two women next had to find a victim.

Since they were both women, and Lilley was young and relatively attractive, they probably could've found some anonymous guy on the streets who would come back to their place, but instead, they made their first significant operational mistake: they chose a victim known to Lenon.

Lenon focused her search on eighteen-year-old Aaron Pajich, who was friends with her adult son. She also knew Pajich from her college classes, which is where the investigators believe she first began to assess his suitability as the murderous duo's first victim.

Pajich was diagnosed with autism, though he was fairly functional and able to attend college. With that said, Pajich's autism meant that he "still inhabited a child's world," according to prosecutor James McTaggart.

McTaggart believes that Pajich's autism is largely why he was chosen as a victim.

The Murder

Lenon approached Pajich in school and invited him to spend the evening with her and Lilley at their house on June 13, 2017. The details concerning how Pajich was enticed to go there alone are not clear, but the possibility of sex may have played a role. Pajich gladly accepted the invitation, having nothing to fear since he was friends with Lenon's son and considered Lenon a friend.

Pajich couldn't have been more wrong.

The evidence shows that not long after arriving at Lilley's house, Pajich was attacked. One of the women garroted the young man while the other stabbed him twice in the chest and once in the neck.

For whatever reason, the women decided not to use the hydrochloric acid to dispose of Pajich's body. They probably forgot to buy proper gloves and masks needed to do such a thing, but regardless, they decided to go with plan B and bury Pajich in their backyard.

They dug a fairly deep hole, dumped Pajich into it, and then poured concrete over the body. Once the concrete was set, they used the tiles. The tiling job was bad, but it did the trick and probably would've concealed their crime indefinitely if it were not for their loose lips and the fact that Pajich was missed by his family and friends.

As Pajich's friends and family grew worried after his disappearance, Lilly couldn't help but brag to people about killing him. Within two weeks, both Lilley and Lenon were arrested and charged with first-degree murder.

The evidence against the women was overwhelming: Pajich's body was found at their residence, and numerous social media and text messages Lilley and Lenon sent each other, before and after the crime, implicated them. The only defense either one had was to place the blame on the other, which they both did, but to no avail.

Jemma Lilley and Trudi Lenon were found guilty of first-degree murder in November 2017. In February 2018, they were both sentenced to a minimum of twenty-eight years in prison.

For Lenon, the sentence is very likely a life sentence, which has not started well for her. She has already endured a couple of attacks at the hands of other inmates.

Sharon Pajich, Aaron's mother, has no sympathy for the pair and believes that anything bad that happens to them is righteous retribution.

"You can't get it out of your head and it will be a lifetime for me," said Pajich. "They deserve everything they get for what they've done."

CHAPTER 7:

THE THOMAS J. GRASSO MURDER CASE

Gary Gilmore was a career criminal who is best remembered for being the first man to be executed in the United States after the death penalty was reinstated under the ruling *Gregg v. Georgia* in 1976. Gilmore was born to a poor family that traveled around the western U.S. looking for work. By the 1960s, Gilmore had compiled an impressive rap sheet featuring his favorite crime: armed robbery.

In 1976, months after the death penalty was reinstated, Gilmore killed two men during the course of two different armed robberies in Utah. He was quickly caught, tried, and sentenced to death.

Gilmore's story up until that point was unremarkable in criminal history. While he was on death row, though, he did something incredible—he forewent all of his appeals and was executed in less than six months.

Gilmore's race to death was chronicled in books and movies due to its unique circumstances, which were mostly not replicated until the early 1990s.

During the early 1990s, Thomas Grasso committed two murders in two different states. Although he did his best to avoid capture, he was eventually caught, convicted, and sentenced to death in the state of Oklahoma.

But the Grasso case was much more complex than Gilmore's.

Like Gilmore, Grasso refused to appeal his death sentence, and the case eventually attracted national media attention. Grasso's case was fundamentally different from Gilmore's, though, because it involved two different states, one of which didn't have the death penalty and whose governor wanted to turn Grasso's fate into a political issue.

Thomas Grasso

Grasso's life mirrored Gilmore's in a number of ways besides how he ultimately died. Like Gilmore, Grasso was a career criminal who drifted around the western states for much of his adult life.

Grasso was born in 1962 to a dysfunctional family that gave him little direction in life. He often found himself in trouble with the law as a juvenile and did time in juvenile correctional facilities before graduating to adult jails and prisons. Although Grasso would do just about any type of crime that could net him some money, his bread and butter was burglaries.

The young criminal spent most of his time in the state of Oklahoma, which is where he met his future wife, Lana Grooms. Married life was not idyllic, though, for Grasso. His choice of occupation often led to conflicts with his wife, not because she had a moral problem with crime, but more so because the income was too unstable—Grasso could make a big "score" and then go weeks before getting anything else.

Grasso, like most career criminals, also had substance abuse problems.

Thomas and Lana constantly fought over finances and substances, which led to a particularly tough holiday season in 1990. Grasso was broke and needed to do something to placate his wife, so he turned to his old standby of burglary.

Two Murders

The Christmas season was shaping up to be a bad one in the Grasso household in 1990. Thomas was broke, and it seemed as though he had exhausted all of his favorite places to rob and burglarize in the Tulsa, Oklahoma area. Frustrated with the situation, Grasso began to consider breaking what is perhaps the number one cardinal rule among career criminals—never strike close to home.

Of course, what is considered "close to home" is relative, but the better criminals know not to hit people and places they are associated with due to the possibility of identification.

Grasso knew this rule and tried to follow it, but he was becoming extremely frustrated the closer it got to Christmas. He began looking at his next-door neighbor, eighty-seven-year-old Hilda Johnson, as a possible target.

Despite her age, Johnson was still pretty active and was able to live alone. She kept her small home nice and clean and was friendly with most of her neighbors, including Grasso and his wife. It was rumored that the elderly woman kept a lot of cash in her home, as many people who lived through the Great Depression did.

Johnson had never had problems with crime in the quiet neighborhood, but there is a first time for everything.

On Christmas Eve 1990, instead of spending the day celebrating with his family, Thomas Grasso was fiending for drugs. He was broke and needed a fix, so out of desperation, he decided to break into Hilda Johnson's home.

He went in through a window, and as he was rifling through Johnson's things, she heard the noise and went to investigate. Like a true predator, Grasso leaped on the defenseless woman and hit her several times before he pulled some Christmas lights down and strangled her to death with them.

The heist and murder netted him twelve dollars in cash and a television set.

He later traded the TV for drugs.

Although Grasso and his wife were interviewed by the police after Hilda Johnson's body was discovered, they were considered possible witnesses but not suspects.

Thomas Grasso had gotten away with murder, but since he was a career criminal, he knew that it was time to leave town.

Not long after he murdered Hilda Johnson, Grasso and his wife moved to New York City, where he had some familial contacts. The couple settled on Staten Island, and before too long, Grasso was up to his old behavior of drug abuse and crime.

But he soon found out that it is tougher in some ways to live as a criminal in the Big Apple.

Although the penalties for crime are tougher in Oklahoma than in New York, the crime rates are lower in Oklahoma, and therefore, people are more trusting, which worked in Grasso's favor. Grasso learned that not only are most New Yorkers leery and distrusting of strangers, but many also have a "siege" mentality where they are actually waiting for something bad to happen.

Grasso earned less as a criminal in New York, which was a problem since the living expenses are much higher than in Tulsa.

After netting a few low-paying scores, Grasso decided to follow a familiar template by targeting an elderly person in his neighborhood. By the spring of 1991, Grasso had noticed that an eighty-one-year-old man in the neighborhood named Leslie Holtz lived alone.

He also heard that Holtz was drawing a nice-sized Social Security check.

Grasso stalked his prey until he thought the time was right, which, similar to his murder of Hilda Johnson, happened to be on holiday.

On July 4, 1991, Grasso broke into Leslie Holtz's home to steal his Social Security check. Unlike the break-in murder more than six months earlier, the career criminal intended to kill the elderly pensioner before taking his money.

Grasso viciously beat Holtz to death, took his check, and calmly left the house.

After dispatching of his victim, Grasso then cashed the check and went to the nearest drug dealer. He spent the next several days getting high, telling more than one person about where and how he got his drug money. Most of the people he told either didn't care or didn't believe him, but people talk, and before too long, the rumor was going around Staten Island that he had murdered a retiree.

Two Convictions

New York City Police homicide detectives took the murder of Leslie Holtz very seriously. The victims' age and the fact that he was attacked in his own home made the crime particularly egregious and difficult for most people to contemplate. The detectives canvassed Staten Island and contacted their network of informants, and one name kept coming up in every interview—Thomas Grasso.

The detectives did a background check on Grasso and learned that he had multiple arrests and convictions for a variety of crimes on his record and that he was also a known drug addict.

They were finally able to get statements from people who claimed that Grasso had bragged about killing Holtz. The information was barely enough for an arrest, but the police thought that they should move before he possibly killed again. The detectives reasoned that since Grasso was a known drug user, he was probably carrying drugs on him, which would be enough to hold him in jail until they collected more evidence.

Thomas Grasso was picked up by the police two weeks after Holtz's murder.

Since Grasso was a career criminal, the detectives conducting his interrogation thought that he would invoke his right to silence, or at least lie to them.

Instead, the detectives got more than a complete confession.

As Grasso sat across the table from the homicide detectives, it was clear that he was a tired, defeated man. He was ready to meet his fate, which in this case had the possibility of death. Grasso looked at the detectives and told them all the details about how he stalked Leslie Holtz for weeks before he forced his way into his home and murdered him. He verified that the murder was committed for drug money and that he picked Holtz because he was old and lived alone.

Grasso thought that Holt was an easy target—it wasn't personal.

The detectives thanked Grasso for his cooperation, and as they were about to lead him away to jail, the killer told them that he wasn't done with his statement.

He wanted to talk about the murder of Hilda Johnson.

The detectives were a bit thrown back by the development, but it wasn't the first time they'd heard a confession from a person who wasn't even wanted for a particular crime. Grasso told the detectives the details about the Tulsa murder, and then, hours later, he was finally transferred to Rikers Island to await trial for the first-degree murder of Leslie Holtz.

Grasso was found guilty in the open and shut case and sentenced to life in prison, with a twenty-year minimum before parole would be considered, on April 21, 1992.

He was promptly sent to the notorious prison, Attica, to do his time.

Not long after Grasso was sent to Attica, officials from Oklahoma requested and were granted his extradition to stand trial for the first-degree murder of Hilda Johnson. A Tulsa jury found him guilty in that case, sentencing him to death.

Like Gary Gilmore more than fifteen years prior, Grasso decided not to appeal his death sentence.

It looked as though Grasso would get his wish and be executed within a year.

A Political Battle over the Death Penalty

Grasso apparently fully expected to be executed within a year, but the case took a strange turn when the Democratic governor of New York, Mario Cuomo, got involved. Cuomo was a staunch opponent of the death penalty and regularly stated in interviews that keeping New York state from bringing back the death penalty was one of the main points of his political agenda.

Cuomo was up for reelection in 1994.

Although Cuomo's polling numbers were good throughout the state of New York in late 1992, and they were very high within New York City, his political advisors believed that he needed to do something to energize his White liberal base. There really wasn't much happening politically in the state of New York at the time, but his allies soon learned about the Grasso murder case.

Cuomo publicly stated that he thought Grasso should be sent back to serve his sentence in New York before serving his death sentence in Oklahoma. Officials in

Oklahoma disagreed and refused to turn over Grasso, who seemingly wanted to be executed anyway.

Sensing that he was gaining political points, Cuomo successfully used legal mechanisms (IAD) to interrupt Grasso's execution and force his return to New York to complete his sentence.

A federal judge agreed with Cuomo's arguments and ordered Grasso returned to New York in 1993.

As Thomas Grasso did his time in Attica prison, his case took on a whole new life in New York's gubernatorial campaign in 1994. Cuomo looked to be a lock for a fourth straight term as governor of New York according to the polls, but a "red wave" was about to sweep the country, giving the Republicans control of both houses of the US Congress and many of the state legislatures and governors' offices as well.

Cuomo's Republican opponent was George Pataki, an upstart state senator, who was of more Hungarian than Italian ancestry and was from the less politically connected "Upstate" part of New York.

Pataki ran on a typically moderate Republican platform—lower taxes, less government, more police—but he also added a pro-death penalty plank to his campaign. The senator vowed to bring back the death penalty if elected governor.

The idea resonated with New Yorkers as polls showed a majority supported the death penalty. As much as it helped Pataki, it also hurt Cuomo, who vetoed several death penalty bills passed by the New York state legislature.

Pataki went on to beat Cuomo by more than three percentage points in what many experts considered an improbable victory.

One of Pataki's first actions as governor was to honor the state of Oklahoma's extradition request for Thomas Grasso. On January 11, 1995, agents with the New York Department of Corrections brought Grasso to the international airport in Buffalo, where he was met by officers with the Oklahoma Department of Corrections, who then brought him back to their state's death row.

Grasso was executed on March 20, 1995.

Besides the incredible legal and political battles over Grasso's life and his Gary Gilmoreesque desire to meet his fate, Thomas Grasso attracted media attention one last time on the day of his execution.

Grasso issued four statements to the press that demonstrated the killer and drug addict had somewhat of an appreciation for literature and philosophy.

The first statement said: "What we call the beginning is often the end, and to make an end is to make a beginning. The end is where we start from."

A few hours later, Grasso released a second statement that read, "For most of us, there is only the unattended moment, the moment in and out of time. And right action is freedom from the past and future also." The second sentence in his statement was taken from T.S. Eliot's "The Dry Salvages."

In his third statement, just three hours before he was executed, Grasso released a poem titled "A Visit with Mystery."

The poem reads:

"Ready, willing, and waiting am I,

Asked for death but could not die.

Each sunrise is one day less,

I'll endure this horrible mess.

When the last sun does sink,

Mr. E will serve a goodbye drink.

On the day our paths do cross it won't take much to see it through,

Just a little toxic brew.

The warden will read my last creed,

And the deadly brew will flow.

As the poison drips into my veins,

And from my body life does drain,

I'll know then once and for all

What 'last call' means when serving Toxahol."

Like most death row inmates, Grasso was given a last meal request. He requested a healthy serving of mussels, clams, a cheeseburger, and a can of SpaghettiOs.

Apparently, the prison was out of the SpaghettiOs brand because, after Grasso was strapped to the gurney and he was asked if he had any last words before they put the needle in his arm, he answered:

"I did not get my SpaghettiOs, I got spaghetti. I want the press to know this."

CHAPTER 8:

THE MURDER OF
KIAYA CAMPBELL

There have been many horrendous crimes committed by juveniles profiled in this series and this volume in particular. Many of these crimes are "thrill kills" where the killer kids picked targets unknown to them. As shocking as these crimes are, they would be much worse if the kids in question picked someone close to them to kill for fun.

Children who kill family members and others close to them break a sacred trust in a way that is fundamentally almost impossible for most people to understand, even criminals.

The most obvious question to arise in such a situation is, why would a child do such a thing to someone they are supposed to care for?

Also, it seems fair to ask, can a child who does such a thing ever be trusted?

These are questions that have recently been asked when a fifteen-year-old Denver, Colorado area boy, Aidan Zellmer, brutally murdered a ten-year-old girl who was entrusted to his care in the summer of 2017. Although the case is yet to be resolved, many issues, such as parenting and juvenile punishment, have already been debated regarding the murder.

Aidan Zellmer and Kiaya Campbell

By all accounts, Aidan Zellmer was a normal teenage boy. He attended Horizon High School in Thornton, Colorado, just outside of Denver. Although he wasn't a great student, he was not a disciplinary problem and got along fairly well with his teachers and fellow students. Growing up, he shared a deep bond with his twin brother Ethan, as the two boys spent most of their time together doing homework and hanging out with their friends.

While Aidan's Facebook account was still active, it revealed normal interests and likes for a kid his age: he was a fan of the superhero Deadpool and the *Chuckie* horror movie franchise.

Although Aidan and Ethan lived with their mother, they were close to their father, Demmie Joseph Olvera. Olvera, who is very religious and has been described as a bit strange by some of his neighbors, had a strong influence on Aidan's life. Aidan clearly looked up to his father, but he received most of his adult supervision from his mother.

Kiaya Campbell was the daughter of Aidan's mother's boyfriend, which is how the two kids knew each other. By all accounts, the two kids got along quite well, but due to their age difference, Aidan was often tasked with babysitting Kiaya. He showed no outward signs of regretting the responsibility, but there was something lurking beneath the surface of the teenager that was extremely violent and antisocial.

Aidan was said to have a dark side that was inexplicable in many ways.

Kiaya, on the other hand, seemed to be an open book of light. The little girl got along with just about anyone, and in her spare time, she enjoyed making YouTube videos. Kiaya would talk about school, her pets, and even Aidan in the videos, some of which went viral. Although she may not have attracted the number of followers as some of the bigger-name YouTube stars, such as PewDiePie, her bubbly personality and good nature made her a definite rising internet star.

All of those dreams were dashed forever on June 7, 2017.

The Crime

Like Aidan, Kiaya lived with her mother most of the time, but spent enough time at her father's that she became fairly close to Aidan. Kiaya's father trusted Aidan with his daughter and, as stated earlier, would often let him babysit her.

With that said, it would be an understatement to say that it was not the best home environment.

The police responded to numerous domestic abuse complaints between Aidan's mother and Kiaya's father, with both children being there on more than one occasion to witness the dysfunction. The home was clearly a chaotic place, but the children seemed to be apart from it.

Until the evening of June 7, 2017.

On the night in question, Aidan and Kiaya made the short walk to the neighborhood convenience store together, as they had done so many other times prior, to buy some candy and soft drinks. On their way back from the store, a heavy but brief downpour of rain blanketed the neighborhood.

As the rain came down, Aidan pulled Kiaya off the street into a grassy, isolated area.

Once he had her alone, Aidan proceeded to beat and rape the little girl, until she died.

Aidan then returned home, wet and without Kiaya. Kiaya's father was immediately worried and asked Aidan where his daughter was. Aidan told him that they were separated in the downpour and that she would probably be along shortly.

Of course, Kiaya never showed up at the house.

Kiaya's dad immediately drove around the neighborhood looking for his daughter, and when he couldn't find her, he called the police. An Amber Alert was issued for the missing girl, and the police interviewed Aidan to determine if she ran away or was abducted.

The police immediately became suspicious of Aidan.

Kiaya's body was discovered the next day, where Aidan had left her. The discovery immediately made Aidan the top suspect because he was the last person to see her alive.

The police questioned Aidan again, but the more he talked, the less credible he seemed because his story continued to change.

Things didn't look good for Aidan Zellmer.

Charges Filed

The police arrested Aidan Zellmer for Kiaya's murder on June 10. Since the proceedings were in juvenile court, cameras were barred from the courtroom, but Aiden's father, Demmie Joseph Olvera, waited for the cameras outside to give a statement. Reporters asked Olvera what he thought about his son's innocence or guilt, but he only replied with a bizarre, cryptic statement referencing God's mercy and returning to God.

Aidan was remanded to a juvenile correctional facility and was officially charged with first-degree murder by the district attorney.

But that marked just the beginning of Aidan Zellmer's legal saga.

The district attorney believed that Kiaya's murder was heinous enough that it warranted charging Zellmer as an adult. Although Zellmer is not eligible for the death penalty due to his age, he faced the possibility of spending the rest of his life in prison.

Zellmer's lawyers argued that their client's mental capacity is truly that of a child and that he didn't understand the gravity of his actions, so therefore he shouldn't be tried as an adult.

On the other hand, the prosecutor argued that the crime was so heinous and premeditated that there is no way that Zellmer didn't know what he was doing, no matter his age.

The judge agreed with the prosecution and certified Aidan Zellmer as an adult in March 2018.

Zellmer was sentenced to life in prison. Zellmer's sentence allows for the possibility of parole after forty years, but with good behavior, he could get out in thirty, Adams County District Attorney Dave Young said.

CHAPTER 9:

THE SOHAM MURDERS

Today, most Western countries like to believe they are forgiving of criminals. It stems from a penological philosophy that stresses rehabilitation over punishment, ideally giving the former offender the chance to make up for their past mistakes by becoming a productive member of society.

The trend began during the 1970s when politicians, social workers, and prison reform advocates presented studies and other evidence that showed criminals were less likely to re-offend if they had more opportunities. The result was the reform movement, not just in prison, but in the entire criminal justice systems in most Western countries.

Prisons were transformed from mere holding pens to institutions that sought to change criminals' outlooks on life through educational and treatment programs.

The courts began implementing diversion programs for first-time offenders that offered probation instead of prison, as well as other forms of "creative sentencing" that aimed to keep people out of jails and prisons.

But there were plenty who wondered if the pendulum had swung too far.

Many believe that criminals now have too many rights. To support their arguments, anti-crime reform advocates pointed to criminal cases routinely being dropped on technicalities, the seeming comfort of many prisons, and the protections that offenders received after prison.

The last point in particular has been a point of debate in the United Kingdom, where, in exceptional circumstances such as crimes committed by children, some offenders are given new identities upon their release from prison as adults, to protect their anonymity and discourage vigilante action.

A number of these issues led to the formation of victims' rights organizations. The 1990s witnessed the institution of sex offender registries in most Western countries as well as criminal background checks for jobs and even housing.

The pendulum swinging back in favor of the victims' rights movement and a tougher view on criminals was propelled by some particularly awful murder cases where the offenders seemingly slipped through the system.

One of these offenders was Ian Huntley, who became the poster boy for the shift back in favor of law and order.

During the 1990s, Huntley was charged with numerous serious criminal offenses in the United Kingdom, including several sex offenses, but was never convicted. Like John Gotti in the United States, no charges ever seemed to stick to Ian Huntley, which proved to cost the lives of two ten-year-old girls in 2002.

Because Huntley was never convicted of any sex offenses, he was allowed to get a job in a position of trust around children.

Huntley's brutal crimes shocked the United Kingdom, which quickly turned to anger when his past was revealed.

A Troubled Life

Ian Huntley was born in 1974 in the Midlands region of England. The often bleak and dreary landscape of the region served as a perfect backdrop to Huntley's often difficult childhood, which was replete with abuse from his classmates.

Huntley was continually bullied for his looks and small size. The bullying began with simple schoolyard taunts but progressed to physical assaults by the time Huntley was twelve. During the 1980s, when Huntley was enduring the bullying, society viewed the concept much differently from now. His teachers told him that he had to do more to be accepted by the other boys, and they told his parents that there was little they could do.

When Huntley was thirteen, the bullying became so intense that his parents transferred him to another school.

The change of scenery proved to be temporarily beneficial, but as with most people who move to avoid their problems, Ian Huntley's problems followed him to his new school.

Although he was not bullied as much, Huntley never seemed to fit in or make permanent friendships at his new school. He also had a difficult time with girls.

It was clear from an early age that Huntley liked girls, but it was equally clear that he didn't know how to act properly around them. He often said and did inappropriate things around girls, such as talking about sex in a disparaging way, which resulted in most girls at his school thinking of him as a weird creep.

In 1990, Huntley had had enough of school, so he quit. He was clearly not college material to begin with, as his grades were average at best, but he also had no intention of going to any trade school. Ian Huntley talked big around his family and the few friends he had about making it big someday financially, but he had no real plans to achieve those riches.

To make ends meet, Huntley mainly worked low-paying labor jobs. He rarely showed any ambition or initiative on those jobs and often quit after just a few weeks. He liked to hang out on the streets of Cambridge, frequenting bars and nightclubs, which is where he learned how to supplement his meager income.

Huntley discovered that many of the businesses in the smaller towns in Cambridgeshire didn't have security alarms at the time, so he took to burglary, stealing cash from safes, and whatever other items he could sell on the black market.

Through his criminal earnings, Huntley was able to save enough money to make himself an attractive marriage prospect, or so he thought.

In 1994, at the age of twenty, Huntley met eighteen-year-old Claire Evans. He was immediately smitten with the younger woman, and after a whirlwind courtship of only a couple of months, the two married.

But Huntley's marriage would prove to be another disappointment in what was mostly a disappointing life.

After just a few days of marriage, Claire left Ian for his brother Wayne.

The betrayal by his wife was bad enough, but the fact that his own brother was a party to the betrayal sent Huntley over the edge. He refused to give his wife a divorce until 1999 out of spite, but more importantly, the event seemed to set in motion Huntley's descent into depravity.

Evil Waiting to Be Unleashed

Not long after Huntley's wife left him in 1994, he embarked on a nearly decade-long odyssey of crime that culminated in the murders of two young girls. Before he committed those crimes, though, Ian Huntley victimized numerous people throughout the Midlands and suffered no legal repercussions.

Although Huntley was not a pedophile strictly speaking, he did have a sexual affinity for underage girls. It is believed that he had sexual contact with about a dozen underage girls from 1995 through 2001 and fathered a child with a fifteen-year-old girl in 1998.

Huntley also honed his skills as a burglar during this period.

While he preferred to break into businesses, he was also known to burglarize unoccupied homes and apartments. For many with Huntley's background, burglary and sex with underage girls can be a toxic and violent combination.

Luckily, Huntley never walked in on any girls while he was robbing a place, which brings up an interesting point—Huntley's criminal sophistication and IQ.

Although Huntley never did well in school and was never considered erudite or even intelligent in the conventional sense, he showed an uncanny ability to evade the police in the plethora of crimes he committed. Huntley was eventually charged with rape and burglary on two separate occasions in 1998, but both times the charges were dropped either for lack of evidence or because the witnesses refused to cooperate.

It is difficult to say just how many crimes Huntley committed throughout the Midlands during the 1990s, but the number may be much higher than previously thought.

While Huntley was in the midst of his decade-long crime spree, he met a twenty-two-year-old woman named Maxine Carr at a nightclub in 1999. The two immediately became involved in a deeply passionate relationship.

In many ways, the two were perfect for each other. Both were average-looking and came from rough backgrounds with substance abuse issues. The result was an abusive yet enduring relationship. Both parties liked to verbally demean and berate each other on a daily basis, and although it was not an "open" relationship, they both cheated on each other on numerous occasions.

Huntley would also use violence from time to time if he didn't get his way.

Despite the problems, they moved in with each other after Huntley landed a job as a janitor at the Soham Village College in Soham in 2001. Although named a "college," the school is actually the equivalent of an American junior-senior high school, which meant that Huntley was around underage girls on a daily basis.

Huntley passed the school's criminal background check with flying colors because he had no convictions.

As part of the position, Huntley was given free housing near the school, and Carr landed a position as a teaching assistant at another school.

All the lucky breaks Huntley received in life were about to end with the murder of two innocent girls.

The Murders

Holly Wells and Jessica Chapman were two typical ten-year-old girls who always had smiles on their faces and were friends with everyone. They both attended the same grade school where Carr worked, so they were familiar, although not necessarily close to Huntley's girlfriend.

Soham is a relatively safe town in a fairly safe county of England, so it was not uncommon to see the girls walking about, but they were always together and never alone.

On the afternoon of August 4, 2002, Holly's family was hosting a neighborhood barbecue, which was well attended and quite festive. Holly and Jessica were sporting matching Manchester United soccer jerseys and having a good time playing with their other friends.

At about 6 p.m., the two girls left the party to take a short walk to the local store to buy some candy.

They were never seen alive again.

While the Wells family was having their neighborhood get together, Ian Huntley was in his house about a half mile away, fuming with anger and hatred. He'd heard rumors that Carr had been cheating on him, and he wanted to find out if they were true. Since Carr was out of town, he had to get confirmation or denial of the rumors via the phone, which apparently frustrated Huntley even more.

The couple had more than one phone conversation on August 4 about Carr's possible infidelity, which she repeatedly denied, but the more she denied it, the angrier Huntley became.

It wouldn't have been the first time she cheated on him, and he had cheated on her in the past, but to Huntley, it was more about control than trust or love. Since he was bullied as a child, Ian Huntley sought to have complete control over his life and all those near him.

Huntley's last conversation with Carr ended abruptly just before 6 p.m.

He paced around the house, seething with rage. Huntley wanted to hurt Carr somehow, but she was miles away.

Then he saw Holly Wells and Jessica Chapman walking down his street.

The details of what he said to the girls and what happened after are open to conjecture. It is generally believed he told the girls he was Carr's boyfriend and lived with her at the house. This was probably enough to get the girls to let their guards down. It also helped that Huntley was not what one would think a scary pedophile would look like.

He was just an average-looking Joe.

Since the girls were on the way to the store to buy some candy, he probably either offered them some candy or money, but told them they would have to go with him to get it.

Once they were in the house, they had only minutes to live.

Huntley later claimed that he had "accidentally" killed both girls. He said that one had hit her head, and the other was screaming so loud that he covered her mouth and accidentally suffocated her.

Few people, including the courts, bought that story.

Based on Huntley's background, it is more likely that he either killed or incapacitated one of the girls while he sexually assaulted and then murdered the other.

After murdering the girls, he brought them to a remote location and burned their bodies before dumping them near a Royal Air Force base.

The girls' parents didn't immediately notice that they were missing due to the large number of people at the party who were coming and going. When the party started dying down around ten pm, they noticed that Holly and Jessica were missing.

They immediately called the local police.

The police came to the Wells' residence and took statements from everyone in attendance. They then widened their net to include everyone in the neighborhood.

Ian Huntley was suddenly in the police net.

The Investigation

As soon as the Cambridgeshire Police received the case of the two missing girls, they feared that they were looking at an abduction. Since most child abductions are committed by someone close to the child, such as a family member or friend of the family, they began their investigation by questioning the Wells and Chapman families.

All of the girls' family members were cooperative and were quickly ruled out as suspects.

The police then went door to door in the neighborhood and questioned every resident, including Ian Huntley.

Huntley told the investigators that he was with Maxine Carr when the girls went missing, which she confirmed. It is not known what exactly Huntley told Carr, but she later claimed that she legitimately believed in her boyfriend's innocence. Carr said she lied because she was afraid of the police framing Huntley.

Few of the British public believed her story.

Part of the reason why no one later believed Carr's excuses was because of the way she carried on immediately after it was announced that the girls were missing.

Of course, every television station and newspaper in the United Kingdom, and a new blog, was covering the case. The parents of the missing girls gave tearful press conferences, and a number of their neighbors were interviewed, including Ian Huntley and Maxine Carr.

Carr especially seemed to relish the limelight, discussing in detail how she knew the two little girls from her job as a teaching assistant. In one statement to the press, Carr said that Holly Wells was "just lovely, really lovely."

Huntley was removed from the initial suspect list after Carr gave him an alibi.

The leads flowed into the Cambridgeshire Police from around the country. For a short time, a theory gained traction that the girls were the victims of another serial abductor and pedophile operating in the area, but that was quickly ruled out.

The investigators then went back to their original suspect list and gave Huntley another look. They discovered that he had numerous arrests but no convictions for a multitude of crimes during the 1990s, including sexual assault.

The big break in the case came when the soccer jerseys that the girls were wearing the day they went missing were discovered on the grounds of the Soham Village College. The evidence was not enough to arrest Huntley, but he quickly became the sole suspect in their probable abduction.

Then on August 17, less than two weeks after they disappeared, the charred remains of Holly Wells and Jessica Chapman were discovered near a Royal Air Force base.

Both Huntley and Carr were brought in for questioning by the police, and after several hours of interrogation, Huntley confessed to the murders. Huntley was charged with two counts of murder on August 20, and Carr was charged the next day with perverting the course of justice.

Huntley faced a potential life sentence, and Carr was also looking at doing significant prison time for giving a false alibi for her cold-blooded boyfriend.

The Trials

Huntley's lawyers' first legal strategy was to try for an insanity defense, but a judge ruled in late 2002 that he was legally sane to stand trial. Although Huntley was able to clean his house pretty well, eliminating any physical evidence, there was plenty of circumstantial evidence pointing toward his guilt.

There was also the confession.

Actually, Huntley and his lawyers hoped that the confession would help him avoid a life sentence. Although he admitted to killing both girls, he claimed that both deaths were the result of a horrible accident.

The jury saw right through Huntley's phony story, finding him guilty of two counts of murder on December 17, 2003. Judge Justice Moses sentenced the child killer to a life term, with a minimum of forty years behind bars.

"The order I make offers little or no hope of the defendant's eventual release," the judge said as he passed sentence.

Although Carr was facing significant time for helping Huntley temporarily evade arrest, the courts believed that she didn't know that her boyfriend had killed the two little girls. Because of that, they allowed her to plead guilty and receive a reduced sentence.

Carr was convicted in December 2003 of perverting the course of justice and sentenced to a term of 42 months. She was released on license in May 2004 after serving approximately 21 months, which is the statutory half-term required under UK sentencing guidelines.

Victims' rights groups were angered that not only was Carr given what they thought was a light sentence for her part in such a heinous crime, but that she was also given a new identity. The indefinite anonymity order granted in February 2005 was deemed necessary by Mr Justice Eady to protect Carr's "life and limb and psychological health" due to numerous threats. This legal protection fueled public anger and reinforced the belief among victims' rights advocates that the system prioritized offenders' welfare over public retribution.

Years later, the same groups grew irate once more when they learned that Carr had married and was now a mother.

The resolution of Carr's sentence led to momentum pushing the pendulum in favor of victims' rights, and once the details of Huntley's past were revealed, it swung even more in that direction.

Fallout

When the pendulum of public opinion began swinging toward law and order after Carr's sentence was announced, it moved even farther that way when Huntley's criminal background was discovered.

It was discovered that before Huntley applied for the Soham Village job, he changed his name to Ian Nixon, likely to mitigate the negative attention his criminal past would bring. He applied for the job in Soham under the name Ian Nixon, although he admitted that he was also known as Huntley.

It is now believed that the local police who did the background check only looked under the name Ian Nixon and not Ian Huntley.

When the British media got hold of this information, a public outcry for answers quickly followed. Victims' rights groups led the charge, and eventually the government initiated an inquiry to see if anyone other than Huntley was to blame for the girls' deaths and what, if anything, could be done to prevent a similar tragedy in the future.

A report published in 2004 about the inquiry criticized the Humberside and Cambridgeshire Police Departments, but no actions were taken.

The Wells and Chapman families obviously lost the most in the ordeal. The victims' families dealt with the murders with incredible poise, never blaming anyone except Huntley and Carr. The government did, though, admit some amount of culpability when they awarded Holly's and Jessica's parents £11,000 in payment.

Victims' rights groups found the payment preposterous due to the low amount.

The fallout for Ian Huntley has been a bit more dramatic and many would argue a bit of poetic justice.

While Huntley was awaiting trial in jail, he tried to kill himself. Most think that it was part of his attempt to be found insane by the courts, but whatever the reason, it marked the beginning of numerous near-death experiences for the convicted child killer.

After his conviction, Huntley was shuffled around a number of Britain's most notorious maximum-security prisons.

His peers have not taken care of him well.

It has been reported that Huntley has suffered regular beatings at the hands of other inmates since his sentence began in 2003, with a number of the assaults being quite serious. In 2005, Huntley was scalded with boiling water by another inmate, which, combined with the beatings, may have been a factor in another suicide attempt in 2006.

He was also stabbed by another inmate in 2010.

Although Huntley has been placed in protective custody, it seems that the inmates there don't like him much either.

Ian Huntley's life sentence could end any day.

CHAPTER 10:

THE KAPIL DOGRA
RAPE CASE

Cell phones have proved to be a mixed blessing in modern society. They have certainly made our lives easier in many ways: one no longer has to wait by the home phone for calls or rely on finding payphones when away from the house.

Mobile phones have also saved lives and helped solve crimes. Witnesses to crimes are able to immediately alert the police, and there are numerous cases where criminals were caught and convicted of crimes thanks to the testimony of cell phone cameras.

But few can deny that cell phones have a negative side.

Cell phones tend to be much more impersonal than speaking with someone in person, with many experts claiming that excessive cell phone use has led to the deterioration of intrapersonal relationships.

Then there are the physical dangers.

No doubt you have heard of more than one case of a fatal car accident caused by distracted drivers talking or texting on a cell phone while driving.

And there are also the more bizarre cases of distracted people walking into or off things that led to their deaths.

The obvious problem is that sometimes our phones bring us into our own personal worlds, a bubble, making us oblivious to the world around us.

This is what happened to a young woman in April 2017 when she was talking on her phone as she walked from a train station near Datchet, United Kingdom. The young woman thought everything was fine, but little did she know that a predator was stalking the area, waiting for someone not paying attention to their environment.

The Case

Kapil Dogra was a man who had an unimpressive background and little future. In April 2017, he was thirty-five years old but had little to show for his life other than a drug addiction and a criminal record.

The British citizen of South Asian descent lived in the city of Reading, where he was quite active in the criminal underworld. He was known to be loosely affiliated with some of the South Asian gangs in the area, some of which focus their attention on sex work and sexual "grooming" of young British girls.

But most of Dogra's criminal activity revolved around him getting his next fix.

Dogra was a known drug addict who committed numerous burglaries and an occasional armed robbery or mugging in order to get high.

Work was a concept unknown to Dogra, although his ability to effectively hold down a job, if he wanted to work, was severely hampered by his heavy drug addiction. So he spent the better part of his days either committing crimes, plotting his next crimes, or getting high.

On the afternoon of April 12, 2017, Dogra's drug addiction and propensity for violence boiled over when he traveled to the neighboring village of Datchet in search of drugs.

Dogra was fiending for a fix when he woke up on the morning of April 12. He was low on money and knew that all of the dealers in Reading would turn him away because he had been buying drugs on credit for some time.

It is only in the movies that drug dealers maim or kill their customers who are delinquent with their payments. Most drug dealers simply refuse to sell their customers any more drugs until they pay up what they owe, or at least pay up partially.

Dogra didn't have enough money to pay any of the dealers he knew in Reading, so he decided to try a guy he used less frequently in the small, quiet village of Datchet, which is just a few miles away. He took the short train ride to Datchet, but when he got there, he decided that robbing someone first would be a good idea.

He lurked around the train station for some time, looking for a victim, but most were either men or women in groups or keenly aware of their surroundings.

All except one.

Dogra noticed an eighteen-year-old woman deeply involved in a conversation on her cell phone. He stalked the young woman like an animal, following her down the street. He carefully flanked the woman and waited for her in some bushes, and then leaped out, put a knife around her throat, and pulled her into the bushes.

As the horrible attack was taking place, the woman had the presence of mind to tell her boyfriend, who she was talking to on the phone, to call 911.

Dogra then raped and robbed the young woman and went on his way to buy drugs.

Dumb Dogra

Kapil Dogra will more than likely never be a scholar, nor will he ever be described as intelligent, even for a criminal. There is no doubt Dogra's drug-addled brain clouded his judgment during his actions in Datchet on April 12, but there is no doubt that his low IQ also contributed to the events.

Even the most average criminal would have recognized the serious flaws in the scheme.

Since Dogra had a criminal record, his DNA profile was in the United Kingdom's national criminal registry.

The United Kingdom is also often touted as the most heavily-surveilled country in the world in terms of the ratio of security cameras to people. Cameras are everywhere, especially in public places such as train stations.

The DNA profile combined with the closed-circuit television footage led to Dogra being arrested just six days after his horrendous crime.

Due to the crime being a brazen, daylight assault, and the fact that the victim was totally minding her own business, it was covered extensively by most media outlets in the United Kingdom. Most reports focused on the fact that Dogra was a drug addict and a repeat offender, but there was a subtext in some articles about the dangers of cell phones.

Due to the conclusive forensic evidence that was stacked against him, there was little defense that Dogra could muster.

In November 2017, Kapil Dogra was found guilty of rape and sentenced to thirteen years in prison. He will have to serve an additional two years of parole after he is released and will be on Britain's sex offender registry for the remainder of his life.

"This was a planned, targeted and violent stranger rape committed by a man, who is clearly ruthless, predatory and dangerous," said the chief Crown Prosecutor for Thames and Chiltern Crown Prosecution Service, Adrian Foster.

Unfortunately, there are numerous other Kapil Dogra types creeping around subway stations and alleys in cities all over the world, looking for people who are distracted from reality by their cell phones.

CHAPTER 11:

THE MURDER OF SHAYLA O'BRIEN/ELSIE SCULLY-HICKS

Some people shouldn't be parents.

This is an unfortunate reality that probably everyone reading this knows to be true. If you haven't come into contact first-hand with someone who shouldn't be a parent, there is no doubt that you have heard about terrible parents. One doesn't need to peruse the news very long to find terrible examples of children being abused or neglected by their parents.

Granted, most of the cases one hears about in the news are extreme in their nature, but it doesn't take away from the fact that there are countless parents who care little about their children.

This is obviously a difficult phenomenon for most people to understand. Parents are supposed to be the providers and protectors of their children and usually give them unconditional love, so when these cases come to our attention, they are rightfully viewed as one of the ultimate betrayals.

The reasons why some parents are abusive toward their children are many and complex, and have filled entire volumes of psychology books. For whatever reason, some people just aren't fit or prepared for the role of parent, which sometimes can be thrust on a person unexpectedly.

Because many children are born to unwanted parents, adoption has been traditionally seen as a good alternative to provide those children with loving homes.

And usually, adoptive parents are some of the most dedicated parents there are.

Children of adoption tend to be well-adjusted on average, and the rates of abuse and neglect toward them are much lower than in traditional families.

But, of course, there are always exceptions.

A recent case from the United Kingdom demonstrates that sometimes adoptive parents can be just as abusive, if not worse, than natural parents.

Matthew and Craig Scully-Hicks

Mathew and Craig Scully-Hicks are a married couple from Britain who met in Portugal in 2008. After seeing each other for nearly four years, the two men decided to marry in 2012 and planned to eventually start a family.

The couple lived a comfortable life in Cardiff, Wales, with Matt working as a fitness instructor and trainer in the area and Craig working in the corporate world. Craig was the primary breadwinner in the relationship, and his job often took him away from home for days and even weeks at a time.

Matt was extremely health-conscious and not what one would call a "party boy," but he did like to socialize with friends, dining out, and visiting cultural attractions such as museums and theaters. He was committed to Craig but enjoyed a certain level of freedom at the same time.

The men appeared to have a solid relationship and were happy.

And they thought adoption was a good idea for them.

By all accounts, they genuinely believed that they could give an unwanted child a good home, but the tragic results of their adoption show that they were woefully psychologically unprepared to be parents.

The social services conducting the adoption only saw two well-adjusted young men, but underneath one of them was a rage waiting to be unleashed.

Shayla's Misery

Shayla O'Brien had little chance in life, and unfortunately, those who were supposed to protect her failed miserably. She was born to a drug-addicted mother in 2014 and quickly put into foster care.

By all accounts, her foster parents treated her well, but she was placed into the adoption pool. Adoptions are tightly controlled by the government in the United Kingdom, and while elements such as familial relations are considered, they are not always the deciding factor.

Shayla's maternal grandmother wanted her to come back home. She knew that her daughter was still unable to care for Shayla—she couldn't even care for herself at the time—but she hoped that by gaining guardianship herself, Shayla would be reunited with her mother one day.

"In January 2015, I started proceedings in the family court to become the legal guardian for Shayla," said her grandma Sian O'Brien. "I wanted to bring her up in a happy, healthy and warm family environment. That was all taken away from me when social services and the family court decided I would not be able to cope."

The courts believed that Sian was too old and had too much going on in her life to give Shayla the kind of care a child her age needs.

Since Shayla was a cute, young, and bubbly little girl, there were plenty of prospective families that wanted to bring her home.

The Scully-Hicks family won the "competition."

The courts ruled that due to their combined incomes, their stable backgrounds, and the fact that Matt would be home most of the time, the Scully-Hicks family would be a good choice. Shayla was legally adopted by the two men on May 12, 2016, and her name was changed to Elsie Scully-Hicks.

Shortly after bringing Elsie home, Craig left on business and would see his adopted daughter very little. Most of the parenting chores were left to Matt, who was unwilling and/or unable to cope with the immense responsibility.

As soon as Craig left, the abuse began.

In the two weeks between May 12 and May 25, Matt brought the toddler to the local emergency room numerous times for treatment of numerous bruises, cuts, and abrasions to her head and body. Every time Matt told the emergency room doctors that the injuries were the result of accidents: she fell down the stairs, she ran into a door, or she hurt herself while he was in the other room.

For some reason, the staff never questioned him much.

The reality is that Matt was using the poor little girl as a punching bag.

Although no one saw Matt physically abuse Elsie, he referred to her in derogatory ways a number of times in front of friends and acquaintances. He was clearly over his head as a parent and frustrated with the situation.

But instead of telling his partner, he gave the impression that everything was fine.

Craig had been largely absent, having been away for much of the two weeks that Elsie was under Matt's charge, and he never questioned Matt's explanations for her numerous hospital visits.

Finally, on May 25, Elsie's little body could no longer withstand the abuse.

Matt brought her to the hospital one last time that day, but she later died. Since the child had died, the hospital staff were required to call the local police.

The coroner's report showed that Elsie died due to severe trauma from being shaken.

Matt Scully-Hicks was promptly charged with murder in the death of his adopted child. It's important to note that, in December 2016, the Family Court exonerated Craig Scully-Hicks of any failure to protect Elsie.

Craig stood by Matthew during the court proceedings, paying for his defense team and attending his trial. Although Matthew had high-quality lawyers in his corner, the forensic evidence was pretty straightforward and clearly indicated his guilt

Possibly out of hubris, Matthew decided that he wouldn't try to plead to a lesser charge or ask for a plea bargain. Instead, he took the case to trial. His lawyers argued that the massive injuries Elsie sustained *could* have been the result of numerous accidents, as he claimed.

Public opinion in the UK was firmly against Scully-Hicks, and he was quite possibly the most hated man in the country in 2017.

The public watched the trial anxiously via the media until the verdict was announced in November 2017—guilty.

No one was really surprised by the verdict, but most were relieved.

Scully-Hicks was handed a life sentence with a minimum of eighteen years to be served behind bars.

"It was Elsie's behavior, your frustration with it which turned to anger, which led you to inflict the serious injuries which swiftly led to her collapse," said Judge Nicola Davies.

Due to the case's high profile and the nature of the crime, numerous threats have been made on Scully-Hicks' life. After he was sent to a Welsh prison, he was placed in a segregated cell block to protect him from the other inmates.

As Scully-Hicks sits in protective custody for twenty-three hours a day, he will have plenty of time to contemplate where his life went wrong and how many lives he's destroyed by his actions. The reality of the situation, though, as terrible as it is, can be summed up in a simple sentence.

Some people shouldn't be parents.

CHAPTER 12:

THE MURDER OF
AME LYNN DEAL

One of the themes in this volume is the terrible phenomenon of child abuse and the many different forms it takes. Some of the cases highlight strangers who abducted and murdered children. Generally speaking, these types of cases seem to resonate longer in the psyches of people because they invoke images of real-life monsters lurking around corners waiting to nab any unsuspecting child.

These are certainly terrible cases, but statistically speaking, they represent the minority of child murder cases.

Most murders of children are committed by those closest to them, those who are entrusted to protect them.

As mentioned in the previous chapter, those who kill children do so for a number of reasons that may seem senseless to a well-adjusted person, but to the child killer, they make perfect sense.

Sometimes the parent is simply in over their head, while other times there is a financial motive.

But sometimes children are murdered out of pure hatred over a period of several months or even years.

Ame Lynn Deal was a little girl who never had a chance at life.

She was born to an extended family of criminals, con artists, and other assorted losers who never accepted her into their demented fold. She was looked at by her father with derision and repeatedly abused by other family members for no conceivable reasons other than envy, hatred, and pure malice.

Ame Lynn Deal's story is truly difficult to understand, but for precisely that reason, it must be told.

Ame Lynn Deal

Ame's short and difficult life began in 2000 in rural Pennsylvania. She was the youngest of David and Shirley Deal's three children, but it was rumored at an early point that David may not have been her father. Although the rumor was never proven or disproven, many believe that it ultimately played a major role in her murder.

David believed that Shirley had cheated on him, so he resented Ame from the day she was born.

The Deals were a poor family, always living on the edge of survival. Neither parent had any real job skills, and their education was minimal. Sometimes they were on public assistance, while at other times they relied on the charity of their families because often both David and Shirley were not working.

Ame and her siblings were emotionally and educationally well behind other kids their ages. They often went to school hungry and wearing dirty clothes.

Shirley later claimed that David was physically and emotionally abusive toward her when they lived in Pennsylvania, but that things got much worse when they moved to Texas.

The Deal family moved to Texas to be closer to David's extended family. Shirley claimed that she thought that David's family would help him find work and that they would be living in the area, but wouldn't be around every day necessarily.

But when they got to Texas, she learned that they would be living in a communal-style arrangement with David's mother, his sister, Cynthia Stoltzmann, and Stoltzmann's adult daughter and her family. Shirley suffered constant physical and emotional abuse at the hands of the extended Deal family until she finally had enough and moved to Kansas.

She left her three children with the Deals.

Years of Torture

Life began as a difficult prospect for Ame Deal, and it only got worse once her mother left.

The Deal family didn't stay in Texas very long, but long enough for Ame to get an initial dose of what she would face in the coming years. She was ignored by her father and constantly berated and belittled by her grandmother and aunt. When it was time to feed the children, Ame was forced to eat after her cousins, usually only getting scraps if she was lucky.

The extended Deal family never stayed in one place very long. They moved from state to state and from city to city throughout the United States in the 2000s into the early 2010s. The constant moves were difficult for all of the Deal children, who were usually forced to live in squalid conditions no matter where they lived.

Although a few of the adults in the family worked, none of them seemed very concerned with basic hygiene or their living conditions.

They also didn't care much about their children's education.

The children were all homeschooled, if that is what one can call it. Apparently, the Deal adults wanted to keep an almost cult-like control over their children, so they refused to send them to public schools. For the most part, they refused to let them associate with children outside of the family.

The Deal clan eventually ended up in the Phoenix, Arizona area in the late 2000s, which proved to be where things got exponentially worse for little Ame.

Most of the family lived in a house they rented, but Ame was forced to sleep outside in a tent, alone. No doubt Ame suffered immense emotional scars as she was essentially abandoned and isolated by her own family. First, her mother left, then her father, grandmother, and aunt forced her to sleep outside like a dog or a cat.

Cynthia Stolzmann became Ame's legal guardian, but after that, things only seemed to get worse for the little girl.

She was routinely beaten by Cynthia for the smallest indiscretions. The punishments became a sort of entertainment for the adults in the Deal household: Cynthia's twenty-three-year-old daughter, Sammantha Allen, and her same-aged husband, John, began slapping Ame around as well.

Cynthia forced Ame to heat hot sauce and/or dog feces if she did something she didn't like, or just because she was bored. She would also make her stand out in the hot Arizona summer sun for hours on end with no water.

Due to the terrible conditions in which the Deals lived, Ame eventually contracted head lice; it was left untreated, causing scabs and scars on her head.

Finally, Sammantha devised a particularly cruel form of torture—placing Ame in a small footlocker for hours at a time. In 2011, Ame was four feet tall, but the locker was only three feet long, which of course meant that the girl would have to contort herself just to fit.

Samantha especially liked to make Ame do hundreds of jumping jacks and run around the block several times in the Arizona heat before stuffing her into the trunk.

Life was truly a living nightmare for Ame.

The general situation at the Deal household was not unknown to their neighbors or the authorities, wherever they lived. Child protective services were called on numerous occasions after neighbors reported seeing the children wandering the neighborhood at all hours of the night, dirty and disheveled. The police were also called to the house more than once.

On July 12, 2011, the police came to the Deal home one last time.

On that day, the police received an anonymous call about a possible assault. When they arrived, they looked around briefly and found the footlocker of torture. They opened it and were horrified to find Ame inside, dead, with numerous bruises all over her body.

The adults initially told the police that Ame had locked herself inside the locker by accident, but when the police pointed out that the lock was on the outside, they admitted they had locked her in there on purpose as part of a punishment.

John and Sammantha Allen were charged the next day with first-degree murder.

The investigation uncovered the magnitude of the abuse and neglect that was primarily directed at Ame, though all of the other Deal kids suffered to a certain extent.

As a result of the investigation, David Deal, Cynthia Stolzmann, and grandmother Judith Deal were all charged with felony child abuse.

David Deal was reportedly seeking funds to bail out his mother and sister immediately following their arrest. This action, prioritizing the liberation of his child's abusers over mourning his daughter, reinforces the family's profound moral dysfunction.

Getting the Needle

All of the Deal adults were remanded to the Maricopa County jail to face trial. Sammantha and John Allen were refused bail, and the others were unable to make bail.

The surviving children were taken by child protective services and put in foster homes.

As Sammantha and John sat in protective custody blocks in the county jail, they received the news that the district attorney was pursuing the death penalty against both of them. The lawyers for both Allens attempted to reach plea bargains with the DA that would spare their clients' lives, but the public outcry was too great.

They would have to take their chances at trial.

Meanwhile, the other members of the Deal family were facing significant prison time, potentially the remainder of their lives, considering their ages, on the child abuse charges.

David was the first of the family to take a deal, pleading guilty to attempted child abuse in July 2013 and receiving a fourteen-year sentence.

Cynthia Stolzmann pleaded guilty to felony child abuse in September 2013 and received twenty-four years in prison and lifetime probation.

Judith Deal, the family matriarch, was given a ten-year sentence and lifetime probation.

Due to publicity and the nature of the case, the Deals will more than likely have to serve their time in a protective custody block where they will be confined to their cells for twenty-three hours a day.

There is a good chance that due to their health and ages, one or more of the Deals will die behind bars.

The most severe sentences were reserved for John and Sammantha, who the courts believe were the most culpable in Ame's death. Sammantha went on trial first, and after a short trial where her lawyers put up little defense, she was found guilty and sentenced to death by lethal injection on August 7, 2017.

Allen shares death row with two other women.

John went on trial a couple of months later and was handed the same verdict and sentence as his wife. He was sentenced to death on November 17, 2017.

CONCLUSION

The crimes profiled in this book demonstrate that, unfortunately, humans have many reasons to inflict pain on other humans—and sometimes, there doesn't need to be a reason at all.

As scholars and experts work to understand the motives that drive criminals, there often seems to be little that the rest of us can do to protect ourselves.

That is not true.

You have already taken tangible steps to protect yourself and your family by reading the pages of this book, as shocking and terrifying as it is in parts. By educating yourself on the scope of depravity that some people have sunk to over the last 100 years, you have effectively taken your head out of the sand.

Enjoy your life, but always remember that there are predators waiting to take advantage of those who are unaware of their surroundings and unwilling to face reality.

TRUE CRIME STORIES

BOOK 5

INTRODUCTION

The dark desires of the criminal mind have been a subject of interest since ancient times. Texts from ancient Egypt and Mesopotamia describe in excruciating detail how those societies dealt with people who transgressed their laws. Later, the Romans and Greeks were some of the first people to really ponder what made someone a criminal. It wasn't until modern times that experts began to truly delve into what drives criminals.

Several new academic disciplines were created as a result, and dealing with convicted criminals became an industry in itself, as witnessed by the birth of modern prisons and departments of corrections.

Unfortunately, despite the fact that governments and private organizations have devoted a vast amount of resources to the problem, it can feel like experts are no closer to understanding what drives criminals today than the ancient Egyptians were 3,000 years ago. Of course, in reality, significant advances in criminal psychology in the past hundred years have provided profound insights into the minds of killers.

Still, crimes will continue to happen, and some of them will be pretty brutal and of a high-profile nature.

Twelve such crimes are profiled in this book!

As with all of the anthologies in this series, it comprises twelve crime cases that perplexed, awed, and horrified the public to such an extent that they became worthy of being considered high-profile crimes. Although the crimes are all different and unrelated, there are some underlying themes and commonalities among some of them.

You will read about two high-profile crimes involving elite families that happened two decades apart and in countries far removed. One case involves the Talwar family in India and how they endured a legal odyssey fighting accusations that they murdered their own daughter. The other concerns the wealthy and successful Haysom family, who were brutally murdered due to the complicity of their own daughter.

Two of the cases involve a geographic area in Texas that is notorious as both a hunting ground and a dump spot for serial killers and other assorted killers.

You will be introduced to two vigilantes who were driven by very different reasons. One wanted to rid Arizona of everyone he considered "scum," while the other wanted revenge against a child molester and to stop the pedophile from striking again.

Finally, a book in this series wouldn't be complete without at least a few cases that can only be considered strange, mysterious, and bizarre. You will read about a young man named William Inmon, who may be America's youngest serial killer, another young man named Orion Krause, who bludgeoned his family to death with a baseball bat before wandering the neighborhood naked, and the mysterious death of Rebecca Zahau.

After reading this book, you may not be any closer to understanding what drives some of the worst criminals in the world, but you will become aware that violence and chaos come in all shapes and forms.

CHAPTER 1:

THE HI-FI MURDERS

Those of you reading this are probably familiar with the term "robbery gone wrong." It is a common term in criminology used to describe the unfortunate instance when an armed robbery turns violent, leaving the victim either injured or killed.

Of course, there are many reasons for a robbery to go wrong, most of which are the result of unintended circumstances and unforeseen situations. For instance, a robbery victim may struggle, and the robber may panic, shooting or stabbing the robbery victim in the process.

Although armed robbery is a violent crime, most robbers don't want to hurt their victims. Complications during an armed robbery bring unintended attention to the robber and quickly change how much prison time a criminal is looking at if caught—in other words, hurting a robbery victim is bad for business.

But sometimes there are robberies that take place where the motivation of monetary gain appears to exist alongside the desire to torment victims.

Instead of a robbery accidentally turning into a murder, these are cases where murders and robberies go hand in hand.

The infamous "Hi-Fi Murders" that took place in Ogden, Utah, in 1974 is one such case. In this case, five innocent people were tortured over the course of several hours, leaving three dead, over what appeared to be the robbery of an electronics store.

A closer examination of the Hi-Fi Murders reveals that the killers truly had no conscience and were driven by bloodlust that could only be sated by cold-blooded murder. Due to the brutality of the crime, it seems as though the killers probably intended to torture and kill their victims from the beginning.

The Hi-Fi Murders is a tragic case of a premeditated murder that occurred alongside a robbery.

The Hi-Fi Shop

The focus of this case involves a cultural phenomenon that was actually quite short-lived when one considers the length of recorded human history: the record shop. Record shops have only existed for about 100 years, but they didn't really become widespread in American cities until the counter-culture movement of the 1960s. Of course, now record shops are almost as rare as records themselves, as the media that people listen to popular music on has evolved from records to tapes to compact discs and finally MP3s and streamed music, essentially making record stores obsolete.

But those of us who remember record stores know that they were much more than just places to buy music.

In the era before cellphones and the internet, record stores served as hangout spots for kids and young people, who often went to the stores to find out about anything from parties to concerts. The non-corporate record shops were often tolerant of this and had no problem letting kids spend hours of their days in the establishments, even if they didn't buy anything.

Many of these record shops also sold stereos and other electronic equipment (often referred to as "High Fidelity" or "Hi-Fi" equipment), making them a one-stop shop for many pre-computer tech junkies.

The Hi-Fi Shop in Ogden, Utah, was one such place.

Located in the middle of one of the most conservative states in the United States, the Hi-Fi Shop provided a sort of haven for many of the kids and young people in the Ogden area. The shop's downtown location proved to be a boon for business, as kids and adults alike who were curious about the quirky store often dropped in for a quick look and walked out with a record. As the name indicates, the Hi-Fi Shop also sold electronic equipment, so it was also popular with local techies.

The owners of the Hi-Fi Shop consciously made their store friendly to the local youth by letting kids hang out there, posting flyers about concerts and other popular youth events, and hiring a number of young people as part-time employees.

On the evening of April 22, 1974, twenty-year-old Stanley Walker and eighteen-year-old Sherry Michelle Ansley were preparing to close the store after a particularly slow day and evening. About the time that Walker and Ansely were about to close, sixteen-year-old Byron Cortney Naisbitt entered the store.

Naisbitt was one of the many local kids who spent much of his free time and money in the Hi-Fi Shop. The owners and employees of the shop liked Naisbitt and allowed him to park in the store's parking lot when he was in the downtown area. When he used the Hi-Fi Shop parking lot, Naisbitt would usually make an appearance in the store to let the employees know he was using a spot.

On the evening of April 22, when Naisbitt entered the store to say hi to his friends, he walked into a brutal murder and torture session that would become a robbery.

The Selby Crew

The criminal crew that descended on the Hi-Fi Shop like a Mongol horde was led by a twenty-one-year-old named Pierre Dale Selby, also known as Dale Selby Pierre. Little is known about Selby's early life, but when he was still a boy, his family immigrated from Trinidad and Tobago to the United States.

Selby was never nominated for the "most likely to succeed" award in high school.

In fact, Selby seemed to be headed for prison as he was picked up for some minor crimes and had a number of run-ins and altercations with his teachers, other students, and the police. So, as was the case with many wayward youth at the time, those close to Selby pushed the idea of the military as a career.

The military would provide discipline, job training, and free room and board, was the thinking.

Selby joined the Air Force, but as with his life in general, he failed to stand out in any positive way.

After joining the Air Force, like with most people in the military, Selby was stationed at a number of bases before he was sent to Hill Air Force Base near Ogden, Utah. Although the base is located in the greater Salt Lake City metropolitan area, the overwhelmingly White and Mormon Utah was a big change for Selby, who was from an overwhelmingly Black Caribbean Island.

But the cultural differences did not prove to be an impediment to what Selby enjoyed doing most—crime.

Not long after being stationed at Hill, Selby immersed himself in the criminal underworld of the base. He became involved in gambling, extortion, and theft, eventually becoming a suspect in the 1973 murder of another airman.

When the Hi-Fi Shop murders took place, he was out on bail on a grand theft auto charge.

Selby's criminal activity in and around Hill earned him the unwanted attention of the military authorities, but it also gained him the respect of a small crew of directionless Black men on the base.

As Selby built his reputation as a budding crime lord, he took a nineteen-year-old man named William Andrews under his wing as his acolyte and eventually as his right-hand man. Like Selby, Andrews, who was from a predominantly Black area of Louisiana, had experienced a bit of culture shock when he came to Hill. He was intrigued by Selby's ability to pull scores and the older airman's natural leadership qualities.

Before too long, nineteen-year-old Keith Roberts joined the crew along with at least two others who may have played a role in the Hi-Fi Murders.

Beginning in late 1973 and early 1974, Selby and Andrews began discussing robbing the Hi-Fi Shop. They reasoned that since the store was always busy, there would probably be a fair amount of cash on hand. The two men also discussed bringing Roberts and others in on the crime to do a large-scale takeover robbery where they would clear the store out of its electronic equipment.

The reality is, though, that the two men were really planning a murder, and the robbery was just secondary.

From the onset of their heist planning, Selby and Andrews were adamant that they would leave no witnesses to testify against them.

And not only did the two men plan to kill all witnesses, they planned to do so in a most heinous way.

Selby and Andrews were fans of the "Dirty Harry" movie Magnum Force, especially the scene where the killer forces a sex worker to drink Drano, killing her almost instantly.

The two men had found their weapon of choice.

The Attack

What took place at the Hi-Fi Shop on the evening of April 22, 1974, can best be described as an attack or a massacre first and then robbery second. Selby and his crew carried out the attack as if they were an armed paramilitary group, or a death squad, and with almost the same effect.

Shortly before the Hi-Fi Shop closed for the night, Selby, Andrews, Roberts, and possibly two or more other men met at a location off the base and drove in two vans to the store. Once at the site, Selby, Andrews, and possibly one other member of the crew burst into the store with guns in a blitz attack. They quickly subdued Walker and Ansley and led them to the basement.

A few minutes later, Cortney Naisbitt unwittingly wandered into the situation and was also subdued and brought to the basement.

Selby's crew could have quickly emptied the cash register, safe, and the entire store of its electronics, but instead, they took their time.

Murder and mayhem were Selby's true desires that night.

The three young people were bound, berated, and threatened in the basement, but the real torture was yet to begin.

When Stanley Walker and Cortney Naisbitt failed to return home that night, their parents began to worry. Both were known to be responsible kids, and even in the era before cellphones, they were known to call their parents if they were going to be late getting home.

Stanley's father, Orren, and Cortney's mother, Carol, went looking for their children at the Hi-Fi Shop around the same time.

Neither knew what they were walking into.

Once all five victims were securely bound in the basement, Selby and his crew conducted a brutal and prolonged torture session.

The first thing that Selby did was to force the five to drink Drano. He later stated to a commutation board that he thought that the caustic base would kill the captives quickly, as it did in Magnum Force. If that is true, then Selby was incredibly dumb, which may have been the case, but it is also likely that he was lying to make himself look better.

Once he administered the deadly cocktail, the effects were apparent.

Selby told his victims that the Drano was a mixture of vodka and sleeping pills, but as soon as the first person took the deadly dose, the others saw the immediate blistering of the lips.

The victims could not keep the Drano down, so Selby and his crew tried to tape their mouths shut!

"I remember the noise they were making, the sound of pain really," Selby told the commutation board.

At that point, it was clear that the Drano was not killing the hapless victims quickly, but instead of finishing them off with their guns, the robbers decided to put the Hi-Fi Shop employees and their families through more pain and misery.

With all five victims writhing in pain from the Drano, Selby grabbed Ansley and took her to a basement bathroom where he raped her. After he got what he wanted from Ansley, he took her back to the others, coldly threw her on the ground, and shot her once in the back of the head, killing her.

Selby and Andrews then turned their fury on the four survivors.

The killers next shot Cortney Naisbitt, who survived a shot to the head but suffered from permanent damage for the remainder of his life. Selby then shot at but missed Orren Walker. Walker was smart enough to feign death, but the trauma of the torture was apparently too much because Selby noticed him still moving.

Selby then attempted to strangle Orren, and when that didn't work, he had Andrews hold him down while he kicked a ballpoint pen through his ear that came out his throat.

Miraculously, Orren Walker somehow survived the attack.

His son Stanley and Carol Naisbitt were not so lucky.

After committing their prolonged torture and murder session, Selby and his crew cleaned the store out of most of its equipment and left.

Orren Walker's wife and other son worried when Orren and Stanley never returned home, so they went to the shop to find them.

Needless to say, they were horrified at what they found.

The police quickly arrived at the scene and cordoned off the shop to conduct their investigation. The Ogden police were shocked at the carnage in front of them. Even the veterans of the department had never seen such a brutal scene, which plagued many of the officers with nightmares for several months and in some cases, years.

The police were even more shocked when they discovered Cortney Naisbitt and Orren Walker clinging to life.

Cortney spent nearly a year in the hospital recovering from his injuries, which ultimately proved to be permanent.

"He was still bright," said Byron Naisbitt about his son after the attack. "(He had) a different kind of brilliance."

Orren Walker would fare much better but would also suffer from lifelong afflictions as a result of the attack on the Hi-Fi Shop.

A Crew of Dummies

Nothing about the idea, planning, or execution of the Hi-Fi Shop heist points to the perpetrators possessing any reasonable amount of standard intelligence or even criminal acumen.

Selby and his crew were not even good criminals!

But then again, the monetary motivations seemed merely to coexist with the pure bloodlust of the crime.

After emptying the Hi-Fi Shop of most of its electronics, Selby and his crew went back to the base to celebrate their score with a number of other airmen. Although they hid most of the stolen equipment in a storage locker, the careless criminals almost immediately began bragging about committing a "big score" after they pulled the Hi-Fi Shop job.

And since the crime was so brutal, it received intense media attention in Utah and was even mentioned in some national media.

This gave the Ogden Police their first major lead.

An airman at the base (who was a police informant) remembered hearing Selby and Andrews specifically discussing robbing the Hi-Fi Shop several months prior and had heard them just after the massacre brag about a "big score," so he gave that information to the police.

As good as that information was, it only put Selby and his crew on their radar. It was not enough to make an arrest.

The next break came when two teenagers found some of the victims' IDs in a dumpster near the base. Instead of letting the uniformed officers immediately take the IDs from the dumpster to catalog as evidence, the local homicide detectives had them secure the dumpster and ordered more cars to the scene.

Before too long, a crowd developed around the dumpster.

Selby and Andrews were in that crowd.

The detectives then arrived, took possession of the IDs, and carefully surveyed the crowd. They noticed two men in particular who looked nervous and out of place. The detectives checked with the local Air Force authorities and learned that the men were Pierre Selby and William Andrews.

Selby's and Andrews' behavior at the dumpster, combined with the informant's statements, was enough for the police to get a warrant to search the men's apartments on base.

The search of Selby's and Andrew's apartments didn't turn up any murder weapon or anything belonging to any of the victims, but an astute detective did think that a receipt for a storage locker was worth checking out.

The detective was right—the locker held the electronics stolen from the Hi-Fi Shop. The discovery was enough to charge Pierre Selby, William Andrews, and later Keith Roberts with multiple counts of first-degree murder.

Selby and his crew were facing the death penalty, and in law-and-order Utah, if convicted, they would likely face the firing squad.

The Trials and Aftermath

Although Orren Walker was the only survivor who was able to testify against Selby and his crew, his testimony, along with the mountain of circumstantial evidence, was enough for a jury to find Selby and Andrews guilty of capital murder.

The jury was split, though, on Roberts.

Roberts' legal team put up a spirited defense and was able to convince the jury that their client wasn't involved in the murders. He was found guilty of armed robbery, served several years in a Utah prison, and was released in 1987. Roberts quickly left the state and was never heard from again.

Many local residents were angered that Roberts wasn't convicted of murder, and there were also questions about why more men weren't charged, if there were more than three men at the Hi-Fi Shop that night, but Selby, Andrews, and Roberts kept quiet.

It worked for Roberts but not so much for Selby and Andrews.

After a short trial, the two men were found guilty and sentenced to death in 1974.

According to the investigation, Andrews was considered "the brains behind the whole deal, the one who organized it," having previously become acquainted with victim Stanley Walker. This suggests a cold, calculated organizational structure established by Andrews, with Selby acting as the primary agent of sadism and enforcement. The crime was a lethal convergence of calculated targeting (Andrews) and extreme violence (Selby), bringing robbery and murder together.

But Selby and Andrews would have to wait several years before meeting the executioner.

In 1972, the United States Supreme Court issued a national de facto moratorium on the death penalty in the Furman v. Georgia ruling. Although states were allowed to keep sentencing convicted criminals to the death penalty, as Utah had done in Selby's and Andrew's cases, they were not allowed to carry out the sentences until they demonstrated that the death penalty was not carried out "arbitrarily" in their respective states. In 1976, the Gregg v. Georgia ruling by the United States Supreme Court essentially allowed the states to resume executions.

Utah was the first state to carry out an execution post-1976.

In 1977, Utah executed convicted killer Gary Gilmore by firing squad for the murder of two men in 1976. Gilmore famously forewent all appeals, which not only made him the first man in America to be executed post-1976, but also the first to be executed by firing squad since 1960.

The people of Utah were mostly happy with Selby's and Andrew's convictions and sentences. However, the leaders of the state office of the National Association for the Advancement of Colored People issued a statement that they thought the men's convictions were unfair.

During the trial, evidence emerged that racism permeated the process, including the discovery of a juror's note stating, "Hang the Nigger's." The trial judge's decision to deny a mistrial and the right to question the jurors regarding this explicit evidence of racial bias was what drove the National Association for the Advancement of Colored People's claim.

For their part, many people in Ogden thought that the Hi-Fi Murders themselves had racial overtones. In the early 1970s, the United States was still experiencing regular bouts of racial violence often perpetrated by groups such as the Black Panther Party and the Black Liberation Army, as well as racial riots in many inner cities.

Although it was never part of the prosecution's strategy and was never brought up at trial, many Utahns believed that the Hi-Fi Murders were at least partially racially motivated

After Selby and Andrews were convicted, sentenced, and sent to Utah's death row, they learned they had few friends—staff or inmates—at the prison. The two men were subjected to daily verbal abuse and the occasional "piss bomb" (cups of urine and feces thrown through the bars of a cell) by other inmates.

The guards, for the most part, let the abuse continue.

Infamous death row inmate Gary Gilmore briefly shared the same tier with Selby and Andrews, leaving the two men with a message before he was led away to the firing squad.

"Adios, Pierre and Andrews, I'll be seeing you directly."

Selby and Andrews, though, would file their maximum number of appeals to prolong their miserable lives. Selby was finally executed in 1987, and Andrews met the grim reaper in 1992.

Both were executed by lethal injection, a method adopted after Gary Gilmore's 1977 execution by firing squad.

Legacy and Loose Ends

The Hi-Fi Murders case has left deep emotional and physical scars on the state of Utah, and some would argue, the entire United States. The case exposed Americans to a new, vicious type of crime that had been largely absent before the 1970s. The Hi-Fi Murders also stoked racial tension that continues to simmer throughout America to this day.

More importantly, the Hi-Fi Murders forever changed the lives of those who were unfortunate enough to find themselves in the middle of the massacre at the Hi-Fi Shop on April 22, 1974.

Survivor Cortney Naisbitt endured a life of pain and misery as a result of the injuries he sustained on that hellish night. He suffered permanent amnesia and was therefore unable to testify against Selby and Andrews at their trials. Cortney was also ravaged with chronic pain that kept him from working. The one bright spot in Cortney's life was his 1985 marriage.

Unfortunately, Cortney died at the age of forty-four in 2002.

"They couldn't find anything," Cortney's father said about his death. "(There was) nothing in the brain, nothing in his body. He just died."

Orren Walker fared far better than Cortney, but he, too, was plagued by chronic pain for the remainder of his life, as well as hearing problems. He recovered enough after the attack to testify at Selby's and Andrew's trials and was instrumental in their convictions.

Walker died in 2000 at the age of sixty-nine.

Since the case attracted nationwide attention, it eventually became the subject of several books and television shows, usually depicted from the perspective of the victims and their families.

Although this incredibly brutal case appears to have been closed, there are still questions regarding more potential accomplices. As stated earlier, Selby, Andrews, and Roberts remained mum in this respect, but the authorities believe there were more involved.

If there were others involved, the chances are good that one or more may still be alive.

CHAPTER 2:

THE ELIZABETH HAYSOM MURDER CASE

No matter how responsible a child or young adult may be, at that age, most people are prone to make mistakes and bad choices in life. Let's face it, we all made or nearly made some dumb decisions when we were growing up concerning our choice of friends, career, or college choices, and use of alcohol and drugs. All of these are common sources of conflict between parents and their children, but perhaps the choice that leads to the most acrimony between kids and their parents is that of boyfriends and girlfriends.

We all want what's best for our children, and often the dates they bring home just don't stack up to our expectations.

But those of you who have children know that you are walking a thin line trying to manage your children's relationships.

If you are too strict and push against a particular person your child has chosen to date, you run the risk of pushing your kid right into Mr. or Ms. Wrong's arms.

On the other hand, if you take too much of a hands-off attitude toward your child's dating, then they may purposely go out with the worst person just for attention.

Truly, it is one of the most difficult aspects of being a parent in the modern world, with no real answer or solution that is "one size fits all." How can there be? Young people's minds are not fully developed to begin with, and their life experiences are minimal at best.

Young people also often use emotion over logic in their decision-making, especially when it comes to their first loves. Young people often believe that their first love is the be-all and end-all of the world and the only person who truly understands them.

When a kid's first serious relationship ends, it is often devastating, but most quickly rebound and move on with their lives. But the highly charged, deep feelings that some kids experience during their first true love can be too much for some to handle.

They do whatever they can to keep the relationship going, even if it means their own destruction.

Some kids descend into a dark world of crime and drugs to appease their first love, often ending with unwanted pregnancies, chemical addiction, and jail time.

Some examples even end in death.

On March 30, 1985, obsessive attachment turned to murder when the wealthy, successful couple Derek and Nancy Haysom were murdered in their own home. There were few leads to begin with, but the brutal manner of the murder, and the fact that the United States was in the midst of the "Satanic Panic," led many at first to think the culprits were members of a Satanic cult.

Once the investigators looked further into the evidence, the ugly truth was revealed. The Haysoms were not murdered by a Satanic cult, but by two young people who felt they could not live apart from each other.

A Privileged Family

If one were to sum up the Haysom family in a few words, wealthy, successful, interesting, attractive, and worldly would be a good start. The Haysoms were multimillionaires, traveled extensively, and were well-educated.

Derek and Nancy knew what they wanted in life, how to get it, and what should be expected from their children. Since they were so successful, they expected their children to listen to them, which they did for the most part, but their daughter was from another generation that they didn't understand.

And they weren't willing to try to understand.

Nancy Haysom was born Nancy Astor Benedict in 1932 in the Blue Ridge Mountains of Virginia. Not long after she was born, Nancy's parents relocated to Arizona, which is where she grew up. Like most women at that time, she got married young to a man her parents approved of and had two sons.

But Nancy had a restless soul and felt constrained by her marriage, so she divorced in the late 1950s, which was before "no-fault" divorces and when divorce in general was still somewhat of a taboo in the United States.

Nancy didn't let the social conventions of the period constrain her as she traveled the world, meeting her future husband Derek along the way.

Derek Haysom was nearly twenty years Nancy's senior. Nancy was immediately drawn to the tall, handsome South African when she met him in his home country in 1960. After talking with Derek, Nancy learned that he had three children from a previous marriage, which was a commonality between them.

But she was more intrigued and attracted to his exploits and ambition.

One would think that parts of Derek Haysom's life were taken from a James Bond novel or a John Wayne movie if they weren't true. As a young man, Haysom joined the army in South Africa—which was part of the British Empire until 1961—and fought in World War II. After the war, Haysom worked briefly in intelligence for the South African government, being involved in operations throughout Africa, before becoming an engineer.

Although Haysom's life as a soldier and intelligence officer was behind him by the 1960s, he continued to travel and live on nearly every continent as an engineer. He even obtained Canadian citizenship while he lived and worked in Nova Scotia as an executive at a steel corporation.

Derek and Nancy married shortly after meeting and had their only child together, Elizabeth, in 1964. Despite Derek being over fifty when Elizabeth was born, the Haysoms didn't think that would be a problem. They both reasoned that their money, influence, and background would make Elizabeth's life easy because, unlike with their previous children, they would be able to give her anything.

And Elizabeth got whatever she wanted!

Spoiled Elizabeth

Elizabeth Haysom was born in the southern African country of Rhodesia, which is now known as Zimbabwe. It became clear at an early point that Elizabeth inherited most of her parents' good qualities—she was physically attractive, intelligent, and had a good personality.

But it also became clear that she had developed one quality that was lacking in her parents—entitlement.

Neither Derek nor Nancy was born into considerable money, with both getting what they had in life through their own merits and connections. They never expected to be handed anything, and both exhibited the standard "Protestant work ethic" throughout their lives.

Elizabeth, though, expected things to be handed to her.

Derek and Nancy made sure that Elizabeth was given the most advantages by sending her to the best schools. They wanted her to be cultured, so they regularly took her on trips around the world.

Although one could say that the Haysoms spoiled Elizabeth to a certain extent, they also had high expectations for their daughter.

For her high school years, Elizabeth was sent to a prestigious and expensive boarding school in the United Kingdom. Not long after school began, the first fissures formed between Elizabeth and her parents. Derek wanted his daughter to follow in his footsteps by focusing on the hard sciences and then studying engineering in college. Nancy agreed with her husband that a science background would be the best route to ensure a solid, lucrative career.

Elizabeth was not interested.

Elizabeth was drawn more to the arts and saw herself as a potential poet or novelist. Although her grades were good in that regard and she showed promise as a writer, her parents were not happy.

Their unhappiness with Elizabeth quickly turned to anger.

Elizabeth's rebellion went far beyond just not choosing her parents' preferred curriculum. She fell in with a wild crowd at the boarding school and quickly found herself experimenting with alcohol, drugs, and sex. It was almost as if she wanted to be caught because she flaunted her indiscretions openly.

She was eventually expelled for drug use and homosexual activity.

The Haysoms were furious when they learned about this, but as much as they may have wanted to discipline Elizabeth, they were unable to find her. She went missing on her own accord in Europe.

Elizabeth was a fairly intelligent young woman, IQ-wise, but she was also worldly, which meant that she had the connections and the background to survive for some time in Europe. She had several friends and acquaintances on the continent and could get by in German, French, and Spanish. Although she was cut off from her parents' money, she quickly found other ways to live.

Elizabeth lived on the largesse of her friends, and when that wasn't enough, she resorted to sex work. It wasn't as if she needed to sell her body—she could have gone home at any time—but Elizabeth was having fun. She continued to party and do drugs across western Europe until her parents finally convinced her to come home.

Derek and Nancy flew to the United Kingdom to get Elizabeth, who was done with her months-long party at that point. Derek had recently taken a high-paying corporate position in Lynchburg, Virginia, and was able to convince Elizabeth that he would pay for her college education if she moved there with him.

Elizabeth enrolled in the prestigious University of Virginia in the fall of 1984.

A young man named Jens Soering also enrolled at the University of Virginia as a freshman in the fall of 1984.

Like Elizabeth, Soering also came from a privileged background. His father was a diplomat with the government of West Germany, and his family had plenty of money, although that is not what got Jens into the University of Virginia. Jens was the recipient of the prestigious Jefferson Scholarship, which is awarded to students based on a combination of high academic success and community involvement. Although Jens' family was wealthy and could have easily paid for his education out of their own pockets, the scholarship provided him with fully paid tuition and a generous stipend.

Soering's future seemed set, but he had a difficult time fitting in with his classmates. Although UVA is considered an elite public university, most of Jens' fellow classmates were Americans who were more "middle America" than blue blood. To Jens, they seemed provincial, insular, and lacking in sophistication.

Needless to say, Jens' classmates didn't regard him too highly.

Most of the freshman class saw Jens as an arrogant European snob and a bore who was insufferable to be around.

At first, Elizabeth Haysom also had a low opinion of Jens, but that changed the more she got to know him. Elizabeth realized that she had less in common with her American "rube" classmates than she did with Jens Soering. She and Jens were both cosmopolitans who didn't fit in with their peers.

Elizabeth also quickly learned that they both hated their parents.

Jens' and Elizabeth's friendship rapidly evolved into a romance. The two co-eds spent nearly all of their free time together, often making promises to each other that they would not live apart.

Elizabeth also began telling Jens that her parents abused her when she was younger. Jens was surprised by the revelation, but he was in love and believed Elizabeth. It was his first true love, so there was little that could sour him on the relationship. Once Pandora's Box was opened, Elizabeth regularly talked about how much she hated her parents and even told Jens, "I wish they were dead."

Still, Jens believed that Elizabeth was possibly exaggerating the difficulties with her parents and that, once he met them, things would get better. After all, how could her parents be disappointed with the son of a diplomat who was going to UVA on a full-ride scholarship?

Soering's background was enough to get him a visit to Haysom's home. Derek was an elderly man by this point, but he was still imposing physically and mentally.

Nancy usually followed her husband's lead, especially in matters regarding their daughter. Although the Haysoms were impressed with Jens' background, they were repulsed by his personality. The Haysoms were immediately turned off by Jens' arrogance, which he was apparently unable to turn off even when meeting his girlfriend's parents, so they demanded that Elizabeth quit dating him.

Of course, Elizabeth was no stranger to disobeying her parents and continued to see Jens. Since she was living in Charlottesville to attend college, there was little that the Haysoms could do to make Elizabeth stop seeing Soering in the short-term, but Elizabeth would have to think of something if she wanted to be with Jens long-term.

Elizabeth told Jens about how awful and abusive her parents were whenever she got the chance. Eventually, Elizabeth only seemed to talk about her parents whenever she was with Jens.

Her talk began to take effect.

A Brutal Attack

March 30, 1985, was a cool night in northern Virginia. The winter lasted a little longer that year, and there was still frost on the ground in the morning. It seemed like the perfect night for Elizabeth and Jens to put their plan into action. They were going to take care of their problem once and for all.

Derek and Nancy Haysom would die that night.

During the afternoon of March 30, Elizabeth and Jens rented a car in Charlottesville, drove to Washington, D.C., rented a motel room, and bought two movie tickets. It was all apparently part of an elaborate effort to set up an alibi in case they needed one. After the pair checked in, Jens then drove back south to "talk" with Elizabeth's parents.

Jens showed up at the semi-rural Haysom house just past 8 p.m. to make his case to the parents.

According to Jens, Derek remained steadfast and adamant that he would never accept Jens' and Elizabeth's relationship. Derek then took things up to another level by threatening to use his vast connections to have Jens expelled from UVA if he persisted in pursuing Elizabeth.

This was too much for the amorous German.

Jens claims that, in a fit of rage, he grabbed a knife from the nearby counter and stabbed the seventy-year-old Derek in the neck. Nancy, who was also in the room during the conversation, screamed and ran for the phone in the kitchen to call for help. Jens chased her down, stabbing her repeatedly until she stopped moving.

As Jens finished Nancy off, Derek rose from the ground and engaged Jens in a life-and-death tussle. Normally, despite his age, the World War II vet could've easily dispatched of scrawny Jens, but the stab wound to his neck proved to be too much. Jens got the best of Derek and hacked him to death.

After killing the Haysoms, Jens washed his hands and quietly left the house. He returned to Elizabeth in D.C.

The Investigation and Flight

The crime scene at the Haysom home was not discovered until several days later, when a concerned neighbor called the police. The responding units were shocked by the brutality of the scene: both Derek and Nancy were nearly decapitated due to all the stab wounds, and the kitchen was covered in blood.

None of the Haysoms' neighbors had noticed anything unusual in the days before or after the murders, which was somewhat to be expected since the Haysoms lived in a relatively isolated subdivision. The lack of eyewitnesses was compounded by the fact that there appeared to be nothing missing from the scene, and there was a lack of physical evidence left by the killer or killers.

Theories about the murders began to flourish.

Some people thought the Haysom murders were the work of a random serial killer, while others, no doubt influenced by the "Satanic Panic" of the time, believed that the perpetrators were a Satanic cult.

The homicide investigators thought from the beginning that the killer or killers were closer to home.

For Jens and Elizabeth, a major obstacle had been removed from their lives, and to all who knew them, they couldn't have appeared happier. When Elizabeth finally met with homicide investigators, she didn't appear bothered and strangely talked about items missing from the house that weren't actually missing. She also made sure to tell the police about the abuse she had suffered at her parents' hands.

The suspicions that the police had about Elizabeth and her paramour were further bolstered when they met with Elizabeth's half-siblings. Her brothers and sisters told the homicide investigators about Jens' and Elizabeth's forbidden relationship and that their sister had quite a few choice things to say about her parents.

They were all sure that Elizabeth was somehow involved in her parents' murders.

In the weeks following the murders, Elizabeth and Jens began to feel increased pressure from the Virginia authorities, so they did what any privileged, cosmopolitan couple would do in their situation—flee to Europe.

The couple reasoned that since they were both intimately familiar with Europe, they could change their identities and avoid the long arm of American justice.

But living on the lam as an international fugitive is easier said than done.

They duo was able to use their passports to catch a flight from the United States to London, England, but they both knew that they would be flagged at airports in the future once warrants were issued for their arrests, which happened not long after they fled.

Obviously, Elizabeth could no longer depend on her family for financial support, and Soering had to sever contact with his family. Since his father was a government official, Soering believed that he would turn him in if contacted. So the pair were reduced to other means to support themselves.

Using connections they had developed years earlier, the pair was able to acquire a number of fake IDs that would allow them to leave the United Kingdom and/or work legitimate jobs.

But neither Jens nor Elizabeth was interested in legitimate work.

They supported themselves in high-priced London by writing bad checks at department and convenience stores. The pair may have possessed above-average IQs, but their criminal sophistication was quite low. They were caught when they tried to pass bad checks at the same locations multiple times.

After they were arrested, the police searched their apartment and discovered books of stolen checks and numerous fake IDs. The pair stayed quiet at first, but with a mysterious West German and American in their custody, the London police knew they were onto something. Before too long, an Interpol report came back with Haysom's and Soering's pictures and fingerprints—the pair's international flight was over.

Among the other items found in the couple's England apartment that were later used in court were a series of letters, written in code, that described the murders.

The pair would face first-degree murder charges in Virginia, which brought with it a possible death sentence in a state that regularly used the death penalty.

But before the couple could go on trial in Virginia, they would have to be extradited from the United Kingdom.

Jens did everything he legally could to keep from being sent back to the United States. His lawyers argued that he shouldn't be extradited because he could face the death penalty, and neither the United Kingdom nor West Germany had the death penalty. Soering then admitted to the murders because he believed he had diplomatic immunity through his father. A high degree of entitlement, born from his privileged upbringing, led to this fundamental legal miscalculation.

Soering then tried to make a deal to have his trial in West Germany.

The Virginia prosecutors weren't willing to budge on most of Soering's demands, but they did agree to forgo the death penalty if the accused killer would relinquish his extradition fight.

Finally, after three years of legal maneuvering, Jens Soering agreed to be extradited to Virginia to stand trial.

Soering was found guilty of first-degree murder in 1990 and sentenced to two life sentences.

Elizabeth decided not to fight extradition and instead returned to Virginia immediately to defend herself in court. Her defense was that Soering did everything and that she only fled with him later because she was scared. After agreeing to testify against Soering at his murder trial, Haysom was allowed to plead guilty to the lesser charge of accessory to murder before the fact in 1987.

Soering continued to proclaim his innocence and filed several appeals, all of which were denied. His efforts did gain him many followers who believed in his innocence.

A number of Soering's supporters have paid for a new forensic analysis to be conducted on the available evidence since DNA profiling was in its infancy at the time. Notably, tests performed in 2009 showed that none of the forty-two pieces of evidence analyzed in relation to the crime could be matched to Soering via DNA.

Release and Deportation

On November 25, 2019, it was announced that both Haysom and Soering would be released, but not pardoned. After over 30 years behind bars, Haysom was paroled and then deported in January 2020 to Canada, where her father, Derek Haysom, had obtained citizenship. Soering was deported to Germany after he was paroled that same year.

Some condemned the killers' releases as a cost-cutting measure by the state of Virginia, while others argued that the parole was valid given the young age of the perpetrators at the time they committed the crime. Having been deported, neither Haysom nor Soering is able to reenter the United States.

CHAPTER 3:

THE MURDERS OF DEBBIE ACKERMAN AND MARIAN JOHNSON

The study of police procedures regarding serial killers is as complex as it is interesting. Beyond examining a particular serial killer's method of operation or signature, perhaps the most important part of an investigation involves actually identifying and capturing a killer.

Some of the most perplexing serial killer cases are ones that were being tracked by the authorities as active, but for some reason, the killer stopped. Experts say that the most common reason for a particular series of killings ending is that the killer was either caught for another crime and in prison, or dead. However, that is clearly not always the case, even if it is the most common reason.

Sometimes, the serial killer simply moves and starts killing in another city or region, as Ted Bundy did.

But when one examines the history of serial killers, there are some who simply quit killing for various other reasons.

Gary Ridgway, the "Green River Killer," is perhaps the best-known case in this regard. Ridgeway murdered up to seventy-one women during the 1980s and 1990s, but he went dormant for several years before he was arrested. His lack of killing in the late 1990s has been attributed to familial obligations.

On the other end of the spectrum, sometimes the police don't even know they have a serial killer until the person is arrested for something else. Because nearly every offender in the United States now has to have their DNA entered into the nationwide CODIS database upon conviction, and in some states when arrested, several unknown serial killer cases have been uncovered in recent years.

And then there are the ones who want to talk.

The reason why incarcerated individuals confess to multiple murders varies. Many are already doing life, or very lengthy prison sentences, so they believe that by confessing to cold cases, they can arrange plea bargains that can get them better living conditions or perks behind bars.

Others do it for notoriety.

Joseph Paul Franklin went on a cross-country murder spree during the late 1970s and early 1980s in the hope that he would start an epic race war. After he was arrested and convicted of killing two Black men in Salt Lake City, Utah, in 1981, he confessed to more than a dozen other murders. He hoped that by doing so, he would inspire others to follow his lead.

Finally, some killers claim to confess to bring closure to their victims' families.

Although these claims are often considered dubious and viewed with skepticism, a number of serial killers have revealed themselves to be so only after being locked up for a considerable amount of time. These killers have claimed that a guilty conscience drove them to confess.

Edward Harold Bell is one such man. Bell was convicted of a high-profile 1978 murder in Texas, after which he went on the lam for fourteen years. After he was captured and sent to prison, most of the world forgot about Bell until he confessed to several other murders in two letters. Bell claimed that he confessed to bring closure to his victims' families, but prosecutors considered his confessions with a grain of salt.

Among the murders that Bell confessed to were those of two Texas girls who may be connected to a string of other murders along the Interstate 45 corridor between Houston and Galveston.

Edward Harold Bell

At first glance, Edward Bell's early life was nothing spectacular, and nothing about it would seem to indicate that he would become a serial killer. But serial killers are known for hiding their dark desires from those closest to them.

Bell was born in 1939 in the small, quiet town of Columbus, Texas. Columbus is an agricultural community about 100 miles west of Houston, where everyone knows each other and little has changed in the years since Bell was born to the present.

Bell was not a troublemaker as a child: he didn't give his teachers any problems and had no run-ins with the police as a juvenile. He was also not known to abuse animals, be obsessed with fire, or be a bed wetter—the so-called "Macdonald Triad" that many experts consider to be an early indicator of a possible serial killer.

Bell graduated from high school without a hitch and went on to college at Texas A&M University. While in college, Bell dated, developed a sizable social network, and was well-liked by those who knew him. He played in the marching band and was known as "Butch" by his friends and acquaintances.

To those who knew Bell during the 1960s, he was a regular, all-American guy.

After he graduated from college and entered the "real world," Bell's all-American exterior slowly began to erode. He moved to western Texas, married, and had three children. Bell supported his family by working in a number of different occupations—he was a trucker, pharmaceutical salesman, and real estate salesman—but none of those professions or his family seemed to quell the problems that were slowly emerging in his life.

Bell was arrested at least a dozen times for flashing young girls between 1966 and 1978 in the states of Texas and Louisiana. It is "at least" because, long before sex offender registries, flashing cases were always treated as misdemeanors and were often dropped in court, or the arresting police officer simply would let the offender go with a warning. There's no doubt that Bell showed signs of being a sexual predator by the 1960s, but those signs were ignored by the authorities.

In those days, the authorities were often more prone to treat people like Bell as mentally ill instead of as criminals. Because of that, Bell was confined to mental hospitals.

Although Bell's numerous flashing offenses landed him in jail on more than one occasion, he never did any serious time. When he was sent to a mental hospital in 1970, his life changed dramatically.

Due to his numerous arrests and his increasingly erratic behavior around their children, Bell's first wife left him. The divorce was a serious blow to the already mentally unstable Bell, but things turned around for him within a short time of being in the mental hospital.

Some American mental hospitals are similar to prisons, with extremely high security and units segregated by sex. Bell was not in one of these hospitals. Instead, Bell was sent to a hospital that was more like a treatment center or retirement home. The food was edible, the patients had plenty of freedom, and most importantly for Bell, the facility was coed.

The thirty-one-year-old Bell immediately set his sights on an attractive seventeen-year-old. He manipulated the already emotionally fragile girl and groomed her to be his next wife. After the couple was released a few months later, they married and moved to the Galveston, Texas area.

The newlyweds told their family and friends that they were planning on starting over by investing in various businesses in the area, one of which was a surf shop that was popular with the local youth.

Once Bell and his wife had bought into the shop, Harold was like a kid in a candy store.

The Brainwash Murders

The beautiful, bikini-clad girls and young women that Bell watched every day from his surf shop were too much for the serial sex offender to resist. He would later claim that his compulsion to commit sex offenses was the result of being "programmed" to do so, first by his father and then by his ex-wife.

"I was 'Brainwashed' into killing Deby [sic] Ackerman and Marian Johnson in 1971," Bell later wrote.

It remains to be seen, and probably never will be proven either way, if this was a genuine delusion from the mind of a mentally disturbed man, or if it was just some bizarre story he concocted to mitigate his status as a serial killer. Either way, it now appears likely that not only did Bell kill those two girls but probably several others as well.

The murders of Debbie Ackerman and Marian Johnson happened in November 1971 near Interstate 45, which is the major highway that connects the Houston metropolitan area to Galveston and the Gulf Coast. Both girls were fifteen-year-old residents of the Galveston area who knew Bell from his surf shop. The surf shop was a popular hangout spot for local teenagers where they often met up to plan their weekends and find out where all the parties were.

Both girls were last seen accepting a ride from a White male in a white van.

Although the driver of the van was never positively identified, it was later determined that Bell owned a white cargo-type van at the time.

It is believed that since the girls knew Bell from the surf shop, they were not on guard when he approached them. He probably offered them a ride to another part of the city, which they accepted without reservation because they knew him and they were together.

Not long after the girls were in his van, Bell's demeanor quickly changed. He pulled out a gun and bound the girls before driving to a remote bayou near I-45. He then raped and shot the girls to death before dumping their bodies in the lonely bayou.

Bell is now believed to be responsible for at least three more I-45 murders, which he claimed were part of his "programmed" killings.

The bones of thirteen-year-old Colette Wilson, who went missing from a summer camp in 1971, and the body of nineteen-year-old Houston native, Gloria Gonzales, were also found in the same bayou location.

Bell also claims responsibility for abducting and murdering sixteen-year-old Kimberly Pitchford in 1971. Pitchford's remains were discovered in the same general location as the others in 1973.

Bell has claimed responsibility for murdering at least six other girls and young women along the I-45 corridor during the 1970s.

The Murder of Larry Dickens

While Bell was killing along the I-45 corridor during the 1970s, the local authorities had no idea that he was responsible; in fact, FBI special agent Robert Ressler had only coined the term "serial killer" and its definition in 1974, so few law enforcement agencies knew how to deal with such an offender.

Bell's case was further complicated by the fact that there were potentially several killers operating in and around the I-45 corridor, using the area as both a hunting ground and a dump spot.

But with someone who is so compelled to commit sex offenses, such as Bell, it was only a matter of time before he committed a serious crime that landed him in prison for a significant amount of time.

It would not be the murder of a girl or young woman that ended Bell's reign of terror, but a young man who was a good Samaritan.

Larry Dickens was a Marine and a youth counselor who enjoyed spending time with his family in his hometown of Pasadena, Texas, which is a suburb of Houston. During the summer of 1978, Larry moved back to Pasadena to live with his mother Dorothy and his sister Dawn. Larry planned to help around the house, making some needed repairs and maintenance, and would be rewarded by getting ample helpings of his mom's home cooking.

On the afternoon of August 24, 1978, Larry Dickens unfortunately crossed paths with Harold Bell.

On the afternoon in question, Larry was mowing the lawn at his family's home as a group of kids rode their bikes up and down the street.

Harold Bell was also in the area.

Bell had been drinking heavily throughout the day and began to feel the urge to commit another sexual offense. After committing countless sex offenses over the course of nearly two decades, Bell had his criminality down to a science. He took his pants and underwear off as he drove around looking for potential flashing victims. He knew exactly which neighborhoods to trawl to find young victims.

He got off the interstate and drove into Larry Dickens' quiet, suburban neighborhood. Bell noticed a group of boys and girls riding their bikes and playing in the street, so he pulled his truck over, got out, and started masturbating in front of the children.

Both Dorothy and Larry saw what was happening, so Dorothy called the police while Larry walked over to Bell's truck and took his keys. When Bell realized what was happening, he became irate and demanded his keys back, but the younger and healthier Larry refused. Knowing that he couldn't physically take the keys back from Larry, Bell pulled out a gun and began shooting the young Marine.

Wounded, but still clutching Bell's keys, Larry retreated to the garage of his family's home, where his mother and sister were. Unfortunately for Larry, Bell followed him, got the keys, and then delivered a final kill shot to Larry's head.

The case immediately made the local news, and Bell was quickly identified. He was caught and charged with murder, but for some reason, the judge gave Bell a $125,000 bail. Bell posted the bail and then went on the run for several years.

Throughout the 1980s, Bell's case was covered from time to time in Houston media outlets, but it was finally picked up nationally when Robert Stack decided to profile it on his Unsolved Mysteries television show. The case aired on a December 1992 episode, with the role of Larry Dickens being played by future A-list actor Matthew McConaughey. The episode generated a lot of tips, and Bell was finally captured in 1993 in Panama.

It turns out that Bell actually owned some land in the small Latin American nation and was panning for gold when he was arrested by the local authorities. He was quickly extradited back to Texas, where he stood trial for the murder of Larry Dickens.

Final Justice?

Bell went on trial for Larry's murder in 1994 and was promptly found guilty and sentenced to seventy years in a Texas prison.

As Bell aged and withered in prison, Texas law enforcement authorities didn't even know that they had a potential serial killer in their midst.

That was until Bell decided to write letters to Harris County (Houston) and Galveston County prosecutors in the late 1990s claiming responsibility for several murders along the I-45 corridor, particularly about "eleven that went to Heaven."

When the prosecutors received the letters, they were immediately skeptical. They didn't believe that Bell had much of a conscience, so that wouldn't have been a reason to admit to the crimes, but they knew he had an ego, so they reasoned that he did so to increase his fame.

The prosecutors also believed that he possibly admitted to the murders to get transferred to a facility with better living conditions. Whatever the reason or reasons, the prosecutors decided against releasing the letters to the public.

The decision proved to be a public relations disaster.

When the existence of the letters was finally revealed in 2011, many of the families of the victims Bell named were rightfully angered. Like all families of murder victims, they want to know what exactly happened to their loved ones, no matter how horrible their last moments were.

"I didn't believe we had sufficient evidence that we could proceed to the grand jury with, and without getting into specifics, that's the decision that had to be made," said former Galveston district attorney Kurt Sistrunk about his office's refusal to release the content of Bell's letters to the public.

On April 20, 2019, Harold Bell died from heart failure in prison, aged seventy-nine.

Today, the families of Bell's eleven other alleged victims are left wondering if they will ever receive justice.

CHAPTER 4:

INDIA'S CRIME OF THE CENTURY— THE MURDERS OF AARUSHI TALWAR AND HEMRAJ BANJADE

The term "crime of the century" has been repeated so many times in the last twenty-five years that it has become a bit of a cliché. To better understand the next case, what makes a crime worthy of having this label should be considered before moving forward.

Many crimes that are worthy of being considered crimes of the century have involved high-profile people, either victims or perpetrators, who have captured the attention of the media and the public. During the 1990s, the Menendez brothers' trials and the O.J. Simpson trial competed for the title in that decade, while the Robert Blake trial earned the moniker in the 2000s. Although the verdicts differed in these cases, that only served to make the cases more memorable and worthy of being"crime of the century."

There have also been some unresolved cases that have become part of folk culture and later earned the title crime of the century despite no trial. The 1962 escape from the notorious Alcatraz prison in California by Frank Morris, John Anglin, and Clarence Anglin certainly qualifies, as does the 1971 skyjacking by the mysterious D.B. Cooper.

All of these cases intrigued the public at the time, and many of them still manage to pique the interest of those interested in true crime. Observant readers will note that some of these cases have been profiled in previous volumes of this series.

Despite being quite different in terms of their details, the above cases all took place in the United States.

Of course, it goes without saying that every country in the world has its own crimes of the century that capture the attention and imagination of its citizens.

Just over ten years ago, India was shocked when it learned about the double murder of thirteen-year-old Aarushi Talwar and forty-five-year-old Yam Prasad "Hemraj" Banjade, which took place in the early morning hours of May 16, 2008. In a country that is more known for temples, elephants, and Gandhi than murder, Indians were not only horrified by the brutality of the crimes, but maybe even more so by the circumstances—Aarushi was a teenager from a privileged family, and Hemraj was her servant.

The ensuing investigation ensured the case not only stayed in the headlines of the Indian media but it was also picked up by news outlets around the world. At times, there seemed to be a lack of evidence, while at other points in the investigation, the evidence seemed to point to multiple suspects.

It would be an understatement to say that the investigation was flawed.

Eventually, the parents of Aaurshi became the prime suspects, but after years of investigation and court proceedings, the authorities seem no closer to identifying the killers in what has become India's "crime of the century."

The Talwars

Rajesh and Nupur Talwar were both successful dentists from the Delhi metropolitan area of northern India. Together, they built a nice practice in the suburb of Noida, running a clinic with another couple, Praful and Anita Durrani.

The Talwars were part of a new generation of emerging wealth in the cities and suburbs of some of India's biggest cities. They took advantage of new economic policies initiated by the Indian government during the 1990s by investing money in real estate as well as the stock market.

The newly-acquired wealth allowed the Talwars to open their clinic and buy a nice home in the suburb of Noida, plus afford other luxuries still out of reach for most Indians.

The Talwars shared the same profession, which was enough for them to overcome their differences in caste background in the caste-conscious nation. Although it is still uncommon for people to marry outside of their caste in India, it is not unheard of, and in the cosmopolitan Delhi area, the Talwars had few problems because of it.

The Talwars also bucked the standard Indian convention of having a large family. The Talwars only had one child, a daughter, Aarushi, to whom they were able to dedicate more time and money as a result. They gave her all of the latest electronic gadgets and sent her to an expensive, prestigious private school.

Besides being able to give their daughter whatever she wanted, the Talwars were able to buy a nice home in a good neighborhood and to hire a full-time driver and a live-in Nepali servant named Hemraj.

Life was perfect for the Talwars until May 16, 2008.

The Murders

The tragedy in Noida began during the afternoon of May 15 when Nupur picked Aarushi up from school. The two spent the afternoon together at their home, talking, watching television, and eating dinner. After dinner, Aarushi went to her bedroom, which was next to her parents' bedroom, to do her homework and use the internet.

Rajesh spent the afternoon at his other job, teaching at an area dental school. After he was done with his classes, Rajesh then stopped by their dental office to do some work before coming home around 9 p.m.

According to the family's driver, Umesh Sharma, he saw all members of the Talwar family and Hemraj in the home just before 10 p.m.

Sharma was the last person other than the Talwars to see Aaurshi and Hemraj alive.

The record of the sequence of events, and the events themselves, after 10 p.m., have been questioned extensively by the authorities since they are primarily based on the testimony of the Talwars.

The Talwars claim that they gave Aarushi an early birthday gift of a digital camera just after 10 p.m. Aarushi was happy to receive the gift and took several pictures before her parents said goodnight and retired to their room next door for the evening. Before leaving, Nupur switched on the internet router that was in Aarushi's room.

The forensic evidence shows that the router was last used just after midnight on May 16.

Just after midnight, one of Aarushi's friends tried texting her but received no response, so she then tried calling the family's landline phone, but it was never answered.

The medical examiners later determined that the time of death for both Aarushi and Hemraj was between midnight and 1 a.m. on May 16.

The evidence shows that Aarushi was attacked in her bed. She was beaten and stabbed to death, and there was possibly an attempt to sexually assault her.

Hemraj was also stabbed to death, but he was killed on the terrace, which is located on the other side of the house from Aaurshi's room.

Both Hemraj and Aaurshi suffered long and agonizing deaths.

The Discoveries

When the Talwars woke up on the morning of May 16, they immediately noticed that a number of things were out of place. Their maid had a difficult time getting in through the front gate and at first thought that it was locked from the inside, but it was later revealed that it was simply stuck.

After letting the maid into the house, the Talwars then noticed a Scotch bottle on the dining room table. Although there was a wet bar in the corner of the dining room, neither of the Talwar parents had made a drink the previous night.

They also noticed that there was what appeared to be blood smudged on the bottle.

At this point, Rajesh and Nupur were beginning to be disturbed by the anomalies within their home, so they walked down the hallway to check on their daughter. They were met with yet another anomaly.

The door on Aaurshi's door was unlocked. Aaurshi usually locked the door at night and opened it in the morning when she got up, but that morning it was unlocked, and as far as both parents knew, Aaurshi was still sleeping.

Unfortunately, Aaurshi would never wake up from her slumber.

Rajesh and Nupur were horrified to find a blanket over their daughter's head, and when they removed the blanket, they discovered that her throat had been slit and her body was lying in a pool of blood.

The Talwars immediately called the police, but they also called their friends and family for support. When the police arrived at the Talwar house, which obviously became a crime scene, it had been forensically contaminated by numerous family, friends, and neighbors of the Talwars.

After finally cordoning off the crime scene hours later, local investigators got to work trying to piece together what had happened to Aarushi and who had done it.

It didn't take them long to come up with a theory.

The investigators argued that just after midnight, Hemraj got drunk on a bottle of Scotch from the wet bar and then decided to rape the young, attractive Aaurshi. Hemraj threatened her with a Nepali knife known as a kukri, and when she resisted, he cut her throat with it and stabbed her several times. Realizing that he would certainly be the prime and possibly only suspect, Hemraj then fled to his native Nepal.

The theory sounded solid, and as the police searched for Hemraj the next day, the Talwars prepared to take their daughter's remains to the Ganges River, to lay her to rest according to Hindu tradition.

While the Talwars were gone, the case took a twist—the partially decomposed body of Hemraj was found on the home's terrace.

It turns out that at about the same time Aarushi was murdered, Hemraj was also stabbed numerous times, had his throat slashed, and was then dragged about twenty feet to the terrace where he was discovered two days later.

At this point, the police had a true mystery on their hands, which was about to become a media sensation in the South Asian nation.

A Confusing Investigation

Although homicide investigators in Delhi, India, may not have the same resources as their Western counterparts, homicide investigation procedures are universal. Homicide detectives from around the world are essentially taught the same tactics when collecting evidence, interviewing suspects, doing stakeouts, etc.

And in any homicide investigation, the first suspect, or suspects, are those closest to the victim.

The Delhi investigators began looking much more closely at the Talwar family.

Although it seemed to the investigators that there was no reason for the Talwars to kill their daughter, they were the ones closest to her.

And the fact that there was no forced entry into the Talwar home made many of the investigators question their innocence.

A more thorough examination of the tainted crime scene, though, seemed to turn up more questions than answers.

The forensic examination of Aaurshi's body determined that she was not sexually assaulted, although the examiner stated that sexual assault could not be totally ruled out either.

The Scotch bottle discovered by Rajesh in the morning had the blood of both victims on it, meaning that it could have been used as a secondary weapon, and there were fingerprints on it, but the prints were too smudged to be of any use.

Several bottles of different types of beer and liquor were discovered in Hemraj's room, although he was said to be a teetotaler.

The fact that Hemraj was dragged twenty feet to the terrace after he was killed also raised more questions. Why would the killer, or killers, go to the effort of moving his body at all if they didn't plan to dispose of it off the premises? Was the killer or killers planning on moving the body, but decided it was too much work when they got to the terrace? Were they spooked by some sounds in the house?

Then there were some other pieces of digital evidence that at first seemed like promising leads, but ultimately proved to be red herrings.

Aarushi's new camera was recovered with several pictures of her and her parents on it, but there were eighteen pictures that were mysteriously deleted.

Both victims' cellphones were stolen. Someone briefly used Hemraj's in the state of Punjab, and Aaurshi's turned up a couple of years later, but the owner was ultimately cleared of any involvement in the murders.

The public began demanding answers, and the more the case became a media sensation, the more the local Delhi police realized they were in over their heads.

They needed to call in experts with better resources.

The Central Bureau of Investigation

Today, due to the constantly evolving nature of crime in the increasingly globalized world, most major countries have a federal police agency that assists local agencies in major investigations. In the United States, the Federal Bureau of Investigation (FBI) serves this purpose, and in India, it is the Central Bureau of Investigation (CBI).

Much like in the United States, murder cases are usually dealt with at the local level in India, but when a high-profile case remains unsolved and stumps the local investigators, the CBI can be requested for assistance.

Within a few days of the murders of Aarushi Talwal and Hemraj Banjade, government officials requested that the CBI take over full jurisdiction of the case. Government officials believed that the CBI, with its vast resources, would be able to solve the murders in a much more efficient manner than local investigators.

Once given the case, CBI investigators wasted no time compiling a list of potential suspects.

Besides looking at Rajesh and Nupur as suspects, CBI investigators considered anyone with access to the Talwar home to be a suspect. The driver and maid were quickly crossed off the list of potential suspects because they both had alibis and no motive for the murders, but a former employee named Vishnu Sharma piqued their interest.

Sharma had previously worked for the Talwars as their live-in servant but was fired and replaced by Hermaj. The investigators reasoned that Hermaj was the primary target in a revenge scenario and that Aarushi was awakened by the commotion and killed to eliminate her as a witness.

The investigators located Sharma and soon learned that he couldn't have committed the murders because he wasn't in the area that night.

The CBI then began to focus its investigation on a number of other suspects, including Rajesh Talwar.

Although there was virtually no evidence linking him to the crimes, he was arrested on May 23. CBI officials gave press conferences where they laid out their flimsy and constantly changing theory as to how and why Rajesh committed the murders.

They stated that they never believed Rajesh could have slept through the murders, even though he and his wife slept under a window air conditioning unit. The CBI theorized that there were two possible motives that drove Rajesh to murder. The first theory involved Rajesh confronting and then killing Hemraj because he was blackmailing him over an affair he was having with Anita Durrani, and Aarushi was a hapless witness. There were numerous holes in this theory, but not more than the second one.

The CBI next stated that the motive may have been an honor killing—Rajesh killed both Aarushi and Hemraj when he discovered they were having an affair.

To bolster their theories, the CBI introduced unconfirmed, salacious statements from a variety of individuals who stated that the honor killing theory was true.

The Talwars countered by pointing out that they were a modern, inter-caste family who would never consider such a thing, even if their daughter were involved with one of their servants, which there was no evidence to support.

Due to the lack of evidence, Rajesh was released on bail on July 12.

After Rajesh was released, the media descended like vultures. The case was in the headlines of every major Indian newspaper, and it was on all of the major television news stations, in several languages, across India. Because of the large Indian community in the United Kingdom, North America, and Australia, and due to the details of the case, the Noida murders also became an international sensation.

The CBI found itself under intense pressure.

They decided to look into Rajesh and Napur's business dealings, which is where they found their next suspect.

After interviewing several of the Talwars' employees at their dentist office, investigators learned that an employee named Krishna Thadarai apparently held a grudge against Rajesh. Several days prior to the murders, Thadarai had been reprimanded for making a mistake at work. According to witnesses, Thadarai threatened to get even with his boss in any way possible.

The statements were enough for the CBI to detain Thadarai in June and bring him into their offices for intensive questioning.

Their interrogation included a polygraph exam, much like what is given in the United States, and what is referred to as a "narco" test. A "narco" test is when the suspect is given a dose of a psychoactive drug, often sodium pentothal—commonly referred to as the "truth serum"—during the interrogation. The narco test method of interrogation is banned in most Western countries but is routinely used by Indian law enforcement.

Needless to say, the police often get a confession from a suspect during a narco test.

After being given the narco test, Krishan Thadarai implicated himself and two other men—Vijay and Rajkumar Mandel. The CBI now had three potential killers but no real motive.

But it soon became apparent that the case against Thadarai and Vijay and Rajkumar Mandel was just as weak as the one against Rajesh Talwar.

The CBI theorized that the three men, led by Thadarai, became involved in a conspiracy with Banjade to exact revenge on the Talwars. For some reason that was never explained by CBI officials, the men decided to focus their wrath on Aaurshi instead of Rajesh. According to this theory, Aaurshi was either killed during an attempted sexual assault or because she overheard Thadarai insulting her father. When she tried to defend him, she was brutally murdered.

Banjade was then killed when he tried to back out of the plot.

There were several problems with this new, tenuous case presented by the CBI.

There was no physical evidence linking any of the men to the house, they all had alibis, and their drug-induced confessions were all very different from each other. Although the CBI initially stood firm by their investigation and arrests of the three men, the top brass in the organization realized that there wasn't enough evidence to get convictions.

The charges against the men were dropped, and they were released from custody in September 2008.

From that point, the investigation into the Noida murders further descended into a maelstrom of ineptness, and some would argue, corruption. The CBI released a report of its investigation into the murders in December that once more seemed to raise more questions than it did answers. Thadarai and the Mandels were absolved of any involvement in the murders, but the finger was pointed at Rajesh again, although this time he was joined by his wife.

The Trial

In the more than two years after Thadarai and the Mandels were released from custody and the CBI report was released to the public, the Noida murders receded from the international headlines. Even in India, more pressing cases took precedence in the media. All of that changed, though, in what many believe was a vindictive move by the CBI.

Although Rajesh was released from jail on bail in July 2008, he was never absolved of his daughter's and his servant's murders. The open-ended, never-ending nature of the case brought an immense amount of stress on the Talwar family and hurt their business.

Also, the Talwars were never able to truly grieve for the loss of their daughter.

On the advice of his lawyer, Rajesh filed a petition with the court to have the case against him formally dropped. Instead, Rajesh was brought back into court, this time with Napur, to face two counts of murder.

The CBI would present its flimsy case to the court and the public in one of the most publicized criminal cases in Indian history.

In Western nations, there is a high threshold that the prosecution must meet before a defendant is charged with a crime, never mind convicted. Although the Indian judicial system is essentially based on and highly influenced by the British model, it is still unique and different from its parent system.

One of its differences is a much lower threshold for arrests and convictions.

The trial against the Talwars began in 2013, and although public opinion was divided concerning their guilt or innocence, the dentist couple acquired a large following of supporters in India and around the world.

The prosecution's case against the Talwars was based primarily on conjecture. They contended that Rajesh heard a noise coming from Aaurshi's bedroom sometime after midnight, and when he went to investigate, he found his daughter having sex with Hemraj. In a rage over what he witnessed, Rajesh grabbed the

Scotch bottle from the wet bar and struck both Aaurshi and Hemraj numerous times, killing them.

Napur then helped him clean up the crime scene.

Of course, there were some key points that the prosecution failed to address. Most obvious was how Aaursh's and Hemraj's throats were cut if they were killed with a Scotch bottle that was not broken. The prosecution also failed to explain how Hemraj's body was moved.

Despite the seemingly weak case, the Talwars were convicted of murder and sentenced to life imprisonment in November 2013.

The high-profile nature of the case ensured that the questionable verdict would be reviewed on appeal. As the Talwars languished in separate Indian prisons, they filed an appeal in 2014. The couple won a subsequent appeal acquittal in 2017 and was acquitted of all charges on October 12, 2017.

Since their acquittal, the Talwars have kept a low profile and gone back to practicing dentistry. Most people familiar with the case, and most of the Talwars' friends and family, believe that the couple has suffered immensely over the last ten years—first when they lost their daughter so brutally, then when they were accused of her murder, and finally when they were convicted of the murders and sent to prison.

But many questions obviously remain.

If the Talwars or none of the other suspects in the case committed the murders, then who did?

Many who are familiar with the case believe that the murders will never be solved. An air of skepticism still surrounds the case, largely fostered by the inept investigation by the CBI, and will probably never subside.

Despite the case's many twists and turns, the family of Hemraj Banjade believes that the Talwars were guilty and that they used their wealth to walk free.

The legal saga remains active, with the CBI admitting an appeal against the Talwars' acquittal in the Supreme Court of India in 2018. Only time will tell if the killers of Aarushi Talwar and Hemraj Banjade are ever caught.

CHAPTER 5:

KRYSTAL BELL AND
THE TEXAS KILLING FIELDS

One of the gorier aspects of a serial killer's behavior is the disposal of victims. Some serial killers tend to leave their victims at the scene of the crime, while the more sadistic types like to take their victims to another location where they can torture them for a period of time before disposing of the bodies.

Often, a serial killer will favor one particular location as a "dump site."

For obvious reasons, dump sites are usually remote locations that allow a serial killer to conceal their nefarious activities far from the watchful eyes of society. Dump sites can be in virtually any isolated area, but some places seem to attract the evil work of serial killers more than others.

Canada's so-called "Highway of Tears" is one such dump site that has apparently attracted multiple killers. At least nineteen murders have been committed along Highway 16 in British Columbia, with the bodies all being dumped in the vicinity, by multiple murders, including serial killer Cody Legebokoff.

Similar to the Highway of Tears is the "Texas Killing Fields," which has already been touched on in this volume in relation to the Harold Bell case. Authorities have recovered the bodies of at least thirty girls and young women along the stretch of Interstate 45 between Houston and Galveston, Texas, since the early 1970s. A twenty-five-acre patch of swamp outside League City, Texas, has particularly seemed to attract evil, as most of the bodies were discovered at that location.

Although Harold Bell claims to have sent eleven young women and girls to their deaths in the Texas Killing Fields, many more met similar fates at the hands of other men.

Thirteen-year-old Krystal Bell was a bright young girl who had her life tragically ended in 1996 when she was abducted, beaten, raped, and strangled to death and then discarded in the Texas Killing Fields. Like so many of the other Killing Fields cases, Krystal's murder became a cold case for many years, but advances in forensic science have recently helped catch her killer.

A Tragic Case

In most ways, Krystal Baker was like any other thirteen-year-old girl in 1996. She liked boys, music, and hanging out with her friends. Although she had a bit of a rebellious streak, she didn't give her family many problems.

As an interesting and somewhat ironic side note, Krystal was the great niece of American icon Marilyn Monroe. Both were unfortunately destined for tragic deaths.

On the evening of March 5, 1996, Krystal was staying at her grandmother's home in Texas City, Texas. Texas City is a working-class suburb of Galveston, where the scenery includes plenty of oil refineries and swamp land.

Texas City also happens to be located adjacent to League City and the Texas Killing Fields.

The night of March 5 was like any other for Krystal: she watched television with her grandmother for a while before walking to the neighborhood convenience store to buy a soda and call a friend on the store's pay phone.

Krystal didn't return to her grandmother's that night.

Several hours later, Krystal's bloody and battered body was discovered in that twenty-five-acre patch of swamp outside of League City. Since she was positively identified as having been in the convenience store that night, the local homicide investigators postulated that she was abducted while walking back to her grandmother's house, driven to the swamp, and then beaten, raped, and murdered.

Although this type of crime was not that uncommon along the I-45 corridor, the age and innocence of Krystal were enough to shock and anger local residents. They wanted justice for Krystal.

But justice would have to wait for technology to advance.

Kevin Edison Smith didn't fit the profile of the type of serial killer who would be stalking the Texas Killing Fields. In 1996, he was only twenty nine years old, had no felony convictions, and was Black in a predominantly White area of Texas.

With that said, there were elements of his background that facilitated a career in serial crime.

Smith was single for most of his life, so he didn't have to answer to anyone and was able to conceal his movements. He lived and worked in seventeen different cities in the states of Texas, Arizona, North Carolina, and Louisiana throughout his adulthood, which gave him access to plenty of victims and anonymity through his many moves.

Galveston was just one of Smith's many stops when he abducted and murdered Krystal Baker in 1996, and although he was as sloppy as he was brutal when he dumped the innocent girl in the Texas Killing Fields, the limits of forensic technology were on his side when he did so.

But ultimately, time was not on his side.

A Cold Case Revisited

Although DNA profiling was available in 1996, it was not very well developed—samples needed to be large enough and well-preserved in order to retrieve a usable profile. Also, as is still the case, the police needed someone to match any usable profile with, so they either needed to have a specific suspect or a sample in the national offender database known as the Combined DNA Index System, or CODIS.

The CODIS system was established in 1998, but it took several years for all fifty states to join the program. In the meantime, Krystal's murder became a cold case and was forgotten by many.

In 2010, detectives with the Chambers County Sheriff's Department were going through the evidence in their storage locker pertaining to a number of cold cases when they came across the dress Krystal Baker was wearing the night she was murdered. One astute detective noticed a stain on her dress and decided to test it.

The stain turned out to be semen, and after it was entered into the CODIS database, it came back as a match for an offender named Kevin Edison Smith, who had recently had his DNA profile entered into the system after a minor drug arrest in Louisiana in 2009.

Just like that, the police had Krystal's killer.

Smith was quickly located, and when presented with the DNA evidence, he almost as quickly admitted to the murder.

Although Krystal's murder was considered a capital crime in the state of Texas because it was accompanied by another felony, rape, the prosecutors withheld pursuing the death penalty. They reasoned that due to the mountain of evidence against Smith, they would surely win a conviction and, along with it, the death penalty. In Texas, that meant that he would surely be executed within ten years, fifteen at the most.

The Chambers County prosecutors, though, were approached by prosecutors and investigators from other jurisdictions where Smith had lived and where they had a number of unsolved murders. The authorities in other jurisdictions wanted to keep Smith alive to potentially clear additional cold cases along the I-45 Texas Killing Fields corridor, where multiple killers have operated.

Smith went to trial, but the verdict was a foregone conclusion. After only thirty minutes of deliberation, the jury convicted him of first-degree murder in April 2012. He was sentenced to life in prison with the possibility of parole after 40 years

Smith's conviction brought a certain amount of closure to Krystal's family, but her mother stated to a local CBS affiliate that it is still difficult to deal with her death and the manner in which she died, twenty years later.

"I dream about her mostly when she was a little girl. And every once in a while when she's a teenager,' Jeannie Baker said. "And she told me one time, she says, 'Mama, I'm just out here hangin' out with my friends. Everything OK.' And I woke up the next day. I wished I could have stayed in that dream a little longer."

Hopefully, Smith can help investigators bring closure to some more families and close some of the unsolved cases involving the Texas Killing Fields.

CHAPTER 6:

THE EMMETT TILL MURDER CASE

The 1988 Hollywood blockbuster film Mississippi Burning introduced millions of people to the era in American history known as the Civil Rights Movement. In the film, and in the real history that it portrays, three civil rights activists were murdered in 1964 in rural Mississippi by members of the Ku Klux Klan and Klan sympathizers for their efforts to register local Black people to vote.

The murders led to FBI involvement in Mississippi to break up the Klan's influence in that state and generated public sympathy throughout the United States for the Civil Rights Movement. The murders also led to greater federal government involvement in civil rights and racial issues, beginning with the *Civil Rights Act of 1964* and President Lyndon Johnson's "Great Society" program.

Today, many see the murders of the three activists as the beginning, or the turning point, of the Civil Rights Movement, but major events were already taking place in the country in the prior decade.

After the American Civil War ended in 1865, the period known as "Reconstruction" ensued in the former Confederate states, whereby many of the men who supported and fought for the Confederacy were disenfranchised. On the other hand, many former slaves were enfranchised, leading to widespread political change across the South and deep racial resentment.

During the late 1860s and 1870s, several different paramilitary groups formed that comprised former Confederates who attacked Black voters and their White sympathizers in clandestine raids. The most notorious and well-known of these organizations was the Ku Klux Klan, but there were a host of others, including the White League and the Red Shirts.

Ultimately, due to a combination of the efforts of the paramilitary groups and acquiescence by the federal government to their actions, White rule was reestablished and Reconstruction was largely abandoned by the late 1870s. The result was that the Democratic Party became the sole party in power in most southern states, which reaffirmed White rule through a variety of different laws that institutionalized segregation of the races and disenfranchised Black voters.

This situation continued largely unchallenged until the United States Supreme Court issued its landmark ruling, Brown v. Board of Education of Topeka, in 1954. The ruling made the state-mandated segregation of schools, and later all public institutions, illegal. The ruling led to large-scale resentment in the South among many Whites and a more than decade-long campaign by activists and the federal government to end state-sanctioned segregation in southern states.

The resistance was fierce and at times violent.

On August 28, 1955, a fourteen-year-old Black teenager named Emmett Till from Chicago was murdered by two White men in a small town in deeply segregated Mississippi. The murder was done due to Till's perceived indiscretion toward the wife of one of the killers, and as a result, many historians now view the young man as one of the first casualties of the post-Brown Civil Rights Movement.

There is still debate over the details of Till's murder, but not about its brutal nature or the effect it had across the South and the entire country.

Emmett Till

It would be an understatement to say that Emmett Till's short life was unstable. He was born in Chicago in 1941 to Mamie Charthan Till and Louis Till. Both of Emmett's parents were originally from the South, but migrated to Chicago along with nearly six million other Black Americans who came to the Midwest and Northeast in what historians know today as the "Great Migration."

Mamie was originally from the Mississippi River Delta in Mississippi, and Louis was from the small town of New Madrid, Missouri, a little farther up the Mississippi River.

Although Chicago gave the Tills more opportunities, Louis was far from being an ideal husband or father.

Louis was known to be a good amateur boxer, and he used those skills to make a little money as a tough guy on the streets of Chicago. He also reportedly used his fists on his wife and cheated on her multiple times with other women.

One night, after Louis had been drinking heavily, he returned home and began beating Mamie, but she had finally had enough. Mamie poured scalding water on

Louis and then called the police and later got a restraining order against her abusive husband.

Louis was unable to control his drinking and obsessive personality. He eventually broke the restraining order and was arrested. In 1943, Louis was facing prison time for breaking the restraining order, but since it was wartime, the judge gave him the option of entering the Army.

Louis Till chose to join the Army.

The military can be a good career choice and often brings stability and discipline to individuals' lives who are lacking in those departments; for Louis Till, the choice proved to be fatal, possibly leaving a large emotional scar on young Emmett.

Like most Black soldiers at the time, Louis served in a segregated support unit well behind the front lines in Allied-occupied Italy. It didn't take him long to meet up with other miscreants, and he was soon involved in theft and black market activities. However, since it was wartime, Uncle Sam needed the warm bodies, so his commanders were willing to look the other way.

Till continued with his criminal activities until he and one of his fellow criminal soldiers raped and killed an Italian girl in 1945. The two men were promptly arrested, convicted, and executed by the United States Army in a military court.

Famous American poet and Fascist sympathizer Ezra Pound was briefly jailed next to Till and mentioned his execution in one of his poems:

"Till was hung

Yesterday

For murder and rape with trimmings"

Emmett was left without a father, but Louis Till was never much of a parental figure anyway.

Mamie didn't waste much time mourning over the loss of her abusive husband, but in late 1940s America, it was difficult, socially and economically, to be a single mother. She met another man, remarried, and moved her family to Detroit. The move proved to be difficult for young Emmett, who, besides the loss of his father, had suffered from some physical maladies as a child.

Young Emmett had contracted polio, which left him bedridden for many months. Even after he recovered, he walked with a slight limp. He also had a noticeable stutter, making him the butt of jokes for his fellow classmates and kids in the neighborhood.

But Emmett was no shrinking violet. He would stand up for himself verbally against any potential bullies, and perhaps taking a cue from his father, would engage in fist fights if need be.

The move to Detroit upset Emmett, who missed his friends and family in Chicago. To make matters worse, he didn't get along with his new stepfather. After a continual conflict arose between Emmett and his stepfather, Emmett was sent back to Chicago to live with family members.

His mother followed him a short time later.

As is so often the case, Mamie's second husband possessed many of the same qualities as Louis Till—he was a philanderer and physically abusive. He also couldn't stand the fact that Mamie had left him, so he followed her back to Chicago.

Mamie's second husband stalked her on the streets of Chicago until eleven-year-old Emmett threatened him with a butcher knife.

Clearly, Emmett learned at an early age how to stand up for himself and his family.

A Visit to Mississippi

During the spring of 1955, Mamie told fourteen-year-old Emmett that he could spend the following summer with family in one of two places—Omaha, Nebraska, or rural Mississippi—and that it was his choice. Omaha didn't interest Emmett much as he thought of it as just a smaller version of Chicago, but Mississippi sounded interesting and exotic.

There was little hesitation—he wanted to visit Mississippi.

Till's family lived in the small town of Money, Mississippi, which is located a few miles from the larger town of Greenwood on the eastern edge of the Mississippi Delta.

Before she sent her son away, Mamie made sure to educate Emmett on the fact that Mississippi was a different world from Chicago, which was far from an exaggeration in 1955. She made sure to explain to him the nuances of segregation and what was expected of young people, both Black and White, in terms of "Southern etiquette."

Emmett seemed to understand the situation, so Mamie sent her son on his way, and he arrived in Money on August 21.

No amount of lecturing could've prepared Emmett for the culture shock and the racial cauldron that he was about to immerse himself in when he arrived in

Mississippi. Although lynchings of Blacks had decreased dramatically in the decades leading up to the 1950s, racial tensions had renewed in the state for a number of reasons.

The landmark ruling Brown v. Board of Education of Topeka was clearly aimed at states such as Mississippi that not only had segregation in schools and other public facilities, but practiced it as a state-mandated policy. The Whites of Mississippi overwhelmingly supported segregation during the 1950s and viewed anyone who opposed the policy, Black or White, as a threat to their way of life. Since most of the lawyers and activists who were opposed to segregation and nearly all of the judges who ruled against it were from outside of the South, Mississippians began to view outsiders with suspicion and even derision.

The ruling did not bring a wave of change to Mississippi; in fact, little changed legally in the years immediately following it. However, anti-segregation activism did slowly begin to take hold in the Magnolia state.

Just before Till arrived in Mississippi, a Black activist was shot in broad daylight in front of a courthouse in southern Mississippi. The victim survived, and although three men were arrested for the assault, they were later released and never went to trial.

The case established a precedent in Mississippi whereby, over the following fifteen years, White pro-segregationists would often not be charged, or if they were, they would be acquitted by all-White juries, in acts of violence and mayhem directed toward anti-segregation activists.

Emmett Till was about to experience this phenomenon first-hand.

Bryant's Grocery

Long before rural Americans flocked to Walmart to buy their groceries and daily needs, "general stores" were a part of the landscape. General stores provided locals with some groceries, basic household goods, and sometimes ammunition for guns. General stores were also a place where locals would meet to find out about upcoming events and to gossip.

The general store in Money was Bryant's Grocery.

Bryant's Grocery was owned and run by twenty-four-year-old Roy Bryant and his twenty-one-year-old wife Carolyn. The Bryants were White while most of their customers, and the population of Money, for that matter, were Black. Many of the customers were local Black children whose parents worked as sharecroppers in the local cotton fields. Some local Black men would also hang out near the store playing checkers on their days off from work.

There were never any problems between the owners and their predominantly Black clientele.

All were polite and all followed the written and unwritten laws and mores of segregated Mississippi at the time. All of that changed on the afternoon of August 24, 1955.

August 24 was a hot, humid Sunday in the Delta. Till was supposed to be at church watching his uncle deliver a sermon to the faithful, but instead, he and a few of his cousins and new friends decided to skip and hang around town.

Emmett and his friends ended up at Bryant's Grocery.

The details of what happened next are still open to debate because many of the witnesses are now dead, and others have changed their stories multiple times.

According to one of Emmett's cousins, Curtis Jones, Till showed the group a picture of a White girl whom he said was a friend from his racially mixed junior high class in Chicago. Living in the South, where segregation was a generational institution and not knowing much about the outside world, the boys teased him, calling Till a liar.

Frustrated, Till then said that the girl was actually his girlfriend.

Some of the boys then dared him to talk to Carolyn Bryant in a suggestive way.

Another one of Till's cousins denied this account and said that Emmett simply went into the store and bought some candy.

One of Till's other friends said that he whistled at Carolyn as he walked into the store.

In Carolyn Bryant's first account of the encounter, she said that Till physically grabbed her, asked her for a date, and said, "I've been with White women before."

She recanted that account years later.

All accounts of the incident agree that after Till left the store, Carolyn ran to her car and retrieved a pistol from her car. Till then ran from the scene, whistling as he did. Some witnesses claimed that Till whistled at some older Black men playing checkers nearby, while others said that he whistled at Bryant once more.

Emmett then returned to his uncle's house, telling him that he wanted to return to Chicago.

Roy Bryant Returns Home

The Bryants' general store was primarily managed by Carolyn and only provided a portion of the family's income. To supplement their income and, at times, to keep the store going, Roy fell back on his other profession of trucking. Sometimes his work as a trucker overlapped with running the store, as he would often deliver goods to and from his store, but when the incident took place between Emmett Till and his wife, he was on a long-haul route delivering shrimp to Texas.

He didn't return to Money until August 27.

When Roy Bryant returned home and learned of the incident, he was furious to say the least. No way would he allow some Black kid to disrespect him and his wife like that.

Since Roy's wife didn't know who Till was, it was up to him to do some investigating. He enlisted the help of his thirty-six-year-old half-brother, J.W. Milam, and a Black man named J.W. Washington to find the kid whom he believed had harassed his wife.

After some aggressive questioning and quite a few threats, Emmett Till's name surfaced.

After stewing in anger for several hours, Roy, Carolyn, and Milam drove to the residence of Moses Wright in the early morning hours of August 28. Wright was a preacher in a local Black church and the great uncle of Till.

Wright told the trio that Till wasn't from Mississippi and that he didn't understand what he did was wrong. He reassured them that there would be no further problems and that Till would probably leave town within the next few days anyway.

This was not good enough for the Bryants.

After Wright was done pleading with the three, Milam calmly took a pistol out of his waistband, pointed it at Wright's head, and told him he wanted the "nigger who did the talking."

Not wanting the rest of his family to face reprisals, Wright turned Till over to the trio.

Milam now aimed the pistol at Emmett's head as they drove through town to the Bryant residence, where they left Carol. Bryant and Milam then proceeded with their captive and picked up two Black men who were employed by Milam.

The two men sat in the back of the truck while they drove to a barn at an isolated location a couple of miles outside of town.

The location allowed the men to torture Till away from the prying ears of neighbors.

Till was beaten, cut, and burned for several hours in that barn. The torture continued until the sun came up, which is when one of the men ended it by shooting Till in the head.

They then dumped Emmett's body into the Tallahatchie River.

Moses Wright almost immediately reported Emmett's abduction to the local sheriff's department, and the authorities actually responded somewhat promptly. Bryant and Milam admitted to abducting Till but said they dropped him off on a corner in town after threatening him. They claimed that they only wanted to scare the teenager for disrespecting Carolyn and for transgressing local mores.

Despite the laws of the South favoring the two men at the time, they were charged with kidnapping.

Till's mutilated body was discovered three days later on the banks of the Tallahatchie River.

The charges against Bryant and Milam were upgraded to murder. The trial would turn out to be one of the first major murder cases of the Civil Rights era, and opinion on it would prove to be as divisive in Mississippi as it was across the country.

The Trial and the Case's Legacy

In the weeks after Till's murder, news outlets slowly began to report on the story. It wasn't that there was a media blackout, but more so that things generally moved more slowly in the decades before the internet and even more so in the always laidback South. Till's murder was considered one of the first lynchings, if not the first, in the post-Brown v. Board of Education Civil Rights era, and therefore, it brought considerable attention to rural Mississippi.

It was unwanted attention for the most part.

The brutal murder was widely condemned by Mississippians, Black and White, pro-and anti-segregationists alike. Even the most militant racists argued that it was a pointless murder that brought undue attention to Mississippi. They argued that the "boy" could surely have been taught a lesson without killing him.

After the initial shock of the murder, it didn't take long for activists on both sides of the segregation issue to use Till's death to forward their causes.

Pro-segregationists argued that the growing Civil Rights Movement was the true cause of Till's death as it led to chaos and discord among the inhabitants of the South, who usually got along with each other and "knew their places."

On the other hand, civil rights activists pointed to the murder as an example of what was wrong with the South and a reason for the federal government to play a more active role in enforcing Brown v. Board of Education by integrating schools and other public facilities.

When Emmett Till was buried in Chicago, his mother elected to have an open casket, demonstrating the extent of the injuries he sustained, which was shown in newspaper articles around the country.

Even before the trial of Bryant and Milam got underway, it proved to have all the hallmarks of a media spectacle. It was the first major criminal trial of the Civil Rights era, which brought newspaper reporters and news crews from all across the United States to cover it.

By late 1955, Mississippi was invaded by an army of journalists.

In the 1950s, court proceedings moved rapidly in most American states. Just over a month after they were charged with murder, Bryant and Milam went on trial in front of a courtroom filled with reporters.

After a five-day trial, the two men were found not guilty by an all-White male jury on September 23, 1955.

After the verdict was read, Milam and Bryant were visibly elated with the decision, while Till's family was devastated. After all, the teenager had been kidnapped, beaten, shot in the head, had a large metal fan tied to his neck with barbed wire, and thrown into the Tallahatchie River—and this was meant to be justice?

The two killers' legal woes were not over, though, as they still had the kidnapping charge hanging over their heads that carried with it a possible life sentence.

The prosecutor elected not to try the men on the kidnapping charge but moved forward with it to a grand jury after they were acquitted of murder.

Given the racial climate at that time, to many, this was no surprise.

About one year after Milam and Bryant were acquitted of Till's murder, the popular Look magazine approached them for a feature article and pictorial. They were both paid nice sums of money for the interview, which apparently added to their level of honesty because they confessed to the murder in detail.

"I stood there in that shed and listened to that nigger throw that poison at me, and I just made up my mind. 'Chicago boy,' I said, 'I'm tired of 'em sending your kind down here to stir up trouble. Goddam you, I'm going to make an example of you—just so everybody can know how me and my folks stand,'" said Milam in the interview.

In the years after his murder, Till was essentially made into a martyr, and to many became a symbol of the inherent inequality and sometimes brutality of the segregated South. Till's death also gave momentum to the emerging Civil Rights Movement.

Historians now credit the murder of Emmett Till with the passage of the *Civil Rights Act of 1957*, which, although minor in its scope, led to the more overarching Acts in the 1960s. Till's death ensured that the federal government would play an active role in the desegregation of the South.

For Till's killers, their lives were set on a steady downward trajectory after their acquittals.

Both men received plenty of public and private support during their trials, but that goodwill quickly evaporated after their confessions were published in Look magazine.

Milam was ostracized and found it nearly impossible to get work in Mississippi, so he moved to Texas, where things weren't much better. He was arrested for several different crimes during the 1960s and 1970s before dying of cancer, broke and alone, in 1980 at the age of sixty-one.

Roy Bryant didn't fare much better than his crime partner. Carolyn left him a few years after the acquittals, and although he stayed in Mississippi, he also had difficulties finding steady employment. Bryant then kept a low profile, claiming that his life was threatened on numerous occasions. He drifted between working low-paying jobs and committing small-time crimes to make ends meet, and occasionally supplemented his income by living on welfare. He was eventually convicted of welfare fraud, for which he served jail time. Bryant died, also of cancer, in 1994 at the age of sixty-three.

Little is known about Carolyn Bryant's life after the trial, other than that she eventually remarried and changed her name. She kept an extremely low profile for most of her life and never gave an interview about the crime—many of her friends and family from her second marriage didn't even know about her involvement.

Carolyn died in 2014 at the age of eighty-six.

The building where Bryant's Grocery once stood was never reopened. Today, only the remains of a derelict building can be seen where the store once stood, much like most of Money, Mississippi. A historical marker stands at the site that briefly tells the story of what went on there that fateful summer day in 1955.

CHAPTER 7:

THE BIZARRE CASE
OF ORION KRAUSE

This series has covered the phenomenon of youth crime in many unique and shocking cases. Different types of youth crime have been profiled that have originated from a diverse range of demographics in cities, suburbs, and even rural areas.

In recent years, many American inner cities have seen senseless acts of violence perpetrated by juveniles and young adults that have often been given more benign-sounding names. A "flash rob" is when mobs of youths ransack stores and inflict wanton acts of violence on unsuspecting people who happen to be in the vicinity.

And the "knockout" game is far from a game but is instead a violent exercise where thugs randomly punch people in the head, hoping to knock them out. The knockout game is not only violently sadistic, but in the United States, also racist or antisemitic, as the perpetrators here are almost always Black and most of the victims are White, Asian, or Jewish.

But White kids in the suburban and rural parts of America have also done their part to ensure that youth violence is a persistent problem.

School shootings in suburban and small-town schools have become much more common in recent years, as have domestic murders and even family annihilations.

A familicide is defined as a mass murder of three or more members of a family committed by another family member. A family annihilation is a familicide is when all members, or present members, of a family are killed in a mass murder event.

On September 8, 2017, a young man named Orion Krause, who seemingly had a bright future, committed one of the most brutal family annihilations in the state of Massachusetts' history. For reasons still not known, Krause beat three members of his family and a caretaker to death with a baseball bat before wandering around the neighborhood naked.

Several further bizarre details of this tragic case of youth violence quickly emerged.

Orion Krause

Twenty-three-year-old Orion Krause was born into an affluent family that by all accounts was stable and supportive. His father, Alexander, and mother, Elizabeth, both came from affluent families and had good jobs that allowed them to live in the upscale and scenic city of Rockport, Maine. The Krauses' summer neighbors included many of the East Coast's elites—the Bush family vacationed not far away in Kennebunkport, Maine, as have numerous other government, media, and finance elites.

High school was easy for Orion, as he did well academically and participated in numerous sports and other activities. He got along well with his teachers and other students, although he was said to be shy and somewhat awkward around girls.

Orion was a particularly talented musician.

He excelled at playing most musical instruments but had a particular talent for percussion instruments. Orion's abilities earned him a scholarship to attend the prestigious Oberlin Conservatory of Music in Ohio for college.

Like the mythological figure and constellation he was named for, Orion Krause seemed to have the world at his knees when he left Maine for college.

On the surface, Krause's college career appears to have gone smoothly. He was a jazz drummer in the school's band and earned good grades. Although he never really developed any deep connections with any of his fellow students, he got along well with most of them, and the faculty all liked the young musician from Maine.

But Orion did have an emerging dark side.

There are numerous reports that he did heroin while in college and that his use of the drug went beyond the experimentation stage. Orion's mother also called the police on him in July 2016 for erratic behavior, although no charges were ever filed.

Despite a few bumps in the road, Orion's life appeared to be headed in the right direction at the end of the summer of 2017.

"I Freed Them"

A reasonable timeline of the events that led up to the quadruple murder on September 8 can be reconstructed.

Orion had been living with his parents in Maine and left their home unexpectedly on September 7. His mother called the police because he took her car, some of her money, and was acting in a frightening and erratic manner. After not having contact with her son for a day, Elizabeth received a phone call from Orion on September 8 in which he said he was alright and that she should come to Massachusetts to get him.

Orion also made a call to one of his former Oberlin professors.

According to the professor, Orion sounded very erratic and disturbed on the phone. The professor was himself disturbed when Orion told him, "I think I have to kill my mom," after confessing to taking her car and money.

The professor tried to calm Orion down and later phoned the police.

Elizabeth picked Orion up a few hours later, but instead of driving straight home to Maine, she suggested that they visit her elderly parents in Groton, Massachusetts.

The modest house, which is located in a quiet neighborhood, was home to eighty-nine-year-old Frank Lackey and his eighty-five-year-old wife, Elizabeth. Their full-time caretaker, sixty-eight-year-old Bertha Parker, also lived at the house.

What happened next is still open to conjecture, but the Middlesex County homicide investigators believe that the massacre began not long after Orion and his mother arrived.

Elizabeth and Orion arrived at the Lackey home during the evening when the couple was seated in the living room watching television. Elizabeth sat down to join her parents, but Orion produced a baseball bat and set to work brutally yet efficiently beating his grandparents and mother with the bat.

All three were later found by the police seated in their chairs, their heads bashed in so badly that their faces were unrecognizable.

It was a blitz assault—they didn't know what hit them.

Parker, though, was apparently in another room or more aware of the situation because her mangled body was found by the driveway. Obviously, she ran outside the house for her life, but the younger and fitter Krause, who was also driven by a homicidal rage, quickly caught and beat her about the head with the bat.

After killing his family and Bertha Parker, Orion then wandered around the neighborhood naked and covered in mud.

It didn't take long for the people of the quiet neighborhood to call the police.

"I'm calling from 42 Common St," neighbor Wagner Alcocer said to the 911 operator. "We have a young guy, about 20 years old, completely naked with mud, he's a little bit crazy, and he keeps saying that he murdered four people. We don't know who he is, we let him stay in the backyard. He needs help."

When officers with the Groton Police responded to the bizarre call, they quickly learned that it was much more than a college kid drunk and/or high on drugs.

"The male was naked and it appeared he had rubbed mud all over his body. The male was also covered in thin cuts. When I approached him I asked, 'Are you OK?' and 'What's going on?' The male stated, 'I murdered four people,'" said responding officer Gordon Candow.

A search of the Lackey's home uncovered the grisly scene. Officers from the normally quiet Groton Police Department and the Middlesex Sheriff's Department were horrified by the sight and smell of the crime scene—everywhere they looked, there was blood, and there was the smell of death in the air.

The bloody baseball bat that was used as the murder weapon was quickly recovered by officers at the scene.

When Orion was brought to the police station, he quickly gave a full confession to the mass murder. When asked why he committed the atrocities, he began acting bizarrely, singing "I freed them" to himself.

Krause was sent to the Bridgewater State Hospital in Massachusetts for a psychiatric evaluation to determine if he was competent to stand trial. Doctors determined that although the young man certainly has some serious mental problems, he was aware of the situation.

A judge ruled that Orion Krause was mentally fit to stand trial in 2018, and in 2021, he was sentenced to life in prison with parole eligibility at 25 years.

CHAPTER 8:

THE DISAPPEARANCE OF SUSAN POWELL

The term "closure" is used quite often in regard to true crime cases, so much so that some argue it is overused. Even in the volumes of this series, yours truly has used the term a number of times in what I believe is an accurate way.

Unfortunately, many people probably can't accurately define the word, let alone how it relates to high-profile crime cases.

The Merriam-Webster Dictionary defines closure as "An act of closing: the condition of being closed."

Obviously, that is a fairly ambiguous definition, but perhaps a simpler definition would be, "the end of something."

When it comes to crime, closure generally refers to the end of a case, but more specifically, it concerns the perspective of the victim or the victim's family. In a murder case, primarily what is profiled in these books, closure would be not only the killer getting caught and sent to prison, but also the body of the victim being recovered for a proper burial. Then there's emotional closure after a traumatic event, which is another matter entirely.

As those of you reading this know, many crime cases do not have closure.

There are a number of cases where a killer is caught and convicted, but the body of the victim is never found. These types of cases are becoming more and more common as states have passed laws that make it easier for prosecutors to convict killers of first-degree murder, even without a body. Although the families of the victims don't have complete closure in these cases, because they are always left to wonder exactly how their loved ones died and where and how they were disposed of, there is at least a sense of finality with the conviction.

Unfortunately, in some rare cases, a body is never found, and there is never a conviction despite the strong beliefs of the authorities that a murder has in fact taken place.

The disappearance of twenty-eight-year-old Utah mother Susan Powell on December 6, 2009, is one such case. When Susan didn't report to work on December 7, her concerned friends and family called the police to report her missing. As is often the case, suspicion immediately fell on her husband, and later on other members of his family, but unfortunately, due to a tragic turn of events, Susan's family will probably never get closure in this case.

Susan Cox and Joshua Powell

Joshua Powell, who was known as "Josh" to his family and friends, was born in 1976 in the Seattle suburb of Puyallup, Washington. Like many people from the Pacific Northwest, Josh grew up hunting, fishing, hiking, and camping, and enjoyed spending much of his free time outdoors. His family was fairly close and were all members of the Church of Latter-day Saints, also known as the Mormon Church. The Mormons have some strict rules, including proscriptions on premarital sex, alcohol, tobacco, and even caffeine. However, the Powell family was known to not follow some of those rules as closely, some even being considered "Jack Mormons."

For his part, Josh was outwardly a good Mormon in his teen years and young adult life and showed quite a bit of promise. He graduated from college in the 1990s with a degree in business. After school, as most good Mormons do, he married a Mormon girl.

Although the marriage failed, the Mormons have no rules against divorce, so the couple amicably ended the marriage and moved on with their lives.

Joshua Powell was destined to meet someone else.

Susan Cox, who was also from suburban Seattle, was five years younger than Josh but otherwise a seemingly good match. Like Josh, she was raised Mormon and wanted to be a good Mormon wife and to give her husband plenty of children.

Not long after the two met, they married in the Mormon temple in Portland, Oregon, in April 2001.

Susan and Josh decided to live in Washington, close to his family, but it became obvious to Susan at an early point that the living situation was a serious problem. Josh's father, Steven, turned out to be a creep and a pervert who was obsessed with his new daughter-in-law. He took numerous pictures of Susan when she was unaware, some of them suggestive, and wrote her several love songs. At first,

Susan was put off by the situation, but as it continued, she grew more disturbed and somewhat fearful.

Josh was either too afraid or simply didn't care enough because, despite his new wife's constant pleas to say something to Steve about his inappropriate behavior, he refused.

Finally, Josh agreed to a compromise of sorts. The couple would move to the Mormon mecca of Salt Lake City, which gave them a legitimate reason to get away from the Powell family.

Josh and Susan Powell moved to Salt Lake City in 2004.

The Powells' first three years in Salt Lake City went well, as Josh was able to find work in the financial sector and Susan worked at various banks in the area. She eventually landed a job at regional bank Wells Fargo, where she was well-liked and respected by her bosses.

The couple bought a new home in the middle-class suburb of West Valley, Utah, located just outside of Salt Lake City, and became actively involved in the Church of the Latter-day Saints there. Since everything appeared to be going well for the Powells, they decided to take the next step and have children.

Mormons, who consider the Book of Mormon and the Bible to be the literal word of God, generally have large families, and it was Susan's desire from an early age to do her part in that respect. Although Josh showed some reservations about having a big family, he eventually agreed, and in 2005, the couple had their first son, Charles. In 2007, Susan gave birth to another son, Braden.

By all accounts, Susan and Josh Powell seemed like the perfect Mormon family—they were young, attractive, and successful with a growing family—but underneath the surface, there were some problems that threatened to destroy everything.

It was later revealed that Josh and Susan had been having financial problems ever since they moved to Salt Lake City. Despite his educational background in finance and business, it turned out that Josh was incredibly bad with money. He spent more than he made, amassing sizable credit card debt over the course of his marriage.

Josh also had a difficult time keeping steady employment.

Although he always presented his employers with a stellar resume, Josh never really seemed to know what he was doing after he was hired. He also never seemed to want to work very much, spending most of his time on the phone with personal calls or on the internet instead of working.

It was rumored that Josh was often calling women to set up illicit affairs.

Still, despite the problems, Susan continued to be a good Mormon wife by standing by Josh.

But would Josh be willing to stand by her?

The Disappearance

Susan Powell was last seen by someone other than Josh on the afternoon of December 6, 2009. Susan and her two sons went to church late that morning and, a few hours later, a friend came over to the Powell home for a short visit. The friend said that Susan was tired, so she left so that Susan could take a nap during the late afternoon.

One of the Powells' neighbors then reported seeing Josh arrive at the house around 8:30 p.m., but they didn't see Susan.

Josh later claimed that he was there to take his sons on a late-night camping trip.

As noted earlier, Susan was reported missing by her family the next day when she didn't drop her sons off at daycare or show up for work. Josh came home later that night after he received a phone call from the local police.

It wasn't immediately apparent to the police what was going on concerning Susan's disappearance: statistically speaking, most "missing" people turn up after a few days. Susan's family, though, was adamant that foul play was involved and, although they didn't immediately point the finger at Josh, they believed that she was abducted.

Because husbands are statistically most often responsible for their wives' disappearances in such cases, Josh immediately became a person of interest. They needed to speak with him to create an accurate timeline and to rule out foul play.

Josh's interview only made him look guilty.

He told the police that he brought his boys out for a late-night camping trip to a campsite near Simpson Springs in northern Utah. The fact that he left late at night was suspicious to begin with, but the story became even more questionable when the police considered that it was an especially cold night in northern Utah.

The police sent detectives and a forensic team out to the location where Josh said they camped, but nothing was found.

Susan's family was initially supportive of Josh because they had no reason not to believe his story, no matter how strange it may have sounded. In the days immediately after Susan's disappearance, Josh spent considerable time with the Cox family, attending a prayer vigil with them and handing out "missing" flyers with Susan's picture outside an NBA Utah Jazz game.

The detectives did not share the Cox family's opinion of Josh Powell.

Less than a week after Susan disappeared, the police continued to put pressure on Josh. As a result, on December 14, Josh "lawyered up" and refused to cooperate anymore with the investigation. Josh Powell was officially named a "person of interest" by the police, which was reported extensively in the Utah media the next day.

Susan's family's view of Josh quickly shifted.

The West Valley Police Department obtained a search warrant for the Powells' home, which turned up some information that did little to clear Josh of any foul play. A drop of Susan's blood was found inside the home, which was not an earth-shattering revelation since people do tend to cut themselves occasionally. However, there was also a drop of an unknown male's blood nearby.

The investigators also found a handwritten note that was determined to be Susan's through handwriting analysis. The note shed light on the Powells' rocky marriage and pointed the finger at Josh as possibly being abusive and a cheater. The police also found copies of multiple life insurance policies on Susan totaling nearly $1.5 million.

To the West Valley investigators, the combination of the note and the policies seemed to indicate a motive for murder: Josh's infidelities were tearing the marriage apart, so instead of divorce, he killed Susan for a cool $1.5 million!

Although most of the evidence that was being compiled was circumstantial, there was a fair amount and more than what some prosecutors have used to win convictions in other murder cases.

Josh also did a number of things in the days before and after his wife's disappearance that at best seemed strange and at worst made him look guilty.

Within the first week of Susan's disappearance, Josh closed all of her bank accounts and cancelled all of her appointments. He also reportedly asked a coworker in the days before Susan's disappearance what would be the best way to dispose of a human body.

Before Josh lawyered up, the investigators were able to speak with his oldest son, who revealed an account of the camping trip that was quite different from Josh's. In his account, Josh claimed that it was only he and his sons who went on the trip, but Charles told the police that his mother went with them as well.

But she didn't return!

Charles' account wasn't enough to arrest Josh, although it did help make him a suspect. Since Charles was not even five years old, it was difficult to trust his account, and it would be even more problematic if he had to take the stand in a trial against his father. Still, less than a month after Susan's disappearance, the West Valley Police firmly believed that they were investigating a homicide and not merely just a missing persons case.

Although several no-body homicide cases have been successfully made by prosecutors over the last twenty-five years in several states in the U.S., investigators and prosecutors will be the first to say that a successful prosecution is much more difficult without a body.

The West Valley detectives began shadowing Josh Powell around town in the days leading up to Christmas 2009—they believed he killed Susan, and they were about to tighten the noose.

Back to Washington

Josh left the Salt Lake City area in the middle of the night with his children days before Christmas to spend the holidays with his family in Washington. After spending a few days there, he returned to Utah with his brother Michael to pack up most of his belongings in order to move permanently back to Washington.

Josh's move to Washington made him look even more guilty in the eyes of the Utah authorities and further divided the already-frayed relationship between the Cox and Powell families.

The Cox family already had their doubts about Josh, but the move confirmed to them that he was somehow responsible for Susan's disappearance. By early 2010, Josh had also severed all contact with the Cox family at his lawyer's request.

But members of the Cox family were not the only ones who thought Josh was a killer.

Josh's own sister, Jennifer Graves, eventually stated that she also believed her brother had something to do with Susan's disappearance.

Members of the Cox family held out hope, though, that Susan was still alive. They thought that there was a slight possibility that, after Josh abducted her, he was actually holding her somewhere and she was still alive.

"The question is, where did he put her and will we find her before she does die?" Susan's father, Chuck Cox, wrote in an email to Utah authorities, according to the police file. "One possibility is that she is still alive, but we need to find her before she does die, if the poison was not a fatal dose, she may...be found."

For their part, the Powell family, minus Jennifer Graves, circled their wagons around Josh. Michael, their sister Alina Powell, father Steve, and Josh did whatever they could in the public eye to make Susan look bad. They created a website that claimed Susan was mentally ill and had left the country for another man.

The Powells' campaign of slander did little to help Josh, and in the end, it backfired. The Cox family filed for custody of Josh and Susan's children, and the Washington authorities began an investigation into Steve Powell for a variety of sex crimes.

Steve Powell was arrested for possession of child pornography in 2011, for which he served time in state prison.

The custody fight also did not end well for Josh. A judge awarded the Cox family primary custody of Charles and Braden in Utah, but they were still allowed to visit and stay with their father on certain weekends in Washington. Things certainly fell apart very quickly for Josh and his family, but he had still avoided prosecution for murder.

In early December 2011, on the two-year anniversary of Susan's disappearance, Josh appeared on an episode of Dateline NBC. Although Josh proclaimed his innocence, it looked forced and hollow, and he looked physically defeated.

The case was clearly wearing on Josh.

At the End of His Rope

2012 began with Josh and Susan's boys living in Utah with her family. Josh was upset and disheartened by the situation, but there was little he could do to get full-time custody. Although he was their only known surviving parent, Josh's dad had recently been sent to prison for sex crimes, specifically possession of child pornography, and Josh was the prime suspect in his wife's disappearance.

Family courts don't look kindly on those types of situations.

Still, the court recognized that he was the parent, so long-distance visitation was arranged under the supervision of social workers.

On February 5, 2012, a social worker brought Charles and Braden to Josh's home in rural Washington. The worker knocked on the door, and Josh answered it immediately, as if he had been waiting. Before the social worker could come inside with the children, Josh shut and locked the door.

The social worker stood outside for several minutes, knocking on the door, but there was no answer. Then suddenly, the social worker was knocked to the ground by a loud explosion.

Joshua Powell had blown up his house with him and his two children in it.

An autopsy revealed that the boys were dead before the explosion from carbon monoxide poisoning, but there were also signs that they had been hacked with a hatchet or machete before they died.

The explosion shocked the Cox family and the Mormon community in Salt Lake City, but it didn't put an immediate end to the disappearance and murder investigation. The press and the public still had many questions about the case, but the West Valley Police had few answers.

Then, in early 2013, the West Valley Police Department declared that the case was officially closed. They stated that they believed Josh abducted and murdered Susan, leaving her remains in an isolated location of the state where they will probably never be discovered. To bolster their claim, they released to the media some notes Susan wrote and a video recovered from a safety deposit box.

"If I die, it may not be an accident, even if it looks like one," said the note written by Susan that was left in a safety deposit box.

The accompanying video showed the Powells' home looking like it had been ransacked by burglars. According to Susan, the damage had been done by Josh in a fit of rage.

"And I had necklaces too, wherever those are [inaudible] got in a rage, as you can see, and broke this, there's studs and pearls and opals in there, broke those and threw all my DVDs and made a mess because he was angry at me about a year or two back," she said.

Although the case was closed, there was no closure for the Cox family. They were unable to give their daughter a proper burial, and her killer would never face justice, at least not in this world. The Cox family would not even be able to learn what happened to their daughter unless someone in the Powell family came forward.

The Utah authorities and the Cox family long believed that members of the Powell family knew more about Susan's disappearance than they let on and that at least one member of the family probably helped Josh dispose of Susan's body.

In particular, the police believed that Michael Powell was somehow involved in the case.

Although the authorities put pressure on Michael, he held the line with the other Powell family members.

The guilt of what Michael had witnessed, and possibly done, was apparently too much for him. He committed suicide by jumping off a parking garage in Minneapolis, Minnesota, on February 11, 2013.

He was probably the last link to any type of reasonable closure the Cox family had.

CHAPTER 9:

THE MYSTERIOUS DEATH
OF REBECCA ZAHAU

Generally speaking, money makes life easier. People with money can live in better neighborhoods, visit better doctors, and have more free time to spend with their families or to pursue their hobbies and other interests.

The aphorism that "money can't buy you happiness" has been uttered an untold number of times, but the truth is, the phrase was probably first said by someone with money.

With that said, money can only buy a person so much happiness, and it can rarely protect a person from unforeseen problems and even tragedies in life.

All the money in the world can't stop a determined murderer from killing someone, nor can it stop all fatal accidents from happening, and the misery that an accident can bring.

Jonah Shacknai learned this the hard way over the course of three days in July 2011.

In the first week of July 2011, Shacknai had it all. He was a multi-millionaire who was the CEO and founder of an Arizona-based company called Medicis Pharmaceutical. Shacknai's income allowed him to marry, start a family, and then divorce in a way that never hurt his pocketbook. He was also able to travel the world, buy a historic mansion in a pricey suburb of San Diego, and meet an attractive, exotic girlfriend.

Jonah Schacknai was wealthy, but more importantly, he was happy.

All of that changed, though, when his son died in an accident in his mansion, and then his girlfriend's body was found hanging in the same location just two days later in an apparent suicide.

All of Jonah Schacknai's money couldn't keep tragedy from striking twice in his home in less than a week.

Two Very Different People

During the 1990s, Jonah Shacknai was an ambitious young man in Arizona who decided to start a pharmaceutical company. He put in long hours, and by all accounts, he did things the "right way," not cutting corners and following all the rules. Within a couple of years, his hard work paid off as he made his company, Medicis Pharmaceutical, a billion-dollar enterprise in the highly competitive pharmaceutical industry.

He married in the early 2000s and, a couple of years later, his son Max was born. Although the marriage ended in divorce, Jonah maintained an amicable relationship with the mother of his only child.

While Jonah wasn't a playboy, he liked to travel and wasn't afraid to spend his hard-earned millions on friends and loved ones.

But Jonah also wasn't afraid to spend money on himself.

In 2007, he bought the "Spreckles Mansion" in the upscale San Diego, California, suburb of Coronado. The mansion is so named because it was first built by tycoon and sugar baron John D. Spreckles in 1901. The historical background of the home impressed Jonah nearly as much as its ten bedrooms, 13,000 square feet, and beautiful view of the ocean.

Jonah truly loved the mansion, but he wanted to share it with someone.

At first glance, Rebecca Zahau appeared to be the perfect woman for a tycoon to have wrapped around his arm. The Burmese woman was attractive, had a good sense of fashion, and was a great conversationalist.

But she also had a bit of a dark side and a somewhat troubled background.

Rebecca Zahau was born in 1979 in the East Asian country of Burma, now known as Myanmar. She lived through political turmoil in her homeland, and although an ethnic Burmese, she was a bit of an outsider at times. She was raised in a protestant family in an overwhelmingly Buddhist country, and although she was never attacked or even harassed because of her religion, she did feel apart from her own people at times.

After she became an adult, she traveled through Europe and had some minor legal problems in Germany before coming to the United States. Most of her immediate family had migrated to Missouri.

Rebecca married in 2002, and although she separated from her husband not long after, the couple never divorced. She met and began dating Jonah in 2008, yet despite her new boyfriend's financial support, she was arrested for shoplifting in 2009.

Rebecca and Jonah were obviously from two very different worlds, geographically and culturally, but they were also in very different places in their professional and personal lives.

Still, Jonah found Rebecca incredibly attractive, and he asked her to move to the Spreckles mansion with him. She gladly accepted.

The Deaths

Rebecca's younger sister came for an extended visit to the mansion during the summer of 2011, so the two got caught up on old times, did a lot of shopping, and spent considerable time at the beach. It was also Rebecca's responsibility to watch Jonah's son, six-year-old Max. By all accounts, Rebecca liked Max and was good with him, which made what happened on July 11 that much more tragic.

On the afternoon in question, Rebecca found Max unconscious at the bottom of the stairs in the entryway of the mansion. Max was rushed to an area hospital but never regained consciousness and died on July 16.

Since the accident happened under questionable circumstances and involved a minor, the police were called to investigate the matter. Rebecca told the police that she was with Max for the entire day and only left him for a few minutes to go to the bathroom. When she got out, he was sprawled out on the floor.

The investigators had no reason not to believe Rebecca's account and theorized that Max probably tripped on something on the balcony and then fell over the railing to his death.

Although the death was ruled an accident, another trauma doctor later claimed that Max suffered injuries to his head before his death. These claims were never substantiated and were rejected by the coroner.

Max's accident immediately thrust Jonah's family into turmoil.

Jonah essentially moved into the hospital to keep vigil over Max in the days before he died, while his brother arrived from Memphis for support.

Adam Shacknai, Jonah's forty-eight-year-old brother, worked as a tugboat captain on the lower Mississippi River. He was known to be a little rough around the edges but was fiercely loyal to his family.

Rebecca picked Adam up at the airport on July 12 and helped him move into the guest house at the mansion. The two got along but didn't say much to each other in what was clearly a stressful and somewhat awkward situation. Adam planned to get a good night's sleep and spend most of the next day at the hospital with Jonah and Max.

On the morning of July 13, Adam woke up and went to the mansion for breakfast, which is when he found Rebecca dead, hanging from the same balcony where Max fell.

Adam immediately called the police, who then processed the scene.

The scene looked somewhat suspicious for a run-of-the-mill suicide.

Rebecca's wrists and ankles were bound, and a shirt was shoved in her mouth as what appeared to be a gag. There was also a message scrawled on a nearby door that said, "She saved him, can he save her."

The message was later determined to have been written by Rebecca.

Jonah later admitted to his ex-wife that the circumstances surrounding Rebecca's death were "undeniably strange," but that he was sure she killed herself out of a sense of "Asian honor." He reasoned that she felt so shamed for allowing Max to die that the only way she could save face was by committing suicide.

Three days later, Max was taken off life support.

After both deaths, Jonah issued a public statement.

"This is a very sad day for our family, as we are again reminded of the enormity of these tragedies," Shacknai said in a statement, which also thanked the police, doctors, and family and friends for their support. "While the investigation is over, the emptiness and sadness in our hearts will remain forever. Max was an extraordinarily loving, happy, talented and special little boy. He brought joy to everyone who knew him, and we will miss him desperately."

He then addressed Rebecca's death.

"Rebecca too was a wonderful and unique person who will always have a special place in my heart," his statement continues. "Nothing will ever be the same for our families after these losses, but with today's information providing some much needed answers, we will try to rebuild our lives and honor the memories we carry with us. Thank you for respecting our privacy as we struggle forward."

Although Rebecca's head showed signs of trauma, the medical examiner ruled her death a suicide.

More Questions

Despite credible medical examiners ruling Max's death an accident and Rebecca's death a suicide, people from both families had their doubts.

Rebecca's family pooled their resources and hired famous medical examiner Cyril Wecht to conduct his own forensic examination of her body. Wecht determined that Rebecca's injuries were caused by manual strangulation and that she was murdered.

Wecht's report was not enough for the San Diego County district attorney's office to bring charges, as they decided that the report was somewhat biased and less accurate than their own medical examiner's report, but it was enough to lay the groundwork for a civil lawsuit.

Rebecca's family sued Adam Shacknai for wrongful death, arguing that he killed Rebecca in revenge for Max's death. The lawyers also argued that Adam sexually assaulted Rebecca, although the coroner's report showed no signs of sexual assault.

The standard for a ruling in a civil trial is much lower than in a criminal trial, so despite a lack of forensic evidence pointing toward Adam's guilt, he was found liable for Rebecca's death.

The jury awarded Rebecca's family $5 million in April 2018, though this was later overturned on appeal.

The San Diego County authorities have not indicated a desire to arrest or charge Adam Shacknai with murder at this time.

There are also some in the Schacknai family who believe Rebecca had more culpability in Max's death. No one thinks she intended to kill the boy, but there are those who believe that her negligence could have been deemed criminal if she had lived.

The reality of this tragic situation is that no matter how much money one may have, terrible accidents can happen, and sometimes those accidents have a ripple effect that is capable of destroying multiple lives.

CHAPTER 10:

THE MARCO FLORES
MURDER CASE

Few would argue that orderly societies need laws. Without laws, there would be anarchy, and not only would everyone's safety be compromised, but society would not be able to function properly or progress. Since humans emerged from the Paleolithic Period and built the first towns over 10,000 years ago, people have philosophized about what the correct balance is between order and justice.

The modern concept of law and order is largely influenced by the Enlightenment philosophers of the eighteenth century, such as Jean-Jacques Rousseau, who wrote in The Social Contract that political authority is given by the people who agree to relinquish a certain amount of freedoms to the government in return for security.

Obviously, just as people sometimes take advantage of their freedom by committing crimes, sometimes the government doesn't hold up its end of the bargain by providing security and protecting the people. When the government consistently fails on its end, the phenomenon of vigilantism can become a problem.

In its most basic definition, vigilantism is when members of society take the law into their own hands to address a perceived crime committed by an individual or individuals that the government has not prosecuted. In orderly, stable societies with little crime, vigilantism is rare, but in failed states, it is fairly common.

The 2010s political instability and hyper-inflation in Venezuela provided many examples of this: there were numerous reports of groups of angry citizens dousing thieves with gasoline and setting them on fire.

In the United States, there has been a long and somewhat romanticized view of vigilantism.

The American Republic was born from rebellion, and in the century following independence, the western frontier was slowly tamed by men and women who were their own law. Americans in the frontier west of the nineteenth century were not afraid to hang a man for horse theft in the absence of any lawman.

Even in more recent decades, there has been a propensity in American courts to view vigilantes with some sympathy.

A notable example in the late twentieth century was when Bernard Goetz shot three would-be muggers on a subway in New York City. Although Goetz was charged with attempted murder, a jury found him not guilty of the charge that could have sent him to prison for decades, instead only convicting him of lesser weapons charges.

American juries, and sometimes even judges, are often willing to give vigilantes reduced sentences, or sometimes not-guilty verdicts, for crimes with extenuating circumstances.

The 2011 murder of Jaime Galdamez was one such case.

There was never any doubt that Galdamez was brutally murdered by Marco Tulio Flores. Flores admitted to the murder and even videotaped himself choking Galdamez to death. At first, the prosecutors thought they had an open and shut case and an unsympathetic client. However, once the details emerged, it became clear that Flores' murder was a vigilante act that could have won sympathy points with a jury.

The case became as complex as it was tragic.

A Brewing Rage

In 2011, Marco Flores was a twenty-one-year-old with a troubled past and not much of a future. He had arrived illegally from El Salvador, and although he lived in the ultra-liberal, immigrant-friendly Boston, Massachusetts area, his legal status and lack of English knowledge prevented him from finding a good job.

Flores had to work menial jobs and was often reliant on other members of the Salvadoran community for help. One of the Salvadorans he met as a child was Jaime Galdamez.

When Flores met Galdamez, at first, the older man seemed to be genuinely nice and helpful. Galdamez helped Flores and his family acclimate to the Boston area and also helped members of the Flores family find work.

Galdamez took a special interest in young Marco.

The reality is that Galdamez had little interest in helping his fellow Salvadorans and really only wanted to get closer to Marco. Galdamez followed the standard

M.O. of a pedophile, grooming Marco by buying him food, electronic gadgets, and other things a young boy would like.

Before too long, Galdamez was sexually molesting Marco.

Like with most children who are victims of sexual molestation, Marco Flores felt too ashamed and scared to tell anyone about the abuse. The fact that he was in the country illegally also added to his silence, which was further exploited by Galdamez. Marco's Latin American background also played a role in his silence. Latin American males are often expected to be hyper-masculine, and Marco believed that admitting to being sexually molested by a man would somehow degrade his masculinity.

When he became an adult, Marco ended the molestation, but the damage had been done.

What Galdamez had done to Marco brewed into a mass of confusion, rage, anger, and hate that was bound to explode.

The Murder

After Marco ended the molestation, he continued to see Galdamez around the neighborhood, although he did his best to avoid him. Marco continued to be close to his family, which inadvertently brought him back into Galdamez's orbit. He heard rumors that Galdamez had become unnaturally close to another child in the Flores family, so he decided to investigate.

He paid a visit to Galdamez's house one day under the pretense that he was there just for a simple visit. When Galdamez got up to use the bathroom, Marco did some investigating and was horrified to find a picture of one of his juvenile nephews.

All of the abuse Marco suffered at Galdamez's hands seemed to come flowing back over him like a tsunami of pain.

There was nothing he could do about what Galdamez had done to him, but Marco wasn't going to let the pedophile victimize another member of his family.

Marco pulled a knife on Galdamez and made him admit to the abuse on camera.

Although Galdamez did admit to the abuse, he did so in a very twisted way that only a child predator would think was right.

"I am a person who loved you, that's all," said Galdamez in his knife-point confession. "I swear. I never hurt you. I never mistreated you. I had sex with you."

Marco then bound Galdamez, dragged him in front of a mirror, and choked him to death with a dog chain. He then set fire to the house but made sure to keep Galdamez's computer.

The computer contained thousands of files of child pornography.

Marco was initially charged with first-degree murder, but when the Suffolk County district attorney's office saw the files, they offered him a plea bargain in 2013. According to the plea bargain, Marco Flores would plead guilty to voluntary manslaughter and serve fifteen years in a Massachusetts state prison.

The plea bargain acknowledged the brutality of the act while mitigating the charge based on the clear extenuating circumstances of a victim striking back against an unpunished predator.

Legal experts also pointed out that the plea bargain was necessary because a sympathetic jury could have seen Marco's vigilante act as reasonable and thus found him not guilty in a trial.

In 2023, Flores was released after serving more than a decade. Proceedings to deport Flores began immediately, though supporters hope to prevent this.

Back at his sentencing, Marco Flores had shown no remorse for the killing.

"I don't feel bad for him," said Marco. "I feel he was a very bad person. It's not like he tried to seek help."

And a sizable percentage of Americans, if not the majority, would probably agree with Marco Flores to some extent.

CHAPTER 11:

THE EXECUTION OF JOE ARRIDY

A common way to gauge a society's enlightenment is according to how it treats its most vulnerable members. Besides the elderly and the young, the most vulnerable people in any society are those with mental and physical disabilities. People with disabilities require support, and they are the most susceptible to being taken advantage of by people with nefarious motives.

When disabilities are identified early in children, they are often placed into inclusive, support, or intervention classes in school. Children with disabilities might also be placed in standard classes to better integrate them into wider society and fulfill their right to an education.

This philosophy is certainly a change from even fifty years ago.

Up until the 1970s, children with disabilities were often taken from their families and placed in state institutions that were little more than warehouses. Many of these children were never seen or heard from again. If they ever did leave these institutions, they were usually ill-equipped to deal with the complexities of the outside world, often becoming victims of crime or becoming criminals themselves.

When people with mental disabilities committed crimes, there was never any thought given to their background, unless they could prove that they were "insane," in which case they would be sent back to a state institution, usually for the rest of their lives.

This attitude began to change during the 1970s as the U.S. government and the individual states began to take a more enlightened view toward people with disabilities, which included the criminal court systems. Tests are now given to criminal defendants to determine if they have the mental capacity to understand the proceedings, and executions of offenders with especially low IQs are banned.

But before the United States took this enlightened view toward people with disabilities, many fell through the cracks, sometimes fatally.

Back in the 1930s, Joe Arridy was a man with a developmental disability who had spent most of his life in state mental institutions. He couldn't grasp basic abstract concepts and could not function on his own in society. Arridy never seemed to be violent, but he was arrested and confessed to raping two girls and killing one in 1936.

At the time, it appeared to be an open and shut case, but a further examination reveals that Joe Arridy was probably one of the unfortunate cases of those with mental disabilities who fatally slipped through the cracks of the system.

A Troubled Life

Joe Arridy was born in 1915 to Syrian Christian parents in Pueblo, Colorado. By all accounts, Arridy's parents were loving and caring people, but they just didn't have the resources or proper education to care for a child with developmental disabilities.

Joe was tested as having an IQ of 46, which placed him in the now-outdated category of "imbecilic," giving him the cognitive ability of a six-year-old child. He didn't utter his first words until the age of five, but well before that time, it was painfully clear to his parents that they would be unable to care for him.

Joe was sent to the—what would be today considered offensively titled— "Colorado State Home and Training School for Defectives" in Grand Junction, Colorado. Although the word "training" was in the title, the emphasis of the school was more on warehousing people with physical and mental disabilities and keeping them segregated from the greater society.

The Arridys took Joe from the home when he was in his early teens, hoping to find him some type of employment in the Pueblo area. Joe was assigned a case worker by the state who checked up on him from time to time. Ultimately, this case worker would give a recommendation as to whether he should be sent back to the institution.

The case worker reported that Joe was known to give oral sex to Black boys around Pueblo, which in his eyes constituted a major problem. But instead of being concerned about Joe's safety and the fact that he was essentially being raped by the boys, the case worker was more worried about Arridy's potential homosexuality.

Joe was sent back to the institution in Grand Junction.

Reports show that Joe was not happy at the institution, probably the result of his being sexually manipulated and assaulted there, as he was on the streets of Pueblo. He ran away twice, the final time in 1936. That time, he left with several other boys who planned to travel aimlessly as hobos on freight railway cars across the western states.

The other boys quickly gave up, but Joe continued hopping trains, which ultimately led to the situation that proved to be his demise.

Brutal Murders

In 1936, Pueblo, Colorado, was a small yet thriving city on the eastern slope of the Rocky Mountains. Although the entire country was ravaged by the effects of the Great Depression, Pueblo suffered far less than other cities and regions because it was located in an agricultural zone—people need to eat no matter the economic situation, and if worse comes to worst, farmers can eat their produce.

Pueblo was also a fairly safe city.

Sure, Pueblo had its crime, but most of it was relegated to certain sections of town and among people who would be involved in criminal activity, whether there was a depression or not. For the most part, random crime was unheard of in Pueblo.

On the evening of August 15, 1936, Riley and Peggy Drain left their two daughters at home—fifteen-year-old Dorothy and twelve-year-old Barbara—to attend a benefit dance on the other side of town. They trusted the responsible Dorothy to look after her younger sister, as she had done numerous times before, and really had no worries about any sort of serious crime coming to their home.

Unfortunately, things went very wrong.

When the Drains returned home from the dance, they found their daughters lying in pools of blood. They immediately called the police and ambulance, but it was too late to save Dorothy. Barbara was hanging on for life in a coma and would eventually survive.

The investigation revealed that both girls had been beaten in their heads, probably with an axe, and then Dorothy was raped. The attacker more than likely intended to kill both girls.

The police had no immediate suspects as it appeared the crime was "random" in the sense that the attacker didn't know the victims, which meant that any woman in Pueblo could be next.

The city was on edge, and the police had no answers. To make matters worse, two weeks later, a similar attack claimed the life of an elderly woman in the same neighborhood.

The only thing that the police had to work with was a report by two women who claimed that what they described as a Mexican man tried to assault them on the night of the Drain attack.

The more the Pueblo Police investigated the Drain attacks, the more they began to think that it was personally motivated. Riley Drain was a supervisor in the local chapter of the Depression-era government organization Works Progress Administration, which meant that he had a lot of power over people's lives. He gave jobs to and took jobs away from men who desperately needed work. As they looked into some of the workers whom Drain had fired recently, they received a tip about one in particular—Frank Aguilar.

Although Aguilar had been fired by Drain recently for a number of reasons, he attended Dorothy's funeral and acted very strangely there, getting in line twice to view her body.

Aguilar also fit the description of the Mexican man who attempted to assault the two women.

Based on that information, the Pueblo Police arrested Frank Aguilar for Dorothy Drain's murder.

At about the same time that Aguilar was being arrested in Pueblo, Joe Arridy was arrested for vagrancy in Cheyenne, Wyoming.

He'd been found wandering the tracks in Cheyenne, apparently waiting for another train to take him out of town. The arresting officer didn't think much of Arridy other than that he was a vagrant who needed to be jailed and then run out of town, but when Sheriff George Carroll got a look at him in the jail, fame and fortune flashed in front of his eyes.

After getting Arridy's vital statistics, Carroll thought it was interesting that Arridy was from the same city in Colorado where two young girls had been brutally beaten, with one being murdered. He read the available reports and decided that Arridy, who had a dark complexion and black hair, fit the description of the "Mexican" the two women saw near the Drain house on the night of the murder.

It didn't matter to Carroll that Aguilar had already been arrested; he decided that Dorothy's murder was a conspiracy.

Carroll pressured Arridy for a confession, but didn't get very far at first. Joe just said whatever seemed to please Carrol, and because of that, his story kept changing. At first, he said he wasn't even in Pueblo, and then, when Carroll got him to admit that he was, he claimed he didn't know who Aguilar was.

After hours of interrogation, Joe finally stated that Aguilar actually did the murder, but that he was in the room when it took place. He said he went along to burglarize the house.

It was enough for Carroll to make his big arrest and get his name in the headlines. Joe Arridy was then promptly transferred to Pueblo to stand trial for Dorothy Drain's murder.

Aguilar later claimed that he didn't know who Joe Arridy was and that the first time he had seen him was in the courtroom.

The trials of Frank Aguilar and Joe Arridy took place quickly, as most did at that time.

Aguilar went on trial first and was found guilty of murder and sentenced to death. He later admitted to the murder of another woman in Pueblo, and researchers today believe he may have been responsible for several more, which would make him a serial killer.

Frank Aguilar was executed on August 13, 1937.

Joe Arridy's lawyer presented an insanity defense based on his history of being confined in state institutions and his recorded low IQ. Although the defense certainly made sense if he had committed or been part of the murder, his lawyer never considered the fact that he was innocent.

Arriday's lawyer never called a witness to testify that Joe wasn't even in Pueblo on the day of the murder, nor did he attack his client's questionable confession.

Joe was found guilty and sentenced to death in Colorado's gas chamber.

Life on Death Row

By all accounts, Joe Arridy had little cognizance of his legal situation, and when he was sent to prison, he acted as if it were just another institution.

Joe Arridy was, after all, quite institutionalized by the time he was sent to death row.

Arridy was later described by Warden Roy Best as "the happiest prisoner on death row" because he did not understand the fate that awaited him on the other side of the tier. While most of the other death row inmates were busy getting their affairs in order, Joe Arridy spent his time playing with toys, including a toy train the warden gave him.

Arridy was well-liked by the other inmates and guards alike, who all seemed to view him as a child trapped in a bad situation. Arridy would often launch his toy train down the tier from his cell only to have it sent back by the other inmates.

Since Joe was unable to realize what was taking place, lawyers offered to handle his appeals pro bono. In an era long before what seems to many to be endless appeals for death row inmates, Arridy received nine stays of execution. There were many people in high places, even back then, who believed that Arridy shouldn't have been on death row.

Despite the support he had, Joe Arridy was finally sent to the gas chamber on January 6, 1939, at the age of twenty-three. Joe was more worried about having to give up his toy train than dying, so the priest told him that he would trade his train in for a golden harp.

In the decades after Arridy's execution, death penalty opponents used his case as an example of how someone with mental disabilities can become a victim of the system. Joe's case has been written about and covered extensively in academic journals and popular publications, proving that some people can touch the lives of others long after death.

In 2011, then-governor of Colorado, Bill Ritter, issued a posthumous pardon for Joe Arridy, pointing out that he probably wasn't even in Pueblo when Dorothy Drain was murdered.

There is a consensus among legal scholars familiar with the case that Joe Arridy was an innocent man and that Frank Aguilar was the sole killer of Dorothy Drain. They point out that, before his death, Aguilar admitted to another, similar murder, and that serial killers who fit his profile nearly always work alone.

Although society unfortunately failed Joe Arridy, his death later served as a catalyst for positive change concerning how people with mental disabilities are treated in the United States.

CHAPTER 12:

THE WANNABE SERIAL KILLER, WILLIAM INMON

Many different serial killers have been profiled in the pages of this series, and if there is one thing that can be said about all of them, it is that most of them show signs of their future vocation at an early age. Some future serial killers exhibit what is known as the Macdonald Triad—bedwetting, pyromania, and cruelty to animals—while others choose to inflict their violent fantasies on their childhood peers.

Nearly every future serial killer displays a noticeable lack of empathy in childhood.

Another common trait nearly every known serial killer shares is that they don't start killing until a little later in life. When caught, most serial killers are in their forties on average, and most don't start killing until they are in their thirties.

Of course, there are always exceptions to every rule.

William Inmon is one such example. Although with three kills, Inmon barely qualified as a serial killer before he was caught, he started at the age of nineteen, which may qualify him as America's youngest serial killer in the modern era.

The Vigilante Killings

William Inmon was born and raised in the Phoenix, Arizona area, but quickly became estranged from his parents. Both his mother and father were heavily involved in drugs and criminal activity, so he was sent to live with other family members and was sometimes in foster care.

As Inmon moved around a lot during his youth, he began to build an elaborate fantasy world where he was a righteous hero whose mission it was to cleanse the world of "scum." He was a fan of action movies and often styled his dress after some of his favorite movie heroes, often wearing camouflage fatigues and carrying large combat knives.

As he entered his late teens, Inmon's "tastes" became more refined as he moved from knives to guns and acquired an interest in history. He especially liked to read about death squads that kidnap and murder their rivals in the middle of the night.

Inmon never had too many friends, and those who did know him never thought much of his ideas, other than that he was a little eccentric.

Most people reasoned: everyone needs a hero, so what's wrong with Rambo?

After Inmon graduated from high school, he decided to move out of Phoenix, far from the scum. He ended up a couple of hundred miles away in a small town named Springerville, Arizona, near the New Mexico-Arizona state line. Inmon found employment in a store in the nearby town of St. John's, Arizona, and although his style of dress was not necessarily popular in western Arizona, he didn't stand out as much as he did in Phoenix.

The people of rural Arizona tend to be self-sufficient and were somewhat sympathetic to some of Inmon's ideas. Inmon, though, was angered when he learned that rural Arizona also had its share of what he considered "scum."

Inmon began his crusade to clear Arizona of those he deemed scum in 2007. His first victim was a seventy-two-year-old man named William McCarragher. Inmon stalked McCarragher for some time, hiding outside of his home on numerous occasions to learn his schedule.

Then, when he thought the time was right, William Inmon fired one shot from his rifle through a window, killing William McCarragher instantly. He later claimed that he murdered McCarragher because he made a pass at him, but there is no way to corroborate that claim, and McCarragher was not known to be a homosexual.

Inmon then went into a "cooling off" period that is indicative of all serial killers, although his was quite long at over a year in length.

The vigilante killer next struck in March 2009 when he killed sixty-year-old Daniel Achten, who was known to Inmon. Achten was a Vietnam War veteran and a known drug user, and Inmon considered drug users scum. Inmon also later claimed that he had a personal grudge against Achten because he killed his dog.

Inmon went over to Achten's house and shot and killed him. After the murder, he burned the body and buried it in his own backyard.

In August 2009, William Inmon claimed his last known victim when he shot and killed sixteen-year-old Ricky Flores. The vigilante killer claimed he killed Flores because of his drug habit, but there was also a financial incentive, as Flores' girlfriend's dad, Jeffrey Johnson, paid him to commit the murder.

William Inmon's reputation as a killer preceded him by August 2009, which is how he was eventually arrested.

As the local authorities were investigating Inmon's first two murders, they began receiving tips about the camouflage-clad young man who wanted to rid Arizona of scum. The circumstantial evidence was enough for the St. John's Police Department to get a search warrant for Inmon's Springerville apartment on August 28, 2009. Not long after the search began, a frustrated Inmon paid a visit to the Springerville Police Department.

Inmon actually believed that it was illegal for a police department from one jurisdiction to serve a warrant in another jurisdiction!

As Inmon complained about the warrant, the Springerville Police Chief got him to open up about his philosophy on life, and eventually, about his crimes. Inmon admitted to all three murders and added that he planned to kill two more drug dealers.

William Inmon was only twenty-one years old at the time of his confession.

Although Inmon was originally charged with murder, the circumstances surrounding the killings were somewhat questionable, and the prosecutor was not so sure he would get convictions on all of them, so Inmon was allowed to plead guilty to the much lesser crime of manslaughter.

Jeffrey Johnson, who paid Inmon to murder Ricky Flores, pled guilty to solicitation of murder, served four years in prison, and was released in 2014.

Inmon was sentenced to twenty-four years in prison in 2011 and has a scheduled release date of 2030. If he survives that long, he will be one of the only serial killers to be released from prison in American history.

CONCLUSION

The world of the criminal mind is as fascinating as it is deep and dark. Most of us never dream of doing the things that the criminals profiled in this book have done, which is perhaps why these stories are so interesting to us.

We want to understand how and why a person can be driven to inflict such pain, misery, and cruelty on other humans.

We are also intrigued to learn how they committed these crimes, especially in the cases where they almost got away with their deeds.

Although fans of true crime will never solve the problems of the world, it is reasonable to say that by reading about these cases, their level of understanding of the criminal mind is increased, in turn benefiting understanding on a general level in society.

No one will argue that knowledge can ever be a bad thing.

So, true crime fans, keep reading and exploring the criminal mind!

EPILOGUE

You've now reached the end of this true crime anthology, having walked through some of the darkest narratives in modern crime history. From infamous slayings to overlooked injustices, the stories in *The True Crime Books Collection: Sixty Disturbing True Stories About Murder And Mayhem (Five-in-One Book)* display the full range of true crime tragedy, curiosity, legal failure, and, occasionally, the perseverance of justice. But where to from here?

True crime is not about glorifying killers or sensationalizing death. It's about looking for understanding—of people and of the systems our society has built to deal with them. It is also about remembering the victims. Whether you knew their names before reading this, or their stories were new to you, you will surely agree that they all matter.

A common theme you may have noticed in many of these cases is the role of the media. Stories like that of Wanda Holloway, the "Texas Cheerleader Mom," or Scott Amedure's death following a TV talk show appearance, demonstrate the dangerous overlap between notoriety and influence. Meanwhile, stories like the Soham Murders or the case of Shanda Sharer reveal how media attention can sometimes deepen trauma for those left behind.

But sometimes media coverage can make a positive difference. In several cases, dogged journalism brought the truth to the fore when institutions failed. The wrongful conviction of Troy Davis, for example, became a rallying cry for criminal justice reform. In the case of Susan Powell, ongoing media coverage kept her name on people's minds even when answers were scarce.

The legal system, too, features prominently in these pages. You'll have seen how it acted as a force for accountability in some cases, while in others, it made errors with devastating consequences. From forced confessions and botched investigations to the complexities of juvenile sentencing and mental health evaluations, the flaws and deficiencies of the criminal justice system are laid bare in these pages.